NORFOLK
HOUSE

MOTOR LEARNING & PERFORMANCE

$\diamond$ FROM PRINCIPLES TO PRACTICE $\diamond$

Richard A. Schmidt, PhD
University of California, Los Angeles

Human Kinetics Books
Champaign, Illinois

Library of Congress Cataloging-in-Publication Data

Schmidt, Richard A.
   Motor learning and performance : from principles to practice / by
Richard A. Schmidt
      p.   cm.
   Includes bibliographical references and indexes.
   ISBN 0-87322-308-X
   1. Motor learning. 2. Perceptual-motor learning.   3. Motor
ability. I. Title.
BF295.S249 1991   90-48919
152.3'34--dc20   CIP

ISBN: 0-87322-308-X

Acquisitions Editor: Rick Frey, PhD; **Developmental Editor:** Judy Patterson Wright, PhD; **Assistant Editors:** Julia Anderson, Valerie Hall, Dawn Levy, and Kari Nelson; **Photo Editor:** Valerie Hall; **Copyeditor:** Peter Nelson; **Proofreader:** Pam Johnson; **Production Director:** Ernie Noa; **Typesetter:** Sandra Meier; **Text Design:** Keith Blomberg; **Text Layout:** Denise Lowry; **Cover Design:** Jack Davis; **Cover Photo:** Dave Black; **Interior Art:** Tom Janowski; **Printer:** Versa Press; **Bindery:** Dekker

Printed in the United States of America   10   9   8

Human Kinetics
Web site: http://www.humankinetics.com/

United States: Human Kinetics, P.O. Box 5076, Champaign, IL 61825-5076
1-800-747-4457
e-mail: humank@hkusa.com

Canada: Human Kinetics, Box 24040, Windsor, ON N8Y 4Y9
1-800-465-7301 (in Canada only)
e-mail: humank@hkcanada.com

Europe: Human Kinetics, P.O. Box IW14, Leeds LS16 6TR, United Kingdom
(44) 1132 781708
e-mail: humank@hkeurope.com

Australia: Human Kinetics, 57A Price Avenue, Lower Mitcham, South Australia 5062
(08) 277 1555
e-mail: humank@hkaustralia.com

New Zealand: Human Kinetics, P.O. Box 105-231, Auckland 1
(09) 523 3462
e-mail: humank@hknewz.com

This text is dedicated to the memory of
Virginia S. Schmidt
and
Allen W. Schmidt,
as a small thanks for all the skills they taught me.

Contents

Preface

For many, there are few things as exciting as a close race, match, or game where the competitors demonstrate nearly incredible levels of skill to achieve victory. For many, there are few things as beautiful as a highly complex, well-controlled skilled action that achieves the performer's exact, intended goal. And, for many, there are few things as satisfying as having been committed to a long-term program of training and skill learning, and then experiencing the thrill of achieving the goal in an important performance.

This book is written for people who feel this kind of excitement about motor skill, and who would like to learn more about the processes underlying skilled performance, how skilled performances are learned, and how to apply the principles of skilled performance and learning in teaching, coaching, and rehabilitation settings. This book is also written for those who have never before considered the complexities involved in teaching motor skills or coaching for maximum performance. This is an introductory text in motor performance and learning for undergraduate college or university students in fields such as physical education, kinesiology, education, psychology, the sport sciences, and physical and occupational therapy. It is intended as a textbook for courses in elementary motor learning or motor behavior. The level of the text is elementary, assuming little prior knowledge of physiology, psychology, statistical methods, or other basic sciences. The concepts from these fields that are critical to understanding motor behavior are introduced as needed, so the flow of the text is not interrupted by these basic background materials.

This text is very different from anything I have tried to write before, and I experienced some difficulty achieving a proper balance between several competing goals. I struggled with decisions about style, organization, and content, and it will be clear that I achieved some goals more effectively than others.

My first goal was to build a strong conceptual understanding of skills, what I term a *conceptual model of human performance*. I started with a simple model of the performer as an information processor, then gradually added elements to the model as they were discussed, and concluded with a larger, integrated, conceptual model that goes beyond the original information processing approach. Upon completion of Part I, the student should have a reasonably coherent view of the conceptual, functional properties of the motor system. A student with a general understanding of how skills operate, the major principles for performance, and how the human motor system learns, will best be able to apply this knowledge to real-world settings. These principles will be most appropriate for maximizing the performance of already learned skills, which typically occurs in coaching settings.

Part II of the text uses this conceptual model to impart an understanding of human motor learning processes. Much of this discussion uses the terms and principles introduced relative to motor behavior in the earlier chapters. This method works well in my own teaching, probably because motor learning is really inferred from changes in motor behavior; it is easy to discuss these changes in terms of the behavioral principles. By the end of the text, there has been a progressive accumulation of knowledge that, in my experience, provides a consistent view of how skills are performed and learned. The applications presented in Part III are more aligned with teaching, focusing on the structure of practice for effective skill acquisition.

Second, I wanted to write a text that could be used by performers, teachers, coaches, and physical therapists to enhance human performance in real-world settings in physical education, sport, athletics, and rehabilitation. This goal demanded careful scrutiny of the many topics presented in these areas. Those topics most relevant to practical application were emphasized, whereas those of less practical interest were excluded.

Many examples of each principle are discussed in the main body of the text. In addition, all the chapters include Practical Applications sections set off from the main textual materials. Strategically located directly after pertinent discussions of principles, these sections indicate applications to real-world teaching, coaching, or therapy settings.

Third, I wanted a presentation style that was simple, straightforward, and easy to read for those without extensive backgrounds in the motor performance area. As a result, the main content does not greatly stress the research and data that contribute to our knowledge of motor skill acquisition and performance. Important points are occasionally illustrated by data from a critical experiment, but the focus is on an integrated conceptual knowledge of how the motor system works and how it learns. However, for those who desire a tighter link to the basic data, I have included sections called Highlight Boxes which describe the important experiments and concepts in detail. At the end of each chapter, I also present a set of self-test questions and a list of key terms as comprehension checks for the reader.

Finally, I demanded that the principles discussed should be faithful to the empirical data and thought in the study area. This goal is not immediately obvious when viewing the text because there are relatively few references cited and few experiments discussed. From my 25 years doing basic research in learning and performance, I have developed what I believe to be a defensible, coherent personal viewpoint (a conceptual model, if you will) about how skills are performed and learned, and my goal is to present this model to the reader to facilitate understanding. My viewpoint is based on a large literature of theoretical ideas and empirical data, together with much thought about competing ideas and apparently contradictory research findings. I have tried to write my perspective as I would tell a story. Every part of the story can be defended, or it would not have been included, but I have not been willing to interrupt the story with justifications, rationales, and critical evidence for most of the points. My goal has been to write the "truth," at least as I understand it, and as it can be understood with our current level of knowledge. I have included at the end of each chapter a brief section describing additional readings, where competing viewpoints and additional scientific justifications can be found.

Thanks should be expressed to several people who helped with this text. First, my longtime friend Rainer Martens was instrumental in convincing me, over several years, that I could actually write such a text. He gave me many concrete suggestions and encouraged my initial efforts; the text would not have happened without his help. Thanks are extended to Gwen B. Gordon for her understanding and encouragement throughout. I would like to thank acquisitions editor Rick Frey, who provided many good suggestions and much encouragement early on in the writing process, and developmental editor Judy Patterson Wright for her critical but constructive comments on the first draft, which became the basis of many fundamental revisions. Appreciation is also extended to Tim Lee and to four anonymous reviewers for their helpful comments on earlier drafts of the manuscript.

Richard A. Schmidt
Westwood, California

Introduction to Motor Performance and Learning

PREVIEW

In the 1970s a petite Russian girl named Olga Korbut captivates the sports world with her feats in women's gymnastics at the Olympic Games, and she becomes a role model for many young girls who suddenly want to learn gymnastics. In the 1980s Jim Knaub, who had lost the use of his legs in an accident, wins several important marathons in the wheelchair division, earning our admiration and respect. From the 1970s into the '90s, David Kiley (shown above) earns the title of "The King of Wheelchair Sports" by winning five gold medals in the 1976 Paralympic Games in Canada, climbing the highest mountain in Texas, and playing on the United States Men's Wheelchair Basketball team five times, as well as by being a top competitor in tennis, racquetball, and skiing. On New Year's Day in 1990, over 105,000 enthusiastic people crowd into a stadium in Pasadena, California, to watch the Rose Bowl football game, and millions more watch the

1

television broadcast. These and many other examples indicate that skills—particularly skills involved in sport—are a critical part of human existence. How people can perform at such high levels, how such skills are developed, and how you can develop some approximation of these skills in yourself, your children, or your students—all of these questions generate fascination, encouraging further learning about human movement.

Here begins a description of the study of motor performance and learning, introducing the concept of skill and discussing various features of its definition. Next the text examines skill classification schemes important for later applications. Finally, to help you understand skills effectively using this book, the logic behind its organization is described: the principles and processes underlying skilled performance, followed by how to develop such capabilities with practice.

STUDENT GOALS
1. To appreciate the varieties of skills and their structures
2. To understand the many aspects of a definition of skill
3. To recognize several classifications of skills
4. To understand the textbook's organization: motor performance followed by learning

The remarkable human capability to perform skills is a critical feature of our very existence. It is almost uniquely human in nature, although various animals high on the evolutionary scale can produce what you might call skilled behaviors (e.g., circus dogs who do complex tricks). Without the capacity for skilled performance, I could not type the page I am preparing now and you could not read it. And for students involved in physical education, coaching, or kinesiology, there would not be the wide variety of sports and athletic endeavors that are so strongly fascinating and exciting.

Human skills take many forms, of course, from those that emphasize the control and coordination of our largest muscle groups, in relatively forceful activities like soccer or tumbling, to those in which the smallest muscle groups must be tuned precisely, as in typing or repairing a watch. This text generally focuses on the full range of skilled behavior because it is useful to understand that many common features underlie the performance of skills associated with industrial and military settings, sports, the re-acquisition of movement capabilities lost through injuries or stroke, or simply the everyday activities of most people. But the major focus is on skilled performances applicable to sports, games, dance, and similar activities that make up so large a part of the scope of human skills.

Most humans are born with the capability to produce many skills, and only a little maturation and experience is necessary in order to produce them in nearly complete form.

Walking and running, chewing, balancing, and avoiding painful stimuli are some examples of these relatively innate behaviors. But imagine what simple and uninteresting creatures we would be if these inherited actions were all that we could ever do. All biological organisms have the remarkable facility to profit from their experiences, to learn to detect important environmental features (and to ignore others), and to produce behaviors that were not a part of their original capabilities. Humans have the most flexibility of all, which allows gaining proficiency for occupations as chemists or computer programmers, for competition in music or athletics, or simply for conducting daily lives more efficiently. Thus, producing skilled behaviors and the learning that leads to their development are tightly intertwined in human experience. This book is about both of these aspects of skills—skilled human performance and human learning.

APPLICATIONS OF KNOWLEDGE ABOUT SKILLS

Because skills make up such a large part of human life, scientists and educators have been trying for centuries to understand the determinants of skills and the factors that affect their performance. The knowledge gained has provided applications to numerous aspects of life, including improving performance in sports and physical activities. Important points apply to the instructional aspects of physical education, where methods for efficient skills teaching and effective carryover to life situations are primary concerns. Also, considerable applicability is possible for improving high-level sports performances and every other kind of physical activity. Of course, much of what coaches do during practices involves, in one way or another, skills instruction. Those coaches

who understand these processes most effectively undoubtedly have an advantage when their athletes take the field.

Human skilled performance involving cooperation among team members.

Other application areas can be emphasized as well. There are many applications in training skills for industry, where effective job skills can mean success in the workplace and be major determinants of satisfaction both with the job and with life in general. Teaching job skills most effectively and determining which individuals are best suited to particular occupations are typical situations where knowledge about skills can be useful in industry.

The principles are applicable to physical therapy and occupational therapy settings as well, where the concern is for the (re)learning and production of movements that have been lost through head or spinal cord injury, stroke, birth defects, and the like. Although all these areas may be different and the physical capabilities of the learners may vary widely, the principles that lead to successful application are generally the same.

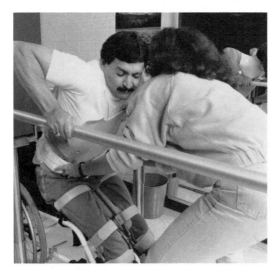

Human skilled performance involving motor control in a therapeutic setting.

SKILL DEFINITIONS

As widely represented and diverse as skills are, it is difficult to define them in a way that applies to all cases. The psychologist E.R. Guthrie (1952) has provided a definition that captures most of the critical features of skills:

> **Skill** consists in the ability to bring about some end result with maximum certainty and minimum outlay of energy, or of time and energy. (p. 136)

There are several important features of this definition to consider. First, performing skills implies some desired environmental goal, such as holding a handstand in gymnastics or completing a forward pass in football. Skills are usually thought of as different from movements, which do not necessarily have any particular environmental goal, such as idly wiggling my little finger. Of course, skills *consist* of movements because the performer could not achieve an environmental goal without making at least one movement.

Second, to be skilled implies meeting this performance goal, this "end result," with maximum certainty. For example, last month while playing darts I made a bull's-eye. But this by itself does not ensure that I am a skilled darts player, because I have not demonstrated that I can achieve this result with any certainty. Such an outcome was the result of one lucky throw in the midst of hundreds of others that were not so lucky. I need to demonstrate that I can produce the skill reliably, on demand, without luck playing a very large role. This is why people so greatly value the champion athlete who, with but one chance and only seconds remaining at the end of a game, makes the goal that allows the team to win.

Third, a major feature in many skills is the minimization, and thus conservation, of the energy required for performance. For some skills this is clearly not the goal, such as in the shot put, where the only goal is to throw the maximum distance. But for many other skills the minimization of energy expenditure is critical, allowing the marathon runner to hold an efficient pace or allowing the wrestler to save strength for the last few minutes of the match. This minimum-energy notion applies to organizing the action not only so the physiological energy costs are lower but also so the psychological, or mental, energy required is reduced. Many skills have been learned so well that the performers hardly have to pay attention to them, freeing their cognitive processes for other features of the activity, such as strategy in basketball or expressiveness in dance. A major contributor to the efficiency of skilled performance is practice, with learning and experience leading to the relatively effortless performances so admired in highly skilled people.

Finally, another feature of many skills is for highly proficient performers to achieve their goals in minimum time. Many sports skills have this as the only competition goal, such as a swimming race. Other skills are more effective if done quickly, such as a boxing jab or a basketball pass. Minimizing time can interact with the other skill features mentioned, however. Speeding up performance often results in sloppy movements that have less certainty in terms of achieving the environmental goal. Also, increased speed generates movements for which the energy costs are sometimes higher. Thus, understanding skills involves optimizing and balancing several skill aspects that are important to different extents in different settings.

In sum, skills generally involve achieving some well-defined environmental goal by

- maximizing the achievement certainty,
- minimizing the physical and mental energy costs of performance, and
- minimizing the time used.

THE MANY COMPONENTS OF SKILLS

The elegant performance of the skilled dancer and the winning actions of an Olympic weight lifter may appear simple, but the performance goals actually were realized through a complex combination of interacting mental and motor processes. For example, many skills involve considerable emphasis on sensory-perceptual factors, such as detecting that a tennis opponent is going to hit a shot to the left or that a baseball pitch is curving. Often, sensory factors require the split-second analysis of patterns of sensory input, such as discerning that the combined movements of an entire football team indicate the play will be a run to the left side. These perceptual events lead to decisions about what to do, how to do it, and when to do it. These decisions are often a major determinant of success, as in deciding whether to take a shot in basketball or where to throw the baseball after fielding a hit. Finally, of course, skills typically depend on the quality of movement generated as a result of these decisions. Even if the situation is correctly perceived and the response decisions are appropriate, the performer will not be effective in meeting the environmental goal if he or she executes the actions poorly.

These three elements are critical to almost any skill:

- Perceiving the relevant environmental features
- Deciding what to do and where and when to do it
- Producing organized muscular activity to generate movements

The movements have several recognizable parts. Postural components support the actions; for instance, the arms of an archer need to be supported by a stable platform to shoot accurately. Body transport, or locomotor, components move the body toward the point where the skill will take place, as in setting for a return on the tennis court, or moving a limb toward a place where the action can occur, as in grasping the horizontal bar after a release. Finally, manipulation components are coupled and coordinated with these other elements and can make up the major focus of the skill, such as the finger and wrist movements in a complex video game.

Here are summarized the three major

kinds of components involved in the production of many skills:

- Postural components provide a "platform" to support the actions
- Body transport components bring the body or limb to the action
- Manipulation components produce the action

It is interesting, but perhaps unfortunate, that each of these skill components seems to be recognized and studied in isolation from the others. For example, sensory factors in perception are studied by cognitive psychologists, scientists interested in (among other things) the complex information-processing activities involved in seeing, hearing, and feeling. Sometimes these factors are in the realm of psychophysics, the branch of psychology that examines the relationship between objective physical stimuli (e.g., vibration intensity) and the subjective sensations these stimuli create when perceived (loudness). Decision-making processes are typically of interest to a different group of scientists in cognitive and experimental psychology. Factors in the control of the movement itself are typically handled by scientists in the neurosciences, kinesiology, biomechanics, physical education, and physiology, often with little concern for the perceptual and decision-making processes. Skill learning is studied by yet another group of scientists in kinesiology or in experimental or educational psychology. A major problem for the study of skills, therefore, is the fact that the several components of skill are studied by widely different groups of scientists, generally with little overlap and communication among them.

To summarize, these are the major processes underlying actions:

1. Sensory or perceptual processes, studied in cognitive psychology and psychophysics;

2. Decision-making processes, studied in cognitive and experimental psychology;
3. Motor-control or movement-production processes, studied in the neurosciences, kinesiology, bioengineering, biomechanics, physical education, and physiology; and
4. Learning processes, studied in kinesiology, physical education, and educational and experimental psychology.

All of these various processes are present in almost all motor skills. Even so, we should not get the idea that all skills are fundamentally the same. In fact, the principles of human performance and learning depend to some extent on the kind of movement skill to be performed. So, the ways that skills have been classified are discussed next.

SKILL CLASSIFICATIONS

There are several skill classification systems that help organize the research findings and make application somewhat more straightforward. These are presented in the following sections.

Open and Closed Skills

One way to classify movement skills concerns the extent to which the environment is stable and predictable throughout performance. An **open skill** is one for which the environment is variable and unpredictable during the action. Examples include carrying the ball against a defensive team in American football, and wrestling, where it is difficult to predict the future moves of the opponent (and hence future responses to the opponent) very effectively. A **closed skill**, on the other hand, is one for which the environment is stable and predictable. Examples include gymnastics routines and swimming in an empty lane in a pool. These "open" and "closed" designations actually only mark the end points of a spectrum, with skills lying between having varying degrees of environmental predictability or variability.

This classification points out a critical feature for skills, defining the performer's need to respond to moment-to-moment variations in the environment. It thus brings in the processes associated with perception, pattern recognition, and decision making (usually with the need to perform these processes quickly) so the action can be tailored to the environment. These processes are supposedly minimized in closed skills, where the performer can evaluate the environmental demands in advance without time pressure, organize the movement in advance, and carry it out without needing to make rapid modifications as the movement unfolds. These features are summarized in Table 1.1.

Table 1.1 Open-Closed Skill Dimension

Closed skills		Open skills
Predictable environment	Semipredictable environment	Unpredictable environment
Gymnastics	Walking a tightrope	Playing soccer
Archery		Wrestling
Typing	Steering a car	Chasing a rabbit
	Playing chess	

Discrete, Continuous, and Serial Skills

A second scheme for classifying skills concerns the extent to which the movement is an ongoing stream of behavior, as opposed to a brief, well-defined action. At one end of this dimension is a **discrete skill**, which usually has an easily defined beginning and end, often with a very brief duration of movement, such as throwing or kicking a ball, firing a rifle, or catching a pass. Discrete skills are particularly important in sport performances, especially considering the large number of discrete hitting, kicking, throwing, and catching skills that make up many popular games and sport activities.

At the other end of this dimension is a **continuous skill**, which has no particular beginning or end, the behavior flowing on for many minutes, such as swimming, running, or pedaling a bicycle. One particularly important continuous skill is tracking, in which the performer's limb movements control a lever, a wheel, a handle, or some other device to follow the movements of some target track. Steering a car is tracking, with steering wheel movements made so the car follows the track defined by the roadway. Tracking movements are very common in real-world skills situations, and much research has been directed to their performance and learning. As discussed later, discrete and continuous skills can be quite different, requiring different processes for performance and demanding that they be taught and coached somewhat differently as a result.

Between the polar ends of the discrete-continuous dimension is the **serial skill**, which is often thought of as a group of discrete skills strung together to make up a new, more complicated skilled action. See Table 1.2 for a comparison summary. Here the word *serial* implies that the order of the elements is usually critical for successful performance. Shifting car gears is a serial skill, with three discrete shift lever action elements (and accelerator and clutch elements) connected in sequence to create a larger action. Other examples include performing a gymnastics routine and following the sequential gates in a skiing race. Serial skills differ from discrete skills in that the movement durations are somewhat longer, yet each movement retains a discrete beginning and end. One view of learning serial skills suggests that the individual skill elements present in early learning are somehow combined to form one larger, single element that the performer controls almost as if it were truly discrete in nature (e.g., the smooth, rapid way a racecar driver shifts gears).

Table 1.2 Discrete-Serial-Continuous Skill Dimension

Discrete skills	Serial skills	Continuous skills
Distinct beginning and end	Discrete actions linked together	No distinct beginning or end
Throwing a dart Catching a ball Shooting a rifle	Hammering a nail Assembly-line task Gymnastics routine	Steering a car Swimming Tracking task

Motor and Cognitive Skills

It is sometimes useful to consider a third dimension, labeled motor and cognitive skills. With a **motor skill** the primary determinant of success is the quality of the movement itself, where perception and subsequent decisions about which movement to make are nearly absent. For example, the high jumper knows exactly what to do (jump over the bar), but the problem is that the movements must be made effectively in order that maximum height be achieved.

On the other hand, with a **cognitive skill** the nature of the movement is not particularly important, but the decisions about which movement to make are critical. For example, in chess it matters little whether the pieces are moved quickly and smoothly; rather, it is important that the player know which piece to move where and when, to maximize the gain against the opponent.

In short, a cognitive skill mainly involves selecting what to do, whereas a motor skill mainly involves how to do it. This dimension, like the others, is really a continuum because there is no completely cognitive skill or completely motor skill (see Table 1.3). Every skill, no matter how cognitive it might seem, requires at least some motor output,

Table 1.3 Motor-Cognitive Skill Dimension

Motor skills		Cognitive skills
Decision making minimized	Some decision making	Decision making maximized
Motor control maximized	Some motor control	Motor control minimized
High jumping Pitching Weight lifting	Playing quarterback Driving a race car Sailing an iceboat	Playing chess Cooking a meal Coaching a sport

Franklin M. Henry, Father of Motor Behavior Research

Prior to World War II, and during the 1950s and 1960s when much effort was directed at military skills such as pilotry, most of the research was done by experimental psychologists on relatively fine motor skills. Little effort was being devoted to the gross-motor skills that would be applicable to many sport performances.

During this time at the University of California, Franklin M. Henry, a PhD trained in experimental psychology but working in the Department of Physical Education, was filling the gap with a new tradition of laboratory experimentation that started an important new direction in research on movement skills. He studied gross motor skills, often involving the whole body, whose performances were intentionally representative of those seen on the play-ing fields and gymnasia. But he used laboratory tasks—whose apparatuses he often built himself in his workshop—that enabled the rigorous study of these skills using methods analogous to those used in experimental psychology. He examined a number of research problems, such as the differences among people, practice scheduling, the mathematical shapes of performance curves, and the roles of fatigue and rest in performance.

Many graduate students educated in this new tradition at Berkeley then opened their own research programs and began to train other graduate students. Henry's direct and indirect influence on the fields of physical education and kinesiology was widespread by the 1970s and 1980s. Without a doubt, his impact has earned him the title of Father of Motor Behavior Research.

and every motor skill requires some preceding decision making. Most real-world skills fall somewhere between the polar ends and are complex combinations of decision making and movement production. Even though most sport skills are weighted quite heavily toward movement, there are strong cognitive and decision-making components in quarterbacking in American football, for example, and in the split-second tactical sailing decisions in racing for the America's Cup. Recognizing this combination of perceptual and cognitive factors with motor control factors has produced several additional labels for skills, such as perceptual-motor skills or psychomotor skills.

Franklin M. Henry at work in his shop in Berkeley (circa 1960).

UNDERSTANDING PERFORMANCE AND LEARNING

In some ways skilled performance and motor learning are interrelated concepts that cannot be easily separated for analysis. Even so, a temporary separation of these areas is necessary for presentation and making eventual understanding much easier. Many of the terms, principles, and processes that scientists use to describe the improvements with practice and learning (the subfield of motor learning) actually come from the literature on the underlying processes in the production of skilled motor performance (the subfield of human performance; the field of motor behavior often includes both motor learning and human performance). Therefore, whereas at first glance it might seem most logical to treat motor learning before motor performance (a person has to learn before performing), it turns out to be awkward to present information on learning without first having provided this background performance information.

For this reason this book is organized into essentially two main parts, the first of which introduces the terminology, concepts, and principles related to skilled human performance and without very much reference to processes associated with learning. The principles here probably most strongly apply to improvement of already skilled performances, which is the goal of coaching. Having examined the principles of how the motor system produces skills, the discussion turns to how these processes can be altered, facilitated, and trained through practice. This involves motor learning, whose principles most strongly apply to teaching motor skills.

Conceptual Model of Motor Performance and Learning

For effectiveness in applying skills information to a variety of settings as well as in generalizing it to novel settings, a relatively consistent overall viewpoint, a "big picture"—a conceptual **model**—should be established. While introducing new topics, this book gradually works toward such a conceptual model, tying together most of the major processes and events that occur as performers produce skills. These models are critical in teaching and coaching, and in science as well, because they embrace many seemingly unrelated facts and concepts, linking them together through a familiar structure, so their appropriate applications are more easily understandable.

Models can be of many types, of course, such as the plumbing-and-pump model of the human circulatory system and the variety of balls that model the structure of atoms and molecules in chemistry. For skills, a useful conceptualization is an information flow model, which considers how to use information of various kinds in producing and learning skilled action. The first portions of the text build this model, first considering how the sensory information that enters the system through the receptors is processed, transformed, and stored. Then, to this is added how this sensory information leads to other processes associated with decision making and planning action. To the emerging model are then added features of the initiation of action as well as of the activities involved while the action is unfolding, such as controlling muscular contractions and detecting and correcting errors. In the second portion of the text, which deals with learning, the model provides an effective understanding of which processes are and are not influenced by practice.

Human Performance Principles

Part I of the text (chapters 2 through 6) is concerned with the major principles of human performance as well as with the progressive development of a conceptual model of human actions. Chapter 2 discusses the nature of information processing, decision making, and movement planning. Chapter 3 considers the detection and processing of sensory information from various sources relevant to movement. Chapter 4 examines the processes underlying the production, or execution, of movement skills that clearly depend on the processes of sensation, perception, and planning, which are added to the conceptual model. Chapter 5 considers some of the basic principles, or laws, of movement performance that form the basis of applications to teaching and coaching, all of which can be understood in terms of the conceptual model. Finally, in chapter 6 the concern is for differences in movement capabilities among people and how these differences allow the prediction of success in new situations; differences among components in the conceptual model help in understanding these differences among people.

Motor Learning Principles

After the conceptual model of the organization of skilled action is relatively well developed and understood, Part II (chapters 7 through 10) examines processes involving skill learning. This division makes understanding motor learning considerably easier because the terminology, concepts, and methods in the field of motor learning are strongly dependent on those gained from studying movement performance. In many instances, learning is spoken of in terms of the changes in the underlying processes in the production of movement skills, so the transition to studying learning in the second half of the text is natural, using consistent terminology and conceptual ideas.

In this second part, chapter 7 treats some methodological problems unique to the study of learning, such as how and when to measure performance, which also have application to measuring performance in analogous teaching situations. Chapters 8 and 9 concern the broad question of how and when

to practice, dealing with the many factors that teachers and coaches can directly control to make practice more effective. Chapter 10 deals with the critical topic of feedback, looking at what kinds of movement information students need for effective learning, when it should be given, and so on.

Finally, Part III (chapter 11) uses the conceptual model to pull together these various principles and processes that have been discussed. This includes the applications of performance and learning principles to relatively complex settings in sports, physical education, physical therapy, and other areas. In all these cases, the well-informed instructor, armed with a consistent understanding of the integrated human motor system, has an advantage in achieving the desired goals of his or her program.

 CHAPTER SUMMARY

People regard skills as an important, fascinating aspect of life. Knowledge about skills has come from a variety of scientific disciplines and can be applied to many settings, such as sport, physical education, industry, and physical therapy.

Skill is usually defined as the capability to bring about an end result with maximum certainty and minimum time and energy. Many different components are involved, major categories being perceptual or sensory processes, decision making, and movement output. Skills may be classified along numerous dimensions, such as (a) open and closed skills; (b) discrete, continuous, and serial skills; and (c) motor and cognitive skills. These classifications are important because the principles of skill and their learning often differ for different categories.

The text's particular organization of materials should facilitate understanding of skills. After an introduction in chapter 1, Part I treats the principles of human skilled performance and the underlying processes, focusing on how the various parts of the motor system produce skilled actions. Part II examines how to modify these various processes by practice and motor learning. Understanding how all of these components can operate together is facilitated by a conceptual model of human performance that is developed throughout the text. Lastly, Part III applies the principles and processes to a real-world teaching situation.

Checking Your Understanding

1. Who is the Father of Motor Behavior Research, and what contributions did he make to the field?
2. How are skills defined? Describe why certainty is such a critical aspect of this definition.
3. Give examples of sports or other real-world activities that are (a) both serial and closed in nature; (b) both continuous and cognitive; (c) discrete, motor, and open.
4. Why is it important to make distinctions between various categories of skills, such as between open and closed skills?

Key Terms

Definitions of the following terms appear on the page(s) shown in parentheses:

closed skill (p. 6)
cognitive skill (p. 8)
continuous skill (p. 7)
discrete skill (p. 7)
model (p. 10)
motor skill (p. 8)
open skill (p. 6)
serial skill (p. 7)
skill (p. 4)

Suggestions for Further Reading

For more on the history of motor behavior research, see a very good review by psychologist Jack Adams (1987), who has been one of the major contributors in this area for several decades. Chapter 1 in my earlier textbook (Schmidt, 1988b) has a brief historical sketch of motor learning in relation to neurophysiology and motor control as well as a more in-depth treatment of how research in physical education and kinesiology has contributed to present knowledge.

Part I

Principles of Human Skilled Performance

Part I is concerned with the principles underlying the production of relatively high-level skilled performances. Whereas some of these skills can be thought of as largely inherited, such as walking, running, and maintaining posture and balance, other skills are profoundly affected by practice, such as steering a vehicle and shooting a basketball. For all these skills, though, Part I focuses on the underlying principles, processes, and mechanisms.

At the same time, Part I begins to develop, or build, a conceptual model of skilled performance, with the goal of giving a more complete overview, or structure, to the principles of how skills are performed. Chapter 2 begins with the notions that humans are processors of information and that performers must make decisions on the basis of this information. This model is added to in chapter 3, where the discussion turns to how sensory information can influence or even determine actions. Chapter 4 includes a number of principles underlying the production of movements, followed by some of the principles governing speed and accuracy of limb movements in chapter 5. Chapter 6 addresses differences among different individuals in their capabilities for skill, and how these differences can be understood in terms of the conceptual model.

By the end of Part I, the conceptual model will be relatively complete and can serve as a useful tool in understanding how the many pieces of the motor system fit and work together to produce actions. These principles lead to the performance enhancement applications summarized in the Practical Applications boxes, which are set off from the main body of the text for emphasis. With a new vocabulary and set of principles of human performance captured in the model, the discussion turns in Part II to how practice and experience can facilitate these processes, further building on the understanding developed in Part I.

Processing Information and Making Decisions

PREVIEW

The batter was ready this time. The pitcher had just thrown three slow curveballs in a row. Although the batter had two strikes against him, he felt confident because he thought the next pitch would be a fastball, and he was prepared for it. As the pitch was coming toward him, he strode forward and began to swing the bat to meet the ball, but he soon realized this was another curve. He could not modify his swing in time, and the bat crossed the plate long before the ball arrived. The pitcher had beaten him again.

How did the batter's faulty anticipation interfere with his performance? What processes were required to amend the action? To what extent did the stress of the game interfere? Certainly a major concern for the skilled performer is the evaluation of information, leading to decision making about future action.

This chapter deals with some of these processes, describing some of the principles of information processing most relevant to skilled performance. The conceptual model of skills is begun, with an information-processing perspective about the decision-making part. This chapter covers such topics as reaction time and the factors that affect it, decision making under stress, the important concept of attention and performance, and memory for skills.

STUDENT GOALS

1. To understand and appreciate the many ways that humans process information
2. To become familiar with the principles of reaction time and the factors that affect it
3. To understand how attention influences performance
4. To apply the principles of human performance to teaching and coaching settings

Without a doubt, one of the most important features of skilled performance is deciding what to do (and what not to do) in particular situations and making these decisions quickly and predictably. After all, the most beautifully executed baseball throw to first base is ineffective if the throw should have been directed somewhere else instead. This chapter considers factors contributing to these decision-making capabilities, including processing environmental information, the ways that this information is coded, stored, and used in decision making, and some of the factors that contribute to the actual decision. First comes a general approach for understanding how the motor system uses information, which will form the basis of the conceptual model of human performance.

INFORMATION-PROCESSING APPROACH

Psychologists have found it useful to think of the human being as a processor of information very much like a computer. Information is presented to the human as input. Various information-processing stages within the system generate a series of operations on this information, eventually resulting in skilled movement as output. This simple information-processing approach is shown in Figure 2.1.

A major goal of cognitive psychologists interested in the control of skills is to understand the specific nature of the processes in the box in Figure 2.1. There are many ways to approach this problem; a particularly useful one assumes that there are discrete

Input

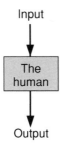

The human

Output

Figure 2.1 The information-processing approach to human performance.

information-processing **stages** through which the information must pass on the way from input to output. For our purposes, here are three of these stages:

- Stimulus identification
- Response selection
- Response programming

Information-Processing Stages

This stage analysis of performance generally assumes that peripheral information enters the system and is processed by the first stage. When this stage has completed its operations, the result is passed on to the second stage, whose result is passed to the third stage, and so on, the process finally resulting in an action, an output. What occurs in some of these stages of processing?

Stimulus-Identification Stage

During this first stage the system's problem is to decide whether a stimulus has been presented and, if so, what it is. Thus, stimulus identification is primarily a sensory stage, analyzing environmental information from a variety of sources, such as vision, audition, touch, kinesthesis, smell, and so on. The components, or separate dimensions, of

these stimuli are thought to be "assembled" in this stage, such as the combination of edges and colors that form a representation of a moving ball. Patterns of movement are also detected, such as whether a stimulus is moving at all, what direction and how quickly it is moving, and so on, as would be necessary for catching a football pass. The result of this stage is thought to be some representation of the stimulus, with this information being passed on to the next stage—response selection.

Response-Selection Stage

The activities of the response-selection stage begin when the stimulus-identification stage provides information about the nature of the environmental stimulus. The response-selection stage has the task of deciding what movement to make, given the nature of the environment. Here the choice from available movements is made, such as either passing the basketball to my teammate or taking a shot myself. Thus, this stage is a kind of translation mechanism between sensory input and movement output.

Response-Programming Stage

This final stage begins its processing upon receiving the decision about what movement to make as determined by the response-selection stage. The response-programming stage has the task of organizing the motor system for the desired movement. Before producing a movement, the system must ready the lower-level mechanisms in the brainstem and spinal cord for action, it must retrieve and organize a motor program that will eventually control the movement, and it must direct the muscles to contract in the proper order and with the proper levels of force and timing to produce the movement

Table 2.1 Characteristics of the Sequential Stages of Information Processing

Characteristic	Stimulus-identification stage	Response-selection stage	Response-programming stage
Function of stage	Detect, identify signal	Select response	Organize, initiate action
Effect of number of S-R alternatives	Minor	Large	None
Type of processing	Parallel	Parallel and serial	Serial
Attention required[a]	No	Sometimes	Yes

[a]See the section on Attention and Human Performance later in this chapter.

effectively. The characteristics of all three stages of processing are summarized in Table 2.1.

Beginning of a Conceptual Model

By including the stages of processing just described, Figure 2.2 adds detail to the simple

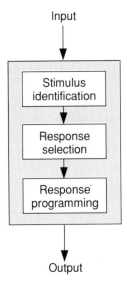

Input

Stimulus identification

Response selection

Response programming

Output

Figure 2.2 The expanded information-processing model showing the stimulus-identification, response-selection, and response-programming substages.

notion of information processing described in Figure 2.1. This structure forms the first part of the conceptual model of human performance to be elaborated throughout the text.

Clearly, these stages are all included within the human information system and are not visible under usual circumstances. However, several laboratory methods allow scientists to learn about these stages. It turns out that reaction time, one of the most important measures of human performance in many situations (e.g., sprint starts), is also a critical tool for understanding how the processing stages operate.

REACTION TIME AND DECISION MAKING

An important performance measure indicating the speed and effectiveness of decision making is **reaction time** (abbreviated RT). RT is the interval of time from a suddenly presented, unanticipated stimulus until the beginning of the response. Measuring RT is important because RT is an actual part of some real-world tasks, such as sprint races, where a starter's gun serves as a stimulus to begin. Following is an old photo of a foot-

Reaction time in a footrace; the starter's gun has fired, yet the athletes are only now getting off their marks after a reaction-time delay (reprinted from Scripture, 1905).

race; the starter has already fired his gun, as you can see by the position of the smoke. Yet, the athletes are all still on the line, only now just beginning to move. This emphasizes the substantial delay involved in RT. Being able to minimize RT in such a situation would give a large advantage.

In addition, RT is thought to be a component of many other activities, where it represents the speed of making decisions and initiating actions. In many rapid skills, success depends on the speed with which the performer can detect some feature of the environment or of an opponent's movement, decide what to do, and then initiate an effective countermove. Such activities are numerous, as in boxing, playing soccer, and driving a race car. Because RT is a fundamental component of many skills, it is not surprising that much research attention has been directed toward it.

But RT has important theoretical meaning as well, which is the major reason it has attracted so much research attention. RT begins when the stimulus is presented and ends when the movement response starts, so it is a measure of the accumulated durations of the three stages of processing seen in Figure 2.2. Any factor that lengthens the duration of one or more of these stages will thus lengthen RT. For this reason, scientists interested in information processing have used RT as a measure of the speeds of processing in these stages. Next is a discussion of how changes in RT inform us about the stages of processing.

Factors Influencing Reaction Time and Decision Making

There are many important factors that influence RT, ranging from the nature of the stimulus information presented to the nature of the movement required of the performer. Some of these factors are considered in this section.

Number of Stimulus-Response Alternatives

My racquetball opponent has a number of good serves all beginning the same way, and

I am frozen for a moment, trying to decide which way to go to return the serve. Why? One of the most important factors influencing the time to start an action, RT, is the number of possible stimuli—each of which leads to a distinct response—that can be presented at any given time. In the laboratory, the situation generally involves several possible stimuli, such as lights, and several responses for the subject to choose from, such as pressing different buttons, depending on which stimulus light is illuminated. This is termed choice RT, where the performer must choose one response from a collection of possible movements selected in advance. The performer receives a warning signal, followed by a foreperiod of unpredictable length (e.g., 2, 3, or 4 seconds [s]). Then the reaction stimulus is suddenly presented. Only then does the performer know which button to press; RT is the time required to detect the stimulus and select and initiate the proper response.

Generally, as the number of possible alternative movements increases, there is a gradual increase in the time required to respond to any one of them, that is, an increase in choice RT. The fastest situation involves only one stimulus and one response; this is simple RT.

Increased response latency due to a greater number of stimulus-response (S-R) alternatives is of critical importance in understanding skilled performances, forming the basis of **Hick's Law** (see the Highlight Box). The increase in RT is very large when the number of alternatives is increased from one to two. As seen in Figure 2.3, RT might increase from about 190 milliseconds (ms) with simple RT to more than 300 ms for a two-choice case—a 58% increase in the time required to process the stimulus information into the response! As the number of choices becomes larger, adding extra choices still increases RT, but the increases become smaller and smaller (e.g., the increase from 9 to 10 choices might be only 20 ms, or about 2 or 3%).

These delays can be of critical importance in determining success in many rapid skills, such as defending against a punch in boxing or intercepting a hockey shot. The entire duration of a baseball pitch might be only 600 ms, and the swing of the bat might take as little as 120 ms; an added 100-ms information-processing delay in detecting the trajectory of a pitch can severely limit the batter's use of this information.

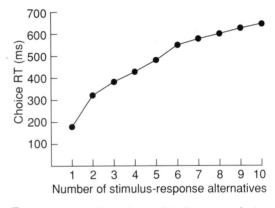

Figure 2.3 The relationship between choice reaction time and the number of stimulus-response alternatives. (Adapted from Woodworth, 1938; data obtained by Merkel in 1885.)

Because reaction delays can be so long, an important strategy in many rapid competitive activities is for the performer to increase the number of stimulus-response alternatives that the opponent must process in order to respond. In baseball, for example, increasing the number of different possible pitches provides considerable extra uncertainty for a batter, delaying processing time, thus giving the pitcher a strong advantage. Your having several possible tennis shots from a given location on the court increases your opponent's uncertainty about which one you will actually hit, delaying the response. Conversely, if you provide your opponent only one alternative, the opponent can do the pro-

HIGHLIGHT

Hick's Law

Over a century ago Merkel (1885, cited by Woodworth, 1938) asked subjects in a choice-RT experiment to press a reaction key when 1 of up to 10 possible stimuli was presented. The stimuli were the Arabic numerals 1 through 5 and the Roman numerals I through V. Each stimulus was paired with one finger and response key. For example, the possible stimuli on a set of trials might be 2, 3, and V (a 3-choice case), and the subjects were to respond with either the right index, right middle, or left thumb when the associated stimulus was presented. Merkel varied the number of possible stimulus-response alternatives in different sets of trials. His results are shown in Figure 2.3, where choice RT is plotted as a function of the number of stimulus-response alternatives. You can see that as the number of alternatives was increased from 1 (simple RT), there was a sharp rise in RT, this rise becoming less steep as the number of alternatives increased toward 10.

Much later Hick (1952) and independently Hyman (1953) discovered that the relationship between choice RT and the logarithm of the number of stimulus-response alternatives was linear. This relationship has become known as Hick's Law, and it holds for a wide variety of situations using different kinds of subjects, different movements, and different kinds of stimulus materials. It is one of the most important laws of human performance. The relationship implies that choice RT increases at a constant rate every time the number of stimulus-response alternatives is doubled (e.g., from 2 to 4 or from 16 to 32). This led to an important interpretation of Hick's Law: Choice RT is linearly related to the amount of information that must be processed to resolve the uncertainty about the various possible stimulus-response alternatives.

cessing very quickly, and you have failed to use a powerful weapon. As a general rule, make your opponent respond to as many likely alternatives as you can, slowing the speed of responding to any one of your possibilities when you finally produce it.

Stimulus-Response Compatibility. An important determinant of choice RT is **stimulus-response (S-R) compatibility**, usually defined as the extent to which the stimulus and the response it evokes are connected in a "natural" way. Catching a bouncing ball is an example of S-R compatibility because the

ball's movement to the right must be mirrored by hand movements to the right.

In the example within Figure 2.4a, the illuminated light calls for the subject to respond in the same direction and on the same side of the body. This is termed a compatible mapping between stimuli and responses. In the example within Figure 2.4b, however, the right light calls for the left hand to be moved and the left light calls for the right hand. The relationship between stimuli and responses is not nearly so natural; this situation is less S-R compatible, or is S-R incompatible.

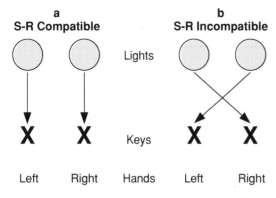

a
S-R Compatible

b
S-R Incompatible

Lights

Keys

Left   Right   Hands   Left   Right

Figure 2.4 Stimulus-response compatibility. The relationship between stimulus and response is more "natural," or compatible, in the situation at the left (a).

It is well established that for a given number of S-R alternatives, increasing S-R compatibility decreases choice RT. This is thought to be the effect of the relative "difficulty" of information processing in the response-selection stage, where the more natural linkages between compatible stimuli and responses lead to faster resolution of uncertainty and hence to faster RTs. The general rules regarding the number of possible stimuli and choice RT still apply to compatible stimulus-response arrangements. However, the amount of increase in choice RT (the slope) is less than it is for less compatible situations. Hick's Law holds for differing levels of compatibility, but the slope is steeper when the naturalness of the linkage, the compatibility, is relatively low.

Amount of Practice. Highly practiced performers can overcome the disadvantages of low S-R compatibility, such as the racing sailor who doesn't even have to think to move the tiller to the right when the boat needs to turn left. Research shows that two major factors affecting choice RT are the nature and the amount of practice. For a given number of stimulus-response alternatives,

PRACTICAL APPLICATIONS

1. An athlete should avoid making stereotyped choices because these can allow an opponent to treat the situation as simple RT and thus to minimize the response delay.
2. In choice situations, the athlete should use many alternative actions to increase the opponent's uncertainty, slowing RT by 50% or more.
3. The athlete should practice to develop new movement possibilities (e.g., additional kinds of handball shots) to increase the number of possible stimulus alternatives to present to the opponent.
4. The athlete should vary the movement alternatives more or less randomly to prevent the opponent from being able to anticipate which will be presented next.

the larger the level of practice, the shorter the RT. Overall, practice reduces the steepness of the increase in RT as the number of stimulus-response alternatives increases. This means that there is only a small effect of practice on simple RT but very large effects of practice on choice RT, particularly when the number of alternatives is large or when S-R compatibility is low. With extremely large amounts of practice, high-level performers can produce reactions that approach automatic processing (see the section on automaticity later in this chapter); these reactions are very fast and are slowed little, if at all, as the number of S-R alternatives increases. Finally, the nature of practice is important here, where practice using consistent mapping, the same stimulus always leading to the same response, is most effective (see chapter 9 for more on this kind of practice).

This effect of practice is essentially the same as the effect of increasing compatibility in that both variables reduce the slope of Figure 2.3's line relating the number of alternatives to choice RT. Thus, the effects of practice seem to make the stimulus-response arrangement "more compatible." Of course, practice has not really done so because the actual S-R compatibility of the task is just as it was in early practice. But the performer *treats* the task as if it were more compatible.

This fits well with practical experience. To a beginning driver, the connection between the presentation of a red light to stop and the response of pressing the brake pedal was very clumsy. However, after thousands of hours of driving practice, the link between the red light and the brake pedal is extremely natural, leading almost automatically to the movement.

Anticipation to Minimize Delays

One fundamental way performers cope with long reaction delays is to anticipate. Typically, a highly skilled performer predicts what is going to happen in the environment and when it will occur, and then performs various information-processing activities in advance; thus, the movement organization system is not required to react after the fact to unanticipated events. The defensive lineman in football predicts that the other team will try a running play, so he moves quickly and stops the play for a big loss.

Highly skilled people know what stimuli are likely to be presented, where they will appear, and when they will occur, so these people can predict the responses required. Armed with this information, a performer can organize movements in advance, completing some of the information-processing activities usually conducted during the response-selection or response-programming stage. This allows the performer to initiate the movement much earlier or at a time consonant with the movements of the environment, as in predicting where and when a pitched ball will arrive at the plate so that it can be struck effectively with a well-timed batswing. Because of these capabilities to anticipate, skilled performers seem to behave almost as if they had "all the time they need," without being rushed to respond to stimuli using the reaction-time processes previously discussed.

Types of Anticipation. Anticipation can be of two general types. It is important to predict what will happen in the environment, such as predicting whether a tennis opponent will hit a lob or a smash in order to get positioned on the court effectively. This is spatial (or event) anticipation. Spatial information allows the performer to organize the movement in advance, so when the signal for action finally does occur, the movement can be initiated with a far shorter RT.

In other situations, it might be clear what is going to occur, but the performer might or might not be able to predict *when* it will occur, such as anticipating the snap of the ball in American football. This is usually called temporal anticipation. Although there is a strong advantage in knowing when some event will occur, not being able to predict what will occur prevents the performer from organizing the movement completely in advance.

Benefits From Anticipation. Spatial and temporal anticipation each provide strong advantages for performance in most skills. If the performer can correctly anticipate both what will occur and when it will occur, however, the advantages become very large. If the defensive lineman in football can predict what play will be run (spatial anticipation) as well as when the snap count will be presented (temporal anticipation), he can initiate his movement simultaneously with the snap of the ball (with a RT of 0 ms); the action will be very effective in stopping the play.

Effective anticipation is not always easy because it requires the performer to have a great deal of knowledge about the opponent's tendencies in various circumstances. Anticipation can, though, bring dramatic gains in performance. For this reason, of course, the opponent will be doing everything possible to prevent the performer from anticipating the stimulus moves. This interplay provides many important strategic aspects in sports.

Several factors affect the capability to predict effectively. One is the regularity of the events. For example, if my racquetball opponent always serves the ball to my (weak) backhand side, I can predict this event and counter it in various ways. Clearly, my capability to anticipate would be minimized if three or four different serves were randomly used instead. Similarly, if the American football quarterback always has the ball snapped on the second of two rhythmical verbal signals, the defensive team can anticipate the critical event and be highly prepared for it. Randomly ordering the snap signals keeps the defensive team from anticipating temporally, yet still allows the offensive teammates (who know the snap count, which is agreed upon in the huddle) to anticipate both temporally and spatially. The goals here are for the offensive team to respond as a single unit to the snap count and to allow the defensive team no capability to anticipate. This provides the offense the greatest relative advantage.

Costs of Anticipating. There are several advantages to anticipation, but, as with most things in life, there are costs as well. The primary disadvantage for anticipation is when the anticipated movement is not the actual one. In American football again, if the defensive lineman anticipates that the snap count will occur on the second sound but

The quarterback and center respond simultaneously to the same signal.

the quarterback takes the snap on the third sound, the lineman could move too early, generating a penalty for his team. In a similar way, anticipating that my opponent will hit the tennis ball to my left allows me to move left to intercept it, only to receive that sinking feeling of seeing the ball go to my right. Clearly, anticipating correctly can result in many benefits, but anticipating incorrectly can be disastrous.

Earlier the notion was discussed that anticipating allows various information processing activities to take place in advance so they do not have to be done after the stimulus. Suppose that a performer has gone through these preparatory processes but now the events in the environment change, indicating that if the prepared movement is initiated, it would be incorrect. First the performer must inhibit, or "unprepare," the already-prepared movement. These processes take time, of course, estimated to be

PRACTICAL APPLICATIONS

1. An athlete should thoroughly practice a skill having important RT components, especially if components are incompatible or if they have many stimulus-response alternatives, because the gains in reaction speed can be very large.
2. The athlete should learn the opponent's actions and tendencies in order to anticipate them both spatially and temporally.
3. If possible, the athlete should view the opponent's play prior to a match, scouting the opponent thoroughly, to appreciate his or her tendencies more completely.
4. During a racquetball match, have the performer try to perform each of several possible serves with about the same frequency, which minimizes the opponent's capability to anticipate.
5. In football, prevent the opponents from anticipating the snap count by randomly varying which sound in the sequence is the snap signal.

somewhere around 40 ms in studies of simple actions. Then the correct action must be organized and initiated, requiring the extremely slow processes and lengthy reaction time. By the time the correct movement finally occurs, the opponent has won that point.

In addition, often the incorrect movement is actually triggered, as you have seen many times in sport events. As before, the performer still has the problem of inhibiting the incorrect action and preparing the correct one. But there is the additional problem that the inappropriate action might be in the incorrect direction, taking the person farther

from the best location and producing momentum in the wrong direction, which is difficult and time consuming to overcome. My actually moving toward the left side of the tennis court for an anticipated shot makes it impossible for me to stop that action and move to the right in time when my opponent hits the shot there instead.

Strategies for Anticipating. The effective gains made when players anticipate correctly, coupled with the large losses when players anticipate incorrectly, produce important strategic elements in many rapid sport activities. One strategy is to do everything to prevent the opponent from anticipating correctly. This can be done by being unpredictable, randomizing which and when movements are made so the opponent cannot effectively anticipate. The opponent who anticipates will be incorrect so often, with disastrous effects, that he or she will not be successful and will be forced to switch to a strategy of merely reacting.

An important principle for many rapid sports events is that, if you can organize your play so that your opponent must *react* to you using the slow, cumbersome reaction-time methods mentioned earlier, then you have essentially won. On the other hand, the opponent who can correctly anticipate has a strong advantage. Your key is randomization, making your movements unpredictable, forcing your opponent to react rather than predict.

Another important strategy is to allow your opponent to anticipate, but then you make essentially the movement opposite to the one anticipated. A racquetball player moves as if to make a soft dink shot near the front wall, causing the opponent to move forward quickly. Then, as part of the plan, the anticipated dink suddenly turns out to be a passing shot that has the opponent badly out of position. Such a strategy is a large part of almost every rapid sport. It is dependent on the fact that if you can lure your opponent into anticipation, you have the advantage because of the large costs of false anticipation.

PRACTICAL APPLICATIONS

1. If the opponent tries to anticipate a tennis shot, an effective strategy is to start one action but abruptly complete a different shot, forcing the opponent into false anticipation.
2. Where errors in choice are too serious to be tolerated (e.g., resulting in a fall in a bicycle race), it is better to avoid anticipating and simply to respond to what actually occurs.
3. If there is little to lose by being incorrect but much to gain by being quick, the performer should anticipate the opponent's moves and strike decisively.
4. In a rapid game, everything should be done to prevent the opponent from anticipating, forcing him or her to respond using reaction time.

Decision Making and Performance Under Stress and Arousal

Stress and **arousal**, the level of excitement stress produces, are common aspects of skill performance situations. This is certainly true of many athletic events, where the pressure to win and the threat of losing are important sources of emotional arousal for players. The level of arousal imposed by a situation is an important determinant of performance, particularly if the performance is dependent on the speed and accuracy of decision making. Next are examined some of the effects of arousal on performance and information processing, with some suggestions of how to enhance performance under such situations.

Inverted-U Principle

You can think of arousal as the level of excitement or activation generated in the central nervous system, low levels of arousal associated with sleeplike states, and high levels associated with the agitated and extremely alert states found in life-threatening situations. The influences of arousal level on performance have been studied for many years; an important principle of arousal's function for performance is the **inverted-U principle**. In Figure 2.5 the level of arousal, on the x-axis, ranges from very low to very high in different situations. Starting from low arousal, increasing the arousal level generally enhances performance, but only to a point. Performance quality peaks at some intermediate value of arousal, and performance actually deteriorates as the arousal level rises further.

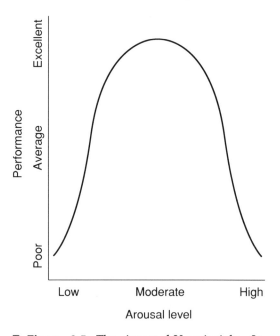

Figure 2.5 The inverted-U principle. Increased arousal improves performance only to a point, after which further increases in arousal degrade performance.

The inverted-U principle is perhaps surprising to many who deal with sports and coaching because it is generally assumed that the higher the level of motivation or arousal, the more effective the performance will be. Coaches often spend a great deal of time before games attempting to raise the team's arousal level, and we hear sportscasters argue that a team's performance was poor because the players were not "up" for the contest. Yet, this general view is contradicted by considerable experimental evidence that a high level of arousal is effective only to a point, but further raising the arousal level actually damages performance.

This effect appears to depend somewhat on the kinds of skills. If the skills require very fine muscular control (as in archery) or have important decision-making components (as in being a quarterback), then the point of maximum arousal is generally shifted to the left of the inverted-U curve, as in Figure 2.6. High and even moderate levels of arousal appear to interfere with fine muscular control and decision making (Weinberg & Hunt, 1976). When arousal levels are low to moderate, cognitively complex skills can be degraded by slight further increases in arousal. On the other hand, many other skills are dominated by large-muscle actions without much fine control or require very little decision making and cognitive complexity, such as power lifting. With such skills very high arousal levels do not worsen performance. The important point is that an arousal level that is too high can be as ineffective as one that is too low, although probably for different reasons.

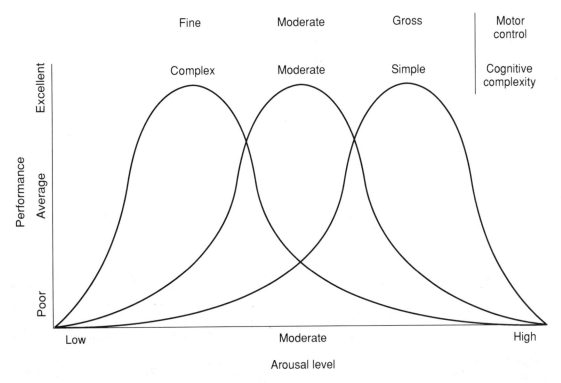

Figure 2.6 The inverted-U principle for different tasks. Optimal arousal level is higher for more simple tasks with more gross motor control.

Even for a given sport (e.g., American football), certain positions (quarterback) have relatively low optimal arousal levels because of important decision-making processes, whereas other positions (defensive lineman) have considerably higher optimal arousal levels because of increased emphasis on maximum force production. It is very important for the coach (a) to assess the skills to be performed in terms of fine control and decision making, and then (b) to generate the optimal arousal level for each skill.

These principles have been recognized and studied recently within the field of sport psychology, where the general problem has been to prepare the athlete for high-level performance by adjusting the arousal level to fit the task requirements. Generally the athlete's arousal level is too high, and various stress management procedures are used to reduce the level of excitement before performance (e.g., Orlick, 1986; 1990). These important techniques for enhancing human performance are just beginning to be understood.

The inverted-U principle can be summarized as follows:

- Increased arousal improves performance, but only to a point.
- Further increases in arousal cause decrements in performance.
- Tasks with high decision-making components or fine motor control have relatively low optimal levels of arousal.
- Tasks with minimal decision-making components or with gross-motor skills have relatively high optimal arousal levels.
- Some people are more easily aroused than others.

Information Processing Under High Arousal

During a 50-yard sprint in his first big meet, a high school swimmer with a very high

PRACTICAL APPLICATIONS

1. If the task involves decision making or fine movement control, try to adjust the performer's arousal to a relatively low level.
2. For a task with large-muscle actions or requiring large levels of force and speed, generate a high arousal level for maximum performance.
3. Analyze a skill for important components that are affected either positively or negatively by high arousal as a basis for altering a player's arousal level.
4. Teach the athlete about the beneficial and detrimental effects of arousal on performance and use effective methods of stress management to bring arousal under control.
5. The coach, whose decision making is often most critical of all, should work to control his or her own arousal level to maximize effectiveness.

arousal level does a flip-turn while 10 feet short of the pool end, leaving him treading water while the others turn and finish the race. Has the high arousal led to faulty performance here? If so, what kinds of processes are impaired? Several ways people process information change when arousal levels are raised, and these processes operate together to help explain differences in performance.

Perceptual Narrowing. One important change in information processing with high arousal is **perceptual narrowing**, the tendency for the perceptual field to shrink. For example, consider how vision changes for the novice in the relatively stressful sport of deep-sea diving (e.g., Weltman & Egstrom, 1966). On land, where the diver can operate under a low level of arousal, the range of possible stimulus sources that can be responded to is relatively wide, representing most of the visual field. However, in a swimming pool, and especially in the ocean, where arousal increases, the visual field becomes more narrowly and intensely focused; systematically fewer peripheral stimuli are detected, with increased attention being directed to those sources most pertinent to, or expected in, the task. This is an important mechanism because it allows the person to devote more attention to those stimulus sources that are immediately most likely and relevant. Perceptual narrowing is not limited to vision but apparently occurs with each of the senses in an analogous way. This phenomenon can also be an effect of drugs, sleep loss, and a number of other factors.

But perceptual narrowing has drawbacks. It can generate effective performance as long as the stimuli that actually occur are the ones that were expected, but it can cause performance to suffer if unexpected stimuli occur. For example, with mild intoxication, perceptual narrowing allows auto driving performance to be "acceptable" as long as the expected events occur. If an unexpected event occurs, however, such as a child suddenly chasing a ball into the street, the driving performance could be extremely ineffective, leading to an accident.

Cue-Utilization Hypothesis. Easterbrook's (1959) cue-utilization hypothesis helps explain these common performance decrements with high arousal. When the arousal level is low and the perceptual field is relatively wide, the performer has access to a wide range of cues, only a few of which are relevant to effective performance, so performance is suboptimal. As the arousal level rises and the attentional focus narrows onto the most relevant cues, more and more of the irrelevant cues are excluded, so proficiency increases because the performer is responding to mostly relevant cues. With further arousal increases, though, the increased perceptual narrowing means missing even some

of the relevant cues, so performance begins to suffer, particularly where the cues are not highly expected. The optimal level of arousal is presumably that where the narrowed attentional focus excludes many irrelevant cues yet allows most of the relevant cues to be detected.

The climber cannot afford to let stress and arousal degrade performance here.

At the highest levels of arousal we find **hypervigilance**, a state commonly called panic. When losing vehicle control in icy conditions, inexperienced drivers often panic, applying the brakes and "freezing" at the wheel, even though they otherwise know this is the wrong thing to do. In a hypervigilant state, decision making is severely limited because of heightened perceptual narrowing, resulting in particularly ineffective performance of nearly any type. At the same time, a high level of arousal also degrades the physical control of movements, actually interfering with the smooth control seen in skilled actions under more relaxed conditions (Weinberg & Hunt, 1976). Although hypervigilant states are relatively rare, it is not uncommon to see a young athlete (or coach!) operating under such a disorienting condition in particularly close competition, and it is not surprising to see the ineffective performance that results.

Summary Break

Some of these effects of increased arousal can be summarized as follows:

- Increased arousal enhances performance, but only to a point, beyond which further increases in arousal are detrimental to performance.
- The optimal level of arousal varies with the task, with skills requiring fine muscular control and decision making suffering the most from high levels of arousal, and skills with large force requirements suffering the least.
- Perceptual narrowing is an important process in high arousal, where reactions to expected cues are enhanced and reactions to unexpected cues are degraded.
- Sport psychologists have developed techniques for stress management whereby an athlete's excessive arousal level can be reduced to an optimal level before performance.

ATTENTION AND HUMAN PERFORMANCE

A very old idea in psychology is that people have some limited capacity to process information from the environment, or to pay **attention**. This section discusses how the concept of attention is related to information-processing capabilities that place limits on human skilled performance.

Attention: Limitations in Information-Processing Capacity

As he is about to serve, a tennis player has his attention distracted by a baby crying in the stands. Attention seems to be limited in that only a certain amount of information processing capacity seems to exist. If it is overloaded, much information can be missed.

Also, attention seems to be serial in that it seems to focus first on this, then on that; only with great difficulty (if at all) can we focus attention on two things at the same time. Sometimes attention is directed to external sensory events (perceiving an opponent's movements), sometimes it is focused on internal mental operations (trying to remember the play that was called), and sometimes it is focused on internal sensory information (sensations from the muscles and the joints). In addition, there are the well-known difficulties in doing two tasks at the same time, as if there were limits in the total capacity to process the information that supports them.

Figure 2.7 shows how the fixed amount of attention (or capacity) must be divided between a "main" task and some secondary activity. When the main task is relatively simple, not requiring much attention, then more attentional capacity remains for other tasks.

This notion has strong implications for understanding high-level skilled performance. In many skills there is an overwhelming amount of information that could be processed, some of it relevant to performance and some of it not (the baby's crying in the example above). The performer's problem is to cope with this potential overload. The performer must learn what to attend to and when, and must shift attention skillfully between events in the environment, monitoring and correcting his or her own actions, planning future actions, and doing many other processes that compete for the limited resources of attentional capacity.

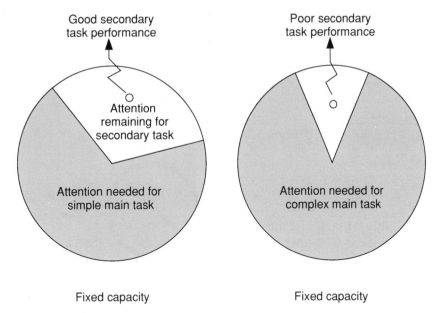

Good secondary
task performance

Attention
remaining for
secondary task

Attention needed for
simple main task

Fixed capacity

Poor secondary
task performance

Attention needed for
complex main task

Fixed capacity

Figure 2.7 Attention remaining for a secondary task is reduced when the primary task is more complex.

It is tempting to equate attention and consciousness, that set of processes of which you are aware. You would probably agree that people are limited in conscious capabilities, but there are still other limitations in information-processing capabilities that do not seem to involve consciousness. A better way to think of attention, therefore, is related to the limitations in doing two things at the same time. Psychologists have approached the limitations in information processing by first trying to understand the separate requirements of tasks that interfere with each other. The idea has been that, if two tasks interfere with each other, then they both demand some access to the limited capacity to process information; that is, they both require attention.

In sum, some of the features that define attention are these:

- Attention is serial, shifting from source to source over time.
- Attention is limited in capacity.

- Attention is effortful and is related to arousal.
- Attention limits the capacity to do certain parts of tasks together.

When Do Tasks Interfere With Each Other?

This section turns to the question of when and under what conditions tasks interfere with each other. One way to understand the kinds of multiple-task interference involves the stages of information processing described earlier (see Figure 2.2). It is useful to ask whether, within each stage, there is interference between two processes competing for the available capacity. As information moves through each successive processing stage, more interference occurs among concurrent activities. Processing can occur in parallel (without attention) in the stimulus-identification stage, but there is much less parallel processing in the response-selection stage. Finally, there is considerable interference among tasks in the response-programming stage, which generates the movement and which can organize and initiate only a single movement at a time.

Stimulus Identification: Information Processing in Parallel

There is much evidence suggesting that information processing in the most peripheral, sensory stages can be done in parallel. With parallel processing, two or more streams of information can enter the system at the same time and can be processed together without interfering with each other. For example, information from different aspects of the visual display, such as the color and the shape of objects, can apparently be processed together without interference.

This finding comes from an analysis of the Stroop effect. Imagine that you are a research subject, asked to respond as quickly as possible only to the color of ink printed on white cards, as in Figure 2.8, pressing one key if it is red and another if it is black. In some cases, the ink is organized into forms irrelevant to color, as with the two forms on the left of the figure. In other cases, as on the right, each of the two colors (red and black) forms the name of the other color. The Stroop effect is the tendency for the set of stimuli on the right to have longer RTs to name the color than those on the left. This effect is taken as evidence that two stimuli—the color of the ink and the word that the ink spells—are initially processed together and in parallel. The interference is caused later on by the two stimuli competing for different responses.

Headphones can carry two separate auditory messages to the two ears. The information can be processed together, even though one message can be ignored intentionally. There is also considerable parallel processing of the sensory signals from the muscles and joints associated with posture and loco-

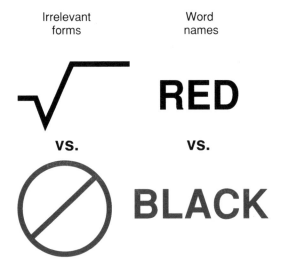

Figure 2.8 The Stroop effect. Relative to responding to ink color in irrelevant forms (left), when ink color and form conflict (right), reaction time to name ink color is slowed.

motion, and people seem to handle these together and without much awareness. The standard view is that, considering the processes occurring in the stimulus-identification stage, sensory information can apparently be processed in parallel and without much interference, that is, without attention. The evidence tends to argue that the processes involving sensory analysis do not contain the source of interference between two separate movement tasks.

Response Selection: Automatic and Controlled Processing

Interference between tasks is never more obvious than when the performer must simultaneously perform two actions each requiring mental operations, such as dribbling a soccer ball while thinking whether a word contains the letter *c*. Such processing activities are thought to be done during response selection because they seem to determine the choice among several possible responses. These activities are governed by **controlled processing**, which is thought to be (a) slow; (b) attention demanding, with interference caused by competing processing; (c) serial, occurring before or after other processing tasks; and (d) volitional, easily halted or avoided altogether. Relatively effortful, controlled processing is a very large part of conscious information-processing activities, involving mental operations among relatively poorly learned, or even completely novel, activities. Having to perform two information-processing tasks together can completely disrupt both tasks. Many examples of this information overload can be seen, such as a golfer whose concentration is disrupted when a partner asks a question.

A separate, very different kind of information processing seems to occur in highly practiced people. In a television interview Peter Vidmar, a 1984 Olympic silver medalist in gymnastics, said he paid attention just to the first trick in his routine; the remainder of the elements occurred "automatically." These elements require only minor adjustments while being run off, allowing Vidmar to focus on such higher-order aspects of his routine as style and form. It is as if much of the information processing necessary in this complex gymnastics routine was fundamentally different from controlled processing, not requiring very much attention (see Table 2.2). This way of dealing with information, **automatic processing**, is (a) fast; (b) not attention demanding, in that such processes do not generate (very much) interference with other tasks; (c) parallel, occurring together with other processing tasks; and (d) involuntary, often unavoidable.

Automatic information processing is thought to be the result of an enormous amount of practice. Your capability to quickly recognize collections of letters as the words you are reading now has come from years of practice, just as Vidmar's capability

Table 2.2 Characteristics of Controlled and Automatic Processing

Controlled processing	Automatic processing
Slow	Fast
Attention demanding	Not attention demanding
Serial	Parallel
Voluntary	Involuntary

to produce his gymnastics routine has. The effectiveness of automatic processing has strong implications not only for many everyday tasks (like reading) but also for high-level performance skills. If automatic, many important information-processing activities can be produced not only quickly but in parallel with other activities, and without disrupting performance.

Production Units. One interpretation of automaticity is that, with practice, a person develops a series of small, specialized "production units" to handle particular information-processing subtasks. Given a specific stimulus, a production unit generates a specific output. For example, after much practice, high-level volleyball players automatically read their opponents' movement patterns to mean the ball will be spiked from, say, the left side (e.g., see Allard & Burnett, 1985). The production units operate on the pattern of information (opponents' movements) to generate a particular output (the internal decision that the play will be to the left). The response-programming stage then takes over to produce the action decided upon.

Costs Versus Benefits of Automaticity. Automatic performances, whose benefits are nearly obvious, are related to processing information in parallel, quickly, and without interference from other processing tasks. But what if the opposing volleyball players in the previous paragraph consistently produce a pattern leading to a play to the left—except on one particular occasion. This time the same pattern unexpectedly leads to a play to the right. The defenders' automatic processing of the pattern would lead to a quick decision and a movement to counter the expected play, a response that is hopeless in combating the play that actually occurs.

Clearly, then, automaticity can have drawbacks, as well as benefits. Although very fast processing is good when the environment is stable and predictable, it can lead to terrible errors when the environment (or an opponent) changes the action at the last moment. Thus, automaticity seems most effective in closed skills, where the environment is relatively predictable. With open skills, so many more patterns are possible that the performer must develop an automatic response to each of them; this is generally possible only after many years of experience.

Practicing for Automaticity. How do people develop the capability to process information automatically? Practice, and lots of it, is a very important ingredient, so you should not expect to see automaticity develop quickly. Practicing for automaticity is generally most effective under a consistent mapping condition, where the response generated is consistently related to a particular stimulus pattern. For example, to stop driving is always the response to a red light. This is in contrast to a varied mapping condition, where a given stimulus sometimes leads to one response, sometimes to another response. An example is the incredible variety of button layouts on TV remote-control units from different brands, where a given function (changing the channel) requires pressing a button in one brand and a different button in another brand. Such a situation

makes it difficult to respond automatically and requires much practice to master. This issue of training for automaticity is covered more completely in chapter 9.

1. Inform the performer that considerable practice under consistent mapping conditions is required to develop automaticity.
2. Use consistent mapping conditions for practice, a given stimulus pattern always resulting in the same response.
3. Emphasize the development of automaticity most strongly in a closed skill, where the stable and predictable environment produces consistent mapping conditions.
4. Instruct the performer that automaticity develops even more slowly in an open skill, where many stimuli must be recognized and responses to them acquired.

Response Programming: Movement Organization Occurs Serially

A fencer moves the foil toward the opponent's shoulder but then quickly alters direction and contacts the waist instead. Responding to the first move, the fake, seems to have interfered with the opponent's speed of responding to the second move, and the point is lost. This suggests strong interference between activities in the later stages of information processing. Much of this view comes from considerable research evidence, in the double-stimulation paradigm, where the subject is required to respond to each of two stimuli presented very close together in time. This paradigm is in many ways analogous to the problem facing the fencer's opponent, who must respond to one move and then another in rapid succession.

Double-Stimulation Paradigm. In this research task the subject might be asked to respond to a tone (Stimulus 1) by lifting the right hand from a key. Then a light (Stimulus 2) might be presented, to which the subject responds by lifting the left hand. The separation between stimuli, the interstimulus interval (ISI), might range from zero to a few hundred milliseconds (a few tenths of a second). Psychologists are usually interested in RT to the second stimulus (RT2) as a function of the ISI.

The general findings from this paradigm are graphed in Figure 2.9, where RT2 is plotted as a function of the ISI. The horizontal line (Control RT2) is the value of RT2 when the first stimulus is not presented at all; it represents the "usual" (without interference) RT to this stimulus. Depending on the length of the ISI, there is a marked delay in the RT2 when the system is also occupied with the first stimulus. When the ISI is about

60 ms, this delay is very large and it can more than double the value of RT2, compared to its control value. As the ISI increases, the delay in RT2 decreases, but there is still some interference with RT2 even with ISIs of 200 ms or more. The processing of the first stimulus interferes seriously with the processing of the second.

Psychological Refractory Period. This delay in responding to the second of two closely spaced stimuli is termed the **psychological refractory period (PRP)**, an important phenomenon in understanding human performance. The system processes the first stimulus and generates the first response. If the experimenter unexpectedly presents the second stimulus during this time, its response is delayed considerably. The current understanding is that there is a bottleneck in the response-programming stage, which can organize and initiate only one action at a time, as diagrammed in Figure 2.10. Any other action must wait until the stage has finished initiating the first. This delay is largest when the ISI is short because the response-programming stage has just begun to generate the first response; this response must be emitted before the stage can begin to generate the second. As the ISI increases, more of the first response will have been prepared by the time Stimulus 2 arrives, so there is less delay before the response-programming stage is cleared.

One more finding is of interest here. When the ISI is very short, say less than 40 ms, the motor system responds to the second stimulus in a very different way. The system responds to the first and second stimulus as if they were one, producing both responses simultaneously. In this phenomenon, termed *grouping*, the early processing stages presumably detect both stimuli as a single event and organize a single, more complicated action in which both limbs respond simultaneously.

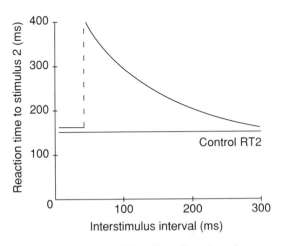

Figure 2.9 The PRP effect. Reaction time to the second of two closely spaced is delayed depending on the interstimulus interval (ISI).

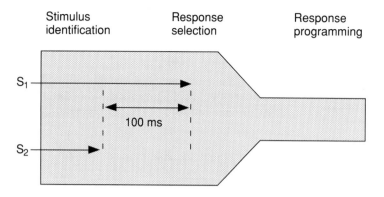

Stimulus 1 enters, followed in 100 ms by Stimulus 2.
Both are processed in parellel until Stimulus 1 reaches
the bottleneck in the response-programming stage, where

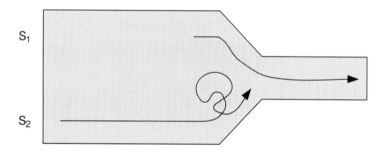

Stimulus 2 must wait until the response-programming
stage is cleared for further processing, so

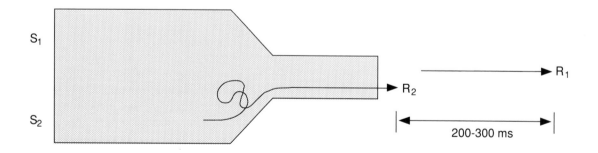

Response 1 and Response 2 are separated by far
more than 100 ms.

■ **Figure 2.10** An information-processing bottleneck in the response-selection stage.

Summary Break

Some of these features of movement production and organization can be summarized as follows:

- When two stimuli calling for separate responses are presented close to each other in time, there is a psychological refractory period, a marked delay in the response to the second stimulus.
- The delay in the second response depends on the interstimulus interval (ISI) and is greatest when the ISI is slightly greater than 40 ms (e.g., 60 ms).
- When the two stimuli are separated by only 40 ms or less, the stimuli are perceived, treated, and responded to as one.
- The delay occurs in the response-programming stage, where only one action can be organized and initiated at a time.

How Does Faking Occur? A basketball player often makes a movement as if to take a shot but then withholds it and actually shoots a short time afterward. An over-enthusiastic defensive player often tries to block the "first" shot and is badly out of position to defend against the actual shot. This example is typical of faking in many rapid sports and games.

The phenomenon of psychological refractoriness just discussed accounts for many of the underlying processes in faking. What actually happens is this: The player taking the shot plans a single relatively complex action that involves a move to begin a shot, a delay to withhold it, and then the actual shot—all done in rapid succession. This movement is organized as a single unit and is prepared as any other movement would be in the response-programming stage. However, the defensive player sees only the first part of this action; this can be thought of as the first

stimulus in the double-stimulation paradigm, and it triggers the response to block the shot. The processing of the first stimulus leads to large delays in responding to the new information that the shot has been withheld, that it is a fake (the second stimulus). The result is that the first response (movement to block) cannot be withheld, and it occurs essentially as originally planned. This creates a very large delay in initiating a second, corrective response to block the actual shot, which is made at about the same time that the defensive player is dropping back to the floor after taking the fake. This all makes the shot very easy, and it makes the defensive player look a little foolish at the same time.

Some principles of faking emerge from research on psychological refractoriness. First, the fake should be realistic, distinct, and clearly perceived, so the defensive player treats it as an actual shot. Second, the single programmed action that contains both the fake and the actual shot should be planned to separate the fake (Stimulus 1) and the actual shot (Stimulus 2) sufficiently to generate a large delay for the response to Stimulus 2. From the data it seems this separation should be somewhere around 60 to 100 ms (see Figure 2.9). If this separation is too short, the defensive player can ignore the fake and respond instead to the actual shot. If the separation is too long, the defender will respond to the second stimulus with an essentially normal RT, and the shooter will have lost the advantage of the fake.

Movement-Output Chunking. Aside from its practical applications, the PRP effect is important for understanding how movement is produced. Two separate actions, each triggered by a separate stimulus, cannot be produced very closely to each other in time. That is, if Stimulus 1 leads to Response 1, considerable time is required before any other Stimulus 2 can generate some different Response

2. If this scheme is accurate, then the movement control system must be putting out a movement into the environment as a chunk, or a burst of activity that exclusively occupies several hundred milliseconds until the next one can be generated. Other research shows that these chunks of activity are separated by approximately 200 ms (Kahneman, 1973) at least. Sometimes when numerous chunks have to be strung together, as in steering a car, the system probably puts out the chunks at a maximum rate of about three per second. These chunks of movement are thought to be organized in the response-programming stage and then run off under the control of motor programs (chapter 4), as shown in Figure 2.11.

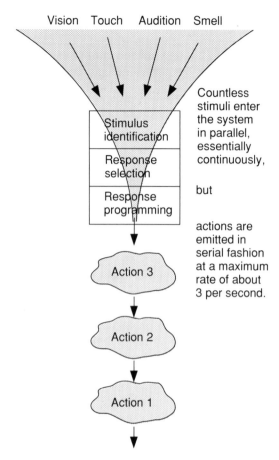

Figure 2.11 Information is provided continuously, but responses are generated in units, or chunks.

PRACTICAL APPLICATIONS

1. To have the opponent take the fake, the performer needs to make the first signal realistic and distinct to increase the opponent's tendency to treat it as a real signal to respond.
2. The separation between the first and second signals should not be too small (less than 60 ms), or the fake can be ignored.
3. The separation between the first and second signals should not be too large (greater than 150 ms), or the second signal can then be responded to almost normally.
4. The performer should experiment with various signal separation lengths in practice to maximize the opponent's delay in responding to the second one.

When Do the Hands Interfere With Each Other?

You have undoubtedly tried to rub your belly and pat your head at the same time, experiencing difficulties in coordinating the two hands. You found that the hands do not "want" to do different things, so you end up patting, or rubbing, both your head and your belly. This example reveals many important movement coordination principles that indicate which kinds of dual tasks are easy and which are essentially impossible. It also tells us about some of the underlying principles of coordination among the limbs.

Role of the Temporal Structures in the Two Hands. One interesting observation is that under many circumstances the hands seem "linked" to each other. It is very easy for the hands to make simultaneous movements if the patterns are the same, and it's even easier if the patterns are mirror images of each other. Try scribbling on a large sheet of paper or blackboard with both hands; you'll see that it is almost trivially easy to make the "same" pattern with the left and the right hands. Analysis reveals that the actions of the two hands have a common time structure, in that muscular forces tend to produce the various submovements at the same time in the two hands. Furthermore, the hands are not anywhere as strongly linked spatially, as you will see if you scribble with large strokes in the left hand and small strokes in the right; yet, they are still strongly linked temporally. These observations and laboratory analyses of similar situations have led to the idea that, especially in relatively unpracticed movements, the system "prefers" to operate in a mode in which the two hands perform the same actions, or at least actions with the same temporal structure.

This point can be made another way. It is particularly difficult to produce movements in the two hands that have different temporal structures, or rhythms. It is very difficult to tap a regular rhythm with the left hand but tap as quickly as possible with the right. It is even difficult to monitor one rhythm and tap a different one with the hand (Klapp et al., 1985). All this suggests that the system prefers to respond with a common underlying time structure. As long as the time structure is the same for the two hands, there is little interference. But if the time structure is different (as in both rubbing your head and patting your belly), then massive interference occurs.

To summarize these ideas:

- Two-handed movements are extremely difficult to perform if the temporal structures are different in the two limbs.
- The system seems to prefer two-handed

movements with the same temporal organization, and producing them is relatively easy.
- If the temporal structures are the same in the two hands, different amplitudes of movement are relatively easy.
- Interference occurs even if the performer thinks about one rhythm while producing another.

Interpretation: Output Chunking. One important interpretation of these findings is that the motor system can produce only a single motor program at one time. This is an extension of the idea expressed earlier that the response-programming stage could organize (during RT) only a single action at a time. But now the focus is on the production of the movement itself, after the RT is completed. Fundamental are the notions (to be developed in chapter 4) that this single movement program has a specific temporal structure inherent to it, that only a single temporal structure can be produced at any one time, and that this temporal structure provides a basis for the temporal organization of the movements of all the limbs it controls. Therefore rubbing your head and simultaneously patting your belly is difficult because it requires different temporal structures; the system tries to control both hands with a single structure but is unsuccessful. Producing a γ (the Greek letter gamma) and a V together presents the same problem (see the Highlight Box on the Gamma-V Experiment). Also, when a performer tries to produce different tapping rhythms, one rhythm dominates, and the dual-task performance is ineffective. However, linking the hands in scribbling is easy because both hands are controlled by the same temporal structure.

From one viewpoint, being able to generate only one action at a time seems to be a serious limitation to human performance. From an ecological viewpoint, however, which emphasizes that humans evolved to

The Gamma-V Experiment

Try this simple experiment for yourself. With a pencil in your left hand, practice drawing small (2-inch) gammas (γ) relatively quickly, without modification during their production. Start with the pencil against the bottom of a ruler laid on the paper, and finish with the pencil against the ruler again. The figure must cross over near the center and have a rounded bottom. When you can do this effectively, use the other hand to draw regular Vs. The procedure is the same except now the figure must not cross over itself and must have a pointed bottom. Most people do not have any trouble producing these figures. It is assumed that each figure is represented by its own well-learned motor program. Also, these are actually two different programs because the temporal structures for the two figures are different: down-up for the V and down-over-up for the γ.

Now try to produce these two figures together, using the same hands as before. You will find, as Konzem (1987) did, that it is very difficult, with results such as those shown in Figure 2.12. Most performers show a strong tendency to make the same figure with both hands or at least to produce certain features of the different figures in both hands (e.g., rounded bottom). They cannot do this dual task effectively even with over 1,000 practice trials. This demonstration indicates that even with separate programs for producing a V and for a γ, these programs cannot be run off at the same time without massive interference between the hands.

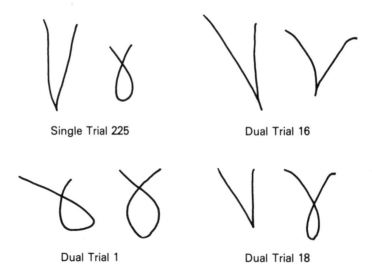

Single Trial 225   Dual Trial 16

Dual Trial 1   Dual Trial 18

Figure 2.12   The Gamma-V Experiment. Results of attempts to draw gammas and Vs either separately (single trial) or together (dual trials) after various amounts of practice. (Reprinted by permission from Konzem, 1987.)

survive in a hostile environment, this mode of movement control is very reasonable. The movement apparatus is organized to produce actions effective in solving environmental problems, such as finding food and escaping from predators. The most relevant action at a particular time, and only that action, is generated. This "protects" the movements from various distractions and allows them to run to completion and thus achieve their goals.

What about athletes, musicians, and industrial workers who can perform two-handed tasks that seem to result in independent movements of the two limbs? It is difficult to see very much in common between what the two hands must do in pitching a baseball. One possibility is that the performer learns to control the hands separately with practice, so one hand can produce a relatively well-learned pattern of actions automatically and the other hand can respond with controlled processing to generate its pattern. A more likely possibility is that the system learns a new program that controls both hands at the same time. How this

process of developing coordination occurs, and what factors influence it, is one of the most puzzling problems for scientists attempting to understand motor behavior; no satisfying answers are available at present.

A moment's reflection will show that all the processes discussed so far involve information that appears to be stored in some way in the central nervous system. Perceiving the flight path of a basketball, producing the muscle commands to execute a somersault, and most other skills we perform require that remembered information be used in the production of the action. The next section discusses the general concept of memory, the system's storage of information for future use.

THREE MEMORY SYSTEMS

An important concept in thinking about skills is **memory**, usually seen simply as the storage of the results of the various information-processing activities discussed so far. The various types of memory and their

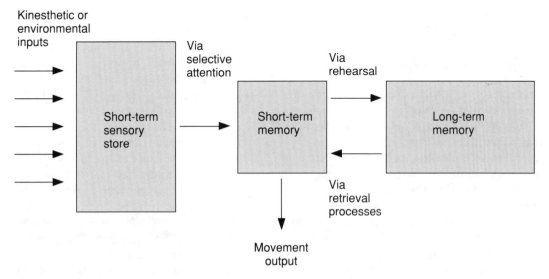

■ **Figure 2.13** Three discrete components of human memory.

characteristics are useful later during the discussion of several aspects of human performance. First are considered three distinct memory systems involved in movement control: short-term sensory store, short-term memory, and long-term memory (depicted in Figure 2.13).

Short-Term Sensory Store

The most peripheral, or sensory, aspect of memory is the short-term sensory store (STSS). Processing in the stimulus-identification stage results in memory of the environmental sensory events, stored briefly in STSS with a maximum duration of about 1/4 s. Numerous streams of information are processed simultaneously, and all in parallel, as argued earlier. A number of STSSs are conceptualized, each with very large capacity, for such things as audition, vision, kinesthesis, touch, and so on. These memory systems hold their information for only a short period of time, perhaps only a few hundred ms, only to be replaced by the next segment of sensory information presented. STSS storage is thought to come before conscious involvement and to result in a very literal form of memory, one very similar to the sensory information itself.

Short-Term Memory

All the information from sensory storage obviously cannot reach consciousness because people are aware of only a tiny fraction of the information available. Thus, a selective attention mechanism selects some sensory information in STSS for further processing; the remainder of the information in STSS is simply lost, to be replaced by more recent sensory information. The final selection for further processing is thought to be related to the information's relevance, or pertinence, to the present task. When someone says your name at a crowded party (a relevant stimulus), your attention is immediately attracted to that source of information and it is processed further. Much learning in high-level sports involves selective attention, directing the senses to the appropriate things as the skill unfolds and avoiding information that would detract from the goal. For example, in catching a football it is important to direct attention to the ball until it is securely caught; only then should attention be shifted to where to run. Thus, learning to ignore a possibly interfering source of information (a potential tackler) is difficult.

Selective attention directs information into short-term memory (STM). STM is thought to be a kind of workspace (termed "working memory" by some authors) where controlled information processing activities can be applied to relevant information. STM is thought to be severely limited in capacity. If STM is thought of as consciousness (which is at least reasonable to do), STM is seen to have a limit of several items. Experiments have shown that, for a remarkable number of different kinds of information inputs, STM can hold at most about 7 ± 2 items, called chunks of information (Miller, 1956), a severe limitation in capacity. This storage is more abstract (less literal) than that for STSS, with the stored information being transformed into more abstract codes (e.g., a printed word might be stored in terms of how it sounds). The information in STM can be held only as long as attention is directed to it, such as by recycling, repeating the information over and over. If attention is directed elsewhere, the STM contents are forgotten, with complete loss in perhaps 30 s. The classic example is the person who looks up a telephone number, fumbles in a pocket for a quarter, and then finds that the number was forgotten from STM (is this why telephone numbers usually contain only 7 digits?). If a coach guides a learner's limbs to a certain position on one occasion, the learner will have a difficult time repeating that position later because the kinesthetic memory will have faded from motor STM in the meantime.

Long-Term Memory

The third compartment of memory is long-term memory (LTM), which contains very well-learned information that has been collected over a lifetime. Experiments show that LTM must be essentially limitless in capacity, as indicated by the vast amount of information that can be stored for very long periods of time. Such information might never be forgotten: You never seem to forget how to ride a bicycle or throw a ball, even after many years of no practice. Probably the only reason you cannot remember someone's name or your old telephone number is not because that information is not stored but rather because you cannot gain access to, or retrieve, the stored information. The coding in LTM is thought to be very abstract, with information coded by elaborate connections to other stored information, by imagery, and by a host of other processes only now being understood.

Information is stored in LTM by controlled processing in STM (such as rehearsal, connecting the information to other information, etc.), so LTM storage is generally effortful. To say that someone has learned something means that information was processed in some way from STM to LTM. This also applies to movement skills, where motor programs for action (discussed in chapter 4) are stored in LTM for later execution. For many motor skills, particularly continuous ones, such as riding a bicycle or swimming, evidence and common experience suggest almost perfect retention after years, even decades, without intervening practice; this is quite contrary to the forgetting seen with

well-learned verbal and cognitive skills (e.g., foreign language vocabulary). However, discrete skills, such as throwing or gymnastics stunts, are more easily forgotten. It is not clear why discrete and continuous skills are so different in their retention characteristics.

 CHAPTER SUMMARY

The human motor system can be thought of as a processor of information, with signals received from the various sense organs, processed through various stages, and output as movements. The system has three main stages: a stimulus-identification stage, which detects the nature of environmental information; a response-selection stage, which resolves uncertainty about what action should be made; and a response-programming stage, which organizes the system for action. Reaction time is an important measure of information-processing speed. Its duration greatly increases with more stimulus-response alternatives (described by Hick's Law), by the naturalness of the relationship between stimuli and their associated movements (stimulus-response compatibility), and by anticipation of the upcoming events. Stress and arousal show an inverted-U relationship to performance: Increased arousal improves performance to a point, with further increases in arousal degrading performance. Tasks having fine motor control and a strong emphasis on decision making have the lowest optimal arousal levels. Attention, the general capacity to process information, is a critical limiter of performance in many situations. The delay in the response to the second of two closely spaced stimuli (the psychological refractory period) suggests that the motor system can organize and initiate only one action at a time, with a maximum rate of about three actions per second.

There is also massive interference between the two hands, which prefer to respond with a common temporal structure. Finally, it is useful to conceptualize three memory systems for holding information: a short-term sensory store, with a limitation of 1/4 s; short-term memory, with a duration of about 30 s; and long-term memory, with very long duration. These ideas underlie the conceptual model of human skilled performance that will be developed further in the next several chapters.

◇Checking Your Understanding

1. Describe the information-processing activities that occur in the stimulus-identification, response-selection, and response-programming stages.
2. What are the negative consequences of false anticipation? Under what conditions should an athlete be encouraged not to anticipate?
3. How does the cue-utilization hypothesis account for the finding that performance deteriorates as arousal increases to high levels?
4. Select an activity with which you are particularly familiar. For optimizing its performance, what level of arousal (high, medium, or low) should you as coach attempt to produce in your players?
5. What is the psychological refractory period? Describe two situations in which there is no added delay in the response to the second of two stimuli.
6. What limitations prevent, or at least make very difficult, the simultaneous production of two different hand movements? What simultaneous hand movements are easy?

◇Key Terms

Definitions of the following terms appear on the page(s) shown in parentheses:

arousal (p. 26)

attention (p. 30)

automatic processing (p. 33)

controlled processing (p. 33)

Hick's Law (p. 20)

hypervigilance (p. 29)

inverted-U principle (p. 26)

memory (p. 41)

perceptual narrowing (p. 28)

psychological refractory period (PRP) (p. 35)

reaction time (p. 18)

stages (p. 17)

stimulus-response (S-R) compatibility (p. 21)

◇ Suggestions for Further Reading

Additional reading on the stages in reaction time can be found in Sanders (1980, 1990). The role of reaction-time research methods in understanding information processing has been reviewed by Posner (1978). Very thorough reviews of attention and human performance are found in Neumann (1987) and Keele (1986). Many of these issues are also treated in Schmidt (1988b, chapters 4 and 5). See also Schneider's work (Schneider, Dumais, & Shiffrin, 1984; Schneider & Shiffrin, 1977) for more on the concept of automaticity.

Sensory Contributions to Skilled Performance

PREVIEW

The wide receiver in American football watches the ball leave the quarterback's hand. With but a few tenths of a second of viewing time, he realizes that he must turn his back on the ball and cut sharply to the left to catch it. He predicts the ball's flight correctly, moves his eyes to focus on it, and times the ball's arrival into his hands. After a few steps he is tackled from behind, senses the ball slipping away, and compensates by grasping it with both hands, all the while trying to maintain balance.

Skilled performers seem able to receive and process vast amounts of information quickly and accurately and to make effective modifications that contribute to skill. How does just a brief glimpse of the ball tell the player where to run? How does he know when the ball will arrive? How is all this information received and processed?

This chapter focuses on some of the many processes that allow high-level performers to detect patterns of information from the environment and base future action on them. The discussion concerns how the motor system uses such information in planning action, correcting movement errors, and regulating performance—first how the system uses sensory information in general, then some of the principles of visual control. Finally, building continues on the conceptual model of human skilled performance.

STUDENT GOALS

1. To appreciate the contributions and limitations of a closed-loop model for human skills
2. To understand the various ways that sensory information is used in movement
3. To become familiar with the particular roles of vision in movement control
4. To continue to develop a conceptual model of movement control by adding the sensory contributions to action

Success in skilled performance often depends critically on how effectively the performer detects, perceives, and uses relevant sensory information. Frequently, the winner of a contest is the one who has most quickly detected a pattern of action in an opponent, as in basketball, or who can sense his or her own body movements and positions most precisely, as in dance or gymnastics. Naturally, coaches direct much effort toward improving the speed and accuracy with which performers detect and process sensory information because these improvements can lead to large gains in skilled performance.

SOURCES OF SENSORY INFORMATION

Information for skills arises from several basic sources, but a major part of this information comes from the environment. This class is typically termed **exteroceptive**, in which the prefix *extero* means that the information is provided from outside the body.

Exteroceptive Information

Chief among exteroceptive information sources, of course, is vision. Seeing serves the important function of defining the physical structure of the environment, such as the edge of a stairway or the presence of an object blocking one's path, thus providing a basis for anticipating upcoming events. Vision also provides information about the movement of objects in the environment, such as the flight path of a ball as well as the time before the ball arrives. Another function of vision is to detect your own movement within the environment, such as your path toward an external object and how much time will elapse before you arrive. Some additional details of visual information are discussed later in this chapter.

The second major kind of exteroceptive information comes from hearing, or audition. Although audition is not as obviously involved in skills as vision, there are many activities that depend heavily on well-developed auditory skills, such as using the sounds of the sailboat hull moving through the water as cues to boat speed.

Proprioceptive, or Kinesthetic, Information

The second major class of information is from the body's movement, usually termed **proprioception**. The prefix *proprio* implies information from within the body, such as positions of the joints, forces in muscles, orientation in space (e.g., being upside down), and so on. A similar class of information is frequently termed **kinesthesis**. The prefix *kines* means movement, and *thesis* means "the sense of." Hence this term refers to the sense of movements of joints, tensions in muscles, and so on, giving data about your own actions. The division between these two concepts has blurred over the years, and they are used almost synonymously today to mean the collection of sensory information from your own body about relative joint positions and movement, muscular tensions, and orientation in space. This information is critically important in performances such as balancing in gymnastics, or holding postures by patients in therapeutic settings.

Several important receptors give information about kinesthesis. The vestibular apparatus in the inner ear provides signals related to movements in space because these structures are sensitive to acceleration of the head and are positioned to detect the head's orientation with respect to gravity. It is not surprising that these structures are strongly implicated in posture and balance.

Several other structures provide information about the limbs. Receptors in the joint capsule surrounding each of the joints give information about distortions of the capsule, hence indirectly about the position of the joint, especially at extreme ranges. Imbedded within the belly of the skeletal muscles are muscle spindles, tiny spindle-shaped structures oriented in parallel with the muscle fibers. Because muscles change lengths when the joints they span are moved, the muscle spindles are thought to provide indirect information about joint position. Near the junction between the muscle and tendon lie the Golgi tendon organs, which are very sensitive to the level of force in the various parts of the muscle to which they are attached. Finally, in most skin areas are cutaneous receptors, including several kinds of specialized detectors of pressure, temperature, touch, and so on. The cutaneous receptors are critical for the haptic sense, the sense of touch.

Each of these receptors does not respond to just one physical characteristic, however. The signal from a particular source, for example, the muscle spindles, provides ambiguous information about joint position because the receptor can be affected by several other physical stimuli (velocity, tension, orientation with respect to gravity) at the same time. For this reason, the central nervous system is thought to utilize a complex combination of the inputs from these various receptors as a basis for kinesthesis. In this way, kinesthesis is not a unitary sense as vision and audition are.

Because of the multiple, complex receptors involved in kinesthesis, perception of movement trajectory can be affected by how the movement is produced. There may be a difference depending on whether the movement was a normal, active action or a passive, guided action, such as when an instructor or therapist moves the passive learner through a demonstration movement. The perception of the proper trajectory of standing up, for example, can be clearly biased if it is presented passively. Also, many guidance techniques, such as artificially manipulating the learner's movements during an action (creating the armstroke in swimming, spotting in gymnastics), can markedly affect the kinesthetic sensations generated. These techniques can be useful at the beginning stages of learning, but because they distort the kinesthetic senses, they could easily be overused in teaching situations.

However, such alterations in kinesthesis are exploited by human-factors engineers in the design of equipment. Adding spring resistance to a car's steering system adds feel, which makes the car easier to control. Supplying aircraft instrument knobs of different shapes and locations makes confusion less likely.

There are many different sources of sensory information for motor control, varying not only in terms of where the information is detected but also how it is processed and used. Even so, the next sections consider this variety of sensations as a single group, focusing on the common ways the central nervous system uses this information for skilled performance.

CLOSED-LOOP CONTROL SYSTEMS

One important way to conceptualize how sensory information functions in movement behavior is by analogy to **closed-loop control** systems, a class of control mechanisms used in countless applications in everyday life. An example is diagrammed in Figure 3.1. A system goal is defined, such as the desired temperature in your house in the winter. Sensory information about the system's output (that is, the room's actual temperature), or feedback, is then compared to the desired temperature in a comparator. Any difference

PRACTICAL APPLICATIONS

1. Passive guidance procedures can be useful for movement demonstrations in teaching situations, but they distort kinesthesis in many tasks, so use them sparingly.
2. Inform the performers about the most relevant sources of sensory information for a particular task, allowing them to focus on the most important information.
3. Asking a learner to describe the sensations received after a movement draws attention to sensory information, developing awareness of the feel of the correct action.
4. These applications can be reversed: Engineers add spring or frictional resistance to vehicle controls to aid kinesthetic sensitivity, increasing performance and safety.

represents an error (e.g., the temperature is too low); this error is brought to the attention of an executive, which decides about action to eliminate or reduce the error. The executive sends a command to an effector, which carries out the action (in this case, turning on the heater). This action raises the room temperature until it equals the reference (goal) temperature (error is now zero), and the executive sends the instruction to switch off the heater. This process continues indefinitely, maintaining the temperature near the desired value.

This kind of system is termed *closed-loop* because the loop from the executive to the effector and back to the executive again is completed by sensory information, or feedback, forming a mechanism regulating the system to achieve a particular goal.

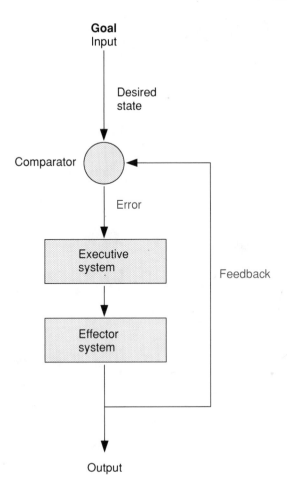

Goal
Input

Desired
state

Comparator

Error

Executive
system

Feedback

Effector
system

Output

■ **Figure 3.1** A closed-loop control system.

The same general processes operate in human performance, as in catching a ball. Visual information about the hand moving toward the ball represents the feedback. Differences between the hand's direction and the desired direction are sensed as errors. An executive determines a correction, modifying the effector system to bring the hand into the proper direction. Of course, in more complicated skills, feedback is a collection of different kinds of sensory information arising from a variety of receptors both within and outside the body. Each kind of information

is compared to a corresponding reference level, and the errors are then processed by the executive level in the system.

In summary, all closed-loop control systems have four distinct parts:

1. An executive for decision making about errors
2. An effector system for carrying out the decisions
3. A reference of correctness against which the feedback is compared to define an error
4. An error signal, which is the information acted on by the executive

CLOSED-LOOP CONTROL WITHIN THE CONCEPTUAL MODEL

These various events fit in the conceptual model for movement control as shown in Figure 3.2. This is simply an expansion of the conceptual model of human performance in the previous chapter, which introduced the stages of information processing (see Figure 2.2). However, now are added the notions of closed-loop control seen in Figure 3.1 to achieve a more complete system, and additional processes are added to suit the model better to a discussion of human motor performance. This conceptual model will be useful not only for understanding the processes involved in relatively slow movements (e.g., positioning a limb in physical therapy) where compensations can be made during the action, but also in relatively fast movements (e.g., a golf swing) where the correction of the error must wait until the movements have been completed.

The parts of the closed-loop model can be seen shaded in red in Figure 3.2. The executive consists of the decision-making processes discussed in chapter 2—the stimulus-

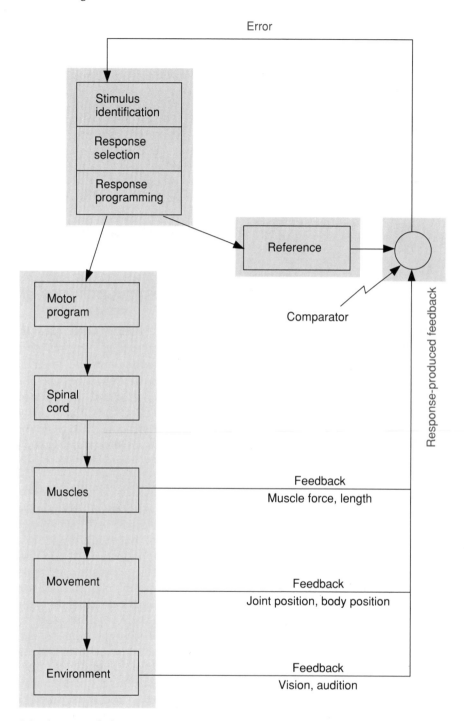

Figure 3.2 An expanded conceptual model of human performance. The elements of the closed-loop control system are integrated with the stages of processing.

identification, response-selection, and response-programming stages. The executive sends commands to an effector system consisting of several parts. One is the motor program, which produces commands for lower centers in the spinal cord, which finally result in the contraction of muscles and the movement of joints (as in a golf swing). At the same time, a reference of correctness is specified to define the sensory qualities of the correct movement, such as the feel of an effective golf drive. This reference represents the performer's expected feedback, that is, the sensations that should be generated if the movement is performed correctly and the environmental goal is actually met. In a comparator, this expected feedback is then contrasted with the actual feedback received when the golf swing is produced. Any differences represent errors in movement, which are signaled to the executive.

The movement results in various sources and types of feedback information collectively termed *response-produced feedback*. When muscles contract, the system receives feedback about forces as well as about the pressures exerted on objects in contact with the skin. Contracting muscles next cause movement and thus feedback from moving joints and the changes in body position with respect to gravity. Finally, movements usually produce alterations in the environment, which are sensed by the receptors for vision, audition, or sometimes even smell, generating yet more feedback. These response-produced stimuli, critically dependent on the production of a particular action by the performer, are compared against their expected states in the comparator. The computed difference represents error, which is returned to the executive. This process refines and maintains the performer's behavior, holding errors at acceptably low levels.

Notice that the stages of processing are critically involved in the closed-loop model in Figure 3.2. Every time an action's feedback goes to the executive for correction, it must go through the stages of processing. This requires attention, time, the bottleneck in response programming, and all of the other difficulties discussed earlier. However, this is not the only way in which feedback can be used; this chapter later discusses various lower level reflexlike loops.

The Conceptual Model and Continuous, Long-Duration Skills

The closed-loop model in Figure 3.2 is useful for understanding the maintenance of a particular state, as is necessary to perform many long-duration activities. For example, simply maintaining posture, where the goal is natural, upright position, requires feedback. Various learned postures might be controlled in the same way, such as positioning the body in a handstand on the still rings in gymnastics. Also, most movement skills involving the various limbs require an accurate, stable posture as a platform. Without this base, the movement, such as throwing darts, would be inconsistent or have insufficient force to be useful. The comparator defines the desired relative positions of the various limbs as well as the general orientation in space.

Other tasks are far more dynamic. For instance, in a continuous **tracking** skill, a performer must follow some constantly varying track by moving a control. A classic example is steering a car, where the steering wheel movements result from visually detected errors in the car's position on the road. Another type of feedback and response is illustrated in a 10-kilometer running race, where small errors in speed (relative to a learned pace) are sensed, leading to corrections that help maintain efficiency. Also, in many tasks the reference of correctness might change continuously over time, as with position of the body at each moment of a slow karate movement, where the goal position changes as the movement unfolds. There are countless other examples, this class of activity being one of the most frequently represented in real-world functioning.

Without a doubt, the closed-loop control models such as that shown in Figure 3.2 are the most effective for understanding these kinds of behavior. In fact, electromechanical devices possessing all of the model's components can be constructed relatively easily, and these nonliving devices mimic the behavior of actual humans relatively well. Thus, understanding how such a model operates provides considerable insight into human performance and allows many important applications. Understanding the model's limitations for movement control is also important, as discussed next.

Limitations in Feedback Control for Performance

The inclusion of the stages of information processing in the system, as depicted in the conceptual model, is a strong advantage because it provides flexibility in movement control, allowing various movement strategies and options, and altering the nature of the movement produced, depending on the particular circumstances. However, these stages of processing provide the biggest disadvantage at the same time: They are very slow, especially with the bottleneck in response programming (as discussed in chapter 2).

Tracking Behavior

One important generalization in chapter 2 was that the stages of information processing require considerable time and attention. Hence the closed-loop system with these processes should be slow as well. The stages of processing were critical components in reaction-time situations, where presenting a stimulus required various processes leading to a movement. The closed-loop model can be regarded in the same way, the stimulus being now the error that drives the executive, and the correction being the movement the executive selects. Numerous studies of tracking suggest that the system can produce separate responses (that is, corrections) at a maximum rate of about three per second. This is about as expected if the system were using reaction-time processes as a critical component, reacting to errors by making corrections.

In the conceptual model each correction is based on a collection of information about the errors that have occurred over the past few hundred milliseconds. This error is processed in stimulus identification, a movement correction is chosen in response selection, and the correction is organized and initiated in response programming. Once this corrective behavior is initiated, it controls the body part until the next segment of error information can be processed. Therefore, tasks with tracks that involve more than three changes in direction per second are typically performed very poorly. It is difficult to chase a baseball rolling and bouncing over a rough surface because its course varies unpredictably and often. For this reason, these closed-loop processes are most relevant to tasks that are relatively slow.

Summary		Break

In general, human closed-loop systems have these characteristics:

- Use of many different sources of sensory information
- Effectiveness for movement control in certain tasks, such as many kinds of tracking, because they are flexible and adaptable
- Limitations in processing speeds, allowing only 3 to 5 compensations per second at most

Discrete Tasks
With Short Movement Times

This general view of movement control fails to explain adequately movement production in skills that are very quick, such as the hitting, throwing, kicking, and batting tasks so common in many sports. In swinging the bat at a pitched softball, for example, the performer first evaluates the environmental situation, then selects a movement to meet the perceived demands. The stages of processing select a program and ready it for initiation. Once started, the response-execution processes carry out that movement more or less as planned. Given that the environment remains in the same state as it was when the movement was organized, the movement should be effective in meeting the environmental demand, so the bat should hit the ball.

But what if something in the environment suddenly changes? For example, if the ball curves unexpectedly, now the batter wants to swing at a different location or perhaps stop the swing altogether. The conceptual model enables an estimate of how much time would be required for this kind of information to influence an ongoing movement. Such information must pass through the stages of processing, therefore requiring several hundred milliseconds before the first modification in the movement can occur.

While these processes that will lead to the abolishment of the movement are occurring, the original movement is still being carried out as originally planned. Therefore, the initial parts of the first movement occur before the batter can initiate the correction to stop the action. If the batter detects the curving ball too late, the original movement is carried out almost completely, resulting in a hopeless miss.

As a general rule, then, with the most rapid human actions, the performer initiates a fully planned movement to achieve the goal. Later sensory information indicating that this movement will be incorrect, and thus should be stopped or radically altered, is processed relatively slowly and sluggishly, so the first few hundred milliseconds of the original movement occur more or less without modification. As you will see later in this chapter, though, sensory information plays an increasingly important and effective role as the movement is made more slowly.

This sluggishness of feedback processing has implications for controlling the moment-to-moment contractions and adjustments in the movement. According to the conceptual model, feedback leading from the rapid movement would not have enough time to be processed before the movement was completed. The feedback thus couldn't influence the fine, moment-to-moment control. More than any other observation, this sluggishness of feedback control has led scientists to believe that most rapid movements must be programmed in advance. In this view, the moment-to-moment control is included as part of the preorganized program and is not dependent on the relatively slow processes associated with feedback. (Feedback can also act reflexively to modify movements far more quickly than indicated here. This aspect of feedback control is discussed later in this chapter; motor program control is considered more completely in chapter 4.)

Finally, these quick actions are initiated in an all-or-none way, more or less like pulling the trigger on a rifle causes a bullet to be fired without the possibility of modification. Once a critical point, a "threshold," has been reached, an internal "go" signal is delivered and the movement is initiated. The system ignores any signal given soon after that internal go signal, and the movement is initiated without interruption. Issuing the go signal effectively passes control from the controlled processing in response selection to the nonconscious processes in response programming. This internal go signal is thought to

The Slater-Hammel Experiment

Arthur Slater-Hammel (1960) conducted an experiment in which subjects held a finger on a key while watching a special timer moving at one revolution per second. The task was to lift the finger from the key at such a point that the clock hand would stop at "8," 800 ms after the clock had started. With a little practice, subjects could learn to anticipate this action and lift their fingers to achieve this goal. On special trials that were unpredictable to the subject, however, the experimenter would stop the clock hand at various places before it reached "8." If this happened, the subject's job was simply to do nothing, that is, to inhibit the finger lift. For those trials on which the clock hand stopped, Slater-Hammel plotted the probability of lifting the finger (i.e., failing to inhibit the finger lift) as a function of the interval size between "8" and where the clock hand had stopped.

The data are shown in Figure 3.3. When the interval before the intended finger lift was relatively large (greater than 210 ms), stopping the clock hand resulted in the subject's inhibiting the movement almost all the time. However, as this interval

decreased, the subjects would lift the finger more and more often, to the point that when the clock hand stopped at "7" (about 100 ms before the intended finger lift), the subject could almost never inhibit the movement. Generally, when the clock hand was stopped about 150 to 170 ms before the intended finger lift, the subject could inhibit the movement successfully only about half the time. This finding can be interpreted to mean that the internal "go" signal is issued about 150 to 170 ms before the intended action. This go signal is a trigger for action, after which the movement occurs even though new environmental information indicates that the movement should be inhibited.

Students in our class-laboratory demonstrations are amazed when they experience this phenomenon. They say that they planned the action, then they saw the clock hand stop, and then—seemingly a long time later—the finger "lifted itself automatically," as if someone else were controlling it. My view is that "someone else" *is* controlling the finger after the internal go signal—the motor program.

---

occur during the response-programming stage, as indicated by the Slater-Hammel (1960) experiment in the Highlight Box.

Following are the major points to remember from this section on feedback control of action and our conceptual model of human performance:

- A closed-loop control system, including the stages of processing as an executive,

is an effective model for understanding continuous, long-duration skills such as tracking, balancing, and slow positioning.

- Once a movement is triggered internally, its control is passed in an all-or-none fashion to the motor program for execution.

- Once triggered, any sensory information indicating that this movement

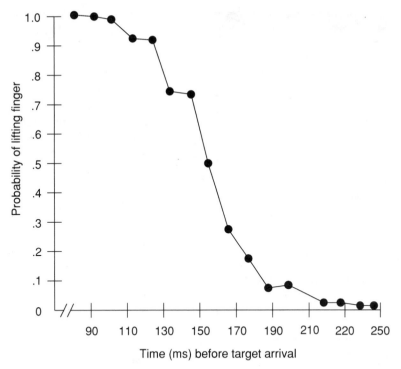

Figure 3.3 The probability of lifting the finger though the clock hand had stopped, plotted as a function of the interval of time before "8." (Adapted by permission from Slater-Hammel, 1960.)

should be inhibited, or altered in a major way, requires approximately 150 to 200 ms before the first modifications are seen.

- Therefore, closed-loop models are generally not effective for understanding the control of rapid, discrete actions.

Reflexive Modulations in Movement Skills

To this point, only one kind of closed-loop processes has been considered: conscious control of actions by sensory information. There are other ways that sensory information is involved in movement control, especially considering the many kinds of corrections, modifications, and subtle changes in skills that occur outside of awareness. These modifications are rooted in the rela-

tively low-level processes in the spinal cord and brain stem and often do not involve conscious control. These modifications are often termed **reflexes**, which are stereotyped, involuntary, usually rapid responses to stimuli. This section deals with how and under what circumstances these lower-level reflex processes can contribute to skills.

Four Kinds of Compensations Can Be Distinguished

Imagine being a subject in a simple experiment. While standing, your task is to hold one of your elbows at a right angle to support a moderate load on your hand, such as a book. You have a dial in front of you to indicate the height of the book, and you have to keep the book at some target position. The experimenter monitors the electrical activities in your biceps muscle by electromyography

(EMG), recording the strength of contraction for later analysis. Suddenly, without your being able to anticipate it, the experimenter adds another book to the load. Your hand begins to drop, but after a delay you compensate for the added load and bring your hand up to the target position again.

What are the processes that contribute to these compensations? A record of the EMG (rectified to make all of the values positive) might look something like that shown in Figure 3.4. There is background EMG activity necessary to hold the limb at the target. After the load is added, several modifications to this background EMG represent the compensations for the added load:

1. M1 responses, with latency of 30 to 50 ms
2. M2 responses, with latency of 50 to 80 ms
3. Triggered reactions, with latency of 80 to 120 ms

4. Reaction time responses (M3), with latency from 120 to 180 ms

M1 Response. First there is a burst of EMG activity about 30 to 50 ms after the added load. This response is brief, not resulting in very much added contraction in the muscle; the limb is still moving downward even after this response. This **M1 response** (or *M1 reflex*, sometimes called the *monosynaptic stretch reflex*) is one of the most rapid reflexes underlying limb control. It is caused by the muscle spindles in the biceps being stretched when the load is added, which results in sensory information being sent to the spinal cord. After traveling to a single connection (or synapse) in the spinal cord, this information is routed directly back to the same muscle that was stretched, causing the increased contraction seen as the small EMG burst. The latency of this correction is very short because the information involves only one synapse (hence the term *monosynaptic*) and has a relatively short distance to travel.

The M1 reflex is thought responsible for modifications in muscle contraction caused by small stretches, such as would be associated with postural sways, unanticipated forces, and the like. As such, the spindle controls muscle length and muscle stiffness (the springlike muscle resistance to length changes when loads are added). These reflex processes are nonconscious and are not affected by the number of possible stimulus alternatives that could be presented—that is, M1 responses do not follow Hick's Law (chapter 2). Perhaps thousands of these modifications can occur simultaneously in parallel to control functions such as limb position and posture. Because these compensations occur simultaneously, in parallel, nonconsciously, and presumably without interference, they do not require attention; they are automatic (chapter 2).

M2 Response. About 50 to 80 ms after the added load comes a second burst of EMG

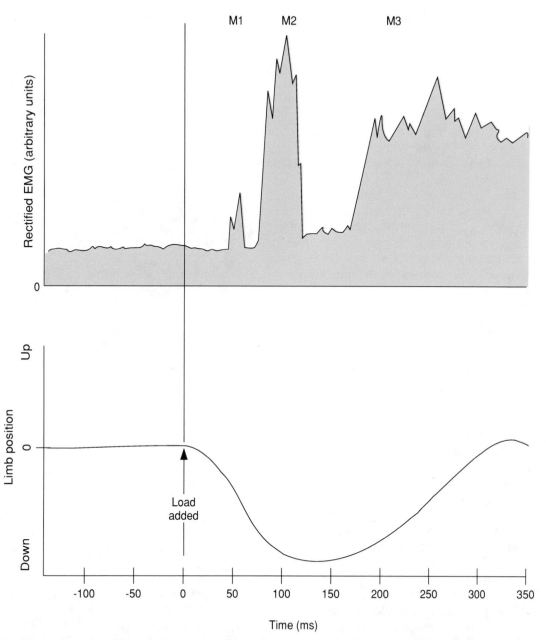

Figure 3.4 Electromyographic (EMG) responses to stretch of the biceps muscle when a load is suddenly applied. Triggered reactions are not shown here. (Adapted by permission from Dewhurst, 1967.)

activity (Figure 3.4). This **M2 response** (or *M2 reflex*, sometimes called the *functional stretch reflex* or the *long-loop reflex*) generates more EMG amplitude than the M1 reflex. It has a longer duration, so it contributes far more to movement compensation than the M1. This response also arises from the muscle spindles and travels to the spinal cord, but then the impulses go up the cord to higher centers in the brain (the motor cortex and/or the cerebellum). Here the impulses are processed, leading to motor impulses being sent down the cord and to the periphery to activate muscles at the elbow joint. This greater travel distance and the additional synapses at the higher levels account for some of the added loop time for the M2.

The M2 response, in combination with the M1, is responsible for the well-known knee-jerk reflex used in neurological examinations and physical therapy. The patient sits on an examination table, with the lower leg hanging down. The doctor taps the patellar tendon under the kneecap, stretching the quadriceps muscle on the front of the thigh, which initiates the reflex response to contract the quadriceps, producing an involuntary extension of the knee.

What are some of the characteristics of the M2 response? Like the M1 response, the M2 is not affected by the number of possible stimuli that could be presented, and thus it does not follow Hick's Law. The M2 is more flexible than the M1, allowing for a few other sources of sensory information to be integrated into the response. One of those sources is the instructional set for the task (information given by the experimenter). In the example, if you had been instructed to "let go" when the added weight was applied (rather than to "resist," as in Figure 3.4), your limb would have achieved a new position without your intervening. The M2 would be almost completely abolished, whereas the M1 response would remain almost unmodified by these instructions.

Thus, the amplitude of the M2 response (called the *gain*) for a given input can be adjusted voluntarily to generate a powerful response when the goal is to hold the joint as firmly as possible, or it can result in almost no response if the movement goal is to release

under the increased load. This capability for modulation is fortunate because it allows the limbs to conform to variations in environmental demands. In skiing, for example, I want my knees to be supple and to yield to sudden bumps, yet in other situations (e.g., wrestling) I might not want any yielding at all (when my opponent moves my leg).

Gain modulation in reflex activities is an important process in controlling leg musculature stiffness in performances like this.

The M2 reflex is a strange kind of response. It is too fast to be called voluntary, which, from the previous section, would require a latency near 150 to 200 ms before the beginning of the action. Yet the M2 can be modified voluntarily by conscious processes, such as those associated with the perception of the upcoming moguls in skiing.

Triggered Reaction. A third type of response (not shown in Figure 3.4), somewhat longer in latency than the M2, has been termed a **triggered reaction**. This action is also too fast to be a voluntary reaction, with latencies of 80 to 120 ms, but it is too slow to be an M2 (or M1) response. It can affect musculature that is quite remote from the actual stimulation site, and it is sensitive to the number of stimulus alternatives, similar to the reaction-time response. And, it can apparently be learned, more or less as an automatic response can be (as discussed in chapter 2).

Triggered reactions are seen in a number of different situations, such as the wineglass effect (Johansson & Westling, 1984). While you are lifting a glass, it begins to slip, its red contents threatening your white rug. These minute slips generate skin vibrations detected by cutaneous receptors in your fingertips, triggering several very fast compensations to stop the slip. First there is increased grip force generated by the muscles in the forearm, causing your hand to squeeze the glass somewhat harder. There is also decreased force in the biceps muscle, slowing the upward acceleration of lifting the glass, also reducing its tendency to slip. These two compensations are coordinated beautifully with each other, being triggered as a single, unitary compensation for the slip. They are faster than reaction time, with latencies of about 80 ms. They also appear to be nonconscious in that you can make these compensations before even being aware that there was a slip. In another example, a wrestler wraps his arm around his opponent's waist. Attempts to escape this hold can be detected by cutaneous receptors in the forearm, which can then lead to rapid compensations to maintain the advantage.

Voluntary, Reaction-Time Response. A final type of response to the added load (another book on the arm) is a voluntary reaction, sometimes called the **M3 response**. Seen as the third burst of EMG activity in Figure 3.4, it is powerful and sustained, bringing the limb back to the final position and holding it there. The latency of the M3 response is around 120 to 180 ms, depending on the task, and it can affect all of the musculature, not just those muscles that are stretched. The M3 responses are the most flexible of all, being modified by a host of factors such as instructions, anticipation, and so on. Of course, the delay in the M3 response makes it sensitive to the number of stimulus-response alternatives, following Hick's Law. Processes underlying these actions involve the conscious activities resulting in increased reaction time (discussed in chapter 2), hence the loop described in Figure 3.2. Because these responses go through the stages of information processing, they occur in a serial fashion and require attention.

Coordinating Compensations for Unexpected Loads. These four kinds of compensations and their major characteristics are summarized in Table 3.1. An important feature is that as the latency of the response becomes shorter, the response becomes

Table 3.1   Characteristics of Different Classes of Muscular Responses to Perturbations During Movement

Response type	Latency (ms)	Flexibility/ adaptability	Role of instructions	Effect of number of choices
M1 response	30-50	Almost none	None	None
M2 response	50-80	Low	Some	None (?)
Triggered reaction	80-120	Moderate	Large	Moderate
Reaction-time response	120-180	Very high	Very large	Large

systematically more rigid, or inflexible. At one extreme is reaction time, which is extremely sensitive to environmental demands but is relatively slow, whereas at the other extreme is the M1 response, which is hardly sensitive to environmental demands but is very fast; the other responses fall in between. This suggests a trade-off between flexibility and speed of response. If more flexibility is needed, more sources of sensory information are taken into account to define the action. Then systematically more information-processing activities must be used, which requires more time.

Reflex Responses in the Conceptual Model

These reflexive modifications in movement control can now be integrated into the conceptual model presented earlier. Figure 3.5 contains the same diagram shown earlier (Figure 3.2) but includes two reflexive pathways to give a more complete picture. With the loop in light red labeled *M1*, feedback about muscle length (stretch) and perhaps muscle tension are fed back to the spinal cord, which returns modifications directly to the muscles without involving any higher systems. This loop is fast, relatively inflexible, and the lowest level feedback in movement control, having minimal contact with any of the higher centers.

The feedback loop labeled *M2*, the long-loop or functional stretch reflex, is shown in dark red. Here feedback about muscle force and length as well as joint position and body position are fed back to somewhat higher centers having to do with the motor programming of the action. Some minor modifications in movement commands can be produced in the motor programming processes, which are sent back to the spinal cord and muscle levels. This loop is slower than that of M1, but it has more flexibility because it interacts with a higher level of control. (In

both of these cases, to keep this diagram relatively simple, all of the comparator and reference portions of the closed-loop process are not shown but are assumed to be present.)

Final Common Path. An important principle of motor control known as the final common path (Sherrington, 1906) is also shown in Figure 3.5. The contributions to the movement arise from three different sources. First, there are the originally programmed commands, shown in black. Added to these are contributions from the M1 response, sensitive to muscle force and length, shown in light red lines. Also, there is the contribution from the M2, sensitive to limb positions and movement as well as muscle force and length, shown in heavy red lines. Therefore, the final common path (or ultimate contribution) of the central nervous system to the muscle contraction force is a sum of all these separate flows of information, each with a different latency and a different relative amount of influence.

Loops Within Loops. Imbedded feedback loops is the important notion that certain closed loops operate totally "within" other closed loops. The M1 response loop in Figure 3.5 can be thought of as operating between the muscle level and the spinal cord level, exerting its influence on the relatively local control of muscle force when an unexpected variation in load is presented. This loop does not have access to higher order information about the goals of the task, but rather it is restricted to the relatively "dumb" task of holding muscle length or stiffness levels constant. This M1 loop cannot be sensitive to information about goal achievement from the outside environment; the M1 simply attempts to hold muscle force and length constant. Any information that the environmental goal is not being achieved must be processed in the "outer" loop (in black in Figure 3.5), which operates through the

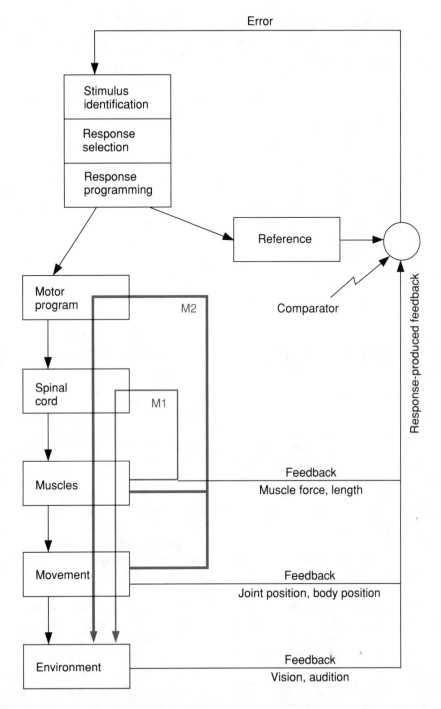

Figure 3.5 The conceptual model of human performance expanded further, here by adding M1 and M2 feedback loops shown in red.

information-processing stages to select a totally new action.

Role of Movement Time. The relative roles of these reflexes depend on the duration of the movement to be produced, as shown in Figures 3.6a to d. The quickest of human actions, such as striking a blow in boxing, with a movement time (MT) of only 40 ms or so, is shown in Figure 3.6a. The "outside" feedback loop (thin black line) would have no capability to complete processing in time to modify that movement, and the M1 response (latency of 30 to 50 ms) has just enough time to only begin to have an influence by the time the movement is complete. The M2 response (latency of 50 to 80 ms) and all other feedback loops with longer latencies are too slow to affect this kind of movement.

As the movement time becomes longer, such as with swinging a baseball bat, which might last 100 ms or so, there is sufficient time for the M1 to be involved. However, the M2 just begins to be a factor in the control of the muscle, and the outer, conscious loop is still far from being included (see Figure 3.6b).

When the movement takes even longer, such as with a forehand tennis stroke, which might take 200 ms, the M1 and M2 reflexes both have sufficient time to contribute to the action. Still, the "outside" conscious loop remains uninvolved in the movement (see Figure 3.6c).

Only when the movement is 300 ms or longer, such as a tennis serve, will the outer loop be involved. Thus, with movement times greater than 300 ms, the picture emerges of control at several levels at the same time, as shown in Figure 3.6d.

Generally speaking, as movement time increases, there is a greater potential contribution from the M1 and M2, relative to the originally programmed output. Given this observation, there should be little surprise that movement time is one of the most important variables in movement control, having a strong limiting influence on the kinds of feedback that can be used and on the relative contribution of these sources of feedback to the movement commands.

Some of these principles can be summarized as follows:

- The very quickest human movements have no possibility of any feedback control until the movement is finished.
- Somewhat slower actions allow lower level feedback control, with increased potential for modulation as movement time increases.
- Slow, continuous, or sustained actions involve a combination of hierarchically ordered loops operating simultaneously.

Choices Among Modes of Control. In many cases, the performer has a real choice among the modes of movement control to use. If the movement is sufficiently long in duration, such as a slow movement in dance, the dancer can preprogram the system, using only the fast, automatic reflexlike processes for control despite the movement's slowness. Otherwise, the dancer may program only a small portion of the action, then override it with the consciously controlled feedback responses in the outer loop of Figure 3.6d. However, shifts to conscious, controlled information processing can have several disadvantages. It is tempting for instructors to suggest that the learner "concentrate" on a particular part of the action or "focus" on a particular source of feedback. This kind of instruction would shift the performer's mode of control toward a more conscious, controlled style in which decisions and modulations about action are handled in a slow, attention-demanding way, actually degrading performance. This general idea—that paying attention to one's actions can actually impair performance—is the very old

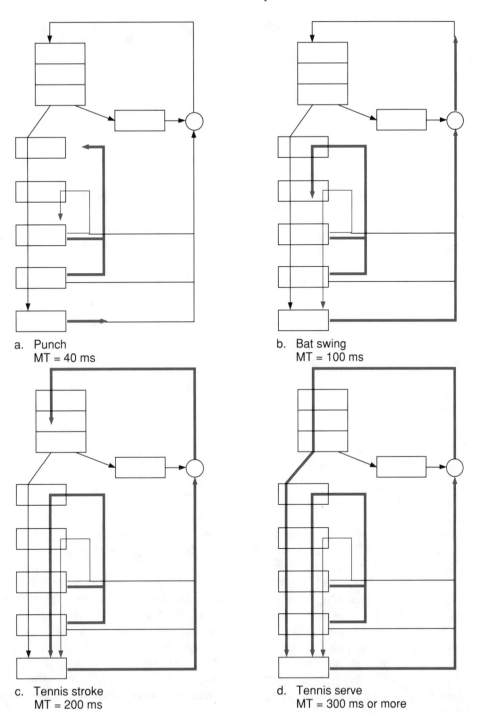

a. Punch
   MT = 40 ms

b. Bat swing
   MT = 100 ms

c. Tennis stroke
   MT = 200 ms

d. Tennis serve
   MT = 300 ms or more

Figure 3.6 The progress of the various feedback loops after movements of different durations. The lowest-level reflex activities are completed first, and the highest-level responses are completed last.

Bliss-Boder hypothesis (Bliss, 1892-1893; Boder, 1935).

This is also related to the ideas presented by Gallwey (1974), whose popular book *The Inner Game of Tennis* emphasized the idea of allowing the movement to "flow." The argument is that some of the best performances seem to occur by simply letting the learned capabilities of your motor system control the action, rather than by intervening with conscious processes. Conscious intervention can lead to overcontrolling actions, such as beginners do when first learning to balance in a headstand. Allowing movements to flow implies the use of preprogrammed movements with corrections only from the inner feedback loops (Figure 3.6a) and with systematically less reliance on the slow, jerky, attention-demanding processes associated with the outer loop. Overreliance on conscious processes in movement can result in what some have termed a "paralysis from analysis," which is certainly not effective for skilled performance.

PRINCIPLES OF VISUAL CONTROL

To some extent, it has been useful in the previous sections to combine all of the sources of sensory information, treating them as if they operated in essentially the same way for skilled performance. But vision seems different. First of all, vision has a very important role for everyday activities, and people deprived of vision have a relatively difficult time functioning in this visually dominated world. Second, vision appears to operate somewhat differently from the other senses in the support of skills. For these reasons, vision deserves a special place of its own in this chapter.

PRACTICAL APPLICATIONS

1. Have the athlete practice responding to perturbing stimuli under consistent mapping conditions to develop rapid, reflexlike capabilities to modify behavior.
2. Instructions to "stiffen the joint" or "let go" are effective in altering the gain of certain reflex pathways, and they easily translate into effective performance changes.
3. In situations where top performance is demanded, avoid instructions or comments suggesting conscious control of well-learned skills; rather, have the learner let it flow.
4. Encourage the learner to develop reflexive processes by avoiding conscious feedback control, forcing practice with lower level fine control by reflexive processes.
5. Be aware of the psychological ploy (and potential disruption to your game) when an opponent asks you how you did something (e.g., your golf swing) so well, prompting you to analyze and think about what you are doing.

Two Visual Systems for Movement Control

Over the past 20 years or so, it has become increasingly clear that two essentially separate visual systems underlie human functioning, rather than just one as it would appear. Visual information is delivered from the retina of the eye along two separate pathways to two different places in the brain, and there is good evidence that these two different pathways of information are used differently in the control of behavior (Trevarthen, 1968). These two systems are

- the focal system, specialized for object identification, and
- the ambient system, specialized for movement control.

Focal Vision for Object Identification

Focal vision is the system you already know about in general terms from personal experience. This system is specialized for conscious identification of objects that lie primarily in the center of the visual field. Its major function seems to be providing answers to the general question "What is it?" Hence you use this system to look at and identify something, such as the words on this page you are reading now. This system contributes to conscious perception of the objects that are focalized, leading to identification and perhaps action. Focal vision is severely degraded by dim lighting conditions, as you know from your attempts to read or do fine handwork without adequate light. These features are summarized in Table 3.2.

Table 3.2 Comparison of the Two Visual Systems

Feature	Focal vision	Ambient vision
Visual field location	Central only	Central and peripheral
Awareness	Conscious	Nonconscious
Effect of low illumination	Degradation	None
General question resolved	What is it?	Where is it?

Ambient Vision for Movement Control

Generally unrecognized is the operation of a second visual system, the **ambient vision** system, thought to be specialized for movement control. Distinct from focal vision, which is sensitive only to events in central vision, ambient vision involves the entire visual field, central and peripheral. Ambient vision operates nonconsciously, contributing to the fine control of movements without your awareness. Clearly, one reason it is difficult to recognize the existence of ambient vision is that it is nonconscious. Even so, there is good evidence that such a system does operate for movement control (see the Highlight Box on the Bridgeman et al. experiment). Ambient vision is not seriously degraded in dim lighting conditions, as focal vision is. This is clear if you attempt to walk on varied terrain in the near-dark; you have no trouble making your way without tripping, even though the light is far too dim to allow reading with the focal system. The ambient system functions to detect motion and position of elements in the environment, and provides information about your own movements in relation to them. Thus, its function is to provide answers to the questions "Where is it?" and perhaps "Where am I relative to it?"

Visual Control of Movement Skills

How is visual information used for movement control, and what factors determine its effectiveness? It is useful to divide this discussion into separate parts, particularly because it deals with the separate roles of the ambient and focal systems.

Focal Vision and Movement

Despite the characterization of focal vision as a system for object identification, it would

The Bridgeman et al. Experiment

Bridgeman, Kirch, and Sperling (1981) have provided some of the strongest evidence for the existence of an ambient system for movement control. Subjects sat in a darkened room in front of a screen on which was projected a rectangle (like a picture frame) and a spot of light inside it. Without the subject's knowing it, the frame was moved back and forth slightly a few degrees, with the dot remaining in a fixed position on the screen inside the moving frame. Under these conditions, the subject reliably experienced the illusion that the dot was moving back and forth within the frame, rather than the reverse, which was actually the case. In terms of the notion of two visual systems, the focal system (the one with access to consciousness) has been "deceived," judging that the dot was moving when it was actually stationary.

Next Bridgeman et al. attempted to manipulate the ambient system. The subjects were instructed that should the frame and dot suddenly be turned off, leaving the room in total darkness, they were to point to the last position of the dot as quickly as possible. Of course, the subject's conscious perception was that the dot was moving back and forth, so if the focal system were being used in controlling the hand, the pointing movements should vary from right to left as well, in coordination with the perceived movements of the dot. To the contrary, when the lights were turned off, the subjects pointed to where the dot actually was, not to where they perceived it to be. The interpretation was that the visual information for the localization of the dot was being used in the nonconscious ambient system, and this system was not deceived by the movements of the frame. This evidence supports the existence of two separate visual systems: the focal system for consciousness biased by the frame movements, and the ambient system for movement control, not biased by the frame movements.

be wrong to conclude that it has no role in movement control. Focal vision has access to consciousness, so it is processed through the information-processing stages discussed in chapter 2, leading to action in much the same way as any other information source. In the conceptual model in Figure 3.2 or 3.5, vision can be seen as just another source of information from the environment, so its only access to the loop would be through the stages of information processing. In one sense, this is obvious. You can look at and consciously identify an oncoming opponent in soccer, which would then lead to the decision to try to avoid him. Focal vision is critically involved here, and failures to identify objects properly can lead to serious errors. This is particularly so in night driving, when the focal system's accuracy (visual acuity) is degraded considerably.

Before realizing there could be an ambient system for movement control, scientists believed that a conscious focal system was the only way visual information could influence action. Under this outmoded view, a baseball batter watching a pitch come toward the plate relied only on the relatively slow processes in the information-processing stages to detect the ball's flight pattern and to initiate changes in movement control. This idea was supported by numerous experiments that seemed to show that visual information requires about 200 ms (or approximately the value of visual reaction time) for processing (e.g., Keele & Posner, 1968) and that visual control of action was particularly slow and cumbersome. However, recent information about the ambient visual system, together with the ideas about optical-flow processes in vision, have markedly changed the understanding of visual information processing for action.

Ambient Vision and Movement Control

Through the theorizing of the late James J. Gibson (e.g., 1966), scientists have begun to ask what aspects of visual information performers process for movement control. A particularly important concept is that of **optical-flow** patterns.

Optical Flow. As you look into a textured environment, each visible feature reflects rays of light, which enter your eye at particular angles, as shown in Figures 3.7a and b. Imagine Objects A and B in this environment, each reflecting rays for an eye located in Position 1 (only one eye is shown for simplification). As the observer's eye begins to move towards Position 2, the angles from

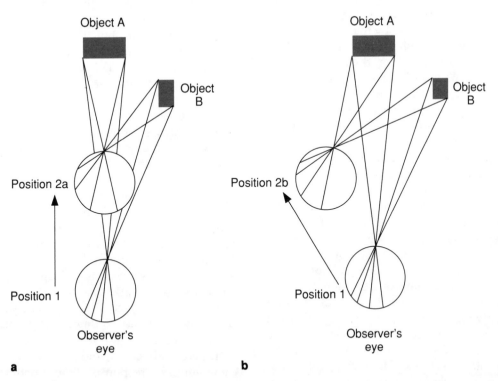

a   **b**

Figure 3.7 Optical-flow information specifies the direction and speed of an observer's eye through an environment containing Objects A and B.

object to eye change over time. These changes are continuous and can be thought of as a flow of light across the retina. The important point is that this optical flow provides the performer numerous important kinds of information about his or her movement in that environment, such as the following:

- Stability and balance
- Velocity of movement through the environment
- Direction of movement relative to objects in the environment
- Movement of environmental objects relative to the performer
- Time before contact between the performer and an object

Assume that the observer is moving directly toward Object A, as in Figure 3.7a. Forward motion is sensed by the increase in the angle between the light rays from the two edges of Object A. (Also, the rays from Object B sweep across the retina.) If the observer were moving backward, these changes would be reversed, indicating opposite motion in the environment. The speed of movement is sensed by the rate of change of the angles between the sides of Objects A and B, with faster movement making more rapid changes in these angles.

In addition to information about the backward-forward dimension, information about subtle differences in the direction of travel is provided by optical flow. In Figure 3.7a, the observer is moving directly toward Object A, so the angles are changing at the same rate across time. In general, moving directly toward an object is perceived when the angles from both sides change relative to the line of sight at the same rate, but in opposite directions. However, if the observer is moving so that the object passes on the right side (see Figure 3.7b), then all of the angles change in the same direction, with

angles from the right side of the object changing more quickly than those from the left.

Presumably, you know how to walk through a forest or how to avoid Rugby tacklers by processing information about the relative rates of change in the visual angles of objects in that environment. The term *visual proprioception* was suggested by D.N. Lee (1980) for the fact that vision (a classical exteroceptor) can provide much information about proprioception, the movement of one's body in space.

Visual proprioception also works for situations where an object, such as a ball, is moving toward a motionless observer. In Figure 3.8a the angles of the rays from the edges of the ball expand at the same rate from each side of the ball, indicating that the ball is coming directly toward the eye. In Figure 3.8b the ball is not moving directly toward the observer, so the angles are all changing in the same direction, but those from the left side of the ball are increasing faster than those from the right. This shows that the ball will pass to the observer's left side, possibly serving as input to the motor system to move the arm to catch the ball.

A special case of this phenomenon is looming, where an object comes directly at your eye and threatens to hit you eventually. We have all had this experience, and the response is a nearly automatic blink of the eye, coupled with a jerk of the head to avoid being struck. Even a newborn baby shows this response if a hand is moved directly at his or her face, even without having ever been struck in the face previously, suggesting that this response is relatively automatic and does not have to be learned. People probably have an innate capability to detect the particular pattern of optical flow that specifies looming; fortunately, effective avoidance reactions are generated as a response to these patterns.

Time-to-Contact Information. The pattern of optical flow from an oncoming object

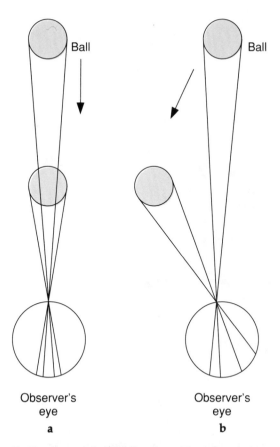

Ball

Ball

Observer's
eye

a

Observer's
eye

b

Figure 3.8 Optical flow provides information about a ball's speed and direction of travel relative to a fixed observer.

such as a ball indicates the time remaining until the object reaches the plane of the eye (Lee & Young, 1985). The retinal image of an approaching object expands as the object approaches, and it expands more quickly as the object approaches more quickly. The optical variable **tau** (τ), defined as the size of this retinal image divided by the rate of change of the image, is proportional to the time remaining until contact. Thus, τ is derived from optical-flow information and is presumably "computed" by the central nervous system to specify timing. This timing information is critical in interceptive actions

involving coincident timing, such as striking or catching a ball, avoiding an approaching car on the street, or preparing the musculature for entry into the water during a dive.

Balance. Early viewpoints emphasized the role of the proprioceptors in detecting sway and loss of stability. For example, when the body sways forward, the ankle joint is moved and the associated musculature is stretched, producing movement signals from the joint receptors and muscle spindles. Also, receptors in the inner ear are sensitive to movements of the head, providing information about body sway.

Recently, however, the role of vision in balance has begun to appear far greater than previously believed. Look straight ahead at an object on the wall. Without shifting your direction of gaze, move your head slightly forward and backward and pay attention to the changes in visual information. You will probably notice that the objects in peripheral vision seem to sweep rapidly back and forth and that these changes are dependent on your head movement.

Lee and Aronson (1974) have shown that balance is strongly affected by varying the visual information, suggesting that the optical flow variables in peripheral vision are critical to balance. In their experiment, the subject stands in a special room surrounded by suspended walls that do not quite touch the floor. The walls can be moved, with the floor kept still, to influence the optical-flow information. Moving the walls slightly away causes the subject to sway slightly forward, and moving the walls closer causes the subject to sway backward. With a little child, an away-movement of the walls can cause the subject to stumble forward, and a toward-movement of the walls can cause a rather ungraceful plop into a sitting position. Moving the wall toward the person generates optical-flow information that ordinarily means the head is moving forward, that is,

■ The moving-room apparatus for studying visual processes in balance. (Lee is second from left.)

that the person is out of balance and falling forward. The automatic postural compensation is to sway backward. Such visually based compensations are far faster than can be explained by conscious processing in the focal system, with latencies of about 100 ms (Nashner & Berthoz, 1978). These experiments suggest that optical-flow information and the ambient system are critically involved in controlling normal balancing activities.

This notion has strong implications for learned postures as well. In performing a handstand on the still rings, where it is important to remain as motionless as possible, the visual system can signal very small changes in posture, providing a basis for tiny corrections to hold the posture steady. It is probably important to train a performer to

fixate the gaze on a particular place on the mat under him or her to see the changes in visual information most easily.

Keep Your Eye on the Ball! It always seemed strange to me that golfers are always reminded to "keep your eye on the ball" during the swing. Keeping your eye on an approaching baseball makes sense because you could detect last-moment information about ball flight as the ball comes close to the plate. But the golf ball is certainly not going anywhere until you strike it, so why should visual information about it help the swing?

The role of optical-flow variables in balance can help to understand this question. It is important to hold the head in a constant position over the ball during the swing, where very small changes in head position are signaled by optical-flow information, just as they are for the earlier examples of balance. Small movements of the head backward during the backswing can be detected rapidly, and small changes in muscle activities can be generated to compensate for these unintentional movements. As discussed in the next section, these changes in musculature through optical-flow information are processed by the ambient system, are nonconscious, and are very fast—far faster than in the case of the visual information used by the focal system in the outside loop in Figures 3.2 and 3.5.

Vision in the Conceptual Model

These principles of visual information processing for movement control can be added to the conceptual model, which is shown revised in Figure 3.9. There are two visual feedback loops added to the earlier version. First there is the loop carrying focal vision (light red). Focal vision is conscious, slow, and attention demanding, so it is logical that this loop passes through the stages of information processing. It can have effects on movement but only after relatively long delays. Also, it is very flexible.

Second is the loop associated with ambient vision, here shown in dark red. Because ambient information is nonconscious, relatively fast, and inflexible, it is fed back to relatively low levels in the central nervous system, considerably "downstream" from the processes that select and initiate movement, but "upstream" from the muscles and the spinal cord. Thus, ambient vision can be thought of as operating at intermediate levels of the system to make minor adjustments in already programmed actions, such as compensation for head movement in the golf swing and alterations in posture to maintain balance on the still rings. The final commands to the muscles are based foremost on the originally programmed action, but notice that this information is supplemented by at least four different feedback loops that signal different features of the movement, of the environment, or of both.

Visual Dominance and Visual Capture

Although vision can make powerful contributions to movement control, it does not always play such a positive role. In many activities, performers have a choice of the modes of control they use, such as the racecar driver or pilot who can monitor the sounds of the engine as opposed to the visual information provided by numerous cockpit gauges. Because vision is such an important sensory source in many situations, however, performers often find that visual control dominates the other senses (**visual dominance**) and that visual information unavoidably captures attention (**visual capture**).

This can often be useful in that visual information is very important in many situations, but in other situations an overreliance on vision can result in ineffective performance. A good example comes from sailboat racing, which is very rich in visual information about the aerodynamic shapes of the sails and the way the wind is flowing over them. This visual information can yield relatively good performance. However, a helmsman focusing on vision is ignoring other forms of information, such as the sounds the boat makes as it goes through the water, the action and position of the hull felt by the "seat of the pants," and forces on the tiller, all of which provide additional useful information about speed—but only if the helmsman is attending to them. To learn to decrease the reliance on vision and share the attentional resources among several of the senses to optimize performance, some Olympic sailors have used blindfolded training methods. When vision

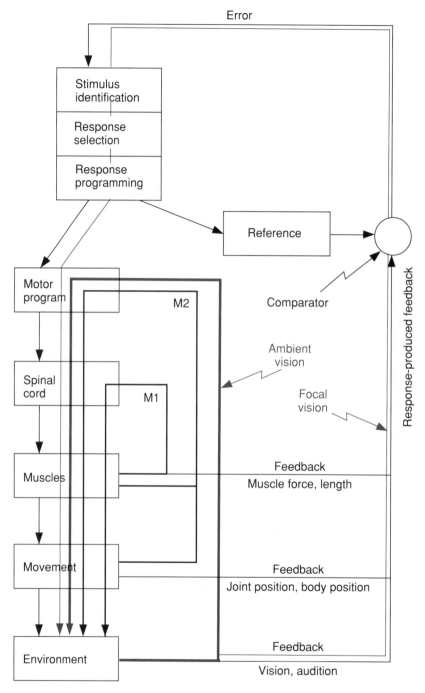

Figure 3.9 The expanded conceptual model of human performance, here including the pathways for focal and ambient vision shown in red.

is prevented for a long time, the sailors develop sensitivity to the less dominant sources of information.

Only part of the difficulty is that visual dominance prevents the additional help of other sensory information: When vision dominates, it sometimes actually leads to poorer performance when other senses are more appropriate. You can see how this might be so in Figure 3.9. If you use vision in a conscious information-processing mode (i.e., the outer loop in light red), processing can be slow and attention demanding. On the other hand, if you use kinesthetic information through the M2 loop, responses can speed up noticeably. Experiments on fencers (Jordan, 1972) suggest just this, where allowing visual information actually slowed performers' responses by shifting attention away from the more relevant kinesthetic senses.

In the same general way, asking a performer to concentrate (consciously) on certain visual events can have detrimental effects on performance. Such a shift to conscious processes would shift control from the relatively fast ambient system to the slower focal system (see Figure 3.9). For example, coaches often use various visual aids for performance, such as telling a batter to initiate the swing when the pitched ball has passed a certain visually determined point in space or when it is a certain measured distance away. Such an instruction seems certain to cause a shift to conscious control by the ambient system, probably resulting in poorer, rather than better, performance. A more natural strategy would be to instruct the performer to watch the ball and to swing when the time "feels right." Such an instruction should encourage the use of the ambient system, allowing the time-to-contact information more reliably derived from optical flow to trigger the response (McLeod, McLaughlin, & Nimmo-Smith, 1985).

PRACTICAL APPLICATIONS

1. In activities such as hitting a golf ball, have the performer watch the ball because this stabilizes the head and therefore the body during the action.
2. In balancing activities such as gymnastics, have the learner focus vision at one point to facilitate optical control of balance.
3. In softball avoid using instructions that would shift ambient visual control to focal control, such as "Respond when the ball is 2 meters away."
4. Encourage the learner to initiate a visually triggered response when it "feels right," emphasizing ambient visual control and the use of time-to-contact information.
5. In many actions, blindfolded practice can prevent visual dominance and can provide improved sensitivity for other sensory control systems.

This is another example of the Bliss-Boder hypothesis, in which performance is hurt by instructions to intervene in natural processes by conscious activities that demand attention and controlled processing. Remember that a high-level performer has developed many elegant, nonconscious processes for detecting and processing visual and kinesthetic information, along with very fast and effective processes for making corrections based on this information. When asked by the coach to pay attention to these processes, the performer is forced out of these nonconscious modes of processing and into the more conscious, controlled information-processing activities, which are usually not very effective for skilled performance.

CHAPTER SUMMARY

The effectiveness with which a performer processes various forms of sensory information often determines overall performance level. Sensory signals from the environment are usually termed *exteroceptive* information, whereas those from the body are termed *proprioceptive* or *kinesthetic* information. For human performance it is useful to think of these signals as operating in a closed-loop control system, which contains an executive for decision making, an effector for carrying out the actions, feedback about the state of the environment, and a comparator to contrast the environmental state with the system's goal.

In the conceptual model of human performance, closed-loop control is added to the stages of information processing discussed in chapter 2. This model is particularly effective for understanding how slower actions as well as tracking tasks are performed. To the conceptual model are then added several reflexlike processes that account for corrections without involving the information-processing stages. In moving from the M1, M2, triggered reactions, and M3 (or reaction time), these responses show systematically increased flexibility but decreased speed.

Finally, vision is considered as a special case of closed-loop control. Two visual systems are introduced—an ambient system for motor control and a focal system for item identification—and the role of the ambient system in balance and in producing and correcting actions is considered. These sensory systems are then integrated into the conceptual model, which helps show how these various sensory events can support or modify skilled actions and under what conditions they operate.

Checking Your Understanding

1. What are the four critical features of any closed-loop system? Describe how this kind of system might operate in the control of joint angle in a human.
2. What is visual proprioception? Explain why an apparent contradiction exists in the joined terms *visual* and *proprioception*.
3. Define and describe the four principal reflexlike responses involved in the movement control compensations for unexpected stimuli.
4. Normally, paying attention to what you are doing aids performance. Under what conditions will attending to your actions actually interfere with performance? Why does this happen?
5. Describe how optical-flow information informs you about the time of arrival of a ball moving toward you. Does this process depend on the size of the ball or its distance?

Key Terms

Definitions of the following terms appear on the page(s) shown in parentheses:

ambient vision (p. 65)

closed-loop control (p. 48)

exteroceptive (p. 46)

focal vision (p. 65)

kinesthesis (p. 47)

M1 response (p. 56)

M2 response (p. 57)

M3 response (p. 59)

optical flow (p. 67)

proprioception (p. 47)

reflexes (p. 55)

tau (p. 69)

◇ **Suggestions
for Further Reading**

Additional information on the functional properties and neurophysiology of the motor system can be found in Brooks (1986) and Houk and Rymer (1981); a somewhat more behavioral orientation is in Schmidt (1988b, chapter 6) and Winstein and Schmidt (1988). Excellent reviews of the role of vision in motor control, particularly with respect to optical flow principles for many sports performances, have been done by D.N. Lee (1980; Lee & Young, 1985).

4 Movement Production and Motor Programs

PREVIEW

Watching the high-hurdler go over the barriers in a meet, I am dazzled by the number of separate actions that appear nearly simultaneously. At each hurdle the athlete stretches forward with the lead (right) leg to clear the hurdle, brings the right arm forward, almost touching the toes, moves the left arm backward with the elbow flexed, brings the left leg to the side with the knee sharply flexed to clear the hurdle, and then brings the right leg down sharply to the ground to initiate the next step.

The hurdler executes many identifiable actions in an instant, with correct sequencing and a coordination among them that give the impression of a single, fluid action. How does the skilled athlete produce so many movements so quickly? What controls them, and how are they combined to form a whole movement? We have the impression that these quick movements are organized in advance and are run off without much feedback.

This chapter investigates the idea of open-loop control, introducing the critical concept of the motor program as the structure responsible for this kind of movement control. Then the various reflex pathways discussed in the previous chapter are examined as to their interaction with motor programs, giving a more complete picture of the interplay of central and peripheral contributions to movements. The chapter also focuses on the concept of generalized motor programs, which can account for the common observation that movements can be varied slightly along certain dimensions (e.g., making a fast or a slow pitch).

STUDENT GOALS

1. To become familiar with the concepts of open-loop control for movement
2. To learn the rationale for and characteristics of motor programs
3. To understand how to generalize programs to allow novelty and flexibility
4. To apply the principles of programming to practical performance situations

In many actions, particularly quick ones produced in stable and predictable environments (e.g., diving, hurdling, dart throwing), most people would assume that a performer somehow plans the movement in advance and then triggers it, allowing it to run its course without much modification or awareness of the individual elements. Also, the performer does not seem to have much conscious control over the movement once it is triggered; the movement just seems to "take care of itself." Perhaps this is obvious. Certainly, you cannot have direct, conscious control of the thousands of individual muscle contractions and joint movements, the degrees of freedom, that must be initiated and coordinated as the skilled action is unfolding. There is simply too much going on for the limited-capacity attentional mechanisms to appreciate.

If these individual contractions are not controlled very directly by processes of which you are aware, how then are they controlled and regulated? In many ways, this question is one of the most fundamental to the field of motor behavior because it runs to the heart of how biological systems of all kinds control actions. This chapter focuses on the ways the central nervous system is functionally organized before and during action and how this organization contributes to the control of the unfolding movement. As such, this chapter is a close companion to chapter 3, which considered the ways sensory information contributes to movement production, although without discussing very much about what the sensory information was modifying. This chapter adds the idea of centrally organized commands that sensory information may modify somewhat. First, though, comes the important concept of a **motor program**, which is the prestructured set of movement commands that defines and shapes the movement.

During this discussion of movement production, some of the important questions are these:

- How is it known that some movements are organized in advance?
- Can movements really be controlled without awareness?
- How are many degrees of freedom organized into workable units?
- How can the capabilities for these actions be learned?

MOTOR PROGRAM THEORY

The concept of the motor program, which is central to this whole chapter, is based on a kind of control mechanism that is in some ways the opposite of the closed-loop system described throughout chapter 3. This type of functional organization is open-loop control.

Open-Loop Control

Figure 4.1 is a diagram of a typical **open-loop control** system. It consists of essentially two parts: an executive level and an effector level.

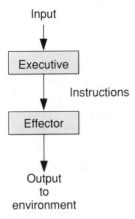

Figure 4.1 Elements of an open-loop control system.

Notice that this open-loop structure has two of the features used in closed-loop control (compare Figure 3.1), but missing are feedback and comparator mechanisms for determining system errors. The system begins with input being given to the executive (or decision-making) level, whose task is to define what action needs to be taken. It passes instructions to the effector level, which is responsible for carrying out these instructions. Once the actions are completed, the system's job is over until the executive is activated again. Of course, without feedback the open-loop system is not sensitive to whether the actions generated in the environment were effective in meeting the goal, and modifications to the action cannot be made while the action is in progress.

This kind of control system is widely used in many different real-world applications, for example, in most traffic signals, where it is effective in sequencing and timing the red, yellow, and green lights that control the traffic flow. If an accident should happen at that intersection, the open-loop system continues to sequence the lights as if nothing were wrong, even though this standard pattern would be ineffective in handling this new, unexpected traffic flow problem. Thus, the open-loop system is effective as long as things go as expected, but it is inflexible in the face of unpredicted changes.

Another example of an open-loop system, which is the basis of the idea of the motor program, is the computer program. In most computers the instructions that form the program tell the machine what operations to do at each step along the way and in what order to do them, and in some cases it specifies the timing of the operations. Although many computer programs are indeed sensitive to feedback, the classical open-loop computer program is not, and the machine follows the instructions to generate various computations without any regard for whether these computations are correct or have met the programmer's goals.

Generally, the characteristics of a purely open-loop control system can be summarized as follows:

- Specific advance instructions give the operations to be done, their sequencing, and their timing.
- Once the program has been initiated, the system sequences through the instructions without modification.
- There is no capability to detect or to correct errors because feedback is not involved anywhere.
- Open-loop systems are most effective in stable, predictable environments where need for modification of commands is low.

Motor Program as an Open-Loop Control System

In a sense, much movement behavior—especially those actions that are quick and forceful, such as kicking and throwing—seem controlled in an open-loop fashion and without much conscious control. The performer in these tasks does not have time to process information about movement errors and must plan the movement properly in the first place. This is quite different from the style of control discussed in the previous chapter, where the movements were slower and strongly based on feedback processes of various kinds.

Open-loop control seems especially important when the environmental situation is predictable and stable, with no changes in

There is little time for corrections here, and the movement needs to be planned and organized correctly from the start.

the environment requiring changes in the planned movement after it has started. Under stable circumstances, human movements appear to be carried out without much possibility of, or need for, modification. This general idea was popularized 100 years ago by the psychologist William James (1890) and has remained as one of the most important ways to understand movement control ever since. The basic open-loop system seen in Figure 4.1, augmented by some of the processes discussed in earlier chapters, gives the general idea of motor program control for movement behavior (see Figure 4.2).

Consider a task such as hitting a pitched baseball. The executive level, which consists of the decision-making stages of the system defined in chapter 2, evaluates the environment in the stimulus-identification stage, processing such information as the speed and direction of the ball. The decision about whether to swing is made in the response-selection stage. The movement is programmed and initiated in the response-programming stage, where details about the swing's speed, trajectory, and timing are determined.

Control is then passed to the effector level for movement execution. The selected motor program is now carrying out the swing movement by delivering commands to the spinal cord, which eventually direct the contraction of the muscles involved in the swing. This movement then influences the environment when the bat contacts the ball.

This view has the motor program as the agent determining which muscles are to contract, in what order, and with what timing. Although the decision-making stages determine what program to initiate and have some role in the eventual form of the movement (e.g., its speed and trajectory), movement execution is not actually controlled by the conscious decision-making stages: There-

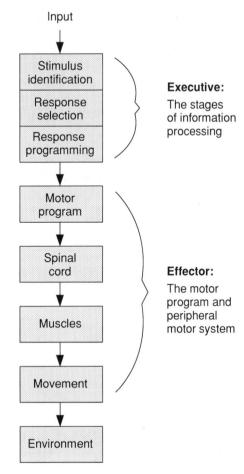

Figure 4.2 An expanded open-loop control system for human performance. The executive level contains the stages of information processing.

fore, the movement is carried out by a system that is not under direct conscious control.

Practice leading to learning skilled actions is thought of as building new, more stable, more precise, or longer-operating motor programs. Initially a program might be capable only of controlling a short string of actions. With practice, however, the program becomes more elaborate, capable of controlling longer and longer strings of behavior, perhaps even modulating various reflexive activities that support the overall movement goal. These programs are then stored in long-term memory (see chapter 2) and must be retrieved and prepared for initiation during the response-programming stage (see Figure 2.13).

One major advantage for the performer using motor programs is that various conscious, attentional processes are used less for movement production. One problem for attention discussed in chapter 2 was movement organization and initiation in the bottleneck in the response-programming stage (review Figures 2.9 and 2.10). But if, after continued practice, the programs run longer and control more skilled behavior, then the response-programming stage is involved less often. This frees various attentional processes to perform other higher-order activities, such as monitoring form or style in gymnastics or dance or attending to the strategic elements in tennis.

OPEN-LOOP CONTROL WITHIN THE CONCEPTUAL MODEL

How does this concept of open-loop control and the motor program fit with the conceptual model of human performance? Figure 4.3 shows the conceptual model used in chapter 3 (Figure 3.9), now with the portions shaded that comprise the open-loop components seen in Figure 4.2. The conceptual model can now be thought of as an open-loop control system with feedback added (not shaded) to produce corrections through the other loops discussed previously. This more complete conceptual model has two basic ways of operating, depending on the task. If the movement is very slow, the control is dominated by the feedback processes. If the movement is very fast, though, then the

---

PRACTICAL APPLICATIONS

1. The quicker an action, the more a learner should be encouraged to plan the movement in advance and produce it as a single unit.
2. In such an action, the learner should be discouraged from trying to intervene in the movement with feedback processes.
3. The more stable and predictable the environment, the more the movement should be organized in advance, produced as a single unit, and feedback-based modulations discouraged.
4. In serial skills, especially where the environment is stable, encourage the learner to combine smaller elements into longer sequences controlled as single units.
5. Encourage the learner to generate longer sequences of elements in order to free attention for other higher-order aspects, such as strategy or style.

---

open-loop portions tend to dominate. Motor behavior is not either open- or closed-loop alone but a complex blend of the two.

For very fast actions, the theory of motor programs is useful because it gives a set of ideas and a vocabulary to talk about a functional organization of the motor system. If a given movement is said to be "a programmed action," it appeared to be organized in advance, triggered more or less as a whole, and carried out without much modification from sensory feedback. This language describes a style of motor control with central movement organization, where movement details are determined by the central nervous system and then sent to the muscles, rather than by peripheral control involving feedback. Of course, both styles of control are

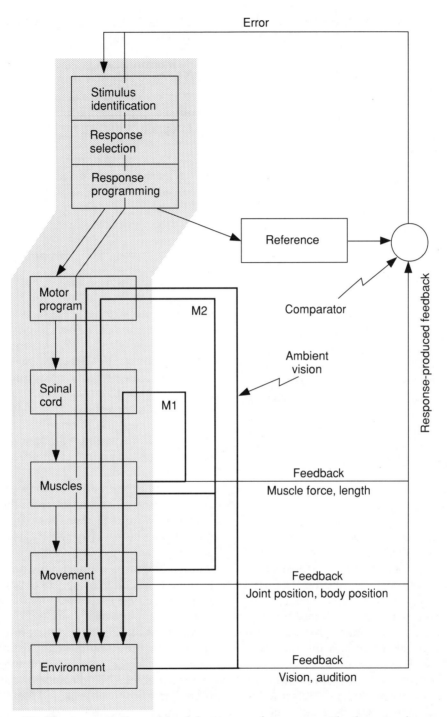

Figure 4.3 The conceptual model of human performance, with the open-loop components highlighted.

possible, depending on the nature of the task, the time involved, and other factors.

Three Lines of Evidence for Motor Programs

Essentially three separate lines of evidence converge to support the theory of motor program control of fast actions. This evidence involves the role of movement complexity for reaction time, experiments on animals with feedback removed, and analysis of electromyographic patterns when the movement is unexpectedly blocked.

Reaction Time and Movement Complexity

When subjects in reaction time situations are asked to respond to a stimulus by initiating and carrying out a predetermined movement as quickly as possible (as discussed in chapter 2), the reaction time depends on the complexity of the *movement* (Henry & Rogers, 1960; see Highlight Box). Recall that reaction time is measured from the presentation of the stimulus until the movement begins, so any added time for the movement itself does not contribute directly to elevated reaction time. However, several features of the movement contribute to its complexity, all of which still affect RT.

- RT increases when additional elements in a series are added to the action: A unidirectional forward stroke in table tennis would likely require a shorter RT than a backswing plus a forward stroke.
- RT increases when more limbs must be coordinated. A one-handed piano chord has a shorter RT than a more complicated two-handed chord.
- RT increases when the duration of the movement becomes longer. A fast swing of a bat taking 100 ms would have a shorter RT than a slower bat movement taking 300 ms.

The interpretation is that when the movement is more complex in any of these ways, reaction time is longer because more time is required to organize the motor system before the initiation of the action. This prior organization occurs, as discussed in chapter 2, in the response-programming stage. The effect on RT by the nature of the movement to be produced is evidence that some of the action is organized in advance, just as a motor program theory expects.

Deafferentation Experiments

Chapter 3 mentioned that sensory information from the muscles, the joints, and the skin are collected together in sensory nerves, which enter the dorsal (back) side of the spinal cord at various levels. A surgical technique termed **deafferentation** involves cutting such an afferent nerve bundle where it enters the cord, so the central nervous system no longer receives information from some portion of the periphery. Sensory information from an entire limb, or even from several limbs, can be eliminated by this procedure.

What are experimental animals capable of when deprived of feedback from the limbs? I have seen films of monkeys with deafferented upper limbs. They are still able to climb around, playfully chase each other, groom, and feed themselves essentially normally. It is indeed difficult to recognize that these animals have a total loss of sensory information from the upper limbs (Taub, 1976; Taub & Berman, 1968). The monkeys are impaired in some ways; they have difficulty in fine finger control, as in picking up a pea or manipulating small objects. On balance, though, it is remarkable how little impaired these animals are in most activities.

HIGHLIGHT

The Henry-Rogers Experiment

One of Franklin Henry's many important contributions was a paper he and Donald Rogers published in 1960. The experiment was simple, as many important experiments are. Subjects responded as quickly as possible to a stimulus by making one of three different kinds of movements. Only one of these movements would be required for a long string of trials, so this was essentially simple RT. The movements, designed to be different in complexity, were (a) a simple finger lift, (b) a simple finger lift plus a reach and grasp for a suspended ball, and (c) a movement requiring a simple finger lift followed by several reversals in direction to targets.

Henry and Rogers then measured the RTs to initiate each of these actions, that is, the interval from the presentation of the stimulus until the beginning of the required movement. They found reaction time increased with added movement complexity. The finger-lift movement (a) had an RT of 150 ms, the grasping move-

ment (b) had an RT of 195 ms, and the movement with two reversals in direction (c) had an RT of 208 ms.

Notice that in each case the stimulus to signal the movement (processed during stimulus identification) and the number of movement choices (response selection) are constant. Thus, because the only factor that varied here was the complexity of the movement, the interpretation was that the elevated RT with movement complexity was caused by increased time for movement programming prior to the action, during the response-programming stage. This notion has had profound effects on the understanding of movement organization processes, and has led to many further research efforts to study these processes more systematically. Most importantly, these data support the idea that movement is organized in advance, which is consistent with the motor program concept.

Sensory information from the moving limb is certainly not absolutely critical for movement production, and it is clear that many movements can occur without it. This evidence suggests that theories of movement control must be generally incorrect if they require sensory information from the responding limb. Because feedback-based theories cannot account for the monkeys' movement capabilities, many theorists have argued that the movements must be organized centrally in motor programs and carried out in an open-loop way, not critically dependent on feedback. In this sense, this deafferentation evidence supports the idea that movements can be organized centrally in motor programs.

This thinking is similar to ideas presented in chapter 3, where some actions were thought to be too fast to allow feedback to be used in their control. For example, in Figure 3.6 a very quick movement is completed before the feedback from that movement can have an effect. Thus, if the movement is quick enough, the motor program controls the entire action; the movement is carried out as though the performer were deprived of feedback. The capability to move quickly thus gives additional support to the idea that there is some central program that handles the movement control, at least until feedback from the movement can begin to have an effect.

Effects of Mechanically Blocking a Limb

A third line of evidence supporting motor program control comes from experiments in which the performer is instructed to make a quick limb action (moving a lever) and the patterns of muscle activity are examined. Figure 4.4 shows an integrated electromyogram (EMG) from a quick elbow-extension movement (Wadman, Denier van der Gon, Geuze, & Mol, 1979). In the normal movement (heavy lines) there is first a burst of the agonist (triceps) muscle, then the triceps turns off and the antagonist muscle (biceps) is activated to decelerate the limb, and finally the agonist comes on again near the end to stabilize it at the target area. This triple-burst pattern is typical of quick movements of this kind.

On some trials the subjects had the movement unexpectedly mechanically blocked by the experimenter so no movement of the lever was possible. Notice what happens to

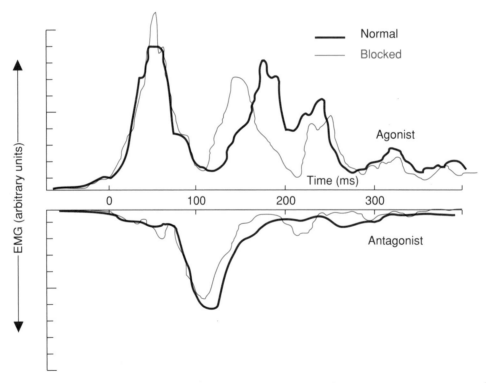

Figure 4.4 Agonist (triceps) and antagonist (biceps) EMG activity in a rapid elbow-extension movement. The lighter traces are from a movement which was mechanically blocked at the outset. (Reprinted from Wadman, Denier van der Gon, Geuze, & Mol, 1979.)

the EMGs (lighter traces). Even though the limb does not move at all, there is a similar initial pattern of muscular organization, with the onset of the agonist and the antagonist occurring about the same times as when the movement was not blocked. Later, after about 120 ms or so, there is a slight modification of the patterning, undoubtedly caused by the reflex activities (e.g., stretch reflexes) discussed in chapter 3. But the most important findings were that the antagonist (biceps) muscle even contracted at all when the movement was blocked and contracted at the same time as in the normal movements.

The feedback from the blocked limb must have been massively disrupted, yet the EMG patterning was essentially normal for 100 ms or so. Therefore, these data contradict theories that feedback from the moving limb (during the action) acts as a signal (a trigger) to activate the antagonist muscle contraction at the proper time. Rather, these findings support the ideas that the movement program organizes EMG activities in advance and that it is run off unmodified by sensory information for 100 to 120 ms, at least until the first reflexive activities can become involved.

Summary **Break**

Here are summarized the three most important lines of evidence for the prior organization of movements via motor programs:

1. Reaction time is longer for more complex movements, suggesting organization in response programming prior to action.
2. Movement capabilities of deafferented animals shows that feedback from the limbs is not critical, suggesting central organization of action.
3. EMG patterning in unexpectedly blocked limbs is essentially normal for 120 ms, suggesting that patterning is not dependent on feedback.

How and When Do Programs Contribute to Actions?

Particularly in rapid movement, open-loop control occurs primarily to allow the motor system to organize an entire action without having to rely on the relatively slow information feedback presented under a closed-loop control mode. Skilled performers appear to organize movements in advance to get it right from the beginning rather than having to modify and correct an initially faulty movement as it unfolds. Several processes must be handled by this prior organization. At a minimum, the following must be specified in the programming process in order to generate skilled movements:

- The particular muscles that are to participate in the action
- The order in which these muscles are to be involved
- The forces of the muscle contractions
- The relative timing and sequencing among these contractions
- The duration of each contraction

Most theories of motor programs assume that a movement is organized in advance by the program's setting up some kind of neural mechanism, or network, that contains time and event information. A kind of movement script specifies certain essential details of the movement as it runs off in time. Therefore, scientists speak of performers "running" a motor program, which is clearly analogous to the processes involved in running computer programs.

A particularly useful analogy or model for a motor program is the common phonograph record. The record defines which sounds are to occur and in what order, the durations and timing (rhythm) of those events, and the relative intensities of the sounds. Not every aspect of the movement is specified in the program as it would be on the phonograph record, however, because there could certainly be reflexive activities that modify the final commands, as discussed in chapter 3. But if you conceptualize a motor program as operating more or less like a record, you have the general idea.

PRACTICAL APPLICATIONS

1. To prevent the disruption of the preprogrammed sequence, avoid asking a learner to attend to various aspects of a rapid action.
2. Encourage the learner to let the movement run its course "automatically," let it flow, in order to facilitate the learning of effective open-loop capabilities.
3. In an unstable environment, abandon open-loop strategies in favor of closed-loop control, emphasizing the processing of environmental information during the action.
4. In sport situations involving simple reaction time, have the performer concentrate on the whole action (which facilitates its programming) rather than on the stimulus.

Postural Adjustments Before Action

Imagine standing with your arms at your sides and an experimenter gives you a command to raise an arm quickly to point straight ahead. What will be the first detectable muscular activity associated with this movement? Most would guess that the first contraction would be in the shoulder musculature, but in fact these muscles' activity occurs relatively late in the sequence. Rather, the first muscles to contract, some 80 ms before the first muscle in the shoulder, are in

the lower back and legs (Belen'kii, Gurfinkel, & Pal'tsev, 1967).

This order may sound strange, but it is really quite a "smart" way for the motor system to operate. Because the shoulder muscles are mechanically linked to the rest of the body, their contractions influence the positions of the segments connected to the arm—the shoulder and the back. That is, the movement of the arm affects posture. If no compensations in posture were first made, raising the arm would shift the center of gravity forward, causing a slight loss of balance. Therefore, rather than adjust for these effects after the arm movement, the motor system compensates before the movement through "knowing" what postural modifications will soon be needed.

There is good evidence that these preparatory postural adjustments are really just a part of the movement program for making the arm movement (W.A. Lee, 1980). When the arm movement is organized, the motor program contains instructions to adjust the posture in advance as well as the instructions to move the arm, so that the action is a coordinated whole. Thus, do not think of the arm movement and the posture control as separate events but simply as different parts of an integrated action of raising the arm and maintaining balance. Interestingly, these preparatory adjustments vanish when the performer leans against a support because postural adjustments are not then needed.

Central Pattern Generator

The idea of motor programs is very similar to that of the **central pattern generator** (CPG), which was developed to explain certain features of locomotion in animals, swimming in fish, chewing in hamsters, and slithering in snakes (Grillner, 1975). Some genetically defined (inherited) central organization is established in the brainstem or the spinal cord.

When this organization is initiated by a triggering stimulus from the brain, sometimes called a command neuron, it produces rhythmic, oscillating commands to the musculature as if it were defining a sequence of right-left-right activities, such as might serve as the basis of locomotion. These commands occur even if the sensory nerves are cut (deafferented), suggesting that the organization is truly central in origin.

An example of a simple network that could account for the alternating flexor-extensor patterns in locomotion is shown in Figure 4.5. Here, the input signal activates Neuron 1, which activates the flexors as well as Neuron 2. Then Neuron 3 is activated, which activates the extensors. Neuron 4 is then activated, which activates Neuron 1 again, and the process continues. This is, of course, far too simple to account for all of the events in locomotion, but it shows how a collection of single neurons could be connected to each other in the spinal cord to produce an alternating pattern.

The notion of the CPG is almost identical to that of the motor program. The main difference is that the motor program involves learned activities that are centrally controlled (such as kicking and throwing), whereas the CPG involves more genetically defined activities, such as locomotion, chewing, and breathing. In any case, there is good evidence that many genetically defined activities are controlled by CPGs.

Integration of Central and Feedback Control

Although it is clear that central organization of movements is a major source of motor control, it is also very clear that sensory information modifies these commands in several important ways, as seen in the revised conceptual model in Figure 4.3. Thus, the question now becomes how and under what conditions these commands from programs and CPGs interact with sensory information to define the overall movement pattern. This is one of the most important research issues for understanding motor control.

Reflex Reversal. In addition to the various classes of reflexive activities discussed in chapter 3 that can modify the originally programmed output (Figure 3.5), another class

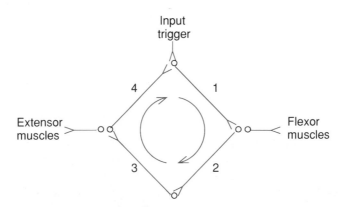

Figure 4.5 A simple network of neurons that could result in alternating flexor and extensor muscle movements in activities like locomotion. Such a network could form the basis of central pattern generators (CPG).

of reflexive modulations has a very different effect on the movement behavior. Several experiments show how reflex activities are integrated with open-loop programmed control. While a cat is walking on a treadmill, the experimenter applies a light tactile stimulus to the top of a foot. This stimulus has different effects when it is presented at different locations in the step cycle. If this stimulus is applied as the cat is just placing its foot on the surface in preparation for load bearing, the response is to extend the leg slightly, as if to carry more load on that foot. This response has a latency of about 30 to 50 ms and is clearly nonconscious and automatic. If exactly the same stimulus is applied when the cat is just lifting the foot from the surface in preparation for the swing phase, the response is very different. The leg flexes upward at the hip and the knee so the foot travels above the usual trajectory in the swing phase.

These alterations in the reflex, reversing its effect from extension to flexion (or vice versa) depending on where in the step cycle the stimulus is applied, has been called the reflex reversal phenomenon (Forssberg, Grillner, & Rossignol, 1975). It challenges our usual conceptualizations of a reflex, usually defined as an automatic, stereotyped, unavoidable response to a given stimulus: Here the same stimulus has generated two different responses.

These variations in response must occur through interactions of sensory pathways and the ongoing movement program for locomotion, the CPG. As just discussed, the CPG is responsible for many of the major events, such as muscle contractions and their timing, that occur in locomotion and other rhythmical activities. In addition, the CPGs are now thought to be involved in the modulation of reflexes, producing the reflex reversal phenomenon. The logic is that the CPG determines whether and when certain reflex

pathways can be activated in the action, as diagrammed in Figures 4.6a and b. During the part of the action when the cat's foot is being lifted from the ground (swing phase), the CPG inhibits the extension reflex and enables the flexion reflex (i.e., allows it to be activated). If the stimulus occurs, it is routed to the flexion response, not to the extension response. When the foot is being placed on the ground, the CPG inhibits the flexion reflex and enables the extension reflex. It does this all over again on the next step cycle and so on. Finally, notice that if no stimulus occurs at all, there is no reflex activity at all, and the CPG carries out the action ''normally'' without the contribution of either reflex.

Enhancing Movement Flexibility. These complex reflex responses are only beginning to be understood, but they undoubtedly play an important role in the flexibility and control of skills. The cat's reflexes are probably organized to have an important survival role. Receiving a tactile stimulus on the top of the foot while it is swinging forward probably means that the foot has struck some object and that the cat will trip if the foot is not lifted quickly over the object. However, if the stimulus is received during the beginning of stance, flexing the leg would cause the animal to fall because it is swinging the other leg at this time. These can be thought of as temporary reflexes in that they exist only in the context of performing a particular part of a particular action, ensuring that the goal is achieved even if a disturbance is encountered.

This feature of a movement program provides considerable flexibility in its operation. First of all, the movement can be carried out as programmed if nothing goes wrong. If something does go wrong, then appropriate reflexes are allowed to participate in the movement to ensure that the goal is met. Also important is the fact that certain reflexes

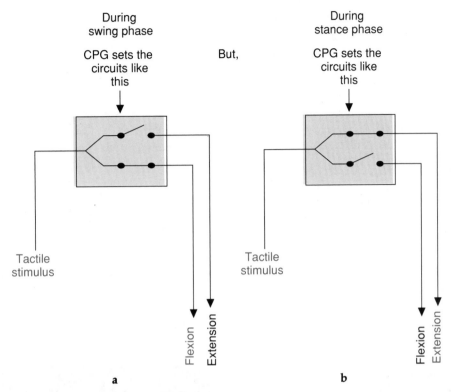

During
swing phase

CPG sets the
circuits like
this

But,

During
stance phase

CPG sets the
circuits like
this

Tactile
stimulus

Flexion Extension

Tactile
stimulus

Flexion Extension

a

b

Figure 4.6 In addition to controlling the leg motion during locomotion, the CPG can inhibit or enable flexion and extension reflexes, depending on the phase of the step cycle.

are *not* allowed to participate in a particular action because the motor program has been organized to exclude them, similar to the reduction of the M2 response by instructions to "let go" (chapter 3). For example, when the tactile stimulus is presented when the cat has just placed its foot down on the support surface, the leg flexion response is not allowed because it would disrupt the system's goal of providing support for the body while the other leg is in the swing phase.

Analogous findings have been produced in speech, where unexpected tugs on the lip musculature during the production of a sound cause rapid, reflexive modulations, with the actual responses critically dependent on the particular sound being at-

tempted (Abbs, Gracco, & Cole, 1984; Kelso, Tuller, Vatikoitis-Bateson, & Fowler, 1984). The critical goals for the motor system in such situations seems to be to ensure that the intended action is generated and that the environmental goal is achieved.

Here are some important generalizations from this section:

- Fast, nonconscious, reflexlike compensations can be triggered by appropriate stimuli during movements.
- The nature of the response can depend on the location of the stimulus in the movement cycle (reflex reversal phenomenon) or on the overall goal of the movement.

- These reflexes are not permanently structured but are organized only as long as that movement is being produced.
- These reflexes are either enabled or inhibited by the motor program or the CPG.

Motor Programs and the Conceptual Model

Motor programs are a critical part of the conceptual model seen in Figure 4.3, operating within the system, sometimes in conjunction with feedback, to produce flexible skilled actions. The open-loop part of these actions provides the organization, or pattern, that the feedback processes can later modify if necessary. Some of the major roles of these open-loop organizations follow:

- To define and issue the commands to musculature that determine when, how forcefully, and which muscles are to contract
- To organize the many degrees of freedom of the muscles and joints into a single unit
- To specify and initiate preliminary postural adjustments necessary to support the upcoming action
- To modulate the many reflex pathways to ensure that the movement goal is achieved

GENERALIZED MOTOR PROGRAMS

The theory of motor programs is very useful for understanding the functional organization of certain kinds of movements. However, motor program theory, at least as developed so far in this chapter, does not account for several important aspects of movement behavior. Perhaps its most severe limitations are the failure to account for novel

movements and for the performer's capability to produce flexible movement patterns.

How Is a Novel Movement Produced?

When I watch a champion tennis player, I am often struck by the amazing capability to produce actions that appear completely novel. The player may be out of position yet return the opponent's shot acceptably with a shot that is completely unorthodox and almost certainly could never have been practiced previously. Even on any play, given the immense number of possible combinations of ball speed, angle of flight, and overall trajectory, as well as the positions on the court of the player and the opponent, each shot must be considered essentially novel in that it has never been performed exactly that way

Sometimes, skilled players make movements they have never made previously.

HIGHLIGHT

Counterpoint: The Dynamical Perspective

The notion of the motor program is not the only theory to deal with movement control. Several investigators have been critical of the program concept on various grounds and have offered an alternative that is generally termed the Bernstein perspective (after Russian physiologist N.I. Bernstein) or the dynamical perspective (e.g., Bernstein, 1967; Kelso, 1982; Kelso & Kay, 1987; Kugler & Turvey, 1986; Turvey, 1977). These critics argue that the program notion assumes too much organization, neural computation, and direct control by brain and spinal cord mechanisms, so that every movement must have an explicit representation stored in the central nervous system. Also, they argue that the program concept does not consider many features of movement dynamics, such as the springlike properties of contracting muscle and preferred frequencies of oscillation of the limb segments.

Investigators from the dynamical perspective hold that the regularities of movement patterns are not represented in programs but rather emerge naturally (that is, physically) out of the complex interactions among many connected elements. This is analogous to the ways in which many complex physical systems achieve organization and structure without having any central program or set of commands, such as the sudden transformation of still water to rolling patterns as it begins to boil and the organization among molecules to form crystals. Just as it would make little sense to postulate a central program for governing the patterns in boiling water, they argue that it is incorrect to think that complex patterns of human motor activity are controlled by such programs.

There is a healthy scientific debate about these issues at present (see Schmidt, 1988a, for my side), and we will probably not see their resolution very soon. Perhaps some combination of these viewpoints will best explain the nature of movement organization. Even so, thinking of the motor system acting as if it were driven by motor programs helps integrate many different findings into a unified structure.

before. Yet, performers make these novel movements with great style and grace, as if producing well-practiced actions.

This raises problems for the simple motor program theory. Recall that in this view a given movement is represented by a program stored in long-term memory. Therefore, each variation in the movement, associated with variations in the height and speed of the ball, the position of the opponent, the distance to the net, and so on, would need a separate program because the instructions for the musculature would be different for each variation. There is literally a countless number of variations; therefore, according to this view, the performer must have a countless number of motor programs to play tennis. Adding to this the number of movements possible in all other activities, the result would be a very large number of programs stored in long-term memory. This leads to what has been called the **storage problem** (Schmidt, 1975, 1988b), which concerns how all of these separate programs could be stored in memory.

There is also the **novelty problem**. Try this: From a standing position, jump up and turn one-quarter turn to the left, touching your head with your right hand and your leg with your left hand while in the air. You have probably never done this movement before, yet you can probably perform it effectively on the first try. Where did the specific program for this action come from? You could not have learned it because you have never practiced this movement. And it is not likely that it was genetically determined because such a movement would have little biological significance in evolution, unlike locomotion or chewing, for example. Motor program theory is at a loss to explain the performance of such novel things.

To summarize, these observations raise two problems for understanding everyday movement behavior:

1. Storage: How (or where) do humans store the nearly countless number of motor programs needed for future use?
2. Novelty: How do performers produce truly novel behavior that cannot be represented in an already stored motor program?

How Can Motor Program Output Be Modulated?

These problems for program theory have motivated a search for alternative ways to understand motor control. There was a desire to keep the appealing parts of motor program theory but to modify them to solve the storage and novelty problems. The idea that emerged in the 1970s was that movement programs can be generalized. The **generalized motor program** consists of a stored pattern, as before. However, this pattern can be modulated slightly when the program is executed, allowing the movement to be adjusted to meet the altered environmental demands.

Over a half century ago, the British psychologist Sir Fredrick Bartlett (1932) wrote about tennis,

> When I make the stroke, I do not . . . produce something absolutely new, and I never repeat something old. (p. 202)

The first part of his statement means that even though a movement is in some sense novel, it is never totally brand new. Each of his groundstrokes resembles quite strongly his other groundstrokes, possessing his own style of hitting a tennis ball (you can probably very easily pick out your favorite sports performer from a film because of his or her unique patterns). The second part of Bartlett's statement conveys the idea discussed in the previous section, that every movement is novel in that it had never been performed exactly that way before.

Variation in Movement Time

What are some of these features that seem to carry over from movement to movement, even though many of the details of the action are different? There are many, but a very important start in answering this question was made by Armstrong (1970) in analyzing the patterns of movements that subjects made in one of his experiments. In Armstrong's experiment learners attempted to produce a pattern of movement at the elbow joint that was defined as a space-time pattern, as graphed in Figure 4.7. The goal movement (solid line) had four major reversals in direc-

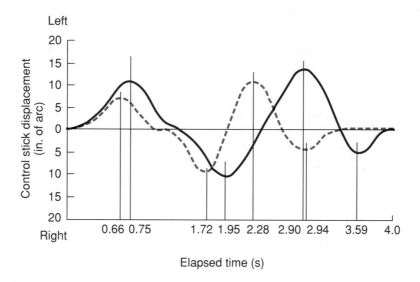

Figure 4.7 The position-time record of performance in an arm movement task. The solid trace is the goal move, whereas a movement that is uniformly too rapid is shown in the dotted trace. (Adapted by permission from Armstrong, 1970.)

tion, each of which was to be produced at a particular time in the action, with the total movement occupying about 4 s.

Armstrong noticed that when the learner made the first reversal movement too quickly (dotted trace), the whole movement was done too quickly. Notice that the graph's first peak (at reversal) was just a little early, with the other timing errors increasing as the movement progressed. This gives the impression that every aspect of the movement pattern was produced essentially correctly but that the entire pattern was simply run off too quickly.

Another way to think of this relationship is this: If you drew the dotted trace on a rubber sheet and stretched the sheet so the final peak lined up with the final peak of the solid trace, then all the other peaks would line up with their respective peaks, too. This aspect of movement control is consistent with the phonograph record analogy of movement programs discussed earlier, where the vari-

ous features of the action (the left-right-left pattern) were programmed on the record. However, there is an important modification: In this case the record has been played too fast, as if the speed of the turntable were accidentally too great. This also agrees with the common experience that we seem to have no trouble speeding up and slowing down a given movement, such as throwing a ball at various speeds.

This indicates that when the movement time is changed, the new movement preserves the essential pattern features of the old movement. Therefore, both movements are represented by a common underlying temporal (and sequential) pattern that can be run off at different speeds.

Variation in Movement Amplitude

The amplitude of movements can also be modulated easily in a way much like varying the time. For example, you can write your signature either on a check or five times as large on a blackboard, and in each case the signature is clearly yours (Merton, 1972). Making this size change seems almost trivially easy. Similarly, the football quarterback throws passes of various distances, which seem to differ mainly in amplitude (and/or speed) of a fundamental throwing action.

The handwriting phenomenon was studied more formally by Hollerbach (1978), who had subjects write the word *hell* in different sizes and measured the accelerations of the pen produced by the forces exerted by the fingers during the production of the word. These accelerations are graphed in Figure 4.8, where a trace moving upward indicates acceleration away from the body and a downward trace indicates acceleration toward the body. Of course, when the word is written larger the overall magnitude of the accelerations produced must be larger, seen as the uniformly larger amplitudes for the larger word. But what is of most interest is that the patterns of acceleration over time are almost identical for the two words, with the

accelerations having similar modulations in upward and downward fluctuations.

This leads to an observation similar to the one just made about movement time. Movements can easily be increased in amplitude by uniformly increasing the accelerations (forces) applied while preserving their temporal patterning. Therefore, two words written with different amplitudes are based on a common underlying structure that can be run off with different forces to produce movements of different sizes.

Variation in Limb Used

A performer can also modulate a movement by using a different limb to produce the action. In the signature example, writing on a blackboard involves very different muscles and joints than writing on a check. In blackboard writing the fingers are mainly fixed, and the writing is done with the muscles controlling the elbow and the shoulder. In check writing the elbow and the shoulder are mainly fixed, and the writing is done with

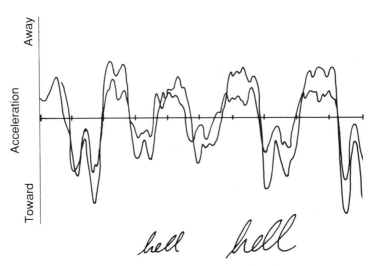

Figure 4.8 Similar patterns of acceleration produced during the writing of the word *hell*, even though one example has twice the amplitude of the other. (Adapted by permission from Hollerbach, 1978.)

the muscles controlling the fingers. Yet, the writing patterns produced are essentially the same. This indicates that a given pattern can be produced even by varying the limb and muscles used as the effector.

These phenomena were studied by Raibert (1977), who wrote the sentence "Able was I ere I saw Elba" (a palindrome, spelled the same way backward as forward) with different muscles. In Figure 4.9, Line A shows his writing with the right (dominant) hand, Line B with the right arm with the wrist immobilized, and Line C with the left hand. These patterns are very similar. Even more remarkable is that Line D was written with the pen gripped in the teeth, and Line E with the pen taped to the foot! There are obvious similarities among the writing styles, and it seems clear that the same person wrote each of them, yet the effector system was completely different for each.

This all indicates that changing the limb

and effector system can relatively easily preserve the essential features of the movement pattern. There is some underlying temporal structure common to these actions, which can be run off with different effector systems.

Summary ◇ Break

There are many more examples that could be mentioned, all of which point to the same general ideas, summarized in the following points:

- Movements can be modified along several dimensions, such as the movement time, the movement amplitude, and the limbs or effector system used for movement production.
- Such modifications seem very easy, suggesting that the novel organization is somehow already available to the performer.
- Even though these changes create differ-

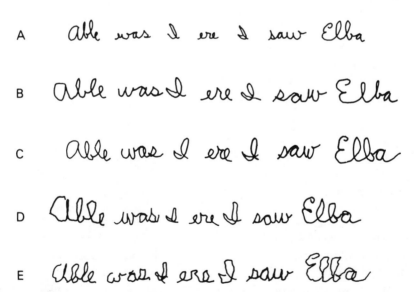

Figure 4.9 Similarities in writing with different effector systems. Line A was written by the right (dominant) hand, Line B with the wrist immobilized, Line C with the left hand, Line D with pen gripped in the teeth, and Line E with pen taped to the foot. (Reprinted by permission from Raibert, 1977.)

ent movements, the underlying temporal pattern can remain remarkably consistent.
- The temporal regularity implies a single underlying structure that can be run off in different ways to modulate movement output.

Identifying Movement Parameters

The theory of generalized motor programs holds that these various movement modulations represent relatively superficial, or surface, features of the movement. The speed of a baseball throw and the spoken volume of a word involve superficial variations of a fundamental pattern. These surface features are specified by quantities called parameters.

Movements are thought to be produced as follows. Based on sensory information processed in the stimulus-identification stage, a generalized motor program for, say, throwing (as opposed to kicking) is chosen during the response-selection stage. This generalized motor program is then retrieved from long-term memory storage, much the same as you retrieve your friend's telephone number from memory. During the response-programming stage, the motor program is prepared for initiation.

One of the necessary processes here is to define how to execute this program. Which limb to use, how fast to throw, and how far to throw must be decided upon, based on the environmental information available just prior to action. These decisions result in the assignment of a few **parameters**, characteristics that define the nature of the program's execution without influencing the overall temporal pattern of movement production. Some parameters include the speed of movement, its amplitude, and the limb used. Once the parameters have been selected and assigned to the program, the movement can be initiated and carried out with this particular set of surface features.

PRACTICAL APPLICATIONS

1. Stress that the learner can easily modify an already learned movement pattern to meet many new movement goals, without having to learn a new movement pattern.
2. Try having the learner speed up or slow down a given movement to reinforce the idea of movement flexibility.
3. Have the learner shorten the overall amplitude of the golf swing to produce a swing suitable for very short shots.
4. Make the learner aware of the relationship between the amplitude or speed of the action and the outcome in the environment.
5. Knowing the relationship between parameters and outcome is useful for determining movement speed values for future movements.

To summarize, quick movements are organized in several steps:

1. Processes in the response-selection stage, based on sensory information, define which movement must be made (throw or kick).
2. The generalized motor program for the chosen action is retrieved from long-term memory.
3. Parameters are specified and assigned to the program in the response-programming stage, and the movement is readied for initiation.
4. The movement is executed according to a relatively rigid temporal pattern,

with surface features tailored to meet specific environmental demands.

◇ CHAPTER SUMMARY

In a person's most rapid actions, where there is no time for the system to process feedback about errors and correct them, a movement is organized in an open-loop fashion—planned in advance and executed with minimal involvement of sensory information. The structure that supposedly carries out this action is the motor program. Several lines of experimental evidence argue for such programs: Reaction time is longer for more complex movements, animals deprived of sensory information by deafferentation are capable of relatively effective movement, and a limb's muscular activity patterns are unaffected for 100 to 120 ms when the limb is unexpectedly mechanically blocked.

Even though the motor program is responsible for the major events in the movement pattern, there is considerable interaction with sensory processes, such as the organization of various reflex processes to generate rapid corrections, making the movement flexible in the face of changing environmental demands. Finally, motor programs are thought to be generalized to account for a class of actions (such as throwing), and parameters must be supplied to define the way in which the pattern is to be executed (such as either rapidly or slowly).

◇ Checking Your Understanding

1. What are the major elements in an open-loop system? Describe the differences between this and closed-loop systems (discussed in chapter 3).

2. Summarize the three lines of evidence for the existence of motor programs.

3. What are reflex reversals? How does the phenomenon tell us about the interaction of open-loop and closed-loop control?

4. How do humans produce novel movements? Are such movements really novel? Explain.

5. What is a generalized motor program? Explain how this idea accounts for the production of movements tailored to environmental demands.

◇ Key Terms

Definitions of the following terms appear on the page(s) shown in parentheses:

central pattern generator (p. 88)

deafferentation (p. 84)

generalized motor program (p. 94)

motor program (p. 78)

novelty problem (p. 94)

open-loop control (p. 79)

parameters (p. 98)

storage problem (p. 94)

◇ Suggestions for Further Reading

Further reading about the evidence for motor programs in humans can be found in Schmidt (1988b, chapter 7), and a treatment of the central pattern generator concept in animals has been contributed by Grillner (1975). Taub (1976) provides a good review of the literature on deafferentation and movement performance. An early discussion of the role of parameters for motor programs is available in Keele (1981) and Schmidt (1975), and a more modern treatment can be found in Schmidt (1988b, chapter 6). A readable account of the dynamical perspective as a rival to the motor program view can be found in Kelso (1982, chapters 10, 11, and 12); a recent treatment of this approach can be found in Jeka and Kelso (1989) and Kugler (1988).

Principles of Motor Control and Movement Accuracy

PREVIEW

While the basketball player is dribbling downcourt, she spots an open teammate breaking for the basket. She knows that a very quick pass will be necessary to get the ball to her, so she throws the ball with extra speed. However, the trajectory is somewhat off, and the pass is intercepted by an opposing player, who breaks for an easy score. Why was the pass inaccurate? Did its being executed a little more quickly than usual contribute to this inaccuracy?

This chapter treats such questions about movement control. First, the text focuses on the generalized motor programs discussed in chapter 4, showing how each is characterized by its own fundamental temporal structure. Some of the most fundamental principles of movement production—analogous to the simple laws of physics—are shown to govern the relationship between movement speed, distance, and accuracy. Some of the underlying causes of errors in movements and ways to minimize them are revealed.

STUDENT GOALS

1. To understand the concept of an invariance in motor control
2. To learn how speed of movement and its amplitude influence accuracy
3. To understand the fundamental causes of inaccuracy in quick movement
4. To apply the principles of rapid actions to real-world settings

The previous chapter discussed motor programs, focusing on open-loop control in action. An important aspect of that discussion was how movements may be altered in their surface features, such as tossing a horseshoe either a long or a short distance or throwing rapidly or slowly. Certain parameters specified prior to movement output determine the particular way the movement will be carried out. This is a critically important feature of movement behavior because it allows us to understand how movements can be tailored to environmental demands while using a well-learned movement pattern (the generalized motor program) as the basis for the action.

This chapter continues this discussion of open-loop control and generalized motor programs. Several observations reveal the underlying structure, or the contents, of these motor programs in long-term memory, and how these movements are represented in the central nervous system. What is it in memory that makes your movements so typical of you? What is the structure to which the parameters are applied? These are a couple of the questions addressed in the next few sections.

Variations in surface features such as load, speed, or grade are accomplished without changes in the fundamental movement pattern.

INVARIANT FEATURES IN A GENERALIZED MOTOR PROGRAM

To begin to discover the nature of representations, we need to know what features of the flexible movement patterns remain invariant, or constant, as the more superficial features (such as movement speed, movement amplitude, and load) are altered. When movement time is altered, for example, almost every other aspect of the movement changes too: The forces and durations of contractions, the speed of the limbs, and the distances the limbs travel all can change markedly as the movement speeds up.

However, what if some feature of these movements could be shown to remain constant even though just about everything else was changing? If such a value could be found, scientists argued, it might indicate something fundamental about the structure of the generalized motor program that serves as a basis for all of these movements, providing evidence for how motor programs are organized or represented in long-term memory. Such a constant value is termed an **invariance**, the most important of which concerns the temporal structuring of the pattern.

Relative Timing: An Invariance

Return to Figure 4.7, which shows Armstrong's (1970) data concerning changes in movement time. The last chapter argued that something about the temporal pattern of the action has remained constant here, even though the actual duration of the movement changed from trial to trial. But what is it?

The answer is suggested in the observation that the whole movement appeared to speed up as a unit. If the movement speeds up uniformly, the constant is a variable called **relative timing** (see Gentner, 1987, or Schmidt, 1985, 1988b for more on these issues). Relative timing is the fundamental temporal structure, organization, or rhythm of a movement pattern, which is independent of its overall speed or amplitude. This is akin to the notion that a waltz is still fundamentally a waltz regardless of the actual speed the music is played. Relative timing represents the movement's fundamental **deep structure**, as

opposed to the **surface features** seen in the easily modified alterations in movement time. This deep temporal organization in movements seems to be invariant, even when the actions are produced at different speeds or amplitudes.

More specifically, relative timing refers to the set of ratios of the durations of several intervals within the movement, as illustrated in Figure 5.1. Consider two hypothetical throwing movements, Movement 1 being performed with a shorter movement time than Movement 2. Imagine that you measure and record the EMGs from three of the important muscles involved in each action (in principle, nearly any feature of the movement could be measured). If you measure several of these contraction durations, you can define relative timing by a set of ratios, each of which is the duration of a part of the action divided by the total duration. For example, in Movement 1, the ratios $b/a = .40$, $c/a = .30$, and $d/a = .60$ can be calculated from the figure. This pattern of ratios is characteristic of this throwing movement, describing its temporal structure relatively accurately.

This set of ratios (the relative timing) is the same for Movement 2, even though Movement 2 is longer, because the values of b/a, c/a, and d/a are the same as in Movement 1. When this set of ratios is constant in two different movements, we say that the relative timing was invariant. Notice that Movement 2 seems to be simply an elongated Movement 1, with all of the temporal events occurring systematically more slowly. This will always be found when relative timing is invariant. According to the theory of generalized motor programs, Movement 2 was produced with a slower timing parameter than Movement 1, so the whole movement was slowed down as a unit but its relative timing was preserved.

One of the important principles of movement control is that, when a rapid movement

Movement 1

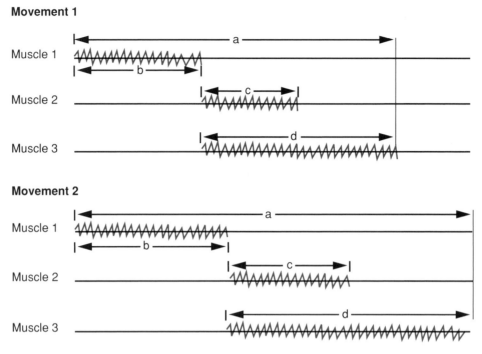

Movement 2

Figure 5.1 Hypothetical electromyographical (EMG) records from two movements, with Movement 1 having a shorter movement time than Movement 2. The ratios of the various EMG durations to total movement time define identical relative timing for the two movements. (Reprinted by permission from Schmidt, 1988.)

is changed in terms of the speed of the action (a fast versus a slow throw), the size of the action (making your signature large or small), the forces with which the action is produced (throwing a heavy versus a light object), or the trajectory of the action (throwing overarm versus sidearm), these alterations seem to be made with an invariant relative timing. Relative timing is invariant across several different kinds of surface modifications, so the form of the movement is preserved even though the superficial features of it may change. There is some controversy about whether relative timing is *perfectly* invariant (Gentner, 1987), but there can be no doubt that relative timing is at least approximately invariant.

Invariant Relative Timing and Classes of Movements

You can therefore think of an activity like throwing as a class consisting of a nearly infinite number of particular movements (throwing overarm, throwing rapidly, etc.). Theory holds that this class is represented by a single generalized motor program, with a specific, rigidly defined relative-timing structure. This program can have parameters in several dimensions (movement time, amplitude, etc.), making possible an essentially limitless number of combinations of specific throwing movements, each of which contains the same relative timing. Further, sensitive observers such as coaches and trained judges can detect these invariances relatively easily (at least in general terms), allowing quick and accurate classification of a movement according to its relative-timing structure.

The previous section suggested that movements of a given type (e.g., a throw) could be produced with the same relative timing by altering a parameter. In fact, the motor system is organized so that the same relative timing is almost required, with a different relative timing very difficult and ineffective to produce. Subjects seem unable (or at least unwilling) to alter this relative-timing structure, tending to produce scaled (faster-slower, larger-smaller) versions of a movement with the same temporal organization as before (Shapiro, 1978).

A common practical situation is for the instructor to ask the learner to make the same movement as on the previous attempt, but to change a small part of it (e.g., make the backswing duration longer in a golf drive). Such a change alters only a "piece" of the generalized motor program, which is extremely difficult to do. The motor system prefers to operate with the original motor program, modifying it as a whole (by changing parameters) from trial to trial, which does not do very much to eliminate difficulties with a particular part of the action. That is one reason why well-learned actions are so hard to modify.

Summary ◇ Break

Some of these elements of the theory of generalized motor programs can be summarized as follows:

- A generalized motor program underlies a class of movements and is structured in memory with a rigidly defined temporal organization.
- This structure is characterized by its relative timing, a set of ratios among the du-

rations of various events in the movement.
- Variations in movement time, movement amplitude, and limb used represent the movement's surface structure, adjusted with different parameters, whereas relative timing represents its deep, fundamental structure.
- Even though a movement may be carried out with different surface features (duration, amplitude, etc.), the relative timing remains invariant.
- Whereas surface features are very easy to alter by parameter adjustment, the deeper relative timing structure is very difficult to alter.

PRACTICAL APPLICATIONS

1. The learner should practice a variety of parameter values (e.g., movement times, distances, directions) of a given action to acquire the capability to assign parameters.
2. Allow the learner to acquire the proper pattern first (relative timing) without undue emphasis on the proper speed or amplitude (parameterization).
3. The learning of relative timing is the hard part, so emphasize it in practice; learning to parameterize is easy once the proper relative timing is established.
4. Altering very well-learned relative-timing patterns is difficult, so correct errors in patterning early in practice.

Different Classes Have Different Invariant Relative Timing

Although relative timing is invariant within a class of movements such as throwing, relative timing differs between different classes of movements, such as throwing and punching. This can be easily seen as an abrupt shift in relative timing when the person changes from one class of movement to another.

Shapiro, Zernicke, Gregor, and Diestel (1981) studied the shifts in relative timing in locomotion. They filmed people on a treadmill at speeds ranging from 3 to 12 kilometers per hour (km/hr) and measured the durations of various phases of the step cycle as the movement speed increased. The step cycle can be separated into four parts, as shown in Figure 5.2. For the right leg, the interval between the heel strike at the left until the leg has finished yielding (flexing) under the body's load is termed Extension Phase 2 (or E_2), and the interval from maximum flexion until toe-off is E_3; together, E_2 and E_3 make up the stance phase. The interval from toe-off until maximum knee flexion is termed the flexion phase (F), and the interval from maximum flexion to heel strike is E_1; together F and E_1 make up the swing phase.

The locomotion data shown in Figure 5.3 are expressed as the proportions of the step cycle occupied by the four phases; the duration of each phase is divided by the total step-cycle time. When the treadmill speed ranged from 3 to 6 km/hr, all subjects walked, each with a particular pattern of relative timing. About half the step cycle was occupied by E_3, about 10% of it was occupied by F and E_2 each, with about 28% occupied by E_1. Notice that as speed increased from 3 to 6 km/hr, there was almost no shift in the relative timing, which is consistent with the discussion in the previous section. When the speed was increased to 8 to 12 km/hr, however, where now all subjects were running, we see that the relative-timing pattern was completely different. Now E_1 had the largest percentage of the step cycle (32%), and E_2 had the smallest (15%). E_3, which had the largest proportion of the step cycle in walking, was now intermediate, at about 28%. Finally, as the running speed increased from 8 km/hr to 12 km/hr, there was a tendency for these proportions to remain nearly invariant.

The interpretation is that there are two generalized motor programs operating here—one for walking and one for running. Each has its own pattern of relative timing, and each is quite different from the other. When the treadmill speed increases for walk-

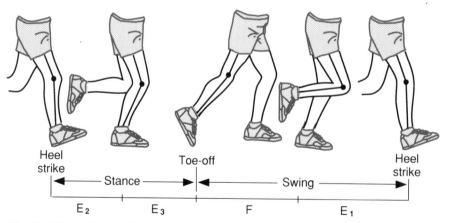

Heel strike   Toe-off   Heel strike

|← Stance →|← Swing →|

E_2 E_3 F E_1

Figure 5.2 Dividing gait into phases for analysis based on the Philippson step cycle. E_2 is time from heel strike to maximum knee flexion, or yield; E_3 is maximum knee flexion to toe-off; F is toe-off to maximum knee flexion; E_1 is maximum knee flexion to heel strike. (Reprinted by permission from Shapiro, Zernicke, Gregor, & Diestel, 1981.)

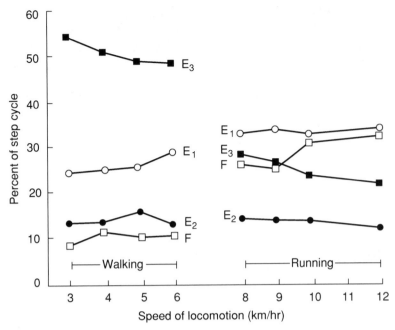

Figure 5.3 The proportion of the step cycle in human gait occupied by each of the phases E_1, E_2, E_3, and F as the treadmill speed is varied. The proportions are different for walking versus running but remain constant within each gait. (Reprinted by permission from Shapiro, Zernicke, Gregor, & Diestel, 1981.)

ing, the parameter values are increased, which speeds up the movement with the same program while maintaining the relative timing. At about 7 km/hr, a critical speed is reached, and the subject abruptly shifts to a running program; the relative timing of this activity is maintained nearly perfectly as running speed is increased further. Other evidence suggests that there is even a third locomotion program as well, used for very fast running or sprinting (not shown here).

Note that the relative timing actually produced by a performer can be thought of as a kind of fingerprint unique to a particular movement class. This pattern can be used to identify which of several motor programs is being executed (Young & Schmidt, 1990a). What would the performer be doing if you observed that the E_3 phase was about 50% of the step cycle and F was about 10%?

Finally, the viewpoint about generalized motor programs provides one kind of solution to the storage problem mentioned in the previous chapter: An infinite number of throwing movements can be produced by a single generalized motor program, so only one program needs to be stored, rather than an infinite number.

Some of these ideas can be summarized as follows:

- A movement class is characterized by a particular relative timing.
- Movements within a class have the same relative timing.
- Movements in different classes have different relative timing.
- A particular relative timing allows a movement to be identified as a member of a particular class.

Phonograph Record Analogy

My favorite analogy for generalized motor programs involves the standard phonograph, where a turntable sends signals from a record into an amplifier, whose output is delivered to speakers. In this analogy, diagrammed in Figure 5.4, the phonograph record itself is the generalized motor program, and the speakers are the muscles and limbs. The record has all of the features of programs, such as information about the order of events (the trumpet comes before the drum), the temporal structure among the events (i.e., the rhythm, or relative timing), and the relative amplitudes of the sounds (the first drumbeat is twice as loud as the second). This information is rigidly struc-

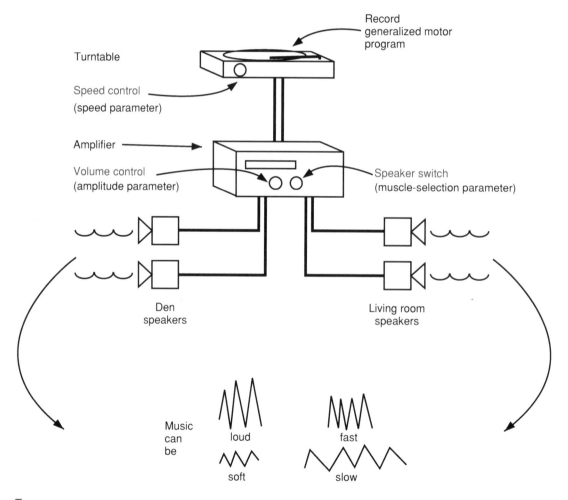

Figure 5.4 The phonograph record analogy to the generalized motor program. The program (record) has a fixed structure, which can be modified at output by the speed control (speed parameter), volume control (amplitude parameter), and speaker switch (muscle-selection parameter).

tured on the record, just as the theory says the analogous information is structured in the program. Also, there are many different records to choose from, just as humans have many motor programs to choose from (throwing, jumping, etc.), each with a different kind of information rigidly stored in it.

Notice, though, that the record's output is not fixed: I can change the speed of output by increasing the speed of the turntable, yet, relative timing (rhythm) is preserved even though the speed of the music is increased. I can change the amplitude of the output by raising the volume, uniformly increasing all the features of the sounds, just as increasing the forces increases a horseshoe toss uniformly. Also, I have a choice of which effectors to use: I can switch the output from a set of speakers in the den to a second set of speakers in the living room; this is analogous to making a handball shot either with the left hand or with the right using the same pattern.

If you think of the theory of generalized motor programs in concrete terms like phonograph records, you can understand most of the important features of the theory more easily. For example, when Shapiro and her colleagues' subjects switched from walking to running (Figure 5.3), they first had to remove the walking "record" and replace it with a running "record." Then they had to parameterize it, like setting the volume, speed, and speaker controls, then initiate it. This kind of characterization helps most people understand the basic idea.

To this point, the discussion has considered how movements are planned and controlled, emphasizing how they can be easily modulated in speed and amplitude by applying a different set of parameters to the generalized motor program. Next are considered the consequences, in terms of success in meeting the movement's environmental goal, of these changes in speed and amplitude.

PRACTICAL APPLICATIONS

1. It is helpful to classify actions to be taught into groups to aid in organizing the teaching process.
2. Use the principles of generalized motor programs and invariant relative timing to help classify skills.
3. If one movement seems to be a speeded-up or smaller version of another with the same general rhythm, assume they are members of the same class.
4. If two movements have different sequences of actions, they are probably members of different classes.
5. Organize practice scheduling based on these classifications, using principles and guidelines discussed later in chapters 8 to 10.
6. If two movements are members of the same class, point this out so the learner can use similar movement patterns for both.

DETERMINANTS OF ACCURACY IN RAPID MOVEMENTS

This section deals with the laws or principles of simple movements, describing fundamental relationships such as how the time required for a movement changes as the distance to be moved increases and how accuracy is affected by movement speed. In many ways these principles are analogous to the simple laws of physics and mechanics, which define the behavior of physical objects in the world. As such, these basic principles form the foundation of much knowledge about movements. One of the most fundamental principles concerns the relationships among the accuracy of a movement, its speed, and its amplitude.

Movement Speed, Movement Distance, and Movement Accuracy

Everybody knows that when you do things too quickly, you tend to do them with less accuracy or effectiveness. The old English saying "Haste makes waste" shows that this idea has been prevalent for many centuries. Woodworth (1899) studied these phenomena early in the history of motor skills research, showing that the accuracy of line-drawing movements decreased as their length and speed was increased. A major contribution to this problem was provided in 1954 by the psychologist Paul Fitts, who described for the first time a mathematical principle of speed and accuracy that has come to be known as Fitts' Law.

Fitts' Law

Fitts used a paradigm in which the subject must alternately tap two target plates as quickly as possible, where the separation between the targets and the width of the targets

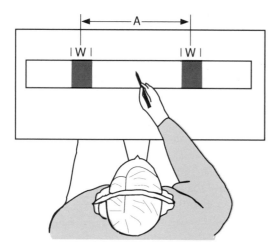

Figure 5.5 The Fitts tapping task. The subject taps as quickly as possible between two target plates of width W, which are separated by amplitude A. (Adapted from Fitts, 1964.)

could be varied in different conditions (see Figure 5.5). The time required for these movements (**movement time** [**MT**]) increased systematically as both the movement **amplitude** (due to distance of target separation) increased and the **target width** decreased. More importantly, though, as shown in Figure 5.6, the movement time was essentially constant whenever the ratio of the target amplitude (A) and the target width (W) was constant, so that a long movement to a wide target was just as rapid as a short movement to a narrow target. These relationships were combined into a formal mathematical statement that has come to be known as **Fitts' Law** (see the Highlight Box in this section for more details).

An important point was that Fitts' Law described the tendency for performers to trade off speed for accuracy. That is, when the accuracy requirements of the movement were relaxed (i.e., with wide targets), movement times were faster than when there were stringent accuracy requirements (narrow targets). This has led to the general notion of a **speed-accuracy trade-off**, the tendency for the substitution of accuracy for speed, as one of the most fundamental principles of movement behavior. This principle has been verified in many different settings (tapping underwater as well as in air), for many different classifications of people (children, older people), and for a number of different body parts (fingers, hands, arms). It even applies to the more modern-day, knob-controlled movements of a cursor across a computer screen. Fitts' Law is truly one of the most fundamental principles in the area of movement control.

Another implication of Fitts' Law is that for a given target size, when movement amplitude increases, the movement time increases as well. Interestingly, this increase is very slight. For example, when the movement distance is eight times as long, the movement time is only doubled. Thus,

HIGHLIGHT

Paul Fitts and Fitts' Law

Fitts (1954) asked subjects to make movements of a handheld stylus between two target plates. In this task, which has come to be known as the Fitts tapping task, the target widths (W) of each target and the amplitude (A) between the targets could be varied in different conditions, and the subject's job was to tap as quickly as possible between the targets while making as few errors as possible (usually less than 5 percent misses). The experimenter would measure the number of taps completed in, say, a 20-s trial, then compute the average time per movement, or movement time.

Fitts found, not surprisingly, that the average movement time increased as the amplitude of the movement increased and as the width of the target decreased. However, Fitts' major contribution was the discovery that the amplitude, the required accuracy, and the resulting movement time could be combined in a simple way that described how these separate factors were related to each other in a variety of combinations. He found that the movement time (MT) was approximately con-

stant whenever the ratio of the movement amplitude (A) to target width (W) was constant. So, very long movements to wide targets required about the same time as very short movements to narrow targets. In addition, he found that the movement time increased as the ratio of A to W increased, either by making A larger, by making W smaller, or both. He combined these various effects into a single equation that has come to be known as Fitts' Law:

$$MT = a + b \left[Log_2(2A/W) \right],$$

where a and b are constants and A and W are defined as before. The relationships between distance, required accuracy, and movement time are plotted in Figure 5.6 for one of Fitts' data sets. The term "$Log_2(2A/W)$" is referred to as the Index of Movement Difficulty (ID), which seems to define the difficulty of the various combinations of A and W. Therefore, Fitts' Law says that movement time is linearly related to the $Log_2(2A/W)$, or that movement time is linearly related to the Index of Movement Difficulty.

added movement distance can be accomplished with only a small increase in movement duration.

This has implications for many tasks in sport. The time for the swing of a baseball bat increases only slightly as the swing's amplitude (and thus velocity) increases, giving potentially much greater impact with the ball. Fitts' Law also has many implications for the design of industrial workspaces, the organization of controls in aircraft and cars,

and the like. A factory worker assembling a telephone will not save very much time by moving the components closer together on the desktop. Some other implications of Fitts' Law for rapid tasks are discussed later in this chapter.

The movements studied under the Fitts paradigm are almost certainly blends of programmed actions with feedback added near the end. That is, the performer generates a programmed initial segment of the action

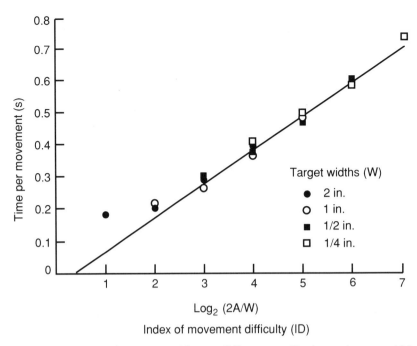

Figure 5.6 These tapping performances with very different amplitudes and target widths follow Fitts' Law. The time per movement is linearly related to the $\log_2 (2A/W)$, or the index of movement difficulty. (Adapted from Fitts, 1954.)

toward the target, processes feedback about the accuracy of this action during the movement, and initiates one (or sometimes more) feedback-based corrections to guide the limb to the target area. As discussed in chapter 2, such visual compensations are probably processed through the ambient visual system and may not be consciously controlled. Thus, Fitts' Law describes the effectiveness of the combined open- and closed-loop processes that operate in these common kinds of actions, where potentially all of the open- and closed-loop processes shown in the conceptual model in Figure 3.9 are operating together.

Finally, it is reasonable to suspect that slower movements are more accurate, at least in part, because there is more time to detect errors and make corrections, as discussed in earlier chapters. Fitts' Law indi-

cates that if the errors are too large, the performer must slow down to reduce them. This suggests that the person can trade off a little speed for a gain in accuracy. Meyer, Abrams, Kornblum, Wright, and Smith (1988) have introduced a nice, formal model of these processes, extending the understanding of Fitts' principles.

In brief, Fitts' Law tells us the following:

- Movement time increases, but only slightly, as the movement amplitude (A) increases.
- Movement time increases as the aiming accuracy requirement increases, that is, as target width (W) decreases.
- Movement time is essentially constant for a given ratio of movement amplitude (A) to target width (W).
- These principles are valid for a wide vari-

ety of different movement environments, types of people, and body parts used.

However, a number of other questions remain unanswered. How, or why, does movement accuracy itself change if the performer is asked to make the movement more quickly? And, for really quick actions, presumably no feedback is involved during the movement, so how can accuracy depend on the number of corrections where there are no corrections? Some of these questions are answered in the next section.

Trading Off Speed for Accuracy

Suppose that you have to make quick action to move your hand or an object, such as a bat, to a target, where spatial accuracy at the target is the major goal. How does your accuracy change as the time for the movement and the distance of the movement vary? Such factors have been studied in aiming movements, where the subject directs a handheld stylus from a starting position to a target, with the movement time and movement distance varying experimentally. The subject is instructed to move with a given movement time, receiving feedback after each movement to help maintain the proper movement time. One set of results from this kind of task is shown in Figure 5.7, where accuracy is expressed as the amount of spread, or inconsistency, of the movement end points about the target area.

Notice that all of these movements are fast, with movement times shorter than 200 ms. From the previous sections, you would expect that such actions are controlled primarily by motor programming processes, with negligible feedback-based corrections along the way. Even with these quick actions, as the movement distance increases, there is a gradual increase in the spread of the movements around the target for each of the differ-

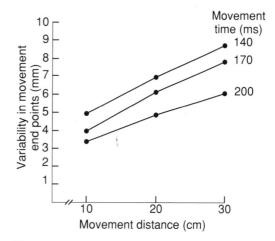

Figure 5.7 Variability of movement end points in a rapid aiming task as a function of the movement time and movement distance. (Adapted by permission from Schmidt, Zelaznik, Hawkins, Frank, & Quinn, 1979.)

ent movement-time conditions. Also, as the movement time is reduced, the inaccuracy of the movement increases. These two effects are more or less independent, as if the effects of increased distance can be added to the effect of reduced movement time to generate aiming errors. This helps explain why the basketball player at the start of this chapter produced an error when she executed a pass too quickly.

These effects of movement distance and movement time suggest that open-loop processes necessary to produce the movement are also subject to the speed-accuracy trade-off. That is, the decreases in accuracy when movement times are short are not simply due to the fact that there is less time for feedback utilization; these effects of movement time occur even in movements too brief to have any feedback modulations at all. Decreases in movement time also seem to have effects on the consistency of the processes that generate the initial parts of the movement, that is, on the open-loop processes necessary to produce quick movements.

This is consistent with the ideas from Fitts' Law. In that situation, if the subject tries to make movements of a given distance too quickly, the result will be too many failures to hit the targets, which is unacceptable in terms of the experimenter's instructions that generally demand errors on no more than about 5 percent of the movements. So, the subject then slows down, decreasing the variability in the movements and hitting the target more often.

These separate effects of movement amplitude and movement time (MT) can be combined into a single expression, more or less as Fitts did in his paradigm. In some of our own research, we found that the amount of movement error, or variability at the target (sometimes termed the **effective target width**), was linearly related to the movement's average velocity, that is, to the ratio of A/MT (Schmidt, Zelaznik, Hawkins, Frank, & Quinn, 1979). For example, in Figure 5.8 the variability in hitting the target (or error) is plotted against the movement's average velocity (in centimeters per second, or cm/s), showing that as the movement velocity increased, the aiming errors increased almost linearly as well. This principle, the linear speed-accuracy trade-off, suggests that for various combinations of movement amplitude and movement time that have a constant ratio (that is, a constant average velocity), the aiming errors are about the same. Thus, increases in velocity and decreases in movement time can be traded off with each other to maintain movement accuracy in these rapid tasks.

Sources of Errors in Quick Movements

Why do even quick movements, where there is little time for feedback processing and corrections, demonstrate more errors as the movement distance increases or the movement time decreases? The answer seems to lie with the processes that translate the motor program's output in the central nervous system into movements of the body part. Earlier sections showed that motor programs are responsible for determining the ordering of muscle contractions and the amounts of force that must be generated in the participating muscles. The "location" of these events are indicated in the conceptual model in Figure 5.9 by the red shading.

■ Aiming variability can have important consequences in many real-world tasks.

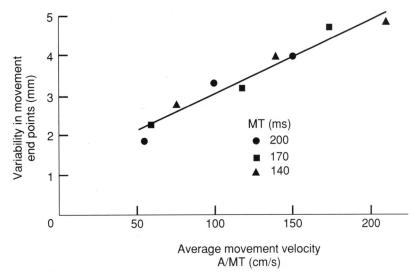

Figure 5.8 Variability of movement end points in an aiming task as a function of the average movement velocity (A/MT). (Reprinted by permission from Schmidt, Zelaznik, Hawkins, Frank, & Quinn, 1979.)

PRACTICAL APPLICATIONS

1. When spatial accuracy is the only goal, the performer should make the movement slower to reduce errors.
2. Spatial errors can be reduced by shortening the movement distance, starting the action closer to the target.
3. Accuracy can be enhanced by making the first part of the action quickly, then slowing the second half of the movement to allow feedback-based corrections near the target.
4. In slower movements, making the movement slower enhances the capability to use feedback, so instruct the performer to pay attention to the movement as it progresses.

How might these sources of error contribute to movement inaccuracy? It has been known for a long time that even if the per-former attempts to produce the same force over and over on successive trials, the actual force produced will be somewhat inconsistent. Today this variability is thought to be caused by the relatively noisy (i.e., inconsistent) processes that convert central nervous system impulses into activation of muscle motor units, ultimately exerting forces on bone through a tendon. Also, there is variability in the contractions generated by various reflex activities, such as the M1 and M2 responses (Figure 5.9).

Of course, the presence of these noisy processes in the system means that the forces actually produced in a contraction are not exactly what were intended by the executive level. This can also be seen in the phonograph record analogy (Figure 5.4), where noise can be introduced in several places by the electronics and wires lying between the information on the record and the eventual activation of the speakers, making the sounds heard slightly different than the sounds originally recorded.

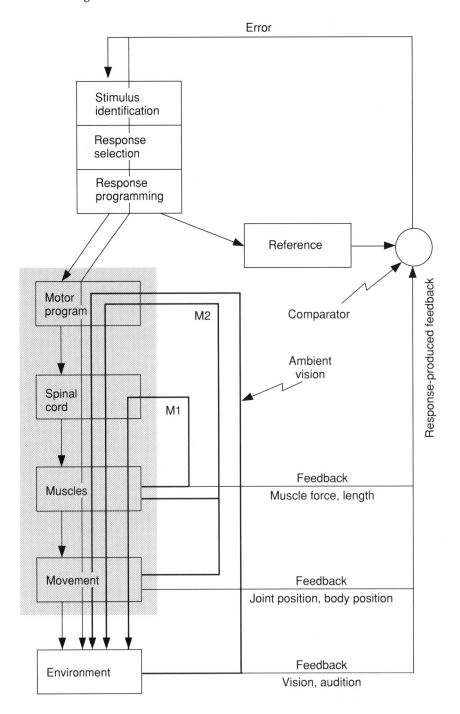

Figure 5.9 The conceptual model of human performance, highlighting the processes associated with variability in rapid movements.

These noisy processes are not constant but seem to change as the required amount of contraction force changes. That is, as the contraction force increases, there is more variability in these forces, as if the noisy processes were becoming larger as well. This can be seen in Figure 5.10, where the variability in these forces, which is interpreted as the size of the noise component, is shown as a function of the size of the contraction, expressed as a percentage of the performer's maximum torque. The noise component generally increases as the amount of force increases, up through about 70% of the subject's maximum. However, when the contractions are very large, approaching maximal values, the amount of torque variability appears to level off again, with perhaps a slight decrease in the force variability in nearly maximal contractions (Sherwood, Schmidt, & Walter, 1988).

shoulders and the trunk to produce forces against the bones, directing the arms and bat toward their goal. The direction of action of some of these muscles happen to be lined up with the intended movement, but most of them are not, aligned at various angles to the action, as shown in Figure 5.11. In most actions gravity acts as one of the contributing forces as well. To complete such an action perfectly, the various muscles must contract with just the right amount of force, in coordination with each other, so that the final combination of force (the resultant force) is in line with the intended movement. Of course, if any of these forces is in error, such as too great a contraction of Muscle 1, the movement's direction will be in error as well, with the movement missing the target.

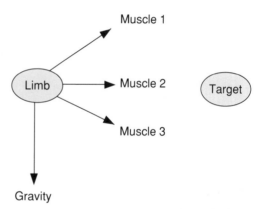

Figure 5.11 A limb being moved by three muscles and gravity toward a target. The eventual trajectory is a product of the many forces acting at a joint.

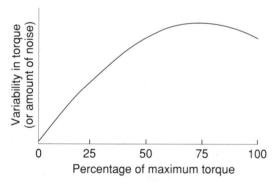

Figure 5.10 An inverted-U relationship between the variability in torque (force) produced and percentage of maximum torque. (A summary of research findings.)

How does this information help in understanding error generation? Consider a movement like hitting a stationary ball with a horizontal swing of the arms and hands, in which a bat is held as in baseball. In such a movement many muscles operate in the

Now, what happens when a given movement is made more rapidly? Of course, as the movement time decreases, the forces exerted against the bones of the arm must increase. When these forces increase (up to about 70% of maximum), Figure 5.10 shows that the noisiness of these forces increases as well. This has the effect of adding a slight error component to the contraction of each of the muscles, causing them to contract slightly differently from how the movement program intended. If these forces are no longer perfectly coordinated with each other, the movement will miss its target to a greater extent. Thus, the movement's inaccuracy increases as movement time decreases, primarily because of the increased noise involved in the stronger muscle contractions.

Here is why increasing the speed of a quick movement interferes with its accuracy:

- The relative contraction forces of the various participating muscles is a major factor in determining the ultimate trajectory of the limb.
- The inconsistency in these forces increases with increased force.
- When movement time decreases, more force is required.
- When amplitude increases, more force is required.
- More force generates more variability, which causes the movement to deviate from the intended trajectory, causing errors.

Two "Violations" of the Speed-Accuracy Trade-Off

As common as the speed-accuracy trade-off phenomenon seems to be for movement behavior, there are several situations where it does not seem to hold, or at least where the principles are somewhat different from those indicated in the previous sections. These situations involve cases where accuracy in timing is the critical feature and where extremely rapid and forceful movements are involved.

Timing Errors. In previous sections the concern has been with situations where spatial accuracy was the major goal, showing how this changes as movement velocity changes. However, many skills have temporal accuracy as a goal, having *when* a move-

ment is done as the most important thing. In such skills a movement must be produced at a particular moment, such as timing an action to block a punch in boxing or pressing the flipper button on a pinball machine to strike the ball.

Still other skills have both temporal and spatial goals, intermixed in complicated ways. Of course, batting a pitched baseball requires accuracy in terms of where to swing to meet the ball (spatial) as well as when to swing (temporal), but batting also demands that the performer be able to time the duration of the swing. Knowing or predicting the action duration allows the batter to determine when to initiate the swing so the bat arrives over the plate at the same time the ball does. So, being able to make a fast movement that consistently occupies a certain amount of time (so that the batter can predict it) is a critical factor in batting effectiveness.

This section is concerned with the temporal component of such skills, discussing the factors that affect this timing accuracy. The temporal component can be isolated somewhat in the rapid task where the performer makes a fast movement, the goal being to produce a particular movement time as accurately as possible. Timing accuracy is studied as a function of changes in the movement distance and the movement time, as well as other variables. It turns out that skills with temporal goals seem to follow somewhat different principles than those having purely spatial goals (Schmidt et al., 1979).

What happens when subjects are asked to produce one of these movements of a given distance, but with the movement-time goal reduced from 300 ms to 150 ms? One might expect that because the velocity of the movement is larger, it would have more error, as was found in Figures 5.7 and 5.8. Not so. Decreasing the movement time has the effect of decreasing the timing error, making the movement more accurate in time, not less. This can be seen in Figure 5.12, in which variability in timed actions increases almost linearly with increases in goal movement time; halving the goal movement time (within limits) tends to almost halve the timing errors. An additional finding is that when the movement distance increases while movement time stays constant, which increases the movement's velocity, timing error hardly increases at all unless the movement is extremely short (Newell, Carlton, Carlton, & Halbert, 1980). Therefore, for skills in which timing error has to be reduced, the main factor is the movement time, which is quite different from skills with spatial goals, as demonstrated in Figures 5.7 and 5.8 (see Schmidt et al., 1979).

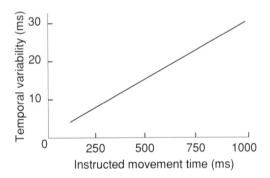

Figure 5.12 Temporal variability as a function of the instructed movement time. As movement time decreases, the movement becomes more temporally stable. (Adapted from Schmidt, Zelaznik, Hawkins, Frank, & Quinn, 1979.)

Here are some principles of movement performance when temporal accuracy is the major goal:

- Increasing speed by decreasing the movement time (with distance constant) decreases, not increases, errors in timing accuracy.
- In most larger movements, increasing speed by increasing the movement distance (with movement time constant) has essentially no effect on timing accuracy.
- In very short movements (a few centimeters long), increasing speed by increasing the movement distance decreases timing errors.
- The primary determinant of timing accuracy is movement time, with longer movement times generating more timing errors.

These findings about timing errors are not as strange as they seem at first, as you will see if you do the following simple demonstration. Take a stopwatch and, without watching, click it twice to try to generate exactly 2 s. Repeat this 9 more times, noting the amount of error you make on each trial. Now do this same task again, but this time try to generate 4 s. After a little careful practice, you should find that the amount of error you make in estimating 2 s will be just about half the amount of error for 4 s. Why? The system that generates these durations (including both the stopwatch and arm movement tasks) are somewhat noisy, or variable, and the amount of this variability increases, or accumulates, as the duration of the event to be timed increases. The motor programming processes that produce the timing are not affected by the increased forces necessary to alter their movement distance, so altered distance does not affect timing error.

Producing a Very Forceful Movement.
Many human movements, especially those in sport, require extremely forceful contractions of muscles, leading to nearly maximal movement speeds, such as in kicking a football or hitting a tennis ball. Making the movement at near-maximal speed is often only a part of the problem because the movement must also have high levels of spatial and/or temporal precision at the same time. It turns out that alterations in movement speed affect

these nearly maximal actions somewhat differently from many of the less forceful actions discussed so far.

Consider a rapid, horizontal, straight arm movement, where a handheld pointer has to be aimed at a target as if it were a ball to be hit. What would happen to the spatial accuracy if the required movement time decreases, so the movements would be closer and closer to the performer's maximal force capabilities? This is similar to your swinging a baseball bat harder and harder, with the limit being your own force capabilities. As you might expect from the speed-accuracy trade-off principles, movements with shorter movement times are less spatially accurate, but only up to a point (about 100 ms), as seen in Figure 5.13 from Schmidt and Sherwood (1982). When the movement time was reduced further, from 100 to 80 ms, which required about 84% of the subject's force capabilities, spatial accuracy began to increase. This produced a kind of inverted-U effect, with very rapid

and very slow movements having the most spatial accuracy and the moderate-speed movements having the least accuracy. This set of data goes against the strict view of the speed-accuracy trade-off, in which faster movements are always less spatially accurate.

How can these movements be so fast yet so spatially accurate at the same time? These movements are very much like those diagrammed in Figure 5.11, where several muscles operate to determine the limb's trajectory. Also, recall that when the forces are very large, approaching maximum, the force variability decreases, as seen in Figure 5.12 by the small downturn near the highest levels of force. Therefore, the nearly maximal movements in Figure 5.13 are operating in a range where the forces are becoming more consistent with increases in force. This low force variability allows these very forceful actions to be very consistent spatially. These are very simple skills, though, and care

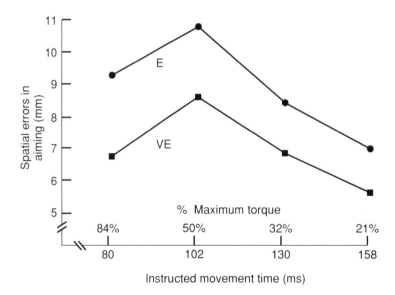

Figure 5.13 Spatial errors in aiming as a function of the instructed movement time. The estimated percentage of maximum torque (force) is indicated above the X-axis. (Adapted by permission from Schmidt & Sherwood, 1982; E = total error; VE = variable error).

should be taken in generalizing the effects to more complicated actions.

In summary, here's what results when a movement requires very high levels of muscular contractions (past 70% or so of the subject's capabilities):

- Increasing speed by reducing movement time can decrease spatial and timing error.
- Adding load to the movement can decrease error, up to a point.
- An inverted-U relationship exists between spatial accuracy and force requirements, with least accuracy at moderate levels of force.

Combining the Principles to Understand Batting

It may seem from the previous section that there are a dizzying number of sometimes contradictory principles involved in these rapid actions. To help in understanding, it will be useful to apply these principles to a common task like batting a pitched baseball. This task requires several of the processes discussed so far, such as anticipation and timing, prediction of the ball's spatial trajectory and arrival time at the coincidence-point, and quick movements that must be both forceful and accurate, so the principles can be applied to various parts of this action. To examine the effects of altering the movement time of the swing of the bat, it will be convenient to hold constant other factors, such as the nature of the pitch and the situation in the game.

Some facts about hitting a baseball are graphically summarized in Figure 5.14. In high-level baseball the pitch requires about 460 ms to travel from the pitcher to the plate (at 89 mph), and the movement time of the swing of the bat is about 160 ms (Hubbard & Seng, 1954). Evidence presented earlier showed that the internal signal to trigger the

---

PRACTICAL APPLICATIONS

1. Instructing the learner to make a baseball swing very slowly to "make contact" can degrade hitting performance and should be avoided.
2. Increasing the weight of the bat, but not so much that the maximal swing slows markedly, can increase spatial accuracy in batting.
3. Have the performer swing the bat almost as quickly as possible, but not so quickly that the movement becomes clumsy and uncoordinated.
4. A batter cannot use visual information in the last one quarter of the ball's flight, so avoid instructions about compensating for last-moment changes in the ball's trajectory.
5. The learner receiving a tennis serve should be encouraged to process information from very early parts of the serve to predict its arrival in space and time.
6. Encourage the learner to use consistent tennis strokes not only in spatial trajectory but also in initiation time and movement time.

---

swing occurs about 170 ms before the movement starts (Slater-Hammel, 1960; review Figure 3.3 in chapter 3 and the associated Highlight Box). With these effects combined, the signal to trigger the action must be given 330 ms before the ball arrives at the plate, that is, 170 ms to prepare the swing and 160 ms to carry it out. Therefore, all decisions about whether or not to swing at the ball must be made well before the ball has traveled halfway to the plate, or after only 130 ms of ball travel. Although there are possible minor modifications in the movement by the

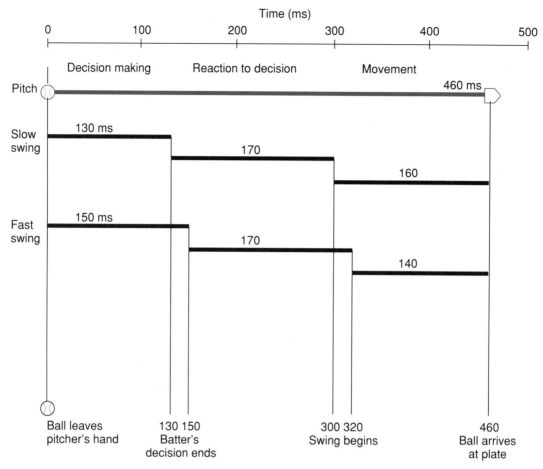

Figure 5.14 Time line showing the critical events in hitting a pitched baseball. The movement time is 160 ms for the slow swing, 140 ms for the fast swing.

visual processes discussed in chapter 3, the majority of the action must be planned in advance and initiated by the central nervous system some 330 ms before the ball arrives.

What happens if the batter decides to speed up the swing, say from 160 ms to 140 ms? Movement time could be made shorter through instructions to make the actual movement faster, to shorten the movement distance by reducing the backswing (a very slight effect), to use a lighter bat, or to change the stance or style of the movement in vari-

ous ways. Several separate factors, which were discussed in the previous few sections, are altered with these changes.

Visual Information Processing. Figure 5.14 shows that shortening the movement time shifts the beginning of the swing, hence the point at which the details of the action have to be specified, to a position later in the ball's flight. This provides additional time for viewing the ball's trajectory, for determining time to contact, and should allow more accurate anticipation of where and when the ball will arrive. And this extra information comes at a point that is maximally useful—when the ball is closest to the batter—making these extra 20 ms (from 150 to 130 ms, or about 3 ft of ball travel) of viewing time particularly beneficial. Therefore, shortening the movement time provides more effective anticipation of the ball's travel characteristics.

Swing Initiation Timing Accuracy. Also, if the swing of the bat is speeded up, the decision about when to initiate the movement is made later and is more temporally accurate. In an experiment on a simulated batting task, shortening the movement time stabilized the initiation time of the movement, as if the batter was more certain of when to start the swing (Schmidt, 1969). Starting the swing at a more stable time therefore translates into a more stable time for the movement end point at the plate, which yields greater movement timing accuracy.

Movement Timing Accuracy. One thing the batter must do in planning the swing is to estimate the duration of his or her own movement. Therefore, the batter selects a movement time, then initiates this action at such a time that the end of the movement coincides with the arrival of the ball at the plate. If the actual movement time is different from predicted, the end of the movement will be too early or late, causing timing errors in hitting the ball. Because reduced movement time increases movement timing consistency (Figure 5.12), the movement's actual duration will be closer to the batter's estimate. This results in greater accuracy in hitting the ball, particularly in terms of the timing aspects (see also Schmidt, 1969).

Movement Spatial Accuracy. Making the movement faster also influences spatial accuracy, as discussed earlier. If the movement is relatively slow, instructions to decrease the movement time have a detrimental effect on accuracy in hitting the ball. However, most batswing movements are already quite fast, near the performer's limits in producing force. Recall that when movements are very fast and forceful, reducing the movement time tends to increase—not decrease—accuracy (Figure 5.13), because the force variability decreases in this range with decreases in movement time (Figure 5.10). Therefore, speeding the movement time when it is already quite fast results in a gain in spatial movement accuracy, giving more frequent ball contact.

Ball Impact. Finally, of course, a faster swing gives more impact to the ball, a critical factor in the particular game of baseball. Increasing the load by having a heavier bat improves spatial accuracy (Schmidt & Sherwood, 1982) and can have only minimal slowing effects on movement speed. Clearly, both added bat mass and a faster movement time contribute to greater impact with the ball.

Summary   Break

Nearly every factor associated with decreased movement times discussed here would be expected to influence the chances of hitting the ball. Perhaps understanding these factors makes it more clear why professional batters seem to swing nearly maximally. Of course, speeding up the swing can certainly be overdone, however, resulting in clumsy, uncoordinated swings that are not very effective in general, especially with children, where the patterns are not well developed.

To summarize, swinging the bat with a faster movement time increases all of the following factors:

- Viewing time of the ball's flight, enhancing predictability
- Stability of the movement's initiation time

- Consistency of the movement time
- Resulting coincident-timing accuracy
- Spatial accuracy of the most forceful movements
- Impact with the ball

PRACTICAL APPLICATIONS

1. In tasks in which an object is to be struck with a bat or racquet, have the learner make a preprogrammed, rapid, ballistic action for the final element that contacts the object.
2. Avoid having the learner "guide" the bat or racquet to the ball using slow, feedback-based movements.
3. Emphasize that the learner should try to make the backswing position and stance as consistent as possible from attempt to attempt.
4. Have the learner make consistent swings, so that movement time, movement distance, and movement speed are as stereotyped as possible.
5. If the movement end point is too early or late, adjust the initiation time of the swing, not the movement time or backswing position.
6. Instruct the learner to make the movement nearly as rapidly as possible, but not so rapidly that control and coordination are degraded.

 CHAPTER SUMMARY

An important idea in motor control is an invariance, a movement pattern feature that remains essentially fixed while many other features are changing. One such invariance is relative timing, a set of ratios among temporal intervals in the action, which indicates the temporal structure of a movement assumed to form the basis of generalized motor programs. Classes of movements are movements that share a given relative-timing structure, such as overarm throwing or kicking.

The accuracy of rapid movements controlled by these programs is influenced by speed and amplitude variations, and these actions display a speed-accuracy trade-off. Increases in speed or decreases in movement time usually degrade spatial accuracy unless the movements are very rapid. On the other hand, decreasing the movement time usually enhances timing accuracy. These effects are caused by relatively noisy low-level processes in the spinal cord and the muscles that make the contractions differ slightly from those originally intended. These effects, combined with feedback-based processes, can be used in the conceptual model of human performance to understand the many features of speed-accuracy trade-offs in human skills.

Checking Your Understanding

1. Explain how a low-level timing error could account for missing the target in dart-throwing.
2. What is relative timing? How can you use measures of relative timing to classify actions?
3. In the Fitts' tapping task, what would happen to the movement time if the movement amplitude doubles while the target width increases by a factor of four?
4. Under what conditions are movements more spatially accurate as the movement time decreases? Explain why.
5. What is the linear speed-accuracy trade-off? How does this principle re-

late to the speed-accuracy trade-off described by Fitts' Law?

◇ Key Terms

Definitions of the following terms appear on the page(s) shown in parentheses:

amplitude (p. 110)

deep structure (p. 103)

effective target width (p. 114)

Fitts' Law (p. 110)*

invariance (p. 103)

movement time (MT) (p. 110)

relative timing (p. 103)

speed-accuracy trade-off (p. 110)

surface features (p. 103)

target width (p. 110)

◇ Suggestions for Further Reading

More evidence for invariances in motor control can be found in Schmidt (1985), and this work is reviewed somewhat more thoroughly in Schmidt (1988b, chapter 8; Young & Schmidt, 1990a). A more advanced discussion of the principles of motor control can be found in Keele (1981, 1986) and Schmidt (1988b, chapter 9). Further details on sources of error in motor control for aiming movements have been reviewed by Meyer, Abrams, Kornblum, Wright, and Smith (1988), who provide an elegant theory of these processes that applies to many different kinds of limb movement situations. And Meyer, Smith, Kornblum, Abrams, and Wright (1990) have written an interesting and readable review of the history of thought about speed-accuracy trade-off effects.

6 Individual Differences and Motor Abilities

PREVIEW

You are amazed when your friend, without any previous golf experience, suddenly takes up the game and nearly beats you. His proficiency is about what yours is after years of serious practice. He continues to improve while you seem stuck at your level. He is clearly different from you in terms of the capability to golf, and he will eventually be much better. Why? What are the underlying differences between the two of you? Will he necessarily be better in other activities as well?

Everyone knows that people are different in countless ways. This chapter focuses on these differences among people, that is, individual differences, in terms of motor behavior. First is introduced the notion of abilities, largely inherited capabilities that underlie the many skills people perform, and a description of their number and nature, how to evaluate them, and how they can help in classifying skills. Finally, the focus shifts to prediction, or how individuals can be selected for certain activities, jobs, or sports on the basis of their underlying abilities.

STUDENT GOALS
1. To understand the notion of individual differences
2. To become familiar with the fundamental nature of motor abilities
3. To use the concept of abilities to classify skills
4. To understand the methods and problems in predicting skills

---

When I was a boy, Charlie Breck used to infuriate me. Charlie could throw a ball faster and farther than anyone around, he could catch and bat well in softball, he was an amazing dribbler and shooter in basketball, and he was a standout runner in football. Charlie clearly had something the rest of us did not, and he used it well to become a fine athlete in high school.

However, I used to take great pleasure in the fact that I was a much better gymnast than Charlie. He was hopeless when it came to doing a kip on the horizontal bar, and I could tumble circles around him. Other kids our age were far better than either of us at still other things, such as riflery, cross-country running, or swimming. Each of us seemed to have inborn capabilities to do certain kinds of skills but little ability to do others.

How can it be that Charlie was far better than I in many things, yet I was far better in others? Are capabilities simply due to practice? What is the nature of these differences among people, where do they originate, and how can they be measured and evaluated? How can the commonsense idea that everyone is different in various ways fit into the concepts of movement behavior developed so far in the text? How can understanding these differences help in making intelligent applications to teaching and coaching?

These questions form the basis of the area in psychology and motor behavior known as individual differences, the science of people's differences in various behavioral capabilities. To this point in the text, the focus has been mainly on the processes and principles operating in people in general, almost as if everyone were the same and followed these principles in the same ways. Contrary to this **experimental approach**, where the focus is on the principles common to all people, the **differential approach** examined in this chapter focuses on the factors that make individuals different from each other. This chapter changes orientation to begin to understand some of these differences—interesting differences that underlie the capabilities for high-level performances in such varied activities as figure skating, lawn bowling, and weight lifting.

STUDY OF INDIVIDUAL DIFFERENCES

Individual differences are defined as stable, enduring differences among people in terms of performance of some task. Two people can differ on some performance test in at least two different ways. First, if the test involves speed in a mile run, for example, one person might be faster than the other on every trial, so you would conclude that the one person is really faster than the other. Second, however, if one person makes a golf putt on one attempt and the other does not, you would probably not be so willing to conclude there is an underlying difference in their putting capabilities. Why not? Because almost anything can happen on a particular trial by chance, and individual differences must be based on stable, enduring performance differences. In the first case, you are confident of stable, enduring differences in the measured behavior, whereas in the second case you are not. Therefore, it should be clear that you can find differences in performance between two people that are not necessarily indicative of individual differences, especially if the performances are somewhat unstable.

Individual differences are present in all skills but are easiest to detect in tasks where the outcome is not highly variable.

To summarize, individual differences in skills have these characteristics:

- Stability from attempt to attempt
- Enduring across time
- Not necessarily indicated by skill differences on a single trial

Studying these stable individual differences involves essentially two related aspects. First, there is the concern for the underlying capabilities, termed abilities here, that determine people's differences in terms of skilled performance, how these abilities can be de-

scribed, and how they are measured and understood theoretically. Second, there is concern for **prediction**, where the abilities are measured and used to estimate (or predict) a person's future skill level at a particular sport or occupation. Being able to predict who will (or will not) be successful in some activity allows the effective guidance of people into certain occupations or sports, and away from others in which they would not be successful.

Therefore, this chapter's treatment of individual differences will focus on these two major components:

1. Abilities, the qualities or traits that underlie skilled performance, and how these abilities explain skill differences among people
2. Prediction, the process of using people's abilities to estimate their probable success in various occupations or sports

ABILITIES AND CAPABILITIES

Scientists who study individual differences in performance generally use the notion of an **ability**, defined as an inherited, relatively enduring, stable trait of the individual that underlies or supports various kinds of motor and cognitive activities, or skills. Abilities are thought of as being largely genetically defined and essentially unmodified by practice or experience.

There can be many such abilities, ranging from visual acuity and color vision, body configuration (height and build), numerical ability, reaction speed, manual dexterity, kinesthetic sensitivity, and so on. Of course, these abilities are spread throughout the motor system. You can see this vividly by turning to the conceptual model of human performance in Figure 6.1, where individual differences in various processes are now highlighted. Some of these involve the many

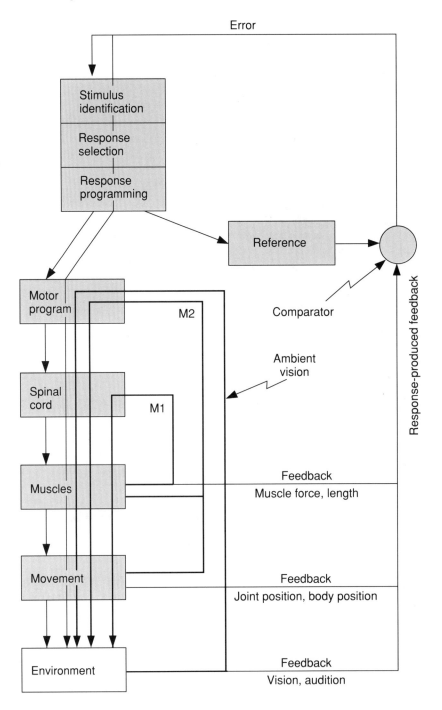

Figure 6.1 The conceptual model of human performance, highlighting several places where individual differences are likely to occur.

aspects of perception and decision making; others involve organizing and planning the action; and others concern the actual production of the movement and the evaluation of feedback that it produces.

Approximately 20 to 30 cognitive and motor abilities have been identified so far, and perhaps a total of 50 will eventually be discovered. All individuals have all of the abilities, but the abilities are stronger in some individuals than in others. That is, I have very poor abilities in hearing but very good long-distance visual ability and average kinesthetic sensitivity. You might have a different pattern of strengths and weaknesses defined by your particular genetic makeup, and these would have implications for the skills in which you would be successful.

The motor and cognitive abilities identified in the research are widely varied and considerably different from each other. The following abridged list is provided to give you an idea about what abilities are being considered (Fleishman, 1957):

- Multilimb coordination
- Spatial orientation
- Finger dexterity
- Arm-hand steadiness
- Visual acuity
- Reaction time
- Movement speed
- Manual dexterity
- Mechanical aptitude
- Kinesthetic sensitivity

Particular tasks use, or rely on, a specific subset of abilities for performance. For example, threading a needle requires near-visual acuity and arm-hand steadiness and does not require strength. Power lifting, on the other hand, requires essentially no near-visual acuity or arm-hand steadiness, but it does require great strength. Think of skill levels in people's many different tasks as based on combinations of a relatively small number

(perhaps 50) of underlying abilities. According to this view, people who are particularly good at a task like javelin throwing happen to have high proficiency in the abilities related to this task. Of course, this does not ensure that this person will have an effective pattern of abilities for some other task, such as fencing, which requires fundamentally different underlying capabilities.

Ability Versus Skill

It is useful to distinguish between the concepts of ability and skill. In common language these words are used more or less interchangeably, as in "You have good ability in [or skill at] something." Notice, however, that scientists generally define abilities as being genetically determined and largely unmodified by practice or experience. Abilities, therefore, can be thought of as the basic "equipment" people are born with to perform various real-world tasks.

Skill, on the other hand, here describes one's proficiency at a particular task, such as shooting a basketball. Skills are easily modified by practice, are countless in number, and represent the particular capability to perform a particular activity. Thus, you could say that Jim has good visual abilities, implying that he can generally see very well, but Jim has developed the specific skill of identifying patterns of movement in football through considerable practice, and this skill has Jim's visual abilities underlying it. Differences between abilities and skills are summarized in Table 6.1.

Abilities as Limiting Factors for Performance

It is helpful to think of abilities as factors that put limits on performance. I will never become a lineman in professional football, regardless of how much time I devote to

Table 6.1 Some Important Distinctions Between Abilities and Skills

Abilities	Skills
Inherited traits	Developed with practice
Stable and enduring	Modified with practice
Perhaps 50 in number	Countless in number
Underlie many different skills	Depend on several abilities

practice, because I do not have the proper body-configuration abilities for this skill. People who are "color-blind" will never be effective in identifying wildflowers, and someone without good balance abilities should probably not be encouraged to join the circus as a tightrope walker. Thus, limitations in the requisite abilities for a particular task limit the level of performance that a particular individual can eventually attain.

On the other hand, even if a novice does not perform very well, leading to the suspicion that he or she does not have the proper abilities for this task, much of this deficit can be made up through effective practice. It would be a mistake to make a firm judgment about someone's abilities for a task when that person has only reached the novice stage. Several factors can change through practice to improve performance (see the section "Patterns of Abilities Change With Practice and Experience," later in this chapter).

How Are Motor and Cognitive Abilities Organized?

Given the idea that there are relatively few abilities that underlie nearly countless separate movement skills, what are these abilities? How can they be described and

PRACTICAL APPLICATIONS

1. Recognizing and appreciating differences among people can be useful in encouraging someone toward or away from certain sports and activities.
2. Do not be too quick to judge individual differences based on observing only a few attempts at a skill, particularly if the performer is a novice.
3. Stable individual differences are very difficult to detect in tasks with high variability (or chance), so employ many trials.
4. Encourage practice to compensate for deficiencies in abilities, but be realistic because the highest performance levels in sport require very strong abilities in the appropriate areas.

measured? To some extent, the answers depend on the particular approach used to study abilities, and some debate exists about the validity of such answers. Some views of motor abilities, and the evidence for and against them, are described in the next few sections.

Is There a General Motor Ability?

One of the earliest views about the structure of human abilities held that skills are accounted for by a single, general factor. In the field of cognitive or intellectual functioning, this general factor is known as intelligence, presumably measured by the *intelligence quotient* (IQ). In the movement field a parallel idea has been termed **general motor ability**.

Abilities to Perform. Early attempts to provide tests that would measure general motor ability were made by Brace (1927: the Brace Test) and McCloy (1934: the General Motor Capacity Test). These tests consisted of whole-body actions that would presumably measure the general capability to perform athletic tasks. In all these tests, a single factor (or ability) was assumed to account for all of a person's skills, so a person with a strong general factor would likely succeed in essentially every task attempted. This is analogous to the old idea that people with high general intelligence can succeed in nearly any cognitive or scholastic task. Further, cognitive ability (intelligence) and motor ability (general motor ability) were thought to be relatively separate, with intelligence not contributing very much to movement skills, and vice versa. Scientists now believe that most of these ideas are wrong, as discussed in the next few sections.

However, this concept of general motor ability appears reasonable at first glance. It agrees with a common observation that a certain few individuals—like Charlie Breck, mentioned earlier—seem successful at most of the popular sports tasks, as if they have an underlying capability to do anything athletic. On the other hand, some people are not successful at any of these activities, leading to the conclusion that these people have a weak general motor ability. Therefore, it might appear reasonable that sport tasks must be based on some common general athletic ability. In this view, the all-around athlete is one who has a very strong general athletic ability, or general motor ability.

This general motor ability notion can be summarized as follows:

- A single, inherited motor ability is assumed.
- This ability presumably underlies all movement or sports tasks.
- A person with strong general motor ability should be effective at nearly any motor task attempted.

As reasonable as it might sound, the concept of a general motor ability is not supported by the scientific evidence and has been dropped as a useful concept.

Abilities to Learn. A concept very similar to general motor ability is that of a generalized capability to learn new skills, which was called motor educability by Brace (1927). Analogous to IQ, the cognitive capability to learn, motor educability was thought to represent some general ability to learn new skills. As with the notion of a general motor ability, though, this notion was not well supported in the literature.

Several lines of evidence fail to support the views of general motor ability (and of general intelligence) and motor educability. The general motor ability view argues that any two motor tasks must have this single motor ability in common because it is supposed to underlie all tasks. Certainly, any two tasks that supposedly measure a subset of motor responding, such as balance, quickness, or speed, should have these underlying abilities in common. Therefore, this viewpoint expects that the correlations computed between any two such tests should be high, either positively or negatively (see the Highlight Box for more details).

Scientists examined both field and laboratory data to determine if high correlations among skills could be found, as the general motor ability view would expect. There are many data sets in the literature, but one by Drowatzky and Zuccato (1967) makes the point particularly well. The authors examined six tests of balance typically found in the physical education literature. A large group of subjects was given all six tests, and the correlations between each pair of tests were computed (15 pairs in all). These values are shown in the correlation matrix in Table 6.2, showing the correlation of any test with any other. The highest correlation in the matrix was between the bass stand and the sideward stand ($r = .31$). All of the other correlations were lower than this, ranging from .03

HIGHLIGHT

Correlation: The Language of Individual Differences

An important concept for understanding abilities is **correlation**, a statistic for measuring the strength of a relationship between two or more tests. Basically, a correlation coefficient (r) is computed from a large group (say, 100 persons), where each person has been measured on at least two different tests. The goals are to determine whether the two tests are related to each other and whether they share any underlying features.

In Figures 6.2a and b are special graphs called scatterplots, with Test A on one axis and Test B on the other. Each subject's score is represented as a single dot on each of the two tests. If the dots tend to lie along a line, then we say that Test A and Test B are related to each other in that scores on one test are associated with scores on the other. In the case at the left, this relationship is positive: Those individuals with high scores on Test A tend to be the same individuals with high scores on Test B. The case on the right shows a negative relationship: Higher scores on A are associated with lower scores on B. The direction of the relationship is given by the sign of the correlation coefficient.

The correlation can range in size from -1.0 to $+1.0$. The size of the correlation indicates the strength of the relationship, or how close the individual dots are to the best-fitting line passing through them. If the dots are close to the line, as in the left figure, the correlation is close to $+1.0$, indicating a very strong tendency for

changes in A to be associated with changes in B ($r = +.90$). If the dots lie relatively far from the line, as in the right figure, the correlation is closer to zero, indicating a relatively weak tendency for changes in A to be associated with changes in B ($r = -.20$). The strength of a relationship is given by the squared correlation coefficient. Thus, the correlation of $-.20$ means that the two tests have $-.20^2 = .04 \times 100$, or 4%, in common with each other. Note that the size of the correlation has nothing to do with its sign, because a strong correlation can be either positive or negative. Finally, a correlation of .00 indicates that the line of best fit is a horizontal line, with a slope of 0, with the dots scattered about it in a random way, more or less in a circular pattern. In such a case, Tests A and B would not be related at all.

Correlations are used in examining abilities. If two tests are related to each other, they have some underlying feature(s) in common. In the study of skills, these common features are assumed to be the abilities that underlie the two tests in question. If the correlation between two tests is large in value (e.g., $\pm .80$), it is concluded that there is at least one ability that underlies them both. On the other hand, if the correlation is near zero, it is concluded that there are no abilities underlying both tests; in other words, the abilities underlying one test are separate from those underlying the other.

to .26. Even the highest correlation of .31 means that there was only $.31^2 \times 100 = 9.6\%$ in common between these two tests, with

over 90% of the abilities underlying the two tests being different. Therefore, it is difficult to argue that there was some single, underly-

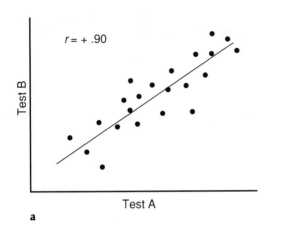

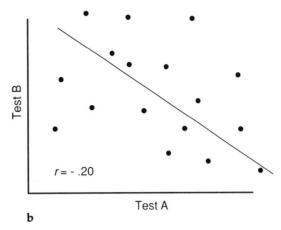

Figure 6.2 Scatterplots showing hypothetical relationships between two tests, Test A and Test B. The relationship is strong and positive at the left, weak and negative at the right.

Table 6.2 Correlations Among Six Tests of Static and Dynamic Balance

	Stork stand	Diver's stand	Stick stand	Sideward stand	Bass stand	Balance stand
Stork stand	—	.14	−.12	.26	.20	.03
Diver's stand		—	−.12	−.03	−.07	−.14
Stick stand			—	−.04	.22	−.19
Sideward stand				—	.31	.19
Bass stand					—	.18
Balance stand						—

Note. Adapted by permission from Drowatzky & Zuccato, 1967.

ing general motor ability that accounted for individual differences in all of these tests. These data do not support the predictions of a general motor ability hypothesis.

The argument for general motor ability is even weaker considering that in this study these are all tests of balancing, spanning a relatively narrow range of human motor capability. Even here, there seemed to be no general ability to balance, with each test measuring some separate ability to control posture. Similar findings have been found with collections of tasks that measure movement speed in a study by Lotter (1960), where the highest correlation between any two tasks was .36. In a study of 50 tests in the Armed Services Testing Program (Fleishman & Parker, 1962), the correlations were generally less than .50 (i.e., $.50^2$, or 25%, in common) unless the tests were practically identical to each other. Taken together, the published literature offers no support for the commonly held belief that movement capabilities are organized with a single, general motor ability. This evidence does not argue against the idea of abilities per se, but it does argue against the idea that there is a single such ability.

This large body of literature on correlations among skills is remarkably consistent in supporting the following conclusions:

- Correlations among different skills are generally very low.
- Even skills that appear quite similar usually correlate poorly.
- This overall lack of correlation among skills argues against the concept of a general motor ability.
- On the other hand, two skills with only minor differences (e.g., throwing 10 m and throwing 15 m) can correlate strongly.

Henry's Specificity Hypothesis

To Franklin Henry (1958/1968; 1961) this evidence suggested that the general motor ability view was simply wrong. In its place, he proposed the **specificity hypothesis**, which argued that movement behaviors are based on a very large number of abilities, perhaps thousands. These abilities were supposed to be independent of each other, so if an individual had a strong ability of one kind, this did not imply that any other ability would necessarily be weak or strong. Also, any given task, such as throwing a baseball, would be based on hundreds of such abilities, some of them strong, some of them weak.

A champion tennis player would be a person who had inherited strengths in the particular abilities relevant for tennis. If she attempts springboard diving, for example, the particular abilities underlying this new task would be different; there is no guarantee her abilities in this area would also be strong. Therefore, she would not necessarily excel in diving, and in fact the best guess is she would be about average, with no special advantage just because she had strong abilities related

---

PRACTICAL APPLICATIONS

1. Just because a student has a low skill level in one task, do not assume that he or she will have a low skill level in another task, even if the two tasks appear similar.
2. Changing the task somewhat can shift the pattern of abilities required, so don't expect an individual to be successful in both situations.
3. Because changing the task slightly shifts the abilities and processes required for success, be careful in designing teaching drills to ensure effective carryover to the goal skill.
4. Fundamental abilities, or lack of them, are difficult to detect and can be masked by a performer's level of experience with the task.
5. If two tasks are different in only very minor ways, then an individual successful in one should also be successful in the other.

---

to tennis. In this way, Henry's hypothesis accounts well for the fact that the correlation is generally low even between very similar tasks.

In summary, the specificity view assumes these points:

- Very many abilities (perhaps thousands) exist.
- These abilities are not related to each other; they are specific.
- A given skill is supported by many of these abilities.
- Different skills have different patterns of abilities with different patterns of strength and weakness.

Henry based most of his thinking on numerous studies that examined correlations among skills similar to the patterns seen in Table 6.2. In seeking additional evidence about specificity, though, he once studied four different populations representing different sport groupings: basketball players, gymnasts, rifle shooters, and people who had never performed on any athletic team. He compared these groups on four novel laboratory skills. If a general motor ability view were correct, then the athletes, who presumably possess strong abilities, should outperform the nonathlete group on the laboratory skills. He found that all of the groups performed essentially similarly, which supported his specificity view and provided even more evidence against the notion of general motor ability.

Modern Perspectives on Abilities

Henry's specificity hypothesis predicts that there should be no correlation between skills. However, most of the evidence available shows that correlations between skills in fact are not zero but rather seem to be very low yet systematically greater than zero. This suggests that some compromise between a general motor ability view and a specificity view should be most effective in accounting for the evidence.

One such viewpoint was provided by Edwin Fleishman and his colleagues in many studies of young American servicemen during the 1950s and 1960s (Fleishman, 1964, 1965; Fleishman & Bartlett, 1969). Fleishman used a statistical technique called factor analysis to organize a large group of tests (e.g., 100) into a smaller group of underlying abilities. These procedures provided a way to discover what the underlying abilities might be, how many there were, and how to measure them. These abilities, like those in Henry's view, are thought to be independent of each other, so your having a particular one that is strong is no guarantee that another of your abilities will be strong also. The major differences between Fleishman's and Henry's views are in the total number of such abilities and how many are involved in a particular task. The list of abilities discovered so far is not complete because it has been based primarily on younger, male subjects manipulating various objects with their hands and arms while seated. No sports performances have been included, such as ones using whole-body activities, so it is difficult to know how the final list of abilities might look. Even so, I suspect the abilities will number between 20 and 50.

Fundamental inherited movement capabilities, your equipment to structure movement skills, can be considered to be based on a relatively small number of underlying abilities. Some of these abilities, together with descriptions of how they are measured and the kinds of skills to which they might contribute, are now indicated:

- *Reaction time.* Important in tasks where there is a single stimulus and a single response, where speed of reaction is critical, as in simple reaction time. An example is a sprint start in a 100-meter dash.
- *Response orientation.* Involves quick choices among numerous alternative movements, more or less as in choice reaction time. An example is batting in baseball, where the nature of the pitch is uncertain.
- *Speed of movement.* Underlies tasks in which the arm(s) must move quickly, but without a reaction-time stimulus, to minimize movement time. An example is swinging a cricket bat.
- *Finger dexterity.* Involves tasks for which small objects are manipulated. An example is threading a needle.
- *Manual dexterity.* Underlies tasks in which relatively large objects are manipulated with the hands and arms. An example is dribbling a basketball.
- *Response integration.* Involved in tasks

where many sources of sensory information must be integrated to make an effective response. An example is playing quarterback in football.

- *Physical proficiency abilities.* Fleishman (1964) also identified several abilities that do not have so much to do with manipulative skills but rather involve what he has termed "physical proficiency." Here nine additional abilities, such as dynamic strength, explosive strength, gross body coordination, and stamina (cardiovascular endurance), have been identified. These are best thought of as being related to what is usually considered "physical fitness."

Myths About Motor Abilities

These ideas about abilities have serious consequences for some of the most common beliefs held by coaches, sportscasters, and the public in general about the structure of movement capabilities. Consider the often-heard type of statement "Sam has good hands." What does that mean? For many people it usually means that, given the many different sport activities in which Sam might participate, his use of his hands is generally effective. However, examine the list of abilities in the last paragraph. Except for physical proficiency, each ability involves the hands in some way, whether to move small or large objects, to press buttons in reaction time, to move quickly to press a button, or to follow a moving target with a handheld apparatus. Yet, each ability is independent of the others. Therefore, there is no general ability to have "good hands"; rather, the abilities needed for a particular task depend on what the hands are asked to do.

Here's another example. We often hear something like "Samantha has great quickness," where the speaker means that Samantha generally responds and moves quickly whenever speedy actions are required. Yet, there are at least three separate abilities to act quickly: (a) reaction time (simple reaction time), where a single stimulus leads to a single response; (b) response orientation (choice reaction time), where one of many stimuli is presented, each of which would require its own response; and (c) speed of movement (movement time), measuring the time of a movement produced without an initiating stimulus (not considering reaction time). Subjectively, each of these abilities involves "quickness." However, these abilities are separate and independent, indicating that there are at least three ways to have the ability to be quick. Therefore, being quick depends on the particular circumstances under which speedy responses are required.

Indeed, just because two tasks appear at first glance to have many general underlying features in common, such tasks might use very different patterns of underlying abilities. As shown later in this chapter, this notion has important implications concerning the prediction of performance in a skill from knowledge about a person's underlying abilities.

All-Around Athletes

Students of motor behavior usually find it difficult to reconcile research conclusions about the lack of a general motor ability with everyday observations that suggest something like general athletic ability. After all, there are many athletes who perform effectively in several sports and it is tempting to conclude that this is because of high general motor ability.

However, there are several factors that can operate to give the appearance of a general motor ability, even though no such ability actually exists. First, some parents are particularly supportive of athletic activities, whereas other parents are not, leading to large differences in the exposure to sports that children receive. Of course, experience and practice at these tasks generate skill, leading the children to join clubs and teams where they receive more practice, and so on. It is easy to see how other children, without this kind of emphasis, could be left out; because they are not skilled, it gives the impression that they have poor ability.

Body configuration is also a factor in many athletic activities. Bigger, stronger children who mature earlier have an advantage at most athletic skills. Again, this leads to more exposure to all these skills and the impression of a general motor ability. Finally, it is risky to make conclusions about the nature of underlying ability by noting only a few of the most visible and highly skilled performers in the world. These people are unusually gifted in most of the specific abilities needed for their sports, and it does not validate a concept of general abilities for everyone else.

In summary, the myth of the all-around athlete is created by several factors:

- Differential parental support for sports and physical activity gives different levels of experience.
- General body-size factors tend to favor larger, stronger, early-maturing children in many sports.
- General personality traits (competitiveness) might contribute to several physical activities.

General Motor Ability Reconsidered: Superability

There may be some way in which a general motor ability does make sense after all. There may be a weak, general factor underlying most movement skills, giving a slight advantage to those individuals with a strong ability. This is sometimes called a **superability**, to distinguish it from the earlier notion of general motor ability. In any case, such an ability must not be very strong, given that the correlations between skills are so generally low. Perhaps abilities for skills are similar to the abilities for intellectual activities: A weak, general intellectual ability is thought to underlie all cognitive functioning, but several specific abilities are far more important (e.g., numerical abilities and verbal abilities).

Be careful, though, because this in no way makes correct the earlier notion that *all* movement capabilities are based on a single ability. There is simply too much evidence against this view, and it has no place in our modern thinking about human motor abilities.

Abilities in the Production of Skills

This section on abilities can be summarized with a diagram of how the important concepts of superability, abilities, and skills are related. Figure 6.3 shows some of the abilities and skills discussed so far (space does not permit complete depiction). Residing at the top of this structure is a superability, which contributes to all the separate motor abilities. Next are the 20 to 50 motor abilities, which provide the specific capabilities to perform.

There are several important features to notice here. A given skill, say that of the race-car driver, is contributed to by a small number of the underlying abilities. Speed of movement, manual dexterity, and reaction time are represented in this skill, whereas other abilities (e.g., response orientation) might not be. This goes along with the view that particular skills are combinations of several underlying capabilities. Also, different skills can use overlapping subsets of abilities. A successful quarterback's pattern of abilities is different from that of the race-car driver; some of the same abilities are used in both

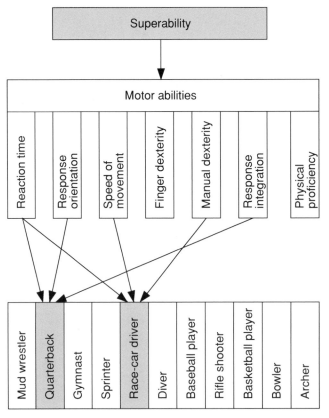

Figure 6.3 Links between a superability, various motor abilities, and selected movement skills. Every task is made up of several abilities, and a given ability can contribute to several tasks.

skills (e.g., reaction time), whereas other abilities are not shared between the two (e.g., finger dexterity). This is necessarily so because there are countless individual skills and only a relatively few abilities that can support them.

Perhaps a workbench analogy will help. Think of abilities as tools of various kinds lying on a workbench. There are many such tools (say, 50), each designed to do a particular kind of job, such as cut a board or drive a nail. Any particular skill or task (such as building a birdhouse) requires a certain set of these tools, and another task (repairing the sink) requires a different set. Some tools are used by both jobs, but the specific combination of tools is different. There are an infi-

nite number of jobs, all of which are handled by different combinations of this limited number of tools. Abilities are the tools you inherited to perform skills.

To summarize the involvement of abilities in the production of skills, the following conclusions can be stated:

- Any given skill is contributed to by several of the fundamental motor abilities.
- Some of the abilities underlying a skill play very dominant roles, whereas others have very weak roles.
- Two different skills have different patterns of underlying abilities.
- Two different skills can have a few abilities in common.

PRACTICAL APPLICATIONS

1. Simply because a student is skilled (or unskilled) in one activity, do not expect him or her to be skilled (or unskilled) in some different activity also.
2. Even within a broad category of skills (e.g., balancing), do not expect performance on one skill to indicate ability to perform well on a different skill.
3. Avoid grouping students for instruction on the basis of performance on published tests of general motor (or athletic) ability. Such an ability does not exist, so the tests are a poor basis for classification.
4. To increase teaching effectiveness, group students for instruction in an activity on the basis of their experience, or skill, in that activity.
5. Parents can contribute to a child's overall athletic capabilities by providing a broad range of sport experiences in early life. They and teachers should encourage many skills to discover the child's strengths.
6. Parents and teachers should be attentive to which skills the child learns particularly easily, which gives evidence of the child's pattern of underlying abilities.

SKILL CLASSIFICATION AND TASK ANALYSIS

Skills were classified in chapter 1 in terms of open versus closed skills, serial-continuous-discrete skills, and so on. The study of individual differences and abilities allows additional skill classifications that are more precise and allow useful practical applications. In addition, these methods allow **task analysis**, in which a task can be divided into its several components, to greatly aid the instructor in organizing the skill for practice.

Classifications are essential for several reasons. First, as emphasized before, the principles of performance and learning are somewhat different for different classes of activities. Therefore, to apply those principles to develop effective methods in teaching, you must be certain that the principles actually apply to the particular class of activities in question. Second, knowing that a task has a strong cognitive component or has a particular emphasis on kinesthetic feel will influence the ways you instruct the learner to go about a task. You can orient instruction and practice methods to particular task requirements, thereby facilitating performance and speeding learning. Finally, task analysis aids in selecting individuals for particular skills or occupations. These important issues about selection are covered in the last section in this chapter.

Therefore, effective classification allows the instructor to do the following:

- Apply appropriate learning principles, which are often specific to a certain class of action, to activities
- Give the learner added assistance in the factors that should be emphasized for effective movement control
- Select individuals for advanced training based on abilities known to be related to the goal task

Abilities as a Basis for Classification

One effective method for task classification is based on the analysis of the activity in terms of its underlying abilities. For example, Figure 6.3 distinguishes between race-car driving and quarterbacking in terms of the abilities that make them up. Quarterbacking is a task with reaction time, response orientation, and response integration components;

race-car driving has reaction time, speed of movement, and manual dexterity components. This is analogous to differentiating between rhubarb pie and a Big Mac by their ingredients. As you can see, this classification of skills by underlying "ingredients" is somewhat more precise than a simple classification, such as open or closed.

Classifications in terms of abilities can be made either casually or formally, with differing precision as a result. On a very casual level, you can simply generate an educated guess about the underlying abilities in a skill by asking yourself—or asking accomplished performers—which actions seem to require which of the abilities. Because teachers and coaches can be very sophisticated about skills, this kind of analysis is not so bad, giving a rough initial indication of the abilities involved. I might guess that race-car driving involves reaction time, speed of movement, and manual dexterity—which is just what I did when I made up Figure 6.3 because no data on race-car drivers are available. This process can be aided greatly by highly skilled experts, who have the advantage of very high-level, intimate familiarity with the skills, which I certainly do not have with respect to race-car driving.

The disadvantage of this method is that very highly proficient performers often do not know how they do what they do. As you have learned, many processes in skills are nonconscious, such as the execution of motor programs and the detection of optical flow patterns; thus, performers do not have good access to them. A pertinent example comes from Polanyi (1958), who found that champion cyclists could not explain the principles of balancing on the bicycle, which was absolutely fundamental to their task. The famous baseball player Ted Williams claimed that he watched the ball rotate right up until the bat struck it, which is probably impossible given what we know about the speed of eye movements, visual information processing, and the like discussed earlier. Much can be learned from champion performers, but you should be prepared not to believe everything they tell you.

Formal Classification Methods

Task analysis can be further aided by flowcharts and other relatively inexpensive paper-and-pencil materials that guide or constrain expert performers into responding somewhat more consistently and reliably than they would if you simply said, "Tell me about it." One such chart is shown in Figure 6.4, taken from Fleishman and Stephenson (1970). An expert would be asked to begin at "Start," answering each question and following the appropriate arrows to the next. If the task were pitching in baseball, for example, an expert might respond "yes" to the first, second, and third questions, leading to the conclusion that this task requires control precision, an ability that contributes to fine control of very forceful actions. Also, it would be clear that reaction time and rate control were not factors here.

This flowchart method has already been used effectively in many military and industrial applications. Certainly there is much room for similar methods in sport settings, but the basic research to develop the exact methods has not been attempted.

PREDICTION AND SELECTION

As indicated early in this chapter, a large part of the work on individual differences concerns prediction of performance or skill. Prediction is everywhere in everyday life. Insurance companies attempt to predict the likelihood that you will have an automobile accident based on your age, sex, kind of car you drive, and driving record. In industry

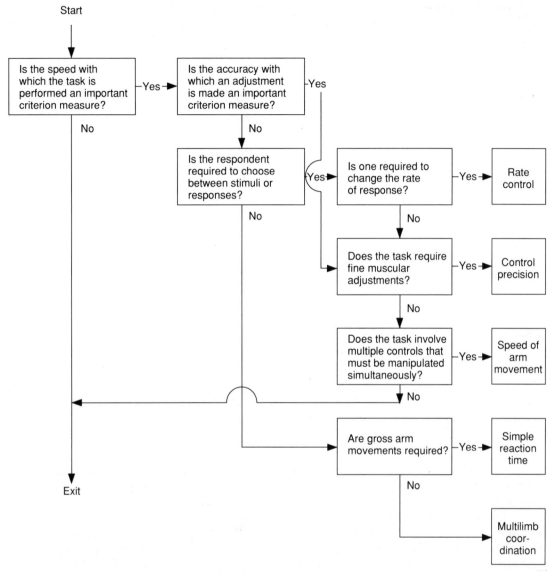

Figure 6.4 A binary flow diagram used as an aid in classifying tasks according to their underlying abilities. (Adapted by permission from Fleishman & Stephenson, 1970.)

a personnel director might want to predict which of several applicants for a job will be most successful after a year's training and experience. In sports, particularly with respect to the Olympic training efforts, a coach might attempt to predict which participants in a youth wrestling program will be most effective as adult wrestlers.

There are several common features to all these examples. First, someone wants to know something about an individual's future performance capabilities. It would be

PRACTICAL APPLICATIONS

1. When possible, interview champion performers to learn techniques that lead to effective performance.
2. Be cautious about what you learn from these interviews because even the most proficient players may not know how they perform, unintentionally giving you misleading information.
3. Become familiar with the fundamental abilities and how they are measured so you can detect individuals with strong (or weak) abilities for a particular activity.
4. If you know that some ability (e.g., speed of arm movement) is critical in a task, emphasize this feature of the skill to the learner ("Try to move faster this time").

simple to estimate who at present is a good performer. It is considerably more difficult to predict who—after growth, maturation, and additional training—will become the most effective. Second, this prediction process requires knowing which abilities are important for the **criterion task**, that is, the ultimate task for which participants would be selected (e.g., Olympic-level wrestling). Third, the process involves measurement (or at least estimation) of the abilities present in the various applicants and decisions as to which of them has the pattern of abilities that matches the criterion skill most completely.

Therefore, all attempts at prediction involve these components:

- Understanding the abilities that underlie the criterion task
- Estimating the strength of these abilities in applicants as indications of their future capabilities in the criterion task

- Estimating the future (or potential) skill level on some criterion task based on present information and its relationship to the criterion

If the individual's potential for eventual skilled performance at some task can be estimated, many advantages can be obtained. People can be directed to those sports, occupations, or activities to which their abilities are best suited, thereby fitting people to the tasks more closely and generating increased satisfaction and success as a result. Of course, everyone could be trained for a long time, and those people who succeed during this training period could then simply be selected. But training is generally expensive and time consuming, and having a way to predict who will not eventually be outstanding performers provides a means for reducing the total amount of training that must be provided for a given task. In this way, training can be more focused on the selected individuals. For those individuals not selected for a particular activity, training can be focused on other activities to which they are better suited.

Who will become a superstar after years of maturation and practice?

This is the rationale for the Olympic training and selection procedures used by many countries recently. The idea is to determine at an early age which of the many children have the abilities and interest necessary to become highly proficient athletes in the various sports, using this determination as a basis to emphasize particular sports, as opposed to others, for them. When the young athletes are selected, extensive training can be provided relatively efficiently for the smaller number of participants who have a strong likelihood of success. Although the system can be criticized on the grounds of being too heavily organized and directive, it does provide a way to select effective performers at an early age. This allows many years of training before the children are too old to compete effectively, as in women's gymnastics, where competitors in their late teens are considered "too old."

Patterns of Abilities Change With Practice and Experience

An important phenomenon to consider when attempting to predict is that the pattern of abilities underlying a particular task changes with practice and experience. At one level this is obvious: For beginners, considerable cognitive activity is involved in deciding what to do, remembering what comes after what, and trying to figure out the instructions, rules, task scoring, and the like. With a little experience, as all players learn the intellectual parts of the task, these cognitive abilities are replaced by more motor abilities related to limb movement.

Consider an activity such as baseball, and assume that it is known which abilities underlie this skill when performers are essentially novices. From Figure 6.5, when the person is a novice, this task is comprised of hypothetical Abilities A, C, T, and P. With additional training at this task, this pattern

of abilities gradually changes, so the expert's pattern of abilities involves Abilities A, C, Q, and R. Notice that two of the abilities, A and C, are present in both novice and expert performers. Other abilities, T and P, drop out to be replaced by abilities not represented earlier, Q and R. Perhaps Abilities T and P were cognitive abilities, which dropped out as practice continued. Still other abilities, X and Z, are never represented in this skill. Remember, the abilities themselves do not change because abilities are by definition genetically defined and not modifiable by practice. It is the use or selection of these abilities that changes with practice.

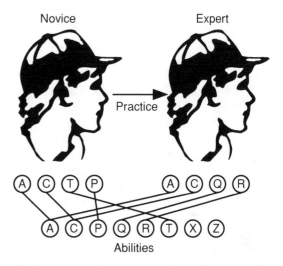

Figure 6.5 The change in the underlying abilities involved in a task as a learner progresses from novice to expert. Some abilities drop out with practice to be replaced by others, whereas other abilities remain.

The difficulty is that although an individual has the ability pattern needed for effective performance at the novice level (A, C, T, P), this will usually not be the proper pattern of abilities required for expert performance (A, C, Q, R). Therefore, selecting people because they are good as novices—or because they have strong abilities in A, C, T, and P, which is the same thing—captures only a part of the job of prediction. Most knowledge about abilities is based on relatively novice-level performances, and little is known about the abilities that underlie very high-level performances, making the task of predicting them particularly difficult.

Selection Based on Performances in Early Practice

This shift of abilities can be a problem if you attempt to select performers on the basis of their performance in early practice. A common procedure is to invite a large group of youngsters to try out for a particular team or activity. After a relatively brief practice period of a few hours, those performers most skilled at these activities are invited to remain on the team, and the others are told that they will not be retained. You can perhaps see the difficulty with this procedure. Referring to Figure 6.5 again, assume that the people who have succeeded at this early stage of practice have strong Abilities A, C, T, and P. These people, after extensive practice, may not be very well suited for high-level proficiency because they may lack strong abilities in Q and R.

The problem is even more serious than this. Consider an individual who has the proper abilities for expert performance (A, C, Q, R), although they may not be apparent without development. This person does not have the proper abilities for novice performance because T and P are not strong, and there is the likelihood that he or she will not even be selected to remain with the team after the brief practice period. Because the abilities underlying a skill change with proficiency level, you stand a good chance of missing the right people if you base selection on performance at the novice level. The solution seems to be to allow many performers

the opportunity to participate as long as possible, so the applicants can gradually move toward their own highest levels of proficiency. Then, evaluating high levels of skill and stable, expert patterns of abilities, you can select more confidently.

PRACTICAL APPLICATIONS

1. Predicting success, especially in athletic settings, is generally neither very effective nor very precise, so use these procedures cautiously.
2. Early levels of practice are characterized by strong use of cognitive abilities, so do not use early performance as a predictor of expert performance.
3. Before making selections for a team, allow as much practice as you can so the performances are based more nearly on expert ability patterns.
4. Because skills are so specific, you should use very different bases for selecting individuals even for two skills that appear similar.
5. When in doubt as to whether a given performer has the proper abilities, withhold judgment and give more practice and experience.

How Effective Is Skill Prediction?

Prediction for future success sounds great in principle, but there are difficulties in actual practice. For example, in various attempts to predict success in activities such as military pilotry, subjects are measured on a large number of **predictor tests**, which are presumably measures of various underlying abilities. The correlation between this battery of predictor tests and the criterion task of pilotry is computed using a technique called multiple regression. These correlations are not usually very high, perhaps .30 or .40; the largest of these correlations ever reported in the literature was only .70 (Adams, 1953, 1956; Fleishman, 1956). Remember, this means that only $.70^2 \times 100$, or 49%, of the abilities underlying the criterion pilotry task are being measured by the test battery, with the remaining abilities underlying pilotry being unknown. The situation is even more dismal in athletics because this problem has received almost no systematic study. The result is that prediction in sport situations is not very effective.

Why is effective prediction so difficult to achieve, even with tasks that have received strong research efforts? Several factors contribute to the problem.

Patterns of Abilities Are Not Generally Known

One difficulty is that the pattern of abilities underlying successful performance of the criterion task are generally not very well understood. Coaches and instructors usually have some general ideas about these abilities, of course, such as the need to be tall in basketball or large in football. Beyond this, determining the abilities for various sport activities is based mainly on guesswork. Related to this is the fact that, even if the abilities were known, no one is certain how to measure them in practice. Therefore, because the abilities underlying a given sport performance are generally poorly understood and difficult to measure, there is little basis for effective prediction.

Many Abilities Underlie a Given Skill

Even if some of a particular criterion activity's abilities were understood and could be measured, there will probably be many other requisite underlying abilities. For example, if 15 of the 50 or so abilities must be measured

to predict effectively, imagine the time and expense in measuring each ability of each of a large group of applicants. Of course, some success at prediction can be achieved using only one or two tests, but the advantage will be relatively small because of the many abilities that are not considered.

Generally, the prediction of success in movement skills is not very effective for the following reasons:

- The underlying abilities in sport performances have not been studied systematically and are not well understood.
- The number of such underlying abilities is probably large, requiring that many abilities be estimated.
- The pattern of abilities shifts with practice and experience, making prediction of expert performances difficult.

 ## CHAPTER SUMMARY

There are many interesting aspects of individual differences among people and how these variations can be understood. A critical concept is that of an ability, which is defined as a stable, genetically defined, enduring trait that underlies the performance of various tasks. An ability is distinguished from a skill, the proficiency in some particular task. The old concept of a general motor (or athletic) ability, where one ability was thought to underlie all motor proficiency, is incorrect. Generally, the relationships (measured by correlations) between skills are low, suggesting that there are many abilities, which are very specific to particular tasks. There appear to be many motor abilities—perhaps 50 or so, when they are all discovered—that will be able to account for performances.

The capability to predict performers' success in some future activity is a critical individual difference consideration, and the success of prediction is based on the notion of abilities. However, even in the most thoroughly studied areas of motor performance, prediction is not very effective because of the incomplete understanding of the fundamental abilities that underlie performance. This is particularly so in sports, where motor areas have received little scientific study. Finally, the pattern of abilities for a particular skill change with practice, requiring caution in attempts to predict a performer's ultimate success on the basis of performances in early practice.

Checking Your Understanding

1. Distinguish an ability from a skill. Why is this distinction important for understanding human performance?
2. What lines of evidence argue against the concept of general motor ability? What about a general ability to balance?
3. Why do correlations provide a "language" for the study of individual differences? Why are they so important?
4. How is the concept of prediction related to individual differences?
5. What factors limit the capability to predict success in common sport tasks? What is needed to improve the situation?
6. What does it mean to say that the pattern of abilities changes with practice? How does this phenomenon alter the ways of predicting success in practical settings?

Key Terms

Definitions of the following terms appear on the page(s) shown in parentheses:

ability (p. 129)
correlation (p. 134)
criterion task (p. 144)
differential approach (p. 128)
experimental approach (p. 128)
general motor ability (p. 132)
individual differences (p. 128)
prediction (p. 129)
predictor tests (p. 146)
specificity hypothesis (p. 136)
superability (p. 139)
task analysis (p. 141)

Suggestions for Further Reading

Additional reading on earlier ideas about individual differences in motor control can be found in Henry (1958/1968), and other treatments have been written by Fleishman (1957; Fleishman & Bartlett, 1969); a short discussion is included in Adams's (1987) review. The concept of individual differences as related to age, race, and gender has been treated by Osborne, Noble, and Weyl (1978), one chapter of which is devoted to these issues for motor behavior (Noble, 1978). A general discussion of the history and nature of motor abilities can be found in Schmidt (1988b, chapter 10).

Part II

Principles
of Skill Learning

To this point in the text, the focus has been mainly on understanding the nature of human movement behavior and control. The major mechanisms underlying skilled performance have been identified, along with the major factors that determine the quality of skilled performance. In addition, throughout Part I, a conceptual model of human performance has been developed that collects these many processes and principles into a single, coherent structure. This conceptual model is not only consistent with the research evidence, but it also provides a way that the information can be easily understood intuitively and can therefore be used effectively for application. By this point you should have a good overview about how the motor system works to produce skilled actions.

Now it is time to put this conceptual model to work to understand how skills are acquired and perfected with practice, allowing athletes to perform at extremely high levels or stroke patients to regain the capabilities to walk. The concepts in chapter 7 used to understand this acquisition process, which is called motor learning, are strongly based on the ideas, terminology, and principles you already mastered and used in Part I. In one way, learning can be thought of as a change in performance. Having a working conceptual model of human performance makes these changes in performance relatively easy to understand. To be sure, there are some new concepts that have to do only with learning, but most are related strongly to concepts in Part I.

The preparations and strategies for effective practice are closely connected in chapters 8 through 10. Chapter 8's focus is on considerations before practice and the strategies for ensuing practice. Chapter 9 turns to the factors associated with practice structure, organization, and alternate practice goals. Chapter 10 examines information feedback, which is so critical for effective practice. Thus, all of these chapters could be considered together as a collection of principles for organizing practice.

7 > Motor Learning: Concepts and Methods

PREVIEW

Imagine that you are an instructor in physical education, charged with teaching a set of sports skills to a group of junior high school students. For grading, you want to measure skill levels at the end of the term, but are puzzled about how to do it. Should your measure for each student take into account the proficiency level at the start of the unit? Should you measure amount learned at the end of a practice hour, when fatigue might influence the measurements? Or should you measure at the beginning of the next hour, by which time forgetting might have occurred? What skills should you ask learners to perform as a test—the same as practiced earlier or slight variations of them?

This chapter concerns motor skill learning, the remarkable set of processes through which practice and experience can generate large gains in human performance. The initial focus is on understanding the concept of learning, establishing some basic ideas about how learning is most effectively defined and conceptualized. Then the text turns to how, and with what standards, one can measure and evaluate the effectiveness of practice, both in laboratory and practical settings with relevance to teaching. Finally, there is discussion of transfer of learning, by which learning acquired in one situation can be used in another.

STUDENT GOALS

1. To understand the concept of learning for motor skills
2. To appreciate some of the problems in the measurement of learning
3. To learn how transfer of learning is related to the study of learning in general
4. To apply the principles of learning measurement to teaching situations

The capability to learn is critical to biological existence because it allows organisms to adapt to the particular features of their environments and to profit from experience. For humans, this learning is most critical of all. Think how it would be to go through life equipped only with the capability inherited at birth. Humans would be relatively simple beings indeed without the capability to talk, write, or read, and certainly without the capability to perform the complex movement skills seen in sports, music, or industry. Although learning occurs for all kinds of human performances—cognitive, verbal, interpersonal, and so on—the focus here will be on the processes that underlie learning the cognitive and motor capabilities that lead to skills as defined earlier.

Learning seems to occur almost continuously, almost as if everything you do today generates knowledge or capabilities that affect how you do other things tomorrow and beyond. However, this book takes a more restricted view of learning, in which the focus is on situations involving practice, that is, relatively deliberate attempts to improve performance of a particular skill or action. Practice, of course, often takes place in classes or lessons, either in groups as might be seen in high school physical education classes or individually as in private ski lessons or physical therapy. Usually, but certainly not always, there is an instructor, therapist, or coach to guide this practice, to evaluate the learner's progress, and to decide about future activities to maximize progress. This focus on practice with an instructor defines an important class of human activities and requires the investigation of the many factors—such as the nature of instructions, evaluation, scheduling, and so on—that collectively determine the effectiveness of practice.

THE CONCEPT OF MOTOR LEARNING

Instructors in charge of practices have a strong advantage if they have a solid understanding of the fundamental learning processes underlying practice settings. An

How do we measure the learning that occurs in instructional settings like this?

important starting point is understanding the nature and definition of learning.

Motor Learning Defined

When a person practices, the obvious result is an improved performance level, which can be measured in any number of ways, such as a higher basketball free throw percentage or a gymnast's higher score on a horizontal bar routine. But there is more to learning than just improved performance. Psychologists have found it useful to define learning in terms of the gain in the underlying **capability** for skilled performance developed during practice, with the improved capability leading to improved performance. Improved performance is then not, by itself, learning. Rather, improved performance is an indication that learning has occurred. This idea can be formalized by a definition:

> **Motor learning** is a set of processes associated with practice or experience leading to relatively permanent changes in the capability for skilled performance.

There are several important aspects to this definition. These are discussed in the next sections.

Learning as the Effect of Practice or Experience

Everyone knows there are many factors that improve the capability for skill performance. However, learning is concerned with only some of these factors—those related to practice or experience. For example, as children mature and grow, their performance capabilities increase. However, these growth factors are not evidence of learning because they are not related to practice. Similarly, gains in cardiovascular endurance or strength could occur in training programs, leading to more effective performance in activities like soccer, but these changes are not related to practice as it is thought of here.

Learning Is Not Directly Observable, but Its Products Are

During practice there are many alterations to the central nervous system, and some of these help establish relatively permanent changes in movement capability. These processes are generally not directly observable, though, so their existence must usually be inferred from the changes in performance they presumably support. It is useful to think of these changes as occurring to the fundamental movement-control processes, discussed in the previous chapters, which are collected in the conceptual model of human performance. Figure 7.1 shows the conceptual model again, this time with some of the human performance processes thought to be influenced by practice.

Some examples of these processes are (a) increased use of automatic processes in analyzing the sensory patterns (stimulus identification) indicating where a tennis ball is aimed; (b) improvements in the ways actions are selected (response selection) and parameterized (response programming) prior to a shot in ice hockey; (c) building more effective throwing motor programs and effector processes in the spinal cord; and (d) establishing

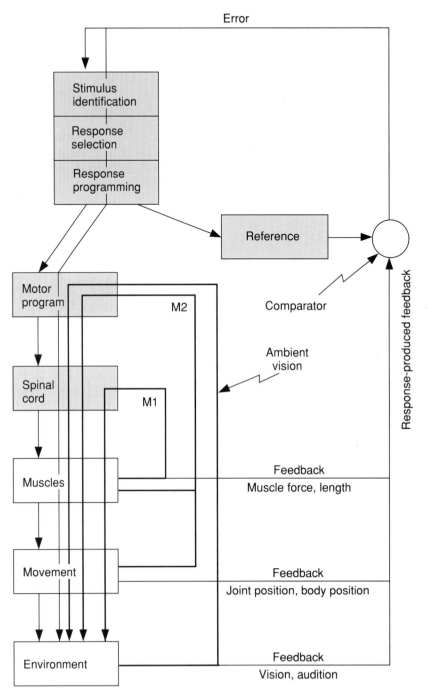

Figure 7.1 The conceptual model of human performance, highlighting some of the major processes subject to alterations during practice.

more accurate references of correctness to aid in balance. In fact, learning can occur at all levels of the central nervous system, but the levels highlighted in Figure 7.1 account for the biggest changes. Of course, all of these processes have been discussed before, but now is simply added the notion that they can be improved in various ways through practice, leading to more effective performance.

Even though the underlying processes are not directly observable, the products of the learning process are. Changes in underlying processes lead to more effective capability for skill, which then allows more skillful performances. Therefore, evidence about the development of these processes can be gained by examining various performance tests. The performance gains on these tests are often assumed to result from gains in the capability to respond.

Relatively Permanent Changes in Skill Indicate Learning

One important qualification must be added. In order for a change in skilled performance level to be regarded as due to learning, the changes must clearly be relatively permanent. Many different factors affect the momentary level of skill performance, some of which are very temporary and transient in nature. For example, skills can be affected by drugs, sleep loss, mood, stress, and a host of other factors. Most of these variables alter skills only for the moment, and their effects soon disappear. For example, alcohol degrades speech and movement performance while the blood alcohol level is elevated, but performance improves to previous levels when the alcohol level is reduced again. Thus, the performance gains from the alcohol state to the no-alcohol state are not due to learning because the changes are too transient and reversible.

In studying learning, it is important to understand those practice variables that affect performance in a relatively permanent way. This changed capability is then a permanent part of the person's makeup and is available at some future time when that skill is required.

An analogy will perhaps be useful. When water is heated to a boil, there are changes in its behavior (performance). Of course, these are not permanent because the water returns to the original state as soon as the effects of the variable (heating) dissipate. These changes therefore would not be parallel to learning changes. However, when an egg is boiled, its state is changed. This change is relatively permanent because cooling the egg does not reverse its state to the original. The changes in the egg are parallel to the relatively permanent changes due to learning. When people learn, relatively permanent changes occur that survive the shift to other conditions or the passage of time. After learning, you are not the same person you were before, just as the egg is not the same egg.

The realization that performance alterations due to learning must be relatively permanent has led to special methods for measuring learning and evaluating the effects of practice variations. Essentially, these methods separate relatively permanent changes (due to learning) from temporary changes (due to transient factors). This idea is returned to in a subsequent section.

To emphasize the features of the definition of learning, the following statements are important to keep in mind:

- Learning results from practice or experience.
- Learning is not directly observable.
- Learning changes are inferred from performance changes.

- Learning involves a set of processes in the central nervous system.
- Learning produces an acquired capability for skilled performance.
- Learning changes are relatively permanent, not transitory.

HOW IS MOTOR LEARNING MEASURED?

For both the experimental effects of learning in the laboratory and the practical effects of learning in the gymnasium or on the playing field, measuring learning and evaluating progress are critical. They are conducted with the same general principles, some of which are presented in this section.

Performance Curves

By far the most common way to evaluate learning progress during practice is through **performance curves**. Assume that for a large number of people practicing some task, performance measures for each of their attempts, or trials, have been collected. From these data, a graph of the average performance for each trial can be drawn, as in Figure 7.2, with successive 10-trial sets of trials grouped to form blocks. These data were generated from a coincident-timing task, which is a laboratory simulation of hitting a baseball with a bat. The curve in Figure 7.2 slopes upward as performance continues, rising quickly at first and more slowly later.

For other tasks the curve slopes downward, such as those in which time or errors are the performance measures. Figure 7.3 involves a task where the subjects attempted to match a complex goal pattern of arm movement. Error in making the proper pattern (termed root-mean-squared error, or RMS error) is the measure of performance, and it is reduced quickly at first and more

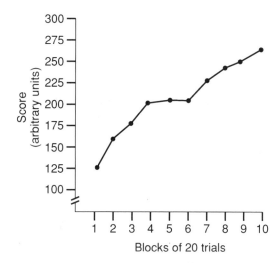

Figure 7.2 Performance curve for a group of subjects practicing a laboratory simulation of hitting a pitched ball with a bat. Scores are analogous to the distance that the ball was hit. (Adapted from Young & Schmidt, 1990b.)

slowly as practice continues. There is a small regression in performance between practice days, due to forgetting and other processes, but after a few trials the learners regained their earlier performance levels and continued to improve. As you can see, performance curves slope upward or downward more or less arbitrarily, depending on whether the measured data increase (distance thrown, amount of weight lifted, etc.) or decrease (errors, time) with practice and experience.

A typical feature of performance curves is for changes to be rapid at first and more gradual later. In some cases the improvements might be essentially completed after several dozen trials, whereas in other cases the improvements could continue for years, although such changes would be very small in later years. This general form of performance curves—steep at first and more gradual later—is one of the most common features of learning any task and is one of the most

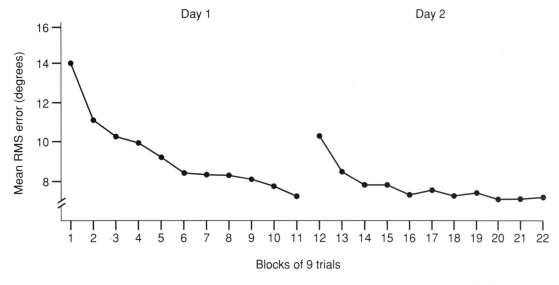

Figure 7.3 Performance curve for a group of subjects practicing an arm-patterning task. Root-mean-squared (RMS) errors indicate how close the movements were to the goal pattern. (Adapted by permission from Winstein & Schmidt, 1990.)

fundamental principles of practice, called the law of practice (Snoddy, 1926). The mathematical form of these curves, how it changes with various features of the task and the nature of the learners, have been discussed in some detail by numerous writers in the skill area (e.g., Newell & Rosenbloom, 1981).

The major points so far about performance curves can be summarized as follows:

- Performance curves are plots of individual or average performance against practice trials.
- Such curves can either increase or decrease with practice, depending on the particular way the task is scored.
- The law of practice says that improvements are rapid at first and much slower later—a nearly universal principle of practice.

Limitations of Performance Curves

There are many useful ways to use performance curves, such as to display a given learner's performance gains or to chart the progress of a gymnastics team's meet scores. At the same time, several potential difficulties require caution in drawing the interpretations from these curves.

Performance Curves Are Not Learning Curves. As useful as performance curves are for charting learners' progress, several characteristics limit their usefulness. First, these are not ''learning curves,'' as if they somehow measured learning. These curves are plots of performance against trials, which (as seen in the next sections) does not necessarily indicate much about progress in the relatively permanent capability for performance, as learning was defined earlier.

Between-Subject Effects Are Masked. One of the main reasons for using performance curves is that they tend to average out the discrepant performances of different learners. By averaging a large group of people together, performance changes in the mythical average subject can be seen and, it is hoped, inferences can be made about general proficiency changes. This is particularly useful in research settings, where differences in improvement for two groups of subjects are studied as a function of different practice methods, for example.

The drawback is that this averaging process hides any differences between people, termed individual differences in chapter 6. Because of this, the averaging method gives the impression that all subjects learn in the same way or that learning is a gradual, continual process. For example, when I was a college gymnast, I tried for most of a year and with only modest success to learn fundamental skills on the pommel horse. My teammate Jim Fairchild had no trouble learning these skills, and he eventually went on to become national champion. He and I were clearly different in rate of improvement and eventual skill level, more or less as seen in

Figure 7.4. Yet, if his and my performances were averaged to form the mean (average) curve in the figure, these important individual differences would have been hidden.

Within-Subject Variability Is Masked. A second drawback to performance curves is that the performance fluctuations within a single person tend to be obscured by averaging procedures. Examining smooth performance curves, such as in Figures 7.2 and 7.3, it is tempting to assume that the individual learners' performances that contributed to the curves progressed smoothly and gradually, also. Of course, smooth individual progression is not always the case. Perhaps you can recall learning some new action where you were trying various strategies and methods in practice: Success was not very likely, proficiency seemed to come and go with specific trials, and your performances were erratic and inconsistent. Sometimes, a learner

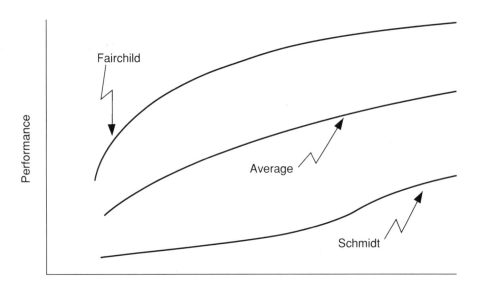

Figure 7.4 Hypothetical performance curves for two learners who improve at different rates. The average curve tends to obscure individual differences.

HIGHLIGHT

Learning Curves—Facts or Artifacts?

In an important article, Bahrick, Fitts, and Briggs (1957) identified a number of artifacts of so-called learning curves. They used a tracking task in which the learners, with hand movements of a lever, practiced following a variable track presented on a screen. The researchers recorded the performances for analysis and later scored them in three different ways. First they defined a narrow band of correctness around the track (5% of the screen's width) and counted the number of seconds out of each 90-s trial that the subject was on target. Such scores, called time-on-target (TOT) scores, measure the subject's accuracy. Next Bahrick et al. estimated TOT for a somewhat larger target (15% of the screen's width), and then again for a very large target (30% of the screen's width). Then they plotted these various TOT scores for each trial, giving the three curves shown in Figure 7.5.

Remember that these curves came from the same performances from the same subjects, who were not aware of the scoring that Bahrick et al. did afterward. If you were to think of these as learning curves, you would be forced into three contradictory conclusions: (a) the learning gains were rapid at first and slower later (30% curve), (b) the learning gains were linear across practice (15% curve), and (c) the learning gains were slow at first and rapid later (5% curve). In fact, there was only one rate of learning experienced by each subject, but it was estimated in three different ways, which led to three different conclusions about the changes with practice. These differences are caused by so-called scoring artifacts, where the measured scores become differentially sensitive to the gains in the internal capability for responding as they move closer to ceiling (90 s TOT) and floor in the scoring range (0 s TOT). This experiment warns of the difficulties in using performance curves as measures of learning.

---

continues for many trials without any measurable success, then a trial with a different movement pattern is instantly successful. Performance change with practice is frequently revolutionary rather than evolutionary, which is not captured by the gradual changes in the average performance curves.

Learning Versus Performance Effects of Practice

Critically important, not only for the experimental study of learning but also for evaluating learning in practical settings, is the notion of learning versus performance effects. According to this view, practice can have two different kinds of influences on performance—one that is relatively permanent and due to learning and another that is only temporary and transient.

Relatively Permanent Effects of Practice

One product of practice is the establishment of a relatively permanent performance

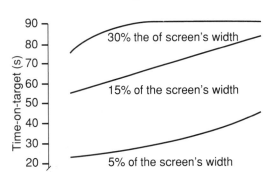

Figure 7.5 Time-on-target performances for one group of subjects on a tracking task, scored with three different scoring criteria. The different scoring methods produced artifacts in the shapes of the performance curves. (Adapted from Bahrick, Fitts, & Briggs, 1957.)

capability, or learning. This effect produces a permanent change in the person—really a change in a collection of processes, as seen in Figure 7.1—that allows the individual to perform a particular action in the future, and which endures over many days or even many years. Essentially, the concern is for discovering those practice conditions that maximize the development of these relatively permanent changes, so these conditions can be used in various practical settings to enhance learning.

Temporary Effects of Practice

However, many practice variations have important temporary effects (either positive or negative) as well as relatively permanent ones. Some of these effects are a result of simply practicing, that is, making the movements necessary to perform the task (e.g., from fatigue). An experimenter or a teacher can generate positive influences by providing praise or instruction. Some effects are positive and contribute to increased perfor-

PRACTICAL APPLICATIONS

1. If possible, avoid using average performance curves to chart team or class progress because they obscure important differences between individual people.
2. Average performance curves should be discouraged because they also hide differences in the rates of improvement for different people.
3. Whenever possible, use individual performance curves to display improvement in classroom situations, avoiding averaging artifacts.
4. Have learners plot their own performance curves, which can lead to increased involvement with the skills and greater motivation to learn.
5. Individual performance curves plotted over several weeks of practice indicate important long-term trends that may be obscured by short-term plots.

mance levels, whereas others are negative and degrade performance somewhat.

Positive Effects. Various kinds of instructions or encouragement elevate performance due to a motivating or energizing effect. As seen in chapter 10, providing the learner with information about how he or she is progressing in the task can have an elevating effect on performance. Giving guidance in the form of physical help or verbal directions during practice can also alter performance. Various mood states can likewise elevate performance temporarily, as can various drugs, such as amphetamines.

Negative Effects. Other temporary practice factors can be negative, degrading performance temporarily. For example, sometimes practice generates physical fatigue, which somewhat depresses performance relative to rested conditions. Lethargic performances can result if practice is boring or if learners become discouraged at their lack of progress, more or less opposite to the energizing effects just mentioned. Numerous other factors associated with practice could exert similar effects.

Summary Break

Practice can have important effects on the learner:

- Relatively permanent effects that persist across many days
- Temporary effects that vanish with time or a change in conditions
- Simultaneous temporary and relatively permanent effects

Separating Relatively Permanent and Temporary Effects

Whenever learners practice, and especially when instructors intervene to enhance learning (e.g., by giving instructions and feedback), it is important to have a way to separate the relatively permanent practice effects from the temporary effects. Assume that you are interested in trying out a new technique for teaching archery in a classroom setting; it involves attaching a special device that gives a warning signal whenever the bow is unstable. This device is not legal for actual competition and is to be used only during practice sessions. Certainly, your evaluation of this new technique's worth for learning will be based on whether it enhances performance relatively permanently, that is, after the device has been removed, perhaps in an archery match. After all, if learning effects disappear as soon as the class is over, the technique cannot have had much advantage as a teaching method.

Frequently, in laboratory settings—and sometimes in practical settings as well—learners are divided into two separate classes or groups. One of the archery classes practices with the new technique, the other with a more traditional method. The two groups might practice under these two different conditions for an hour, the students recording their performances on all of their shots. You average all of the learners' scores, each group separately, and plot performance curves, essentially as was done in Figures 7.2 and 7.3. Such a plot might look like that in Figure 7.6, where the average number of bull's-eyes is plotted for successive blocks of 10 practice trials.

Which condition is best for learning—the new method or the old one? This might seem like a silly question. Looking at the graph reveals that the students using the new method improved their performance in practice more rapidly than the students with the old method, and their final performance level was higher, also. It seems obvious that the new method is better. The difference might be because the new method generated more learning than the old method, which would be most interesting. As recently argued, however, the performance difference between these two groups might be only a temporary performance effect, which might disappear as soon as the device is removed.

The problem can be posed more systematically in the form of hypotheses about the two conditions:

Hypothesis 1: The new group learned more than the old group (the new group had developed a stronger relatively permanent capability for responding than the old group by the end of practice).

Hypothesis 2: The new group learned the same amount as the old, but the new group had a temporary advantage (the new group had developed the same level of the relatively permanent capability for performance as the old group, but

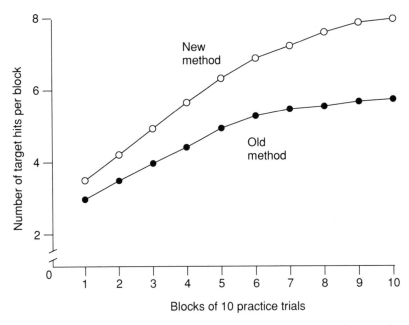

Figure 7.6 Hypothetical performance curves for two groups practicing archery under a new and an old method.

their performance is enhanced temporarily by the information or motivation provided by the device).

Which of these two hypotheses is correct? The answer, based only on the data in Figure 7.6, is unknown. The information given permits no way to tell whether the advantage of the new group is due to some relatively permanent (learning) effect or to some temporary (performance) effect that is likely to disappear as soon as the device is removed. This is a critical problem because there is no real basis for deciding which learning method is better. However, additional procedures permit separation of learning and performance effects.

Transfer Designs in the Laboratory and the Real World

A transfer design can separate the relatively permanent and temporary effects of a vari-

able. This method has two important features. First, the temporary effects of the variable (the new archery device) must be allowed to dissipate. In this example, the temporary effects of the device (if any) might be largely informational or motivational, acting mainly during actual performance, so very little time for dissipation would be needed. As a result, any temporary effects would have dissipated by the next day. (Other variables could have temporary effects with much longer times for dissipation, such as a week or a month.) Second, the learners are tested again under equivalent conditions, either both with or both without the new device. This is done to equalize any temporary effects for this test, preventing one group from generating more of the temporary effect during the test itself than the other group. Otherwise, the results would be difficult to interpret.

One solution is to give a transfer test, or a **retention test**, the next day, the two groups practicing under the same conditions. Because the interest is mainly in the effect of the device on performance when the device is removed (e.g., for competition), the decision is to test both groups without the device (alternatively, both groups could be tested with the device). Here's the logic: If the temporary effects have dissipated by Day 2 and any differential temporary effects are not allowed to reappear, then any differences observed on Day 2 should be due to relatively permanent effects acquired through the device on Day 1. Therefore, the learning effects of the device are not evaluated during Day 1 but rather on Day 2, when the temporary effects have disappeared, leaving the relatively permanent effects behind to be revealed on the test.

The essential features of a transfer design can be summarized as follows:

- Allow sufficient time (rest) for the supposed temporary effects to dissipate. The amount of time varies depending on the particular nature of the temporary effects.
- Test learners again on a transfer test, both groups under identical conditions.
- Any differences on this transfer test are due to a difference in the relatively permanent capability for performance, that is, in learning.

Outcomes With Transfer Designs

Consider the possible Day 2 outcomes of the hypothetical experiment just described. A few of these possibilities are shown in Figure 7.7, labeled Transfer Outcomes 1, 2, and 3 on the x-axis. In Outcome 1 the Day 2 performances of the two groups are different by

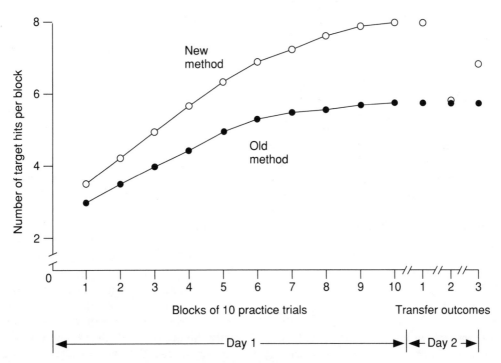

Figure 7.7 The effect of the new and old learning methods on learning is evaluated on a transfer test. Three possible outcomes on the transfer test are shown at the right.

approximately the same amount as was present at the end of the trials on Day 1. In this case, all of the difference between groups on Day 1 was due to a relatively permanent effect because allowing the temporary effects (if any) to dissipate did not change the groups' relative status at all. Conclusion: The new method is better for learning than the old method.

Now consider Outcome 2 in Figure 7.7, where the Day 2 performances of the two groups are essentially the same but at the level of the old group on Day 1. Here, when the temporary effects dissipated, all of the Day 1 difference between the groups dissipated as well. This leads to the conclusion that all of the Day 1 effect of the method was due to some temporary elevating change, and none was due to learning. Conclusion: The new method elevates performance over the old method temporarily, but it has no lasting effect on learning.

Finally, examine Outcome 3, where the Day 2 performance of the group practicing under the new method is better than that of the group with the old method, but not as good as on Day 1. It can be argued that some of the difference between the Day 1 performances of these groups was due to temporary effects because dissipation reduced the difference somewhat. However, not all of the Day 1 difference was temporary because some of it remained on Day 2 after the temporary effects dissipated. Conclusion: The new method elevates performance temporarily over the old method, but it also produces some lasting effects on learning.

Evaluating Learning in Practical Settings

The issues just discussed may seem, at first glance, to relate mainly to learning evaluation in research situations. However, transfer designs form the basis for learning evaluation in many teaching situations as well. For example, when a learner practices some skill, the proficiency level reached at the end of an hour may not reflect very well the actual performance capability achieved. Because practice and various factors involved in it may also affect performance temporarily, they may mask the underlying acquired capability for responding. Only through some kind of a retention or transfer test, after the dissipation of any temporary effects, will the true level of student achievement be evident.

A related issue concerns evaluation for the purpose of grading. If a student's grade in some activity is related to amount learned, then basing the grade on performance toward the end of some practice session would be unwise. The learning level would tend to be masked by various temporary practice effects. A far better method would be to evaluate the student's progress on a delayed retention or transfer test, administered sufficiently long after practice that the temporary effects of practicing had dissipated.

In addition, people may be affected differently by these temporary factors—yet another form of individual differences. For example, a student more susceptible to fatigue than others will show larger temporary decrements in performance during the practice phase, perhaps leading to the false conclusion that learning progress has been slow. However, evaluating the learning level by a delayed test under relatively rested conditions shows a better representation of actual learning progress.

It is even possible that Dan, who performs less well than Pete in the practice phase, may actually perform better in a delayed test phase. If you were to evaluate learning in the practice phase, you would have concluded that Pete learned more than Dan, when exactly the opposite would be found in the retention phase. For such reasons, learning should usually be evaluated under testing conditions relatively remote from the training conditions and probably when the subject is well rested.

1. Performance levels during the practice phase are altered severely by various temporary factors, so do not use such levels for evaluation and grading.
2. Use a transfer or retention test to evaluate the level of learning achieved by a member of a class of learners.
3. This test should be relatively separated from the practice phase and probably conducted under relatively rested conditions.
4. Achievement levels of different individuals for grading should be evaluated under delayed, rested conditions, not at the time of practice.
5. Temporary effects can either elevate or depress performance, so be prepared to see either performance gains or losses on a retention test when these effects have dissipated.

Transfer of Learning

An important variation of the ideas about learning discussed so far concerns the **transfer of learning**. As the name implies, this concept involves the application of learning achieved in one task or setting to the performance of some other task, which is usually called the criterion task. For instance, in the example with the archery device, the question was whether practice with the device transferred to competition performance. Transfer is a particularly important notion for instructors concerned about practice design and learning efficiency. Teaching for trans-

fer, or organizing practice and instruction to facilitate transfer of learning, is an important goal for most instructional programs.

Role of Transfer in Skill Learning Settings

Transfer is involved anytime students practice one task version with the idea that learning achieved there will be useful on some other task version. Consider drills, for example. Having football players practice blocking with padded dummies assumes this experience will benefit the task of blocking real players in a football game. Shooting practice free throws under rested conditions assumes this experience will transfer to shooting free throws in game situations, where fatigue is usually present. In each of these situations, the transfer from drill to criterion skill situation must be substantial. If it is not, practicing the drills could be largely a waste of time.

Transfer is also involved when instructors modify skills to make them easier to practice. For example, relatively long-duration serial skills, such as doing a gymnastics routine, can be broken down into their elements for practice. Practicing the stunts in isolation must benefit the performance of the whole routine (the criterion) made up of the individual stunts. However, in more rapid skills, such as a tennis serve, it is usually not so clear that breaking down the skill into ball-toss and ball-strike portions for part practice will be effective. Practice of the part must transfer to the whole skill. The principles of transfer applicable to such situations are dealt with in chapter 9.

How Is Transfer Measured?

Measuring transfer of learning is closely related to the learning measurement discussed earlier. Essentially, what is wanted is to estimate the performance level of some skill (the criterion task), with the relatively permanent effects of learning separated from any temporary performance effects. However, rather than asking how practice variations of a given task affect learning, transfer concerns the amount of learning on a criterion task that can be achieved by practice on some *other* task.

Suppose you want to know whether practicing golf at the driving range transfers to the actual game of golf, which is the criterion skill. Consider three hypothetical groups of subjects with different kinds of practice experiences. Group 1 practices 4 hr at the driving range, whereas Group 2 does not receive any practice. Also consider Group 3, which practices 4 hr at miniature golf. After these various practice activities, all groups transfer to (are tested on) five rounds of actual golf. The results of this hypothetical experiment are shown in Figure 7.8, where the average

scores for the five rounds of golf are plotted separately for the three groups. Assuming that the groups are equivalent at the start of the experiment, the only reason for the groups to be different on the first (and subsequent) round of golf is that the previous experiences have somehow contributed to, or detracted from, golf skill. Therefore, the focus for transfer would be on the relative differences among the groups on the criterion task.

Figure 7.8 shows that Group 1, which had received earlier practice at the driving range, performed more effectively than Group 2, which had no previous practice. This difference is usually measured on the first trial, or at least on the first few trials, before the additional practice on the criterion task can alter the skill levels very much. In this case, we would have said that the driving range experience transferred positively to golf be-

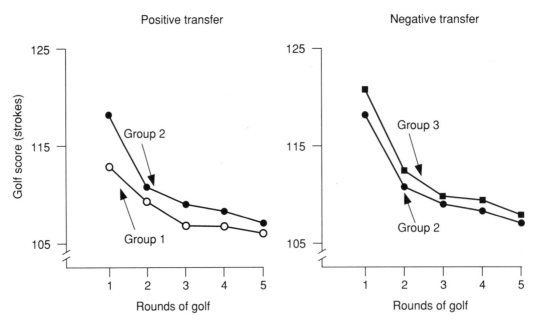

Figure 7.8 Performance in golf as a function of prior experiences. Before actual golf, Group 1 practices at the driving range, Group 3 practices at miniature golf, and Group 2 receives no practice.

cause it facilitated golf performance over and above no practice. If this were an actual experiment, you might conclude that the skills developed on the driving range were applicable in some way to those on the golf course.

Transfer can also be negative, as you can see in the right portion of Figure 7.8. Notice that Group 3, which had practice on the miniature golf task, performs more poorly on the rounds of golf than Group 2, which had no prior practice at all. In this case, miniature golf experience transferred negatively to golf performance. If this would have happened in an actual experiment, you might conclude that the skills in miniature golf are systematically different from those in actual golf, leading to disruptions in the golf game.

Finally, a rough estimate of the amount of transfer can be generated from performance curves such as in Figure 7.8. Considering the amount of gain of the group with no prior practice (Group 2) as a standard amount learned in this task (that is, 118 − 108 = 10 strokes), then the improvement accomplished on the other tasks can be estimated. Group 1 started with a score of 114 strokes, 4 lower than Group 2 at the start of practice. That is, 4 out of the 10 strokes of improvement in golf were accomplished by driving range practice. Positive transfer was 4/10 × 100 = 40%, expressing this gain as *percentage transfer*. The same thing can be done for negative transfer. The initial performance of Group 3, with prior miniature golf experience, was 3 strokes worse than for Group 2, with no prior experience. The negative transfer was −3/10 × 100 = −33%.

These **percentage transfer** statistics are not perfectly reliable, however, because they are badly distorted by all kinds of temporary factors and differences in task scoring that affect the performance measures. However, they are generally useful for comparing the amounts of transfer experienced in different conditions (early and late in practice) or in different kinds of tasks (continuous and discrete) where the measures of performance might not be directly comparable. These ideas about transfer are returned to in chapter 9 in the discussion of the various practice conditions for learning.

Here are some of the major points for the concept of transfer:

- Transfer can be estimated as the gain (or the loss) in proficiency in one task as a result of practice or experience in another.
- Transfer can be either positive or negative, depending on the particular tasks involved.
- Transfer can be estimated roughly as the percentage of gain on the criterion task that resulted from practicing on the prior transfer task.

Transfer as a Criterion for Learning

The previous sections on measuring learning have perhaps left the impression that the only way to measure the relative amount learned is by performance on some delayed retention test. This is probably the most important way to estimate learning, but other ways are possible, and some are even preferable in some situations.

The essential issue is what we want learners to be able to do after training. In some cases, learners are trained to be proficient at a specific task with a limited range of variations. You provide instruction in softball pitching—a particular distance to a particular target area—so this specific action will be learned. You don't care very much about pitching to targets half as large or half the distance away. Where the criterion is performance on a particular task, the idea of giving delayed retention tests on the particular action to measure progress seems perfectly reasonable. However, other criteria for training are sometimes important.

Teaching or Training for Transfer: Near Transfer. One critical aspect of many training settings is the extent to which the practice transfers to different yet very similar settings in the real world. This is generally termed **near transfer**, the learning goal being a task relatively similar to the training task. For example, a basketball coach trains her players during the practice week to execute plays, but she cannot practice against the opposing Bearcats until they arrive to play the game on Saturday night. She hopes the practice will transfer to the novel skill of playing a new team. Sometimes instructors have to train learners to perform in situations very different from practice settings such as performing well against the Bearcats' new defense, which is totally unexpected and which her team has not seen previously. Being able to perform in such unexpected and unpredictable conditions is one mark of a highly skilled player or team.

Training Fundamental Capabilities to Move: Far Transfer. Sometimes instructors want to train learners to develop more general capabilities for a wide variety of skills, only a few of which are actually experienced in practice. This is usually termed **far transfer** because the eventual goal is quite different from the original practice setting. For example, elementary school children are taught to ice-skate in physical education classes; these skills may eventually be used many years later in figure skating, ice hockey, or simply recreational settings. Therefore, the goal of the class is not so much associated with the effectiveness of skating at that time but in the eventual transfer to other situations. Another example is learning to throw, jump, and run; the main concern is the extent to which these activities transfer to future activities involving throwing, jumping, and running but occurring in very different settings.

In all these situations, the evaluation of training effectiveness is not based exclusively on how well the learners master the skills during actual practice. Rather, if transfer to relatively different activities is the goal, the most effective training program will be that which produces the best performance

Often the best measure of the transfer of learning from practice activities is performance in the criterion task (a game or a match).

PRACTICAL APPLICATIONS

1. In evaluating training, first decide what the criterion skill, or goal behavior, is for learning—specific skills, near transfer, or far transfer.
2. If the goal is specific skill, evaluate progress with a delayed retention test involving that particular skill in the setting in which it is to be used.
3. If near transfer is the goal, give a transfer test involving a performance variation different from that in practice.
4. If far transfer is the goal, actual evaluation in practical settings is difficult because such transfer is likely to be small and difficult to detect.
5. In evaluation during practice, place less emphasis on the mastery of specific skills and more emphasis on the transfer performance that is the real goal of practice.

on some transfer test performed in the future—one that may involve quite different skills from those actually learned in class. Here, the effectiveness of a training program is measured by the amount of transfer to some different activity.

◇ **CHAPTER SUMMARY**

Motor learning is defined as a set of processes associated with practice that lead to relatively permanent changes in performance capability. As such, the emphasis is on the determinants of this capability, which supports or underlies the performance. Hence, factors that affect performance only temporarily tend to be confused with factors affecting this underlying capability, which

makes the use of "learning" curves somewhat risky for evaluating learning.

However, temporary and learning effects can be separated by using transfer or retention tests. In experiments on learning, learners practice under different conditions in acquisition; after a delay, they are tested on the same task but under identical conditions. This procedure focuses attention on the performance in the retention tests as measures of progress. Transfer, closely related to learning, is where practice on one task contributes to response capability in some other task. Transfer can be positive or negative, depending on whether it enhances or degrades performance on the other task. It can also be near or far, depending on how different the criterion is from the practice activities.

◇ **Checking Your Understanding**

1. What are learning curves? Describe three features that make them unreliable for estimating learning.
2. Suggest three variations in practice that might enhance performance only temporarily.
3. In evaluating learning for grading purposes, when should you give progress tests? When should you not give them?
4. Identify and describe a practical situation in which transfer of learning is the critical practice goal.
5. Describe the differences between near transfer, far transfer, negative transfer, and positive transfer. Can far transfer ever be negative?

◇ **Key Terms**

Definitions of the following terms appear on the page(s) shown in parentheses:

capability (p. 153)
far transfer (p. 168)

◇ Suggestions for Further Reading

More information on the measurement of learning can be found in Schmidt (1988b, chapter 11). Special applications to physical therapy are discussed in Schmidt (in press). An analysis of learning curves is given by Newell and Rosenbloom (1981), and applications to instruction in sports can be found in Christina and Corcos (1988).

8 Preparations and Strategies for Designing Practice

PREVIEW

Jenny's tennis serves seem to be getting worse and worse. As her coach, you feel that her ball toss is inconsistent in height and placement, which is requiring her to alter her serving motion to contact the ball effectively. You consider various strategies to solve her problem, one of which is having her practice the ball toss in isolation.

This sounds good, but you are concerned that, practiced unnaturally in isolation, the toss will become so distorted that it may not contribute much to the overall serve. And will the time spent in this part practice be worthwhile in relation to how much it affects the serve? How do you decide? In designing a program of instruction for learners—either individually or in a class—instructors face a nearly overwhelming number of decisions about how to organize practice.

This chapter focuses on issues related to the strategies for ensuing practice—what to say in your instructions, how to give demonstrations, how much practice to provide, how students should practice, when they should rest, and other questions. This chapter presents the principles addressing these questions and then suggests applications for various teaching situations.

STUDENT GOALS

1. To understand the features of practice that determine the amount learned
2. To appreciate the role of instructions and demonstrations before practice
3. To learn the important variables that define effective physical and mental practice
4. To apply these principles to many real-world practice settings

Imagine you have just been assigned to teach a group of students a particular set of skills. How would you organize your practice sessions? What would you say to motivate your students to learn? How would you schedule physical practice and rest time? In what order will you present skills, and how much practice will you allow on one skill before moving to the next? Countless prepractice questions like these affect how you plan instruction, and this chapter presents the principles that let you solve these problems of how and when to practice.

Practice, or various kinds of experience, at particular skills is a broad concept, difficult to specify precisely. Practice can occur at many different times and places, under varying conditions, and it can be either almost unintentional or highly guided and structured. Many features of practice settings can be varied systematically to make practice more or less effective, and many are under the direct control of the teacher or the coach. Of course, your being armed with principles of movement performance and learning will facilitate

such decisions, equipping you to make wise choices about structuring practice to produce the most effective outcomes—usually the maximization of learning.

The discussion of practice principles begins by considering a general description of the practice stages that learners go through from novice level to becoming experts. This general framework for practice provides a basis for many decisions about practice organization to be considered later.

THE STAGES OF LEARNING

It is useful to consider three relatively distinct stages that can be identified in the learning process: (a) the verbal-cognitive stage, (b) the motor stage, and (c) the autonomous stage (Fitts & Posner, 1967). These stages should not be confused with the information-processing stages discussed in chapter 2. Rather, they are descriptors of the different levels of skill development.

Verbal-Cognitive Stage

In the **verbal-cognitive stage**, the task is completely new to the learner. As a beginner on the sailboard, I was bewildered by the many decisions I had to make about how and where to stand, how to hold the sail, and how to balance; I was fascinated by the many different ways I managed to fall. As the stage name implies, the learner's first problem is verbal and cognitive, in which the dominant questions are about goal identification, performance evaluation, what to do (and what not to do), when to do it, how to stand or grasp the apparatus, what to look at, and a host of others. As a result, verbal and cognitive abilities (discussed in chapter 6) dominate at this stage. Figuring out what to do and generating a beginning attempt at it are critical.

Instructions, demonstrations, film clips, and other verbal (or verbalizable) information are also particularly useful in this stage. One goal of instructions is to have the learner transfer information from past learning to these initial skill levels. For example, many skills have similar stance requirements, so instructions that bring out already known stances should be useful for teaching a new one. Also, several previously learned movements can be sequenced together to approximate the desired skill (e.g., dribble the basketball, run, jump, and shoot a lay up), and provide a start for later learning. Gains in proficiency in this stage are very rapid and large, indicating that more effective strategies for performance are being discovered. Do not worry that performance at this stage is halting, jerky, uncertain, and poorly timed to the external environment; this is merely the starting point for later proficiency gains.

Some learners engage in a great deal of self-talk, verbally guiding themselves through actions. This activity demands a lot of attention and prevents the processing of simultaneous activities, such as overall game strategies and elements of form. This verbal activity is effective for this initial stage, though, facilitating a quick, rough skill approximation, and it should drop out later.

Motor Stage

The performer next enters the **motor stage**. Most cognitive problems have been solved, so now the focus shifts to organizing more effective movement patterns to produce the action. In this stage my windsurfing skill level quickly rose from that in the verbal-cognitive stage. I began to display consistent stance and control, my confidence improved, I started to work on smaller details of the task, and I continued to improve rapidly. In other skills requiring quick movements, such as a tennis stroke, the learner begins to build a motor program to accomplish the movement requirements. In slower movements, such as balancing in gymnastics, the learner constructs ways to deal with response-produced feedback.

Several factors change markedly during the motor stage, associated with more effective movement patterns. Performance improves rapidly. Some inconsistency from trial to trial is seen as the learner attempts new solutions to movement problems. Consistency gradually increases, though, and the movement begins to be grooved and stable. Enhanced movement efficiency reduces energy costs, and self-talk becomes less important for performance. Performers discover environmental regularities to serve as effective cues for timing. Anticipation develops rapidly, making movements smoother and less rushed. In addition, learners begin to monitor their own feedback and detect their errors. This stage generally lasts somewhat longer than the verbal-cognitive stage, perhaps for several weeks or months with many sport skills or even longer if the learner is having difficulty.

Autonomous Stage

After much practice, the learner gradually enters the **autonomous stage**, involving the development of automatic actions that do not take attention (chapter 2). Here the motor programs are well developed and can control the action for a relatively long time, as with the gymnast who runs off several seconds of activity as a single programmed unit. Programming longer movement sequences means triggering fewer programs during a given time, decreasing the load on attention-demanding response-initiation processes. I never entered the autonomous stage in windsurfing, but those who are there clearly display very skilled sail-handling in high winds, with plenty of reserve attention to think about strategies in a race or surfing on large waves.

The stage brings increased automaticity in the sensory analysis of environmental patterns, where the early signs of a play unfolding in football are detected quickly and accurately. The decreased attention demand frees the individual to perform higher-order cognitive activities, such as decisions about game strategy or the form or style in activities such as dance and figure skating. Self-talk about the actual muscular performance is almost lacking, and performance often suffers if self-analysis is attempted. However, self-talk continues in terms of higher-order strategic aspects. Self-confidence increases, and the capability to detect one's own errors becomes more developed.

Performance improvements are slow, because the learner is already very capable when this stage begins. However, learning is far from over, as shown in industrial studies; for example, Crossman (1959) found that the speed of making cigars on a production line continued to increase even after 7 years, or after 100 million cigars! There are often gains like improved automaticity, further reduced physical and mental effort in skill produc-

tion, improved style and form, and many other factors not so directly related to actual physical performance.

Summary Break

Here are some key phrases that characterize the three learning stages just discussed:

- *Verbal-cognitive stage:* The learner determines what to do and what the goals are, improvement is rapid, movements are jerky and fragmented and based on previous learning, decision-making processes and self-talk predominate, and attention demands are very high.
- *Motor stage:* The learner begins to develop specific motor programs for the actions, consistency increases rapidly, anticipation and timing improve, self-talk begins to decrease, and gains in performance are somewhat slower than in the first stage.
- *Autonomous stage:* The learner has become very proficient, attention demands are greatly reduced, the movements and sensory analyses begin to become automatic, emphasis is placed on strategic or stylistic aspects of performance, and continued gains in skill come relatively slowly.

SOME CONSIDERATIONS BEFORE PRACTICE

Several important aspects of the practice setting occur very early in the process. In fact, many of these processes occur before any physical practice at all, such as concerns for motivation for learning, instructions, and demonstrations.

How to Motivate for Practice

Instructors often have the impression that the learner's motivation is not a problem, that a student would obviously want to learn a particular skill. However, some students do not always share instructors' goals for learning. A student who is not motivated at all will not practice, and little or no learning can result. A motivated student devotes greater effort to the task, with more serious practice and longer practice periods, leading to more effective learning. How can instructors provide this motivation to learn?

Introduce Skills to Provide Motiva...

It is important to s... a skill would be useful for the st... n. Many high school students a... iented to the traditional team ... as basketball and baseball, an... ult to be interested in other a... ffective instructor might poi... here will come a time in the stu... when team games are less imp... more recreational skills will be use... , golf, tennis, and canoeing). Providing a future application gives the students more purpose and direction in learning. Along similar lines, when I was in high school, an instructor showed our class a movie of Olympic-level volleyball before an instructional unit in that activity. I was shocked that volleyball was far more than that silly game we had played in elementary school, and I developed a strong desire to learn it. Such motivational techniques are widely varied and easily applied, and seem to be used by the most successful instructors.

Goal Setting for Learning

Another important motivational method is **goal setting**, where learners are encouraged to adopt performance goals for themselves. This method has had numerous applications, particularly in industry, and it has strong implications for learning in sport and physical education (Locke & Latham, 1985). In an experiment by Locke and Bryan (1966), subjects were given instructions either to set standards (goals) for themselves or simply to "do your best." Figure 8.1 shows the benefits of the goal setting instructions. There was

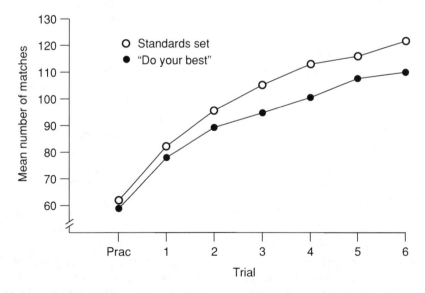

Figure 8.1 The effect of goal setting on performance. Learners encouraged to set their own goals outperformed those told only to "do your best." (Adapted by permission from Locke & Bryan, 1966.)

no transfer test here, so it is not clear that these were relatively permanent learning effects (see chapter 7), but at least it is clear that there were strong benefits for performance.

Apparently, being forced to commit oneself to a goal is strongly motivating. The instructor should encourage the learner to set realistic goals, ones that can be reasonably achieved with practice and effort. The learner can become discouraged by not even approaching goal levels that are too high. Yet, goals that are too easy to meet can result in lack of motivation.

Presenting the Task: Conveying the General Idea

After giving various motivational instructions, it is time to deal in more specific ways with the particular skill to be learned. The first step is to use a method that gives the student an overall picture of the skill, including a description of generally how to attempt the new action. Several procedures are useful in this regard, such as instructions, modeling, and demonstrations.

Instructions

Giving instructions is a feature of nearly every teaching setting. Instructions are usually spoken (although they could be written) and provide information about the very first aspects of the skill. How the skill will be used in the game and tips on where and how to stand, how to hold the apparatus or other implement, what to look at, and what to do are frequently parts of the typical instruction. Information about what is likely to happen also helps, such as a statement like "You will feel a firm tug in your shoulders during this movement." Considering the difficulty students have with no instructions at all, these procedures are critical for raising skill level in very early practice. Simple, direct statements

PRACTICAL APPLICATIONS

1. Try to determine what stage of learning the student is in, so you can adjust teaching methods and instructions accordingly.
2. Use demonstrations, film loops, videotapes, photos, or other aids freely during the verbal-cognitive stage, when the learner is just getting the idea.
3. For initial orientation to a skill, describe when or how a particular skill is used, perhaps by referring to a famous athlete.
4. Enhance motivation for learning by explaining how a particular skill can be useful later in life in various recreational settings.
5. Use goal setting to generate student motivation because students bring more effort to the task when committed to achieving their own goals.
6. Rather than selecting the students' goals for them, encourage the students to select and become committed to their own realistic goals.

that start people off on the right track are certainly effective in the long run, too.

Instructions can be overdone, though. One problem is that words are a relatively crude, imprecise way of describing the subtle aspects of movements, so verbal descriptions are probably best suited only for the most elementary features. Try describing the Fosbury Flop, a high-jumping technique, to people who have not seen it, and the problem will be obvious. Along similar lines, many advocate explaining skills in terms of their biomechanical, or physical, bases, using concepts such as transfer of momentum and action-reaction. Some of this may be useful, but it assumes that learners understand the physical principles well enough to apply them to the new skills. In any case, knowing such principles may not be very important for performance; circus dogs perform wonderful skills without very much sophistication in college physics.

Verbal instructions often provide too much information in a short period of time, so the learner has trouble remembering what was said when it comes time to practice. Recall that short-term memory for once-presented materials (chapter 2) is limited in capacity to a few items, with rapid forgetting (in about 30 s or so) and much interference from other information. Much of the instructions is lost by the time of the first performance attempt.

All this implies strongly that instructions should be brief and to the point, emphasizing one or two major concepts. Try to make instructions more meaningful by relating them to other things that the student has already learned, increasing transfer to the new skill. Spacing instructions throughout the first few minutes of practice—giving only the most elementary instructions first, then finer details as the practice continues—minimizes forgetting. All these considerations are particularly relevant for the younger learner, who is more limited than the adult in information-processing capacity.

Observational Learning: Demonstrations and Modeling

Good companions to prepractice instructions are various visual aids, such as still pictures of proper actions, film clips or videotapes of successful performances, and demonstrations by skilled students in the class or by the instructor (**modeling**). Skill information can be transmitted easily this way because it is not so limited by the use of words. This procedure comes under the general

PRACTICAL APPLICATIONS

1. Verbal instructions are useful in early learning, but only if they are straightforward and direct and do not present too many concepts.
2. Distribute verbal instructions throughout practice, emphasizing the most fundamental ones first and the less critical ones later.
3. Explaining even the most elementary biomechanical, physical, or physiological bases of actions is minimally useful in the initial stages of practice.
4. When in doubt, usually minimize verbal instructions and substitute active practice; have the student get the idea and try it.
5. Use previously learned movements or concepts in instructions to increase transfer to the new skill ("Hit the handball just as if you were throwing it").
6. Define key points that the learners can check for themselves later in practice, such as "straight elbow" in the golf backswing.

heading of **observational learning**, in which the learner gains information simply by watching another's performance. How observational learning works without active movement on the part of the learner is a question that has raised considerable debate. But there can be little doubt that a considerable amount of learning, particularly early in practice, comes from studying and imitating others' actions. Capitalizing on this in instructional settings is a good procedure.

Apparently, whether the model is a peer or a coach is only of minor importance. Whoever does the modeling must display the critical skill features. Of course, demonstrations and modeling cannot be effective if the observer is not paying attention or if the physical arrangement makes detecting the relevant information difficult. If the learner cannot see the demonstrated movement, or can see it only from behind, observational learning will suffer. Modeling can be used in conjunction with instructions, the teacher pointing out critical features as the action unfolds. Emphasizing how the hands are moving or how the feet are coordinated with the hands during a particular phase of the action can be effective.

Like instructions, models and demonstrations can provide too much information for the learner to focus on what is really critical at his or her stage of proficiency. It thus is usually wise to use cuing techniques, in which the instructor tells the learner what to observe and what not to observe. Saying to the learner, ''Don't focus on how hard the swing is for now but rather on how the hips lead the action of the arms,'' would be a useful cue.

BASIC PRINCIPLES OF PRACTICE

Assume that you have begun the actual (physical) practice phase and are now confronted with several decisions about how to organize practice. This section presents several important points in the design of the learning environment.

Most Important: Amount and Quality of Practice

It almost goes without saying that the most important variable for learning is practice itself. With the highest skill levels shown by champion athletes, the amount of time, effort, and practice that went into preparation is very impressive. For example, Kottke,

---

PRACTICAL APPLICATIONS

1. Supplement instructions with demonstrations, live modeling, videotape, film, or photographs of effective actions.
2. During a model's demonstration, the instructor should cue important points to direct the learner's attention to the most relevant aspects of the performance.
3. Suggesting what not to observe in the demonstration can be effective in directing attention to relevant aspects.
4. Alternate short periods of practice with demonstrations, allowing rest while new information is emphasized from the model.
5. In teaching children, try the simple statement ''Do this'' followed by a demonstration, minimizing complex instructions.
6. Employ models and demonstrations to demonstrate common mistakes, ineffective form, or faulty strategy, but probably not in the earliest stages of learning.

Halpern, Easton, Ozel, and Burrill (1978) estimated that across 15-year careers in their respective sports, a quarterback in professional football throws 1.4 million passes and a basketball player shoots 1.0 million baskets! It is clear that a high level of practice is critical for sophisticated skill development, so the athlete who really wants to be successful should be prepared to maximize the amount of practice. There's no easy way around it.

But the amount of practice time is not the only concern here. Certainly, the *quality* of this practice is critical, too. A student can exert much effort over many hours in ineffective practice, emerging with little to show for it except boredom and frustration. It is critical to organize and structure practice effectively. The next several sections cover some features of effective practice.

Learning Versus Performing During Practice

Perhaps it is obvious that, when learners acquire a new skill, they do so by doing something different than they had done earlier. The processes leading to learning require that the learner change something in the movement patterning, hopefully so the performance becomes more effective. Yet, when giving learners instructions or directions concerning what to do during practice, teachers and coaches frequently encourage them to "do your best" on each practice attempt. This generates two conflicting practice goals: *performing* as well as possible in practice (Goal 1) and *learning* as much as possible in practice (Goal 2).

Conflicting Goals During Practice

The learner who attempts to perform as well as possible (Goal 1) tends to be inhibited from modifying movements from attempt to attempt, which detracts from learning as much as possible (Goal 2). The approach for maximizing performance, repeating the most effective pattern discovered so far, is not effective for learning because it discourages experimentation. Some way to separate the processes inherent in these two goals seems necessary to make learning efficient.

Practice Sessions and Test Sessions

One way to separate these conflicting practice goals is to provide two fundamentally different activities during practice—practice sessions and test sessions (see Table 8.1).

Table 8.1 Learner Goals for Practice and Test Sessions

Practice goal	Self-test goal
Change movement pattern	Stabilize movement pattern
Search for optimal pattern	Use best previous pattern
Stress single-trial performance	Stress overall performance

Practice Sessions. First, provide practice sessions where you instruct the learners simply to avoid repeating what has been done earlier. Tell the learner to try different styles of movement control to discover some more effective pattern of action. You can guide the learning by suggesting specific ways to alter the movement, helping the learner eliminate inappropriate patterns. The learner should know that performance quality is not critical during this practice period, and that the only goal is to discover some new way to execute the skill that will be more effective in the long term.

Test Sessions. Of course, the measure of learning progress is a test of some kind. After several minutes in the practice session, the instructor could announce a switch to a test session, where the next five attempts are a "test." In the test session the learner performs as well as possible, using the best estimate of the movement pattern for the most proficient performance. After the test session the learner has some idea of his or her progress and can return to the practice mode to continue searching for more effective movement patterning. Such tests could be formally evaluated and graded, but they would also be effective if given only for the student's own information. Why not have the learner write down his or her own test scores, perhaps even charting the progress over several days or weeks?

Summary Break

Dividing a class session into practice and test phases has several benefits:

- This division separates the conflicting goals of practicing and performing, making each more effective.
- Practice periods become more efficient because the student can attempt many different movement styles without worrying about performance.
- Self-test periods are motivating, giving learners information about their rates of progress for comparisons with themselves or others.
- Dividing the session into different activities provides a break that helps keep the session interesting for the learner.

PRACTICAL APPLICATIONS

1. Divide a class period into alternating phases—practice phases for learning and self-test phases for students to evaluate their progress.
2. For a practice phase the goal is to try various approaches in a search for new movement patterns, deemphasizing the goal of performing well.
3. For a self-test phase the goal is to perform as well as possible, using the most effective methods discovered to that point.
4. Alternate practice and test phases frequently to eliminate repetition and boredom.
5. To enhance motivation, have the student keep progress records on these self-tests.

Guidance Techniques

Guidance techniques are a large class of common methods in which the learner is guided in various ways through the movement patterning. They have several goals, the main one being to reduce errors and ensure that the proper pattern is carried out. This is particularly important when the movement is dangerous, as in gymnastics, where harmful falls can be prevented by various spotting methods, or in swimming, where fearful beginners can use flotation devices. Guidance is also useful for training with expensive equipment, where mistakes can be costly as well as dangerous, as with learning to drive a car or fly an airplane.

Types of Learning Guidance

Guidance methods vary widely in different settings. Some forms of guidance are very loose, giving the learner only slight aids to

Physical guidance can be useful, but if overdone it can interfere with the natural progress of the movement, inhibiting learning.

performance. Examples are the coach who talks the learner through a football play and the dance instructor who gives verbal cues to help the student remember a new dance sequence. Other forms of guidance are far more powerful and invasive. An instructor can physically constrain the learner's movements, such as the therapist who channels the patient's movements into the proper path, preventing a serious fall. There are also many mechanical performance aids that physically constrain movement patterns.

Each method provides the learner with some kind of temporary aid during practice. The hope is that learning, as measured by performance in the future without this aid, will be enhanced. Research has provided a reasonably clear picture of when, under what conditions, and for what kinds of skills guidance procedures should be most and least effective.

How Effective Is Guided Practice?

A classical experiment giving much insight into some of the processes involved in guided practice was conducted three decades ago by Annett (1959). He had subjects learn to produce a given amount of pressure against a hand-operated lever. During the movement one group of subjects received additional visual guidance on a display showing the amount of pressure currently being exerted in relation to the goal pressure, whereas another group of learners did not. During practice the guidance (feedback) facilitated performance. However, on a retention test with the guidance removed, the guidance group performed very poorly, with some subjects pressing so hard on the apparatus that it was damaged! Subjects who had learned the task with this aid were unable to perform without it. (See also the section on Dependency Producing Properties of Feedback in chapter 10.)

This points up an important principle of guided practice. Guidance, almost by definition, is effective for performance when it is present during practice. After all, guidance, such as helping a beginner through a golf swing, is designed to help the performer make the correct action, to prevent errors, to aid in confidence, and so on, so there is little surprise that performance, as measured in the acquisition phase, benefits from guidance. But the real test of guidance effectiveness is how well subjects do without it, and here is where guidance procedures often fail. When guidance is removed for retention tests, performance usually falls to the level of, or often below, that of a group that never had guidance at all. That is, guidance is not a very effective variable for learning.

These are the important points to remember about guidance:

- Guidance is very powerful and effective when applied in practice, that is, guidance is a strong performance variable.
- In a retention test with guidance removed, learners who received earlier guidance perform no better than, or even worse than, learners who did not; that is, guidance is not a strong learning variable.

Processes in Guided Practice and Retention

How can these principles of guidance be understood? Probably the best interpretation is that during practice where guidance is present, the learner relies too strongly on its powerful performance enhancing properties, which actually changes the task in several ways. Physical guidance modifies the feel of the task. When the instructor tells the learner what to do, decision making changes. Also, the learner is not provided the opportunity to experience errors, nor to correct errors either during the present movement or on the next movement.

Because guidance facilitates performance so well, the learner comes to rely on guidance as a crutch. That is, guidance tends to block practice on component processes that are necessary when the guidance is later withdrawn. The problem is that the learner seems to be doing fine as long as the guidance is present. But the criterion is usually skill performance with guidance removed, as in a future match or game. The learner will have failed to acquire several skill aspects necessary to perform in the retention test or competition without guidance.

On the other hand, the learner who does not receive guidance, forced to struggle somewhat more during practice, does not perform as well during the acquisition phase. But this person *learns* the capability to perform effectively without guidance and thus outperforms guided learners on a retention test.

Notice that this interpretation is really a statement of the specificity view discussed earlier (chapter 6). If guided practice changes the task requirements markedly, this task is not really the same task it was under the unguided conditions. If these modifications are large (as in very strong physical guidance procedures), then practice on the guided version can be thought of as involving practice on a different task than practice on the unguided version. Under the specificity view, practice on the guided version will be effective for a retention test under guided conditions, but it will not be effective for a retention test performed under unguided conditions. This fits with the principles of transfer discussed later in this chapter, where transfer tends to be maximized when tasks are similar. Guided and unguided versions of the same task are thought of as being dissimilar, leading to poor transfer between them.

Conditions Where Guidance Can Be Effective for Learning

The previous sections suggest that guidance is not effective for learning and should be avoided as a practice method. However, there are several situations where guidance can benefit performance and learning.

Early Practice. In very early practice, when the learner is developing the most primitive ideas of the task, guidance procedures could be useful. They help present the basic features of the skill, give a rough indication of what to do, and start the learner on the way to making the first attempt on his or her own. Guidance procedures can easily be

Spotting in gymnastics. The spotter provides only as much help to the performer as needed.

overdone, however, and should therefore be removed as quickly as possible, probably at about the point that the learner is just capable of performing the task independently.

Dangerous Tasks. Another exception is dangerous situations. Physical guidance, such as the spotting belts frequently worn by gymnasts learning new stunts, can prevent a slip or fall that could cause an injury. In the absence of a belt, instructors or other students can provide physical guidance at critical points in the skill, such as when a gymnast is being helped through a movement. As the performer gains proficiency, the amount of guidance can gradually be reduced, and the instructor can still quickly intervene to prevent a fall.

These procedures also have the advantage that they decrease fear, which is the "great crippler" in such activities. Learners confident that they will not be injured during attempts can concentrate more effectively on the movement pattern and how to produce it more smoothly and efficiently. This works very well in beginning swimming, where a partner with a long pole walks along the pool deck, holding the pole just above the learner's hip. As long as everything goes well, the pole is not used. The learner who requires assistance, though, can simply reach up to grasp it. The pole can actually continuously touch the severely frightened learner's hip so he or she can be certain it is there. Such methods give a secure, relaxed learning atmosphere, but one without various devices (e.g., floats) that interfere with the dynamics and feel of the strokes. As before, guidance should be removed as quickly as possible to prevent the learner from acquiring a dependence on it.

Mental Practice

One useful addition to the collection of activities in a practice session is to ask the learner to mentally rehearse skills to be learned, without actual overt physical practice. In such **mental practice**, sometimes called mental rehearsal, the learner thinks about the

■ Spotting belts can be very helpful for guiding gymnasts through dangerous stunts.

PRACTICAL APPLICATIONS

1. Use physical or verbal guidance procedures to help the learner overcome skill patterning problems in the earliest learning stages.
2. Because the feel and the dynamics of the movement are usually markedly altered by guidance, thus changing the task, use guidance sparingly.
3. Withdraw guidance as soon as the learner can perform the skill independently to avoid a learned dependence on the guidance.
4. Employ guidance in dangerous tasks to prevent injury, but withdraw it as soon as the learner can perform the skill safely without it.
5. Use guidance procedures to reduce the learner's fear of injury, thus providing more relaxed and enjoyable practice and making learning more efficient.

skills being learned, rehearses the steps in a sequential skill (e.g., a skating or dance sequence), and imagines doing the actions successfully, perhaps even winning the state championship.

Can this method actually contribute to learning? Until the past few years, scientists in the motor learning field had very much doubted that learning could actually be accomplished through mental practice. The understanding of practice and learning at the time held that overt physical action was essential for learning. It was difficult to understand how any learning could occur without movement, active practice, and feedback from the movement to signal errors.

However, evidence from various experiments has convincingly demonstrated that mental practice procedures actually generate motor learning (see Feltz & Landers, 1983,

for a review). Figure 8.2, from Rawlings, Rawlings, Chen, and Yilk (1972), shows that a mental practice group learned almost as much as a physical practice group and far more than a no-practice control group (see also the Highlight Box on mental practice on page 185). Other studies show that randomly alternating mental practice with physical practice, rather than giving it in a blocked fashion, is even more effective for learning (Gabriele, Hall, & Lee, 1989).

How Does Mental Practice Work?

There are several theories of how mental practice generates new task learning. One early idea was that mental practice facilitated the cognitive-symbolic elements of the skill. For example, a tennis player could decide what shot to take, a baseball player could think how to grip the bat, and a skier could rehearse the sequence of turns in the ski run. These cognitive elements were thought to be present only in the very early stages of learning (the cognitive stage discussed earlier); thus, mental practice effects were limited to early learning as well. Although learning cognitive elements is undoubtedly a major factor in mental practice, evidence such as that in Figure 8.2 suggests that there is more than just this.

Another theory concerns evaluating possible movements and mentally experiencing their consequences. For a complex game, such as basketball or American football, you can rehearse a particular play, imagining what your opponents will do and how you will react. Imagining different execution patterns and the consequences of each provides a kind of strategy learning useful later in actual practice.

An older notion is that the motor system produces contractions of the participating musculature, but far smaller than the size necessary to produce action. With this view, the "movement" is carried out in the central

The Curious Benefits of Mental Practice

One of the most convincing examples of mental practice's effectiveness for learning comes from an experiment by Rawlings, Rawlings, Chen, and Yilk (1972). The task was the famous pursuit-rotor tracking task, where the subject attempts to maintain contact between a handheld stylus and a rotating target on a turntable-like surface. Performance is scored as time-on-target, the time out of a 30-s trial that the stylus contacted the target. In the experiment, all subjects had overt physical practice on Day 1. Three groups of subjects were treated differently for the next 8 days. One group had more physical practice as before. A second group received no practice. The third group had mental practice, where the subjects were instructed to imagine successful performance at the task. All groups were then tested again on Day 10.

The data from the three groups are shown in Figure 8.2. The physical practice condition showed the typical day-to-day increases for this task. The Day 10 data, which can be considered a retention test of learning, showed that the no-practice condition resulted in almost no improvement over the 8 experimental days. The interesting finding is that the mental practice group improved almost as much as the physical practice group, far more than the no-practice group. This task involves acquiring new patterns of coordination in order to follow the target, not simply learning new verbal-symbolic aspects of the task, so such data go a long way to convince us that mental practice was contributing to real motor learning. The challenge has been to understand how such learning improvements could occur without physical practice or feedback about errors.

nervous system, providing "practice" even without body movement. Although EMGs show some evidence of weak electrical activities during mental practice, these EMGs do not resemble those from the actual movements very closely, making it difficult to understand how these electrical activities alone could enhance learning.

Finally, mental practice can build confidence, allowing the performer to gain control of harmful emotional states such as stress and anxiety. For years many champion skiers, gymnasts, quarterbacks, and others have engaged in mental rehearsal before important competitions. Imagining successful performance tends to produce relaxation; the person focuses on what is required to perform well rather than harmfully focusing on what might happen if performance fails. Although these processes have mainly been related to high-level athletes, they could also apply to novices, whose levels of anxiety and fear can also be very high.

Mental practice could have effects at several places in the motor system, as indicated in the conceptual model in Figure 8.3. Any one or several of these hypotheses could correctly explain mental practice effects. Whatever the final explanation, it is clear that mental practice enhances skill learning.

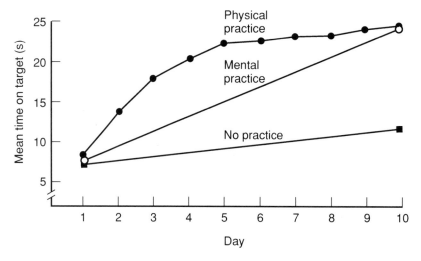

Figure 8.2 Some effects of mental practice on performance and learning. Mental practice produced nearly as much learning as physical practice. (Reprinted by permission from Rawlings, Rawlings, Chen, & Yilk, 1972.)

These hypotheses for mental practice efficacy can be summarized as follows (see also Gabriele et al., 1989; Heuer, 1985):

- Mental practice could involve practicing the cognitive, symbolic, decision-making aspects of the skill.
- Mental practice could allow the learner to rehearse possible actions and strategies, estimating the probable outcomes in the actual situation.
- Mental practice could allow minute muscular contractions, far too small to produce action, that simulate the real movement.
- Mental practice could build confidence for subsequent performance, allowing effective management of stress and anxiety.

How to Use Mental Practice

The learner needs to be instructed carefully in the methods of mental practice. It is not enough simply to suggest that the learner go somewhere and practice mentally, but systematic procedures should ensure that such practice is done effectively.

The learner should move to a quiet, relaxing place, and focus clearly on the movement task. This in itself requires some practice because it is difficult to be calm and focused on command. The learner should imagine the event in as vivid a way as possible, even in color and with all of the sounds and other sensations of the actual event. The movement should be allowed to unfold in real time, the sequence of activities imagined clearly as they progress in the skill. Finally, the learner should imagine success in the action, avoiding images of failure and seeing him- or herself accomplishing the goal. For additional tips for maximizing mental practice, see Orlick (1986, 1990).

Performed this general way, mental practice is a particularly effective way to rehearse skills. Such activities can take place almost anytime, such as between practice trials, between days of practice while relaxing at home, and when riding to and from school on the bus. Mental practice requires no apparatus, allowing a large group of learners to

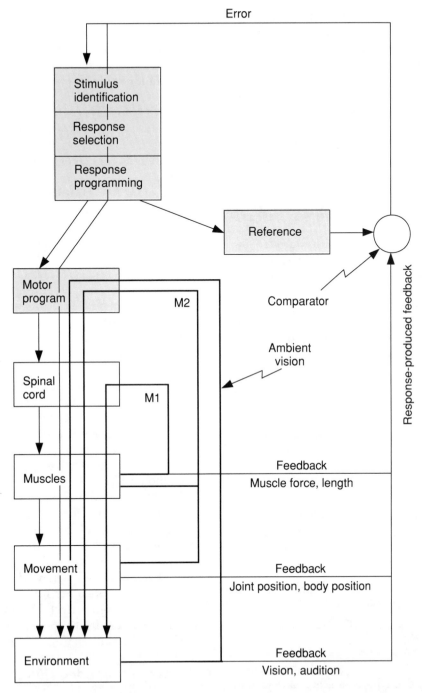

Figure 8.3 The conceptual model of human performance, highlighting the major processes where mental practice is thought to occur.

perform it at the same time. There is no doubt, though, that some combination of mental practice and physical practice is more effective than either alone, and the clever instructor will find ways to intertwine the two practice modes to provide maximal gains, such as urging mental practice during the rest phase between trials of a fatiguing task or to break up a long string of repetitious physical practice.

Whole Versus Part Practice

Some skills are enormously complex, such as a gymnast's routine and the activities in basketball; even pole-vaulting and javelin-throwing seem very complex to novices. Clearly, in such situations the instructor cannot present all aspects of the skill at once for practice because the student would be overwhelmed and would likely grasp almost none of it. A frequent approach is to divide the task into meaningful units that can be isolated for separate **part practice**. The goal is to integrate these practiced units into the whole skill for later performance. This is not as simple as it may sound because there are several factors that make integrating the learned units back into the whole skill somewhat difficult.

Therefore, the question is how to create subunits of skills and how they should be practiced for maximum transfer to the whole skill. It is a simple matter to divide skills into parts. You could separate a gymnastics routine into the component stunts; you could divide the pole-vault into run-up, pole-plant, and vault segments. Each subpart could even be divided further. But the real question is whether these parts, practiced in isolation, will be effective for learning the whole skill, which is the overall goal. Thus, part practice is based on the transfer of learning principles defined in chapter 6 (see also chapter 9): Will the subunit transfer to the whole task that contains it? How much (if any) class time should be spent on part practice, and would this time be more effectively spent practicing the whole task?

At first glance the answers to these questions seem obvious. Because the part of the task practiced in isolation seems the same as that part in the whole task, the transfer from the part to the whole task would seem to be almost perfect. This may be so in certain cases, but there are other situations in which transfer is far from perfect. These differences in part practice effectiveness depend on the nature of the skill.

Serial Skills of Long Duration

In many serial skills, the learner's problem is to organize a set of activities into the proper order, as with the gymnast who assembles a routine of stunts and the ski racer who must execute several turns in a row. Practicing the specific subtasks is usually effective in transferring to whole sequences. Part transfer works best in serial tasks of very long duration and where the actions (or errors) of one part do not influence the actions of the next part. That is, part practice is most effective when the parts are performed relatively independently in the whole skill. The learner can devote more practice time to the troublesome parts without practicing the easier elements, making practice more time-efficient.

However, in many serial skills in sport, performance on one part frequently determines the movement that must be made on the next part. If the ski racer comes out of a turn too low and fast, this affects the approach for the next turn. Little positioning errors on the beam in one move determine how the gymnast must perform the next one. If a part-part interaction is large, as it might be if the sequence is run off quickly, modifying a given action as a function of performance on a previous action is an important component of the skill. However, interactions between parts of the whole skill cannot be practiced and learned in isolated part practice. The gymnast might be able to do all of the individual stunts in her routine, but she still might not perform an effective routine in a meet because she never learned to modify each component movement based on the previous one. The relationship between the degree of interaction between the task's components and the effectiveness of part practice is depicted in Figure 8.4.

Discrete Skills of Short Duration

Any skill is in some sense serial because certain pieces of it come before other pieces, such as hitting a baseball, which contains step, hip-turn, and swing elements. At some point, though, these individual parts, when viewed separately, cease to be parts of the

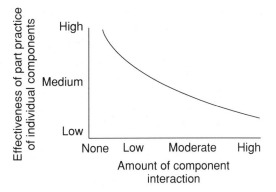

Figure 8.4 Part practice effectiveness decreases markedly as the interaction among task components increases.

whole skill. It is as if dividing a swing into smaller and smaller arbitrary parts destroys a critical aspect that allows the parts to be characterized as parts of a swing; that is, the division seems to disrupt the essential features of the action. Practice at these subparts could be ineffective, even detrimental, to learning the whole task.

Several experiments suggest that practicing parts of a discrete task in isolation transfers little if any to the whole task (e.g., Lersten, 1968; Schmidt & Young, 1987), especially if the task is rapid and ballistic in nature. This is probably related to the fact that the components in rapid tasks usually interact strongly, which means less effective transfer (Figure 8.4). In fact, transfer from the part to the whole can even be negative in certain cases, so practicing the part in isolation could be worse for the whole task than not practicing at all!

This evidence suggests that when very rapid skills are broken down into arbitrary parts, these parts become so changed from the "same" parts in the whole task that the part practice contributes very little to the whole. In tasks like hitting a golf ball, for example, practicing the backswing separately from the forward swing changes the dynamics of the action at the top of the back-swing, which is dominated by actively lengthening muscles whose springlike properties allow the downswing to be smooth and powerful. Therefore, practicing the back-swing in isolation, which eliminates the role of these springlike muscle properties, is quite different from the same backswing in the context of the whole skill.

Motor Programs and the Specificity Principle

According to the motor program concept introduced earlier, quick actions are controlled essentially open-loop, with the decisions about the action's structure being programmed in advance. Performing only a part of this action, particularly if the part has different dynamics (e.g., in the golf swing) when performed in isolation, requires using a different program, one that is responsible for only the part. Practicing this part program contributes to performance of the part in isolation, but it will not contribute to production of the whole movement, which is based on a different motor program. Thus, in part practice the learner develops two separate movement programs—one for the part and one for the whole task. This is consistent with Henry's (1959) specificity view of movement learning, in which isolating a part and changing it slightly to practice it separately shifts the underlying abilities to the point that it is no longer related to the original part in context of the whole skill (see chapter 6).

Progressive Part Practice

Even with very rapid actions, though, some part practice might be helpful, particularly if the action's elements are many in number and provide difficulty for the learner to sequence properly (as in the approach for bowling or javelin throwing). Very early part practice might be beneficial. However, to minimize the problems of learning actions that do not transfer to the whole, many instructors use **progressive part practice**. In this method the parts of a complex skill are presented separately, but the parts are integrated into larger and larger parts, and finally into the whole, as soon as they are acquired.

Gymnasts often use a practice method where Trial 1 involves the last stunt in a routine (the dismount), Trial 2 adds the move just previous to it, Trial 3 adds the next earlier movement, and so on, until a long sequence of moves is strung together. In other skills it is usually best to begin practicing the whole task as soon as it can be executed reasonably well, avoiding practicing the parts in isolation. Of course, for very slow, serial tasks, in which the parts do not interact with each other, part practice will be effective (Figure 8.4), but for rapid actions, shifting the learner quickly to the whole action is best.

The principles of part practice can be easily summarized:

- For very slow, serial tasks with no component interaction, part practice on the difficult elements is very efficient.
- For very fast, programmed actions, practice on the parts in isolation is seldom useful and can even be detrimental to learning.
- The more the components of a task interact with each other, the less the effectiveness of part practice.

Scheduling Practice and Rest Phases

Certainly, scheduling practice is a major concern in designing a program of instruction. This includes how many days per week skills should be practiced, whether to provide lay-off days, how much practice to give on each day, and how much rest to provide during

PRACTICAL APPLICATIONS

1. For a serial task of very long duration, have the learner practice the most troublesome parts in isolation, later switching to the whole task.
2. If the task has parts that interact strongly with each other, have the learner practice these parts together to learn their interactions.
3. Be careful using separate practice of two simultaneous parts of a skill (e.g., hand and foot motion in dance), because the coordination between them cannot be learned when they are separated.
4. In a very rapid skill, where the action appears to be controlled as a single programmed unit, never use part practice, and have the learner practice the whole task from the outset.
5. In a very complex action, beginning with part practice can be useful for a short period, but employ progressive part methods to reach the whole action as quickly as possible.

the practice period so fatigue does not become a problem. Some of these questions have been studied in the laboratory, revealing interesting and useful implications.

How Often to Practice

In supervising the long-term practice of movement skills, as in coaching an athletic team, you must first decide how often per week the learners must practice. On the one hand, your goal as a coach is usually to prepare the learners maximally in a fixed amount of time before the first meet or game. In some activities, the number of weeks of practice before the competitive season is limited by the rules. This emphasis would suggest providing as much practice as possible per week, concentrating it to maximize the practice time.

However, as shown by Baddeley and Longman (1978) with typing skills, there is undoubtedly some upper limit to the amount of practice per day (2 hours was too long) because long practice periods can be very tiresome, with minimal gains as a result. In other skills where there are various ways of breaking up the practice (different plays in football, different events in track and field), the amount of practice per day could probably be increased without loss of efficiency. An interesting point in the Baddeley and Longman study was that the most popular practice schedule (2 hours per day) was the one that produced the *least* learning, so students do not always know which procedures are best in terms of the overall goal of learning.

Provided that the amount of practice per day is reasonable, there is no evidence that practicing every day is less effective than, for example, practicing every other day. Even if negative effects were present, they would likely be relatively unimportant relative to the need to produce effective learning quickly, such as to prepare for the season opener with the Bearcats in 4 weeks. Of course, practicing every day for months or years can lead to boredom and burnout. But for most common tasks, a reasonable amount every day is highly effective for learning because there is ample opportunity to rest and evaluate one's performance on a given practice day before turning to the next. An exception should probably be made for tasks that produce extreme muscle soreness; more between-practice rest is needed. Overall it is safe to say that for most learning environments, providing practice as often as is practical generally maximizes learning and does not lead to motivational or other problems in learning.

Work and Rest Periods During a Practice Session

Unlike the questions raised concerning scheduling practice over a week, issues concerning organizing practice and rest during a single practice session have been studied a great deal in the laboratory. For the purposes here, we can define two classes of practice, based on the relative amounts of practice and rest provided, called massed and distributed practice in the literature.

Massed practice provides relatively little rest between trials. For example, if a task has practice trials 30 s long, a massed practice schedule might call for rest periods of only 5 s or perhaps no rest at all (so-called continuous practice). On the other hand, **distributed practice** calls for much more rest, perhaps with the rest period between trials being as long as a trial itself (30 s in this example). There is no fixed dividing line between massed and distributed practice, but massed practice generally has reduced rest between practice trials, whereas distributed practice has more rest.

Researchers interested in massed and distributed practice (see Lee & Genovese, 1988, for a recent review) have generally been concerned with effects of physical and particularly mental fatiguelike states on learning effectiveness. For a given number of practice trials, decreasing the amount of rest between trials reduces the time available for dissipation of fatigue, degrading performance on the next practice trial and perhaps interfering with learning processes operating on this trial. Many experimenters used a fixed number of practice trials in an acquisition session, varied the amount of rest between these trials, and then measured learning on a retention test under identical conditions of practice. It turns out that the principles governing the effects of these work and rest schedules are different for discrete and continuous tasks.

Discrete Tasks. Nearly all the massed practice experiments have involved long-duration continuous tasks (see the next section), but a few have had relatively rapid discrete tasks. Generally, when the task involves performance trials that are only a few tenths of a second, as in a throw or a kick, it is very difficult to make the rest periods short enough to affect performance. In the laboratory, even when the rest periods were made as short as 300 ms, seemingly far shorter than for any real-world practice session, there has been either no decrement in performance or learning or perhaps even slight advantages for massed conditions (see Carron, 1967; Lee & Genovese, 1988). It is best to say that for these discrete tasks, such as shooting a basketball or fielding a baseball, there is no evidence that reducing the rest time through massed practice degrades learning, and it may even benefit learning in some cases.

Continuous Tasks. By far most massed and distributed practice research has involved continuous skills analogous to real-world tasks such as swimming or cycling. In these tasks, fatiguelike states have much more opportunity to build up within a trial, so decreasing the rest between trials has larger effects on recovery from fatigue and on subsequent performance. This can be seen in Stelmach (1969), where two groups of subjects on a Bachman ladder-climb task had either 0 s or 30 s rest between trials. Figure 8.5 shows that decreasing the rest between trials degraded performance greatly and slowed the rate of improvement during the acquisition session. However, when subjects were allowed to rest for 4 min and then were given a transfer test with 30 s rest between trials, most of the difference between conditions had disappeared. Generally, this and numerous other experiments allow the conclusion that massed practice degrades performance but affects learning as measured on a transfer test only slightly. Most of the

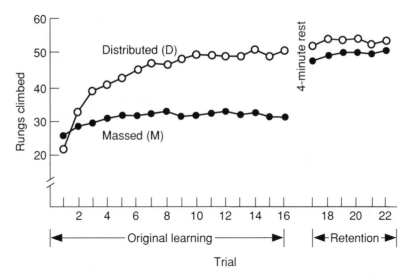

Figure 8.5 Performing and learning the Bachman ladder task under massed and distributed practice (0 s and 30 s rest between trials in acquisition). All subjects were then tested with 30 s rest in a transfer test of amount learned. (Reprinted by permission from Stelmach, 1969.)

effect of reduced rest in practice is due to temporary, fatiguelike processes that dissipate quickly with rest, and these processes appear not to degrade learning very much.

| Summary ◇ Break |

These principles of massed and distributed practice can be summarized by stating that reducing the rest between practice trials generally has the following effects (Lee & Genovese, 1988):

- For rapid, discrete tasks, almost no effect on performance or learning and maybe even a slight benefit to learning
- For long-duration continuous tasks, strong detrimental effects on performance during practice because of buildup of fatiguelike states
- For continuous tasks, only slight negative effects on learning as measured on retention or transfer tests

Theoretical and Practical Implications.
These findings raise a number of tough ques-

tions for understanding the nature of practice, particularly the role of fatigue in learning. By the end of the practice period, the subject under massed conditions is far more fatigued than the subject under distributed conditions, which is evident in reduced performance (Figure 8.5, left). Then how can the subject perform so poorly during practice, yet *learn* essentially as much as the subject under more rested conditions? It is not clear why, but it appears that fatigue is not a particularly potent variable for reducing learning—it mainly affects performance temporarily.

There are many practical implications of this research. First, because even very high levels of fatigue lead to very efficient learning, fatigue during the practice session is not a worrisome problem. It would be good to explain to the learner that even though fatigue may come during practice, he or she is still learning effectively. Inform the student that the learning gained under fatigue will be evident in the future, after the temporary fatigue effects are gone. However, in a task that is relatively dangerous (e.g., gymnastics), fatigue can be a problem, generating a sloppy performance that could lead to a serious accident. The instructor should be careful that such a practice session contains sufficient rest for performance not to be seriously degraded by fatigue.

Practice Periods of Fixed Duration. For various theoretical reasons, most investigators have studied massed, as opposed to distributed, practice in experiments with fixed numbers of practice trials. The problem is different for the teacher or coach, where the practice period is fixed in length (e.g., 45 min) and the concern is to maximize learning in the time available. There is a trade-off: For a continuous task, there is a slight learning advantage with relatively rested practice. However, increasing the rest between trials decreases the number of trials included in the fixed-length period, and reducing practice reduces learning. So, the problem is to find a combination of practice and rest that provides as much practice time as possible without producing so much fatigue that learning is degraded.

Graw (1968) studied different combinations of practice and rest, so the percentage of time actually in physical practice was either 20, 30, 40, 57, or 77% of the total 30-min practice period. He examined this schedule with two different continuous tasks—the stabilometer balance board and the Bachman ladder task—and tested for learning on a transfer test given on the second day. Figures 8.6 a and b, show the results. For the stabilometer task (where smaller scores are better), the optimal condition for learning was that with 57% of the time in practice (see Figure 8.6a). For the Bachman ladder task (larger scores are better), the 30% practice condition was best (see Figure 8.6b). It is clear from these results that there is no single optimal practice-rest ratio for all learning tasks: The ladder task was learned most effectively

when most of the time was spent resting, whereas the stabilometer task was learned best when most of the time was spent practicing.

What are the task differences that determine which schedule is most effective for learning? One important factor is the energy requirement of the task. In the Bachman ladder task, the energy costs associated with high-level performance are relatively large because the learner must climb the freestanding ladder quickly and repetitively for the trial's duration. Furthermore, in this task the energy costs increase with increasing skill level, the performers climbing higher and faster as they improve. In the stabilometer task, on the other hand, the energy requirements are relatively lower because

PRACTICAL APPLICATIONS

1. Before initiating training, classify tasks as continuous or discrete and in terms of likely energy costs.
2. With a discrete task, reduce the rest pause between trials to increase the number of trials in a practice session.
3. Long practice periods each day can be detrimental to learning, especially if only one task is being learned and practice can become tedious (e.g., place kicking in football).
4. For a continuous task with high energy requirements (e.g., hurdling), choose a practice schedule with relatively more time in rest than in practice.
5. In a high-energy continuous task, give demonstrations or urge mental practice during the relatively long rest periods to utilize overall practice time more effectively.
6. For a dangerous task, provide relatively more rest so fatigue does not result in accidents and injuries.

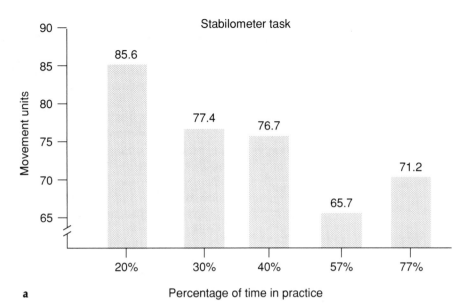

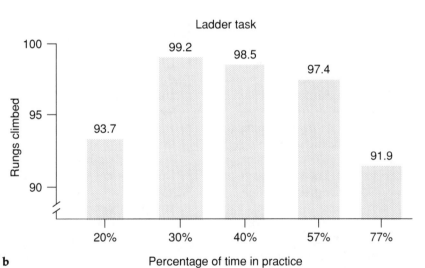

Figure 8.6 Performance on a Day-2 transfer test for groups with different percentages of total time spent in physical practice on Day 1, plotted for the stabilometer task (a) and the Bachman ladder task (b). (Adapted by permission from Graw, 1968.)

stable balancing requires very little movement of the major muscle groups. The energy costs in this task decrease with rising skill level, quite opposite to the Bachman ladder task. The high energy requirements of the Bachman task suggest that the performer would benefit from more rest, fatigue levels increasing markedly with more massed practice. The low energy costs of the stabilometer task allow more practice in a fixed period, with less time resting. There may be other relevant task dimensions here as well.

These findings underscore the need for the instructor to perform a task analysis to tailor the practice conditions to the various relevant task requirements. It is important for the instructors to know the tasks very well, understanding the energy costs as well as other difficulties the learner is likely to experience. These considerations guide decisions about practice organization.

 CHAPTER SUMMARY

As people practice they generally pass through three stages of learning: a verbal-cognitive stage, in which cognitive and decision-making processes predominate; a motor stage, where the movement patterns are better developed and actions become more proficient; and an autonomous stage, where the movements are refined and the performance starts to become automatic. Before practice the instructor can enhance learner motivation in several ways, such as by stating the importance of the skills to be learned and asking the learner to set his or her own performance goals. The learner can receive additional prepractice help through instructions, demonstrations, modeling, films, videos, and other procedures that define the skills to be learned.

Actual physical practice is critical in learning, of course, but it must be done effectively or much time will be wasted. Guidance techniques, where a learner is directed through the task either physically or verbally, are useful for very early learning, but they can be overdone if the learner becomes reliant on them. Mental practice, imagining a task without actual physical performance, is effective for learning, especially where the task demands much cognitive involvement.

Complex actions can be broken down into components for part practice, which is especially effective in slow, serial skills where the components do not interact strongly.

Long practice periods focusing on only one skill could become boring and should be avoided, but there is no reason to space practice periods by more than one day unless the learner develops physical problems (e.g., muscle soreness). Within a practice period, increasing the amount of rest between trials enhances learning slightly in continuous skills, but it has minimal effect in discrete skills. However, increased rest subtracts physical practice time from a practice session. There is no single optimal practice-rest ratio; this value varies for discrete versus continuous tasks and with the movements' energy requirements.

⬦ Checking Your Understanding

1. Distinguish the important features of the verbal-cognitive stage, the motor stage, and the autonomous stage of learning.
2. What procedures could you use to motivate a group of high school girls learning field hockey?
3. Describe some conditions under which you would want to use physical guidance for teaching golf putting.
4. How does mental practice enhance learning? Are its effects limited to enhancement of verbal-cognitive skill processes? Explain.
5. Make a list of 10 different sports skills and rank them according to how effective part practice would be for learning them. What is the most important feature that determines your ranking?
6. For what kinds of skills does the amount of rest provided between practice trials seem least important? Most important?

◇Key Terms

Definitions of the following terms appear on the page(s) shown in parentheses:

autonomous stage (p. 174)

distributed practice (p. 192)

goal setting (p. 175)

guidance (p. 180)

massed practice (p. 192)

mental practice (p. 183)

modeling (p. 177)

motor stage (p. 173)

observational learning (p. 177)

part practice (p. 197)

progressive part practice (p. 190)

verbal-cognitive stage (p. 173)

◇ Suggestions for Further Reading

Additional information on the motivating properties of goal setting in a variety of learning environments can be found in Locke and Latham (1985), and in Locke, Shaw, Saari, and Latham (1981). Research on mental practice phenomena has been reviewed by Feltz and Landers (1983) and by Heuer (1985), leading to several hypotheses about why mental practice is effective. More on the interesting topic of modeling has been provided by McCullagh, Weiss, and Ross (1989). Lee and Genovese (1988) have thoroughly reviewed the abundant literature on massed and distributed practice. More on part practice, and on issues related to this chapter generally, can be found in Schmidt (1987, 1988b, chapter 12).

Organizing and Scheduling Practice

PREVIEW

The skills instructor is puzzled and concerned. She has just finished teaching a unit of gymnastics in which her students were to learn 12 stunts during a series of 1-hour sessions. So her learners could concentrate fully on each stunt during the learning sessions the instructor decided to provide practice on a single stunt for repeated trials, then shift to a second stunt for more practice, and so on. The students seemed to perform relatively well during practice, but when the skills test was given a few weeks later, the students appeared to have lost much of what they had learned and did not perform well at all. Why could the students not retain the level of performance seen in practice? Should the instructor have given more practice? Was the practice scheduling not optimal?

This chapter continues chapter 8's theme of how to structure practice for effective learning. This chapter focuses on the actual organization of the practice sessions, showing how two or more tasks can be practiced together to facilitate learning and retention and how systematically varying practice of a given task increases generalizability. Some alternative goals of practice are also considered, such as developing automaticity and detecting errors. Also discussed are how instructional methods and simulators facilitate transfer to other tasks.

STUDENT GOALS

1. To understand the principles of randomizing practice for effective learning
2. To become familiar with methods for varying practice to increase generalizability
3. To recognize alternative practice goals of automaticity and error detection
4. To apply these principles to numerous real-world teaching situations

---

It comes as little surprise that increasing practice time, or increasing the efficiency of a given amount of practice time, is a major goal of instructors interested in practice effectiveness. Practice time is not the only factor, however: The quality of practice must also be considered. Thus, it is important to structure or organize a given amount of practice to maximize its effectiveness.

ORGANIZING PRACTICE

There are countless ways to organize practice, of course. Understanding how these variations affect learning and trade off with each other is potentially complicated. Yet, there are several common features of practice sessions that have been studied a great deal in the scientific literature, and understanding how these variables affect learning takes us a long way toward devising effective practices.

Practicing Several Tasks: Blocked and Random Practice

In many real-world settings, the instructor's goal is to teach more than a single skill in a week, often in a single practice period. Many different football plays may be presented and practiced within a session, for example; tennis serving and volleying as well as the more usual groundstrokes can all be practiced during the hour. The question confronting the teacher or coach is how to sequence the practice at these various tasks during the practice session to maximize learning. Two variations have powerful effects on learning: blocked and random practice.

Blocked and Random Practice Scheduling

Suppose that your student has three tasks (Tasks A, B, and C) to learn in a practice session, and that these tasks are reasonably different, such as three different gymnastics stunts, or tennis serves, volleys, and groundstrokes. A commonsense scheduling viewpoint would be to practice all trials of one task before shifting to the second, then to finish practice on the second before switching to the third. This is **blocked practice**, where all the trials of a given task (for that day) are completed before moving on to the next task. Blocked practice is typical of some drills where a skill is repeated over and over, with minimal interruption by other activities. This kind of practice seems to make sense in that it allows the learners to concentrate on one particular task at a time and refine and correct it.

In **random practice**, on the other hand, the order of task presentation is randomized, so that practice of the various tasks is interleaved, or mixed, across the practice period. The learner can rotate among the three example tasks so, in the most randomized case, the learner never practices the same task on two consecutive trials.

HIGHLIGHT

The Shea and Morgan Experiment

John Shea and Robyn Morgan (1979) conducted a groundbreaking experiment that revolutionized the way scientists think of the processes involved in practice. Following some of the original ideas of William Battig (1966), they had subjects practice three different tasks that involved rapid movements of the hand and arm, each task with a different predetermined sequence. One group of subjects practiced the tasks in a blocked order, where all Task A practice was completed before moving to Task B, which was completed before moving to Task C. Another group practiced in random order, where the trials of the three tasks were mixed randomly. Both groups had the same amount of practice on Tasks A, B, and C, but they differed only in the order in which these tasks were presented.

The results are presented in Figure 9.1. First notice that during acquisition the blocked condition was far more effective for performance (with faster times) than the random condition. Shea and Morgan tested for learning by conducting retention tests after 10 min and 10 days. Consider the retention test requiring random test trials, shown as the circles in the figure. There was a large advantage for the subjects who had learned the task under random conditions (open circles). This

suggests that, even though the blocked group outperformed the random group in acquisition, the random group learned more.

However, this result could have been due to the fact that the random group received practice under the same conditions in both acquisition and retention, giving them a special advantage in the retention test. This specificity hypothesis was tested by giving half the subjects a retention test under blocked conditions, shown as the squares in the figure. Again, the subjects who practiced under random conditions in acquisition (open squares) outperformed those who practiced under blocked conditions in acquisition (filled squares), contradicting the specificity hypothesis.

These data surprised scientists in the field by showing that even though random conditions result in poorer performance than blocked conditions in acquisition, random conditions produce more learning, regardless of whether the subsequent learning test was under random or blocked conditions. The challenge recently has been to understand how conditions that degrade practice performance can produce more learning, and considerable interest in this phenomenon has resulted from this early work.

What are some of the effects of these two different practice schedules on learning? Numerous recent experiments have generated very surprising findings that seem to contradict standard views on practice. The first of

these studies was done by Shea and Morgan (1979; some of this experiment's details are described in the Highlight Box in this section). Basically, two groups of subjects practiced three different rapid, sequential

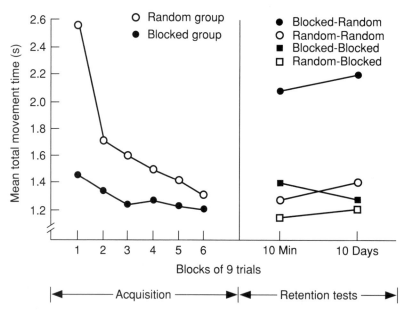

Figure 9.1 Performance on movement-speed tasks under random and blocked conditions. Relative amount learned is indicated on the transfer tests at the right. (Reprinted by permission from Shea & Morgan, 1979.)

arm-movement tasks under blocked or random trial conditions. As seen in the acquisition (left) portion of Figure 9.1, there was a clear performance advantage throughout practice for subjects under blocked conditions. When the subjects were given either a blocked or random retention test to evaluate learning, however, *random* practice always proved more effective than blocked practice. The surprising point is that even though random practice subjects performed poorer than blocked practice subjects in the acquisition phase, the random practice resulted in more learning. These findings have been validated several times in the laboratory and where physical education skills (three different serves in badminton) were to be learned in a classroom situation (Goode & Magill, 1986).

Some of the important points from this research can be summarized as follows:

- Blocked trial conditions lead to more effective practice performance than random conditions.

- However, when subjects are given a retention test, those who had random practice in acquisition outperform those who had blocked practice.
- Therefore, even though random practice is less effective during practice, it is better for learning than blocked conditions.
- The benefits of random practice are evident in both random and blocked retention tests, but especially in the former.

Why Random Practice Is So Effective

The research just discussed shows that organizing practice in a random way—which, relative to blocked practice, systematically degrades performance in the practice or acquisition phase—has beneficial effects on learning (as measured on a retention test). Most conventional viewpoints, which suggest that learning should be maximized by those conditions that make learners most proficient in practice, appear to be seriously challenged by these newer findings. There are several interesting new hypotheses to explain these results.

Forgetting, or Spacing, Hypothesis.

A forgetting hypothesis is one view of how random practice facilitates learning. This hypothesis holds that when the learner shifts from Task A to Task B, the processes generating the solution to Task B cause the solution generated on Task A to be forgotten. When Task A is presented again in a few trials, the learner must generate the solution anew; therefore, performance in practice is relatively poor. Yet, this solution-generation process is assumed to be beneficial for learning. In blocked practice, on the other hand, the performer remembers the solution generated on a given trial and applies it to the next trial, which minimizes the number of times the learner must generate new solutions. Therefore, performance on blocked practice is very good because the solution, once generated, is remembered on a series of trials. Yet, learning is poor because the learner does not have to repeatedly generate the solution to the task on every trial.

This view can be understood more fully with an analogy (after Cuddy & Jacoby, 1982). Suppose that as a 10-year-old you want to learn to do long-division in your head; the three tasks are 21/7, 18/2, and 12/4. In a blocked practice condition, your first trial is 21/7, and you struggle to come to the answer, 3. On the next trial you receive 21/7 again, but without going through the processes to generate the solution again, you simply remember the previous answer, 3. The same thing happens on Trial 3, and so on. Your performance in blocked practice becomes essentially perfect because you have remembered the solution. However, you have not been forced to do the mental processes necessary to *generate* the solution (except on the first trial, of course).

In a random practice condition, on the other hand, you receive 21/7, then 18/2, then 12/4 on Trials 1, 2, and 3, respectively. On Trial 4 you receive 21/7 again; by this time, you have forgotten the solution to this problem, so you are forced to generate it again. Your performance is much slower and more difficult now, but your learning is enhanced because you have been forced to generate solutions on every trial.

This is one way to understand how systematically degrading (relative to blocked practice) performance during practice actually enhances learning. Generating solutions has been termed **retrieval practice** because the learner is forced to retrieve the necessary performance information from long-term memory, actually receiving practice at the skill of retrieving (Bjork, 1975, 1979; Landauer & Bjork, 1978). Such retrieval practice leads to more effective performance in future situations requiring these retrieval operations.

What are the solutions for motor problems that correspond to the example's arithmetic solutions? Recall that in the conceptual model of human performance, when a movement is generated, a generalized motor program must be retrieved from memory, then parameters must be selected to define how to execute the movement (how rapid, forceful, large, etc.). The program and its selected parameters are a kind of solution. During random practice the learner must retrieve a different program and parameterize it on each trial because the previous selections have been forgotten; this facilitates practice at retrieval and parameterization of the programs. With blocked practice, the learner can use the same program and parameters almost without modification on successive trials, thereby avoiding the effortful regeneration processes critical for learning.

More Meaningful and Distinctive Learning.

Shea and Zimny (1983) interpreted the beneficial effects of random practice somewhat differently. They argued that changing the task on every random practice trial made the tasks more distinct from each other and more meaningful in the learner's memory. As revealed in subject interviews after the experiment, random condition subjects tended to relate the task structure to already learned materials (creating meaningfulness), such as discovering that Task B had essentially the shape of an upside-down Z. Also, they would make distinctions between tasks, such as ''Task A is essentially like Task C, except that the first part is reversed'' (creating distinctiveness). The blocked-practice subjects, on the other hand, tended not to make such statements, instead talking of running off the performances more or less automatically. Presenting a task repeatedly did not require that task differences and similarities be noted. According to this hypothesis, increased meaningfulness and distinctiveness produces more durable memories for the tasks and, thus, increased performance capabilities.

Summary Break

The beneficial effects of random practice over blocked practice appear to be due to several factors:

- Random practice causes the learner to forget the short-term solutions to the movement problem after each task change.
- Forgetting the short-term solution forces the learner to generate the solution again on the task's next trial, which is beneficial to learning.
- Random practice forces the learner to become more actively engaged in the learning process, by preventing simple repetitions of actions.
- Random practice gives the learner more meaningful and distinguishable memories of the various tasks, increasing memory strength and decreasing confusion among tasks.

Practical Implications of Random Practice Effects

One of the most important implications of the work on random practice concerns repetition. How often have you heard that learners should practice some task ''over and over until they get it right,'' as if a massive number of repetitions was somehow going to stamp in the correct movement?

Repetition. Repetition is deeply rooted in many traditional training methods, like with the basketball coach who has her players shoot 100 free throws at the end of practice or the tennis coach who has his students do serve after serve from the same position on

A common form of blocked practice, producing good performance at the time but not very effective for long-term learning.

the baseline. Hitting a bucket of golf balls at the driving range with the same club over and over is another example. All these situations essentially involve blocked practice, clearly shown in the laboratory research to be relatively ineffective for long-term learning.

Blocked Practice Gives a False Sense of Skill.

The paradox of blocked scheduling is that it makes performance very effective during practice without creating lasting learning. The learner achieves many minor, temporary adjustments in factors necessary for performance maximization (such as the level of arousal and the focus of attention), the environment is very stable and predictable, and the learner fine-tunes the movement parameters from trial to trial. This leads to artificially high levels of performance and leaves the learner with a false sense of accomplishment. My golfing friends tell me they can "do anything" at the driving range, implying that they have risen to some new level of skill. When they return to the golf course to test their skills, though, their games are no better than before the driving range practice. Why?

Criterion Version of the Skill.

One answer is that the criterion version of the skill—the particular actions and setting (or context) for which the learner is ultimately practicing—is frequently very different from the blocked practice done in practice. For example, the basketball free throw and the handball serve in competition (the criterion skills) are performed only once or twice at a time (except for rare penalty situations in basketball and a string of aces in handball). These skills are called for just after regular, varied court play.

On the golf course (the criterion context), one never hits two golf shots in a row with the same club (unless the ball goes in the lake on the first one), and most shots are preceded by a long walk (or a search for the ball, in my case). In golf the problem is to decide which club to use, how large a swing

to take, how to adjust the stance on the sloping ground, and so on, requiring the solution of a particular almost novel movement problem, not just a minor variation of what was done a few seconds earlier, as in blocked practice. Furthermore, the golfer gets only one chance to make this shot, with no possibility of modifying it on the next trial. Blocked practice at the driving range does not simulate the criterion skill very well. In most real-world skills, the criterion version is quite different from the skill repeated over and over in practice, as summarized in Table 9.1.

Table 9.1 Features of a Skill in Competition and in Blocked Repetitions in Practice

Competition (criterion) skill	Blocked, repetitious practice
Preceded by regular, varied play	Not preceded by regular, varied play
Generate solution on each trial	Generate solution only on first trial
Only one chance for success	Many chances for success
Not repeated on successive trials	Repeated on successive trials
No corrections allowed on next trial	Corrections allowed on next trial

The fact that blocked practice does not rehearse the almost random characteristics of the criterion skill is not the only factor operating here, however. Recall that in the Shea and Morgan (1979) study (Figure 9.1), random practice was more effective than blocked practice even when the learners were subsequently tested on the blocked version of the task. In practical terms, even if the criterion skill is performed under blocked conditions (e.g., rifle shooting at a fixed target and distance for 100 trials in a match), it is still slightly more effective to practice the task under random conditions. However, in most skills, where the criterion skill is done under more or less random conditions, random practice is far more effective than blocked practice.

How to Use Random Practice in Instruction

For the very first attempts at a new skill in the verbal-cognitive stage, blocked practice might be slightly more effective than random practice (Shea, Kohl, & Indermill, 1990), perhaps because the learner needs repeated attempts to produce the action successfully just once. Very soon after the learner has acquired a rough approximation of the movement, however, blocked practice should be abandoned in favor of random practice.

After this initial learning stage, the instructor should do everything possible to structure practice to avoid repetitious blocked practice. One way is to provide instruction on several tasks in the same class session, rotating the class members among them. Springboard divers at UCLA, for example, practice a different dive on each successive attempt, rotating through the various dives to be practiced that day. Football players should not practice the same play over and over; instead, they should switch among the various plays scheduled for that session. A golfer should never hit two consecutive shots with the same club at the driving range, and perhaps should avoid the driving range altogether.

It is not essential that the tasks presented in a random practice session be similar to each other. In fact, the research evidence suggests that the benefits of random practice are enhanced by large task differences on successive trials. This fosters forgetting the solutions of each task before resuming its practice on a later attempt. As with other sit-

uations—involving fatigue, for example—it is probably beneficial to inform the learners that random practice does not allow performing up to their potential. Assure the learners that their performances in the criterion conditions, whatever they might be, will be maximized by random trial scheduling in practice.

PRACTICAL APPLICATIONS

1. In the first few trials of practice at a skill, block the practice to enhance performance quickly.
2. Once the performance is roughly approximated, perhaps after only a few trials, shift to random practice.
3. If the criterion conditions of the skill are themselves random (e.g., in golf), never use blocked scheduling conditions beyond very early practice.
4. Even if the criterion skill is performed under blocked conditions (e.g., rifle shooting), use random practice; it is still slightly more effective than blocked practice.
5. In a classroom situation, practice several skills during the hour, rotating among them frequently to avoid blocked practice.
6. Explain to the learner that random practice causes decrements in immediate practice performance but actually enhances learning and retention performance.
7. Drills, particularly those with unvarying repetitions, are generally ineffective for learning and should be avoided in practice.

Variable Practice

Consider now the many situations where only a single task is to be learned, such as passing a football or shooting a basketball. How should you go about structuring practice for such situations?

Classes of Tasks: Motor Programs and Parameters

Recall from chapters 4 and 5 that throwing is not a single movement at all but is a collection, or class, of movements. Being skilled at passing a football, for example, involves the capability to produce many different throwing distances, arched and flat trajectories, throws to stationary and moving targets, and many other variations. Even with these variations, there is something fundamental, consistent, and characteristic about a football pass, such as the particular grip on the ball, the step and the follow-through, the arm action, the wrist movement producing a spiral, and so on. Earlier, these features were called invariances. An action can easily be detected as a member of a particular class of actions because it has the same invariant features. Also, these features differ between classes. Members of a class have these characteristics:

- Common movement sequencing among the elements
- Common temporal, or rhythmical, organization
- Usually (but not necessarily) the same body parts used
- Differences only in terms of the values of surface features (e.g., speed), specified by different movement parameters

Return now to the conceptual model of human performance developed in Part I, shown again in Figure 9.2. Action patterns are governed by generalized motor programs, each with an almost invariant temporal organization. Once learned, a generalized motor program for football passing can be applied to many specific passing situations through the specification of movement

parameters in the response-programming stage, defining how the movement is carried out in a particular instance. Therefore, some of the learner's problems in passing effectively are to evaluate the environment, decide what kind of pass is required in this particular case, and then specify the proper parameters to the program to produce the proper version of the football pass. The parts of the conceptual model involved in this process are shown in Figure 9.2. How does the performer learn to specify these parameters properly?

Parameter Learning Through Variable Practice

Variable practice, rehearsing many possible variations of a movement class, establishes competence throughout a dimension. Figure 9.3 graphs the distance dimension in the football pass. On the horizontal axis are all the possible distances to throw the football, with a maximum of 40 yd for the learner. All the different throwing distances require that the same generalized motor program be used. However, different sets of parameters must be specified to adjust the throwing forces and speeds to propel the ball particular distances. For a 10-yd throw the passer must select parameters in the low range; a 40-yd pass requires parameters in the very high range. Selecting the wrong parameters makes the pass too long or too short, and the most effective quarterback will have best learned to match the parameters to particular situations.

When the student is faced with learning to produce a class of actions, it follows that practice should be structured to be variable, taking into account the many possibilities actually experienced in the criterion version of the skill (e.g., in a football game). In one way this is just common sense. If the quarterback's only game requirements are to pass 10, 20, and 30 yd, naturally a coach needs to

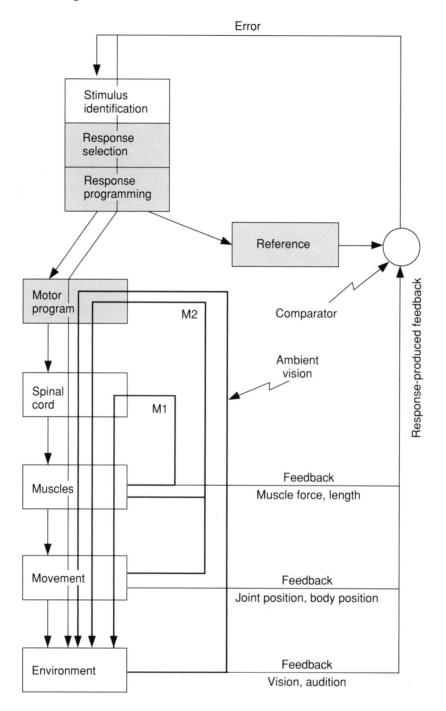

Figure 9.2 The conceptual model of human performance, highlighting the processes where random practice effects are thought to occur.

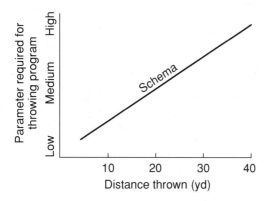

Figure 9.3 Hypothetical parameters to make football passes of different distances. Larger parameter values produce longer throws.

provide practice at these particular distances. This is a variant of specificity view (Henry, 1958/1968), in which one must learn specific actions to accomplish specific goals. There is a grain of truth to the specificity view, which encourages the instructor always to tailor practice close to the circumstances of the criterion task performance. However, there is much more learned in variable practice than just the specific movements actually practiced.

What Is Learned in Variable Practice?

Assume that a group of learners receives practice with parameters for 10, 20, and 40 yd during an acquisition session. They are then given a transfer test where the throwing distance is 30 yd. In a sense, this will be a novel task: The learners never received practice at this particular distance. At the same time, this task is not novel at all because the learners practiced at distances surrounding 30 yd. The laboratory evidence and common sense both indicate that learners can throw this novel distance with no difficulty at all, almost as if they had practiced the 30-yd distance many times before.

What does the specificity view say about this result? If people learn exactly what they practice, as a strict specificity view would have it, then people should perform effectively at the particular distances they practiced, but they should fail at a novel distance they had not specifically practiced previously. The fact that learners do not fail at such novel distances is evidence that they acquire much more than just the specific actions practiced, developing some general capability to produce a class of actions, a capability that is not strongly tied to the particular versions they practiced.

Schema Learning

Practice at a selection of specific throwing distances somehow produces learning that generalizes to all of the throwing distances in the class. One conceptualization to account for this is schema theory (Schmidt, 1975), in which the learner acquires a set of rules, the **schema**, that relates the throwing distances to the parameter values necessary to produce those distances. Referring to Figure 9.4, suppose the learner begins by generating Parameter A, which leads to a throwing distance of 15 yd. On a subsequent attempt, the learner chooses Parameter B, which leads to a throw of 36 yd, then Parameter C, leading to a throw of 24 yd, and so on. With each throw, the learner associates the parameter value with the distance thrown (seen as points on the figure), forming a general relationship or schema between parameter values and distance thrown. This schema is represented by the diagonal line that comes closest to passing through the points on the graph. With each successive throw, the schema is updated, so after hundreds or thousands of throws, the schema relating distance thrown to parameters should be very stable and strong.

How is this schema used? The learner who wants to pass a football gauges the required

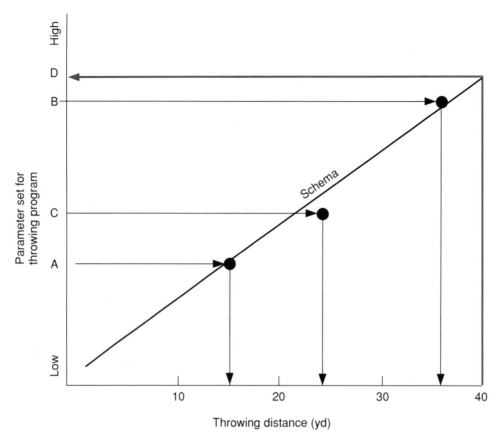

Figure 9.4 The schema relating parameter values to the distances of a football pass. To produce a pass of 40 yd, the schema selects a parameter with value D.

movement distance, say 40 yd. The learner uses the schema in the response-programming stage to estimate the parameter values for that trial. In terms of the graph, the learner goes up (red arrow) from the 40-yd mark on the horizontal axis of Figure 9.4 to the schema line, then moves left to detect the parameter value associated with that distance, shown as Parameter D. A parameter with value D is then delivered to the generalized motor program for throwing, and the movement is produced (also see Figure 9.2).

This process generates a movement with parameter values based on the learner's past experience in using this program. Most important, this process allows the learner to make a movement he or she has never made previously. Suppose that this learner had never produced a 40-yd pass before. No problem: The learner simply provides the best estimate of the required parameter values from the schema, then runs off the motor program with this value. Viewing the process this way, it is not difficult to understand how a person can produce a skilled movement that has not been specifically practiced earlier.

Variable Practice Produces Schema Learning

Considerable evidence suggests that variable practice plays a role in developing schemas. The typical research paradigm contrasts two groups of learners: One is a constant-practice group, practicing only a single member of a class of tasks; the second is a variable group, practicing several members of the class of tasks. Both groups have the same amount of practice, but they differ in the practice variability they receive.

The constant group typically outperforms the variable group during the acquisition phase. This is not surprising because a learner can produce a single version of a movement more effectively than four versions, particularly if these versions are intermixed, as they usually are in research. However, when adult subjects are switched to a novel version of the task on a transfer test, the group that received variable practice performs at least as well as the constant group, and frequently slightly better. When children are the subjects, the variable group is usually more skilled at the novel test than the constant group (e.g., Kerr & Booth, 1978).

This evidence has been interpreted to mean that learners acquire schemas when practicing, and that variable practice enhances their development, allowing more effective novel task performance in the future.

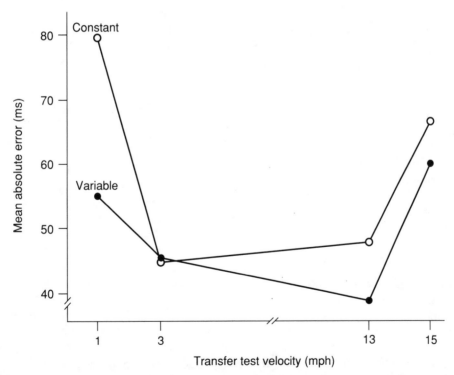

Figure 9.5 Mean absolute timing errors in a coincident-timing task for constant- and variable-practice groups in acquisition. Subjects were trained at 5, 7, 9, and 11 mph and tested at 1, 3, 13, and 15 mph. (Reprinted by permission from Catalano & Kleiner, 1984.)

In other words, variable practice enhances **generalizability**, allowing the performer to apply learning to actions not specifically experienced in practice. This can be seen again in Figure 9.5 (from Catalano & Kleiner, 1984), where groups rehearsed a coincident-timing task at 5, 7, 9, or 11 mph under constant or variable practice conditions. With transfer tests on task versions not experienced previously (at 1, 3, 13, 15 mph), variable practice led to much smaller errors and hence greater generalization. Of course, many sports and games require athletes to produce actions they have never experienced previously, and variable practice is one way to maximize a player's capability to respond effectively.

When organizing variable practice, the instructor should be careful not to exceed the boundaries of the generalized motor program being taught. For example, when required to throw very short (a lob less than 5 yd) or very long (an all-out "bomb" of 50 yd), the example learner might abandon the throwing program and substitute a different program for the short or long movement. These programs for extreme movements have their own parameter sets that must be learned, and so we should not expect transfer to a different program for midrange movements. A given program's boundaries are exceeded if the action patterning changes markedly near the extremes of a movement's range, although such changes are sometimes hard to spot.

Practicing in Slow Motion

A frequently used method for motor learning is to have the learner practice a skill in slow motion, such as taking several seconds to complete a tennis serve or using very slow swimming strokes as in dry land drills. Slow-motion practice can be viewed from several perspectives, one of which is transfer from the slow-motion task version to the normal-speed version. The fundamental

---

PRACTICAL APPLICATIONS

1. When a performer learns a particular class of tasks (e.g., throwing), vary the practice along some dimension such as throwing distance, speed, or direction.
2. Construct the variable-practice experiences to span the range of variations experienced in the eventual criterion skill performance.
3. Whenever possible, present the skill variations in random order and avoid blocked repetitions of the variations.
4. Use your familiarity with a skill to detect when a task variation has exceeded the boundaries of the motor program, which is seen as a distinct change in movement patterning.
5. Do not make a practice task variation so large that it exceeds the range of the generalized motor program.
6. Encourage the learner to make the same fundamental pattern on each variation, allowing only the surface features (e.g., speed, amplitude) to be altered to achieve the various goals.

---

concern is the same as that discussed with respect to part practice in chapter 8: Is the slow-motion version really the "same" skill as the normal-speed version, so practice on one of them transfers to the other? Of course, a specificity view would argue that the slow-motion version would be changed too much from the normal version for very effective transfer.

However, slow-motion practice is valuable in terms of schema learning. A generalized motor program has an overall speed parameter chosen to determine how slowly or quickly to execute a given movement pattern. If the movement is slowed down slightly, the same generalized motor program can be used as in the normal-speed version. Slow-motion practice can thus be viewed as a kind of variable practice. Particularly with a student early in the learning process, practicing a slower skill version reduces errors and allows somewhat more effective control.

Be careful, though. If the movement is slowed down too much (e.g., a tennis serve that lasts 5 s), its essential dynamics are destroyed. The learner will abandon the normal serve program for one that accomplishes this particular slow-motion goal. In such extreme cases, slow-motion practice will not effectively generalize for learning the normal-speed action.

Distinctions Between Random Practice and Variable Practice

At first glance, the evidence makes random and blocked practice, discussed earlier in this chapter, appear to be just another example of variable and constant practice, being discussed here. However, there are several major differences between these practice schedules. Furthermore, the related mechanisms influencing the learning process seem very different as well (Wulf & Schmidt, 1988).

Random and Blocked Practice. Random and blocked practice may involve several very different tasks. In random practice, it does not matter how different the tasks are across practice because the major consideration is that no two tasks be repeated on consecutive trials. The differences between random and blocked practice is in the order in which these tasks are received. Random practice causes gains in learning through trial-to-trial forgetting of the solutions to the movement problem, through more meaningful and distinctive representations, or both.

Variable and Constant Practice. Variable practice involves skills that are all members

of a particular class of actions, such as passing a football. The versions of the task experienced in acquisition may vary along several dimensions, such as the throwing distance or the movement speed. **Constant practice** involves only a single variation or dimension within a given class of actions. Compared to constant practice, variable practice involves more variations of the movement class. Learning gains are caused by the more effective development of a schema relating the parameter values of the movement variants to their outcomes in the environment.

Summary Break

The following is a summary of the differences between random/blocked and variable/constant practice schedules:

- Random practice may involve tasks from different classes, whereas variable practice involves variations from a single class.
- Random and blocked practice both involve several different tasks, but with different orders of presentation.
- Variable and constant practice involve different practice experiences within a single class of actions.
- Random practice enhances learning by causing increased generation of movement solutions or enhanced meaningfulness of movement representations, whereas variable practice generates more effective schemas.

Combining Variable and Random Practice Schedules. The benefits from random over blocked practice, and from variable over constant practice, can be combined to produce further learning gains. You could give 100 trials of variable practice at throwing a football two different ways—in either a blocked or a random presentation order. With a blocked practice order, you might give 20 trials at 20 yd, 20 trials at 30 yd, and so on, one task version repeated on 20 successive trials. With a randomized practice order, on the other hand, you might give one trial at 20 yd, one at 30 yd, one at 40 yd, back to one at 20 yd, and so on for the same total number of trials per distance. T.D. Lee (1988) found that the gain from variable practice compared to constant practice was far greater if the variable practice was random across trials rather than blocked. Perhaps, because requiring different parameters on different trials forces the subject to regenerate a new parameter on each trial, producing greater parameter learning results.

Random and variable practice can be merged even further. Suppose you have a series of randomly ordered variations of a single task class, still throwing a football. If these passing variations were interspersed with a second task, say punting, evidence suggests the benefits would be even larger (Lee, Wulf, & Schmidt, 1990). The learner would not only have to generate a new parameter on each trial but also a new motor program (throwing versus punting) as well. Presumably, these generation processes are extremely beneficial for learning. With the proper combination of variable practice and random ordering, stronger gains in learning might be produced than with variable or random practice alone.

NUMEROUS BENEFITS OF PRACTICE

Obviously, a major goal of practice is performance, to develop the capability to do some skill on future demand. However, there are several other benefits of practice that leave the learner with capabilities not so directly related to actual task proficiency.

Automaticity

When I watch some high-level sports performers, I am intrigued that the often com-

PRACTICAL APPLICATIONS

1. In early learning, give the learner practice at skills slowed somewhat to increase movement control, but be sure not to exceed the range of the generalized program for the normal-speed version.
2. In the performer's very early learning of a single movement class, repeat a given variation for small blocks of several trials before moving to the next version.
3. Somewhat later in learning a single movement class, randomize the variations from trial to trial rather than giving them in a blocked order.
4. Except in the earliest practice stage, alternate between two or more movement classes (e.g., throwing and kicking) in the same session, generating a random practice schedule.
5. After initial stages of practice, switch tasks on every trial if practical, and never repeat a task on successive attempts.
6. When two or more classes of actions are to be practiced, mix them to generate random practice scheduling of the classes, with variable practice on each.
7. Do not use variable practice sessions as a basis for testing; learning should be evaluated on transfer tests on a subsequent day, perhaps with novel task variations.

plex information processing necessary for performance is done so quickly and effortlessly, sometimes almost as if the performer were not even paying attention. In chapter 2 this mode of control was defined as automatic processing, or automaticity, where information processing was relatively attention free, parallel as opposed to serial, fast, and frequently unavoidable or "involuntary" (see Table 2.2). This kind of processing, developed during the autonomous stage of practice discussed earlier, has great importance for movement skills. The basketball player for whom dribbling has become automatic can devote attention to finding the open player for a pass rather than to controlling the ball. The dancer whose moves have become automatic can concentrate on the expressive performance aspects so critical at high levels.

Developing Automaticity

It is important to emphasize that automaticity develops relatively slowly, so a great deal of practice is needed before automatic action patterns emerge. A good estimate is that about 300 trials under the most favorable conditions are necessary for automaticity (Schneider, 1985). This number is larger for a task with more uncertainty and complexity and if the practice conditions are not so favorable. What are some of these practice factors that determine the development of automaticity?

Consistent and Varied Mapping. For effective practice for automaticity, consistently mapping the stimulus (or sensory) information to the goal action is critical. Consistent mapping means that any particular stimulus will always lead to the same response. With varied mapping, on the other hand, a given stimulus sometimes leads to one response, sometimes to another response. American football players often watch game films to learn to detect an opposing team's action patterns. If they are to develop automaticity in this specialized form of information processing, some feature of a given pattern of action (e.g., the movement of the guard during a run to the right) should always lead to a particular outcome and to no other. The coach can help by pointing out which features of the pattern are uniquely related to a particular outcome, then by providing ample practice at detecting this feature in the films.

As a result of practice with consistent mapping, the learner develops a special-purpose detector that can pick out a single feature from a complex sensory environment, resulting in far faster pattern recognition and quicker initiation of the proper response in the game. With varied mapping, however, such processes do not develop, or at best develop at markedly slower rates.

These ideas can be summarized as follows:

- In practice with consistent mapping, where a given stimulus always leads to the same action, automaticity develops with several hundred attempts.
- In practice with varied mapping, where a given stimulus sometimes leads to one response and sometimes to another, automaticity develops more slowly or not at all.

Be careful not to confuse the concepts of varied mapping and variable practice, discussed earlier in this chapter. Varied mapping refers to the variable connection between a stimulus and its response. Variable practice refers to systematically varying the goal of a given movement, such as varying the distance or speed to throw a ball. Note that with variable practice the mapping is always consistent; a given stimulus (a throwing distance goal) is always linked to a given response (a throw of that distance). So variable practice is actually a form of consistent mapping and effectively leads to automaticity.

Random Practice. Suppose there are several skill aspects in which you want your fencing student to become automatic. There are four different movement patterns that an opponent could produce, each requiring a different quickly initiated response. You want your student to respond automatically when any of these patterns occurs in a match. Automaticity practice for such situations should be random, as discussed earlier in this chapter. With four different patterns to be detected, present them in a randomized order, never repeating one on consecutive trials. Random practice more actively involves the information processing activities leading to automaticity, whereas blocked practice allows the learner to avoid them (Schneider, 1985). Practice should be with random order, but with consistent mapping of each pattern, for maximum development of automaticity.

Part-Whole Practice and Automaticity.
Recall from chapter 8 that breaking a skill into its parts for part practice is often risky, the isolated part perhaps not transferring to the "same" part imbedded in the whole skill. Yet, a useful method to develop automaticity is to identify those aspects of the whole task that could be automated and to practice them separately (see Schneider, 1985). One example is the sensory analysis of football team movements, which could be evaluated in films, the player focusing only on analyzing and classifying the opponent's movements. Ask the viewer to discriminate as quickly as possible whether a given play will develop into a pass or a run. Be sure to use consistent mapping with random practice. Similarly, ask a tennis player to judge whether an opponent's serve will travel to the right or the left and to indicate a response as quickly as possible.

The general steps involved in the structure of part practice for automaticity are as follows:

1. Analyze a task into its component parts, particularly those involving rapid pattern analysis.
2. Decide which components could benefit from increased automaticity.
3. Provide randomly ordered, consistently mapped practice of the parts in isolation.

PRACTICAL APPLICATIONS

1. Be prepared to devote considerable practice to developing automaticity because it develops relatively slowly.
2. To develop automaticity most quickly, always use consistent mapping in practice, with a given sensory event leading predictably to the same decision or movement output.
3. If a given stimulus pattern appears to lead to two different movement responses in a game, search for some more detailed feature of the pattern that distinguishes between the responses needed.
4. In Application 3, if you can't find additional detailed information, do not attempt to train automaticity because the stimulus could trigger inappropriate movements and errors.
5. If there are several situations for which automaticity is desired, randomize practice among them; avoid blocked, repetitious practice.
6. Analyze a complex task into its parts, determine which could be performed automatically, and give randomly ordered, consistently mapped practice of each in isolation.

Error Detection Capabilities

Only moments after contacting the ball, and without even looking, the champion golfer has that sinking feeling that this shot is a bad one. How does she know this? She generally gains this information through her **error detection capability**, a special learned mechanism for detecting her own performance errors.

Error detection capabilities can be thought of as an alternative goal of practice. When the instructor is present during practice, this capability is not critical because the instructor can point out movement patterning errors and suggest corrections. However, when the learner attempts to transfer this skill to another context, such as an actual match, the instructor is usually not available or allowed to provide this correction information. The learner who is able to detect and analyze errors independently, and thus make corrections of grip or stance on subsequent attempts, will be a far better performer. This capability makes the learner self-sufficient, which is one overall goal of practice.

How Error Detection Capability Is Learned

Learning to detect errors is perhaps similar to learning an action, but with somewhat different processes. The golfer who detects her own errors is being sensitive to response-produced feedback, to the wide range of information produced by the movement itself. Such information can be kinesthetic, about the movements and forces in the muscles and joints, the feelings of the ball contact, and shifts in balance. It can be visual, with the movements of the limbs evaluated in relation to each other and to the environment. It can be auditory, where the sound of the race car's engine is monitored. Other tasks produce different sensations, but almost all tasks are richly associated with response-produced feedback that potentially informs the learner about success.

Learning error detection means learning sensitivity to the particular patterns of response-produced feedback related to the performance outcome. The feel of the steering wheel when the race car is turning a corner may indicate that the car is not in proper balance. Through practice and experience, the driver learns which sensations from the machine indicate good and bad handling and which are irrelevant. With enough experience the driver can even describe alterations to the mechanics to improve the vehicle's performance.

Facilitating Learning to Detect Errors

A general procedure for acquiring error detection capabilities is to become sensitive to response-produced feedback. The learner might not notice and subsequently process this information unless the instructor draws attention to it. One way to draw attention to the movement's feedback, for example, is to require the learner to describe, or estimate, the number of performance errors prior to receiving information about the actual outcome.

The learner's subjective estimation can be applied to a variety of different situations. For example, in a riflery or archery task, ask the learner to guess where the missile struck the target before you give accuracy information. Ask the learner to describe certain features of the movement just produced, such as elbow straightness or whether the finger release of the bowstring was clean. Forcing the learner to report on such movement aspects means the learner must devote attention and effortful processing to the feedback produced by the response. This forces greater familiarity with the particular feedback, leading to the capability to detect errors.

Be careful, though, that your instructions do not force attention to response-produced feedback *during* the movement. The performer would then be attending to sources of feedback other than the ones critical for performance. However, after the movement is completed, ask the learner to describe some feature of the movement to draw attention to the sensations the movement has just produced.

Movement outcome is often obvious shortly after the movement is produced, such as the accuracy of a basketball shot or the location of a baseball pitch, so asking the learner to guess about the outcome would be essentially meaningless. But what if the outcome information were blocked from the learner? In basketball you could screen the basket from the shooter just after ball release. In sailing a helmsman often practices blindfolded (with another, nonblindfolded person also in the boat), forcing the helmsman to detect information about the boat's performance kinesthetically. Such procedures require learners to process their own response-produced feedback, leading to learning error detection capabilities.

Once the learner can detect errors, the problem is to learn to make effective corrections. A golfer detecting consistent hooking should make small adjustments to bring the shots into line. Some kinds of adjustments are more effective than others, and an inappropriate adjustment in an important match could lead to even worse performance than before. This, then, represents a second goal for the instructor—to make sure that learners are able not only to detect their own errors but also to know what to do about them.

Learning to Transfer and Generalize

Generalization and transfer are important practice goals. Generalization means that the learning acquired in practice can be applied to, or transferred to, other goal situations, such as a game or a match. An instructor cannot be satisfied if the students can perform only task variations they have specifically rehearsed. The instructor wants them to be able to generalize specific learning to the many novel variations they will face in the future. The concern is to organize practice to maximize generalization.

Recall from chapter 6 that transfer was defined as the gain or loss in the capability to respond in one task as a result of practice or

| PRACTICAL APPLICATIONS |

1. Try to develop the learner's capability to detect and correct errors, which contributes to an important alternative goal of practice.
2. Ask the learner to estimate a movement's outcome before giving objective feedback, directing attention to subjective, response-produced feedback.
3. Blocking the learner's knowledge of movement outcome (e.g., with a screen, a blindfold) enhances processing of response-produced feedback.
4. Analyze a skill to determine which of the many sources of feedback is most relevant in signaling errors, then direct the learner's attention to it.
5. Delay giving feedback about movement outcome for several seconds, because instantaneous feedback degrades the development of error detection capabilities (chapter 10).

experience in some other. Transfer is positive if it helps performance in another skill, negative if it degrades performance, or zero if it has no effect at all. This text has discussed transfer in several different contexts (e.g., part practice), but the issues surrounding transfer, and particularly maximizing transfer by adjusting teaching methods and styles, are much farther ranging than emphasized so far and need to be discussed here.

Transfer and Similarity

An old idea in psychology and motor learning is that transfer of learning between two tasks increases as the *similarity* between them increases. One idea was that of identical elements, where learning certain elements in one situation transferred to another skill using the same elements. As simple as this idea might sound, there have always been problems with it. One is that the concepts of similarity and elements are never explicitly defined. For example, is throwing a baseball more similar to passing a football than shooting a basketball? What exactly are the elements involved?

There is a sense in which the notions of similarity and identical elements can guide in designing teaching environments. The most fruitful approach seems to be to identify those skills that have similar movement patterning. For example, throwing short and long distances have obviously similar temporal and spatial patterning, and the two actions look almost identical except for the speeds and forces involved. Something about patterning seems fundamental; when patterning is the same, the movements are called similar. Pitching a baseball overarm and pitching a softball underarm seem to involve different patterns, though, so you might not classify these two skills as being similar. (Fundamental, underlying patterns was the notion behind generalized motor programs in chapters 4 and 5, and schema learning, considered earlier in this chapter.)

Fundamental Movement Patterning. Many have suggested that the so-called overarm pattern underlies throwing a baseball, serving in tennis, spiking a volleyball, and many other actions requiring forceful overarm movements to strike or throw an object. All these involve rotation of the hips and shoulders and ballistic actions of the shoulder-arm-wrist, ending finally with wrist-hand action to accomplish the particular goal. An analogous idea common among gymnasts is that certain fundamental actions (e.g., the sharp hip extension in the kip) can be applied to almost any apparatus event requiring such an action. In both these examples, if practice

is given at one variant of the class of movements sharing the same general pattern, then the learner should be able to transfer the learning to any other variant using this same pattern. Of course, practicing a kipping action would not transfer to an overarm action, or vice versa, because these skills use very different patterns, belonging in separate movement classes.

Perceptual Elements. Similarity is evident in the numerous perceptual elements underlying collections of tasks, sports, and games. For example, racquetball, squash, paddleball, and handball all require playing a ball's rebound off the walls of a four-walled court (plus the ceiling and floor), resulting in many common features about rebound speed, direction as a function of ball speed, the initial angle, the ball's spin, and so on. Learning to intercept flying balls of various kinds (baseballs, footballs, tennis balls, etc.) depends on learning the common features of ball flight, which are based on the principles of physics. Learning to react to such problems in one situation provides much transfer to other situations where the perceptual elements are similar.

Strategic and Conceptual Similarities. Similar strategies, rules, guidelines, or concepts are present in many different activities. For example, various court and racquet sports have similar rules, as do different gymnastics and diving events. Strategic elements such as controlling or guarding territory are similar in games like basketball, American football, soccer, ice hockey, field hockey, and lacrosse. Needing to generate passing lanes along which one player may safely pass an object to a teammate without an interception, not to mention finding the open teammate, are important general ideas in many activities. You can identify many other classes of similar concepts in the variety of skills and sports that you ask your students to learn.

Summary ◇ Break

Overall, the concept of similarity among skills involves several classes of common features:

- Common movement patterning
- Common perceptual elements
- Common strategic or conceptual elements

Teaching for Transfer of Learning

The general idea of teaching for transfer involves not only maximizing transfer from earlier learning but also selecting those methods and ways of organizing practice that maximize transfer and generalizability. This section considers ways to enhance generalization through practice organization. As you will see, these methods are particularly useful in early practice, when skill learning has just begun. The principles of transfer for later practice are dealt with soon after.

Point Out Similarities Among Skills. It is often obvious to you, but not necessarily to your learner, that a particular skill being presented for the first time is similar to another one learned earlier. Point out these similarities, using statements such as "The arm action in this tennis serve is like that in an overarm throw" or "The kip action here on the rings is just like it was on the horizontal bar." Borrowing an action pattern from earlier learning gives the student an advantage in the new skill, particularly in early learning.

Use Teaching Cues to Emphasize Transfer. Similarities can also be emphasized by various teaching cues, such as "Throw the racket head at the ball," which makes the action seem similar to overarm throwing. In gymnastics it is helpful to use consistent la-

bels for skills, like emphasizing the fact that kips on the horizontal bar, on the rings, and on the mat are really the "same" skill; refer to them all as kips. Also, many skills have similar mechanical principles, such as shifting momentum in throwing or needing a wide base of support for maximum balance. Remind the learner how these principles applied to earlier learned actions: "Let your hip rotation lead your arms in the golf swing, just like you do in baseball."

Pointing out similar patterns of action in various skills can be used to facilitate learners' early transfer of learning.

Emphasize Transfer to Future Skills. It is tempting to think of transfer as contributing only to the skill that the learner is attempting at the moment. It works the other way, too, though. In the practice of a given skill, ask the learner how to apply a particular strategy or concept to some new setting. Some methods, such as variable practice, have this characteristic as a goal, today's specific techniques being at least partly directed to future generalizability. In children's motor learning, movement educators have children roll over a mat in as many ways as possible, hoping to build a general capability to perform whole-body movements. Such exercises should lead to learning that generalizes effectively.

PRACTICAL APPLICATIONS

1. Analyze the skills you teach to discover patterns of similarity that can provide a basis for transfer; it pays to know your skills.
2. Search especially for common movement patterns, such as an overarm pattern in both baseball throwing and volleyball hitting or a kipping pattern in many gymnastics events, as a basis for transfer.
3. Particularly in the early phases of instruction, emphasize features of the present skill that are common with skills that have been well learned earlier, increasing transfer.
4. In addition to movement patterning, point out similarities in cognitive elements of skills, such as rules, concepts, mechanical principles, and strategies that could transfer.
5. Organize practice to generalize to future situations by providing variable practice of skills.
6. Ask the learner how the principles being learned in current practice could apply to future activities, thereby increasing generalization to other skills.

Principles of Motor Transfer

The transfer principles just discussed apply best when the learner is just beginning to learn a skill. When the skills become more developed, the amount of transfer from earlier learning drops markedly. This is because, with continued practice and increased capability, a skill becomes more specific and shares less with other skills of the same movement type. In early practice an overarm throw and a tennis serve do seem similar, and relating them does help the novice get the idea critical to initial attempts. However, everyone knows that a tennis serve and an overarm throw are *not* the same thing, and at higher levels of proficiency, the two skills become more distinct. What, then, are the principles of transfer for later stages of learning?

Motor Transfer Is Generally Small, but Positive. Between two reasonably well-learned tasks that appear somewhat similar, there is usually very little transfer. The transfer that does appear is usually positive, the skills generally facilitating each other to some extent. But the amount of transfer is generally so low that transfer ceases to be a major goal of practice, in contrast to the earlier practice stages, where transfer was a major goal. Therefore, teaching a particular Skill A simply because you would like it to transfer to Skill B, which is of major interest, is not very effective, especially if you consider the time spent on Skill A that could have been spent on Skill B instead. Transfer is fine when received for free in early practice, but it usually requires too much time in later practice.

Drills and Lead-up Activities. The principle just mentioned applies to using various **lead-up activities** or drills. These actions are usually not of interest in themselves but are considered only as means to another goal, the transfer to another skill. Learning to step through tires on the ground is a common drill for football running backs, and various gymnastic stunts are common lead-ups for criterion stunts. Generally, learning such preliminary activities does not transfer well to the goal movement because they are not sufficiently similar. The instructor usually does well by giving practice only on the goal movement, when practical.

No Transfer of Basic Abilities. A common misconception is that fundamental abilities (chapter 6) can be trained through various drills or other activities. The thinking is that, with some stronger ability, the athlete will see gains in performance for tasks with this underlying ability. For example, athletes are often given various ''quickening'' exercises, with the hope that these exercises would train some fundamental ability to be quick, allowing quicker responses in their particular sports. Coaches often use various balancing drills to increase general balancing ability, eye movement exercises to improve vision, and many others. Such attempts to train fundamental abilities may sound fine, but usually they simply do not work. Time, and often money, would be better spent practicing the eventual goal skills.

There are two correct ways to think of these principles. First, there is no general ability to be quick, to balance, or to use vision, as discussed in chapter 6 on individual differences. Rather, quickness, balance, and vision are each based on many diverse abilities, so there is no single quickness ability, for example, that can be trained. Second, even if there were such general abilities, these are, by definition, genetic and not subject to modification through practice. Therefore, attempts to modify an ability with a nonspecific drill are ineffective. A learner may acquire additional skill at the drill (which is, after all, a skill itself), but this learning does not transfer to the main skill of interest.

Negative Transfer Is Not Common. A frequent concern in skills learning is negative transfer, the degradation in some skill because of practice or experience in another. Tennis players say that racquetball or badminton practice over the winter degrades their tennis skills by the time that the first match of the spring comes along. Their idea is that racquetball and badminton actions are just different enough from tennis strokes to cause negative transfer to tennis. This could be, but it fails to consider the fact that there has been an entire winter without tennis practice, so some forgetting of tennis strokes will naturally occur in any case—badminton or not.

The laboratory evidence suggests that negative transfer hardly ever occurs in motor activities. True, an experimental subject can degrade one skill by practicing another specifically designed to interfere, but this is not a usual situation in the outside world. Most of the skills people learn become so specific with practice that they eventually do not transfer either positively or negatively between themselves. The weight of evidence favors the view that negative transfer is not a practice problem to be concerned about. Again, however, for very early learning, when skills are more general in nature, the student can receive negative transfer from prior learning, so instructions should include warnings to avoid treating Skill A like Skill B because they might interfere with each other.

Simulation, Simulators, and Transfer

Transfer principles are commonly used in the area of simulation. A **simulator** is a practice device designed to mimic certain features of a real-world task. Simulators are often very elaborate, sophisticated, and expensive, such as devices to train pilots to fly aircraft. But simulators need not be elaborate at all, such as a putting cup for the living room floor. Simulators can be an important part of an instructional program, especially when the skill is expensive or dangerous (e.g., learning to fly a jetliner), where facilities are limited (e.g., a golf course), or where real practice is not feasible (e.g., using baseball pitching machines to replace a live pitcher).

Remember that the overall goal of simulation is for the learning in the simulator to transfer to the criterion task. Thus, a simulator will be effective only to the extent that substantial transfer to the criterion occurs. Because transfer increases with similarity, this idea has naturally led to the notion that simulators should be realistic, possessing as much visual, auditory, and movement similarity to the criterion task as possible. Therefore, it is not surprising that many simulators are very expensive. If the simulator and the criterion task were very different, requiring different processes for control, learning in

the simulator would not transfer effectively to the criterion task.

A related consideration is how much transfer is produced by the simulator in relation to the time spent there. Consider Figure 9.6, showing the hypothetical performance curves on a baseball batting task for two groups of subjects. The simulator group begins practice on the main task after 3 hr of practice on a batting simulator, whereas the no-simulator group receives no prior practice on the simulator. There is much positive transfer from the simulator to the batting task, seen as the gain in probability of a hit from .30 to .50. The simulator seemed to save about 1.5 hr on the main task in that the simulator group started at a level (.50) that took the no-simulator group 1.5 hr of practice

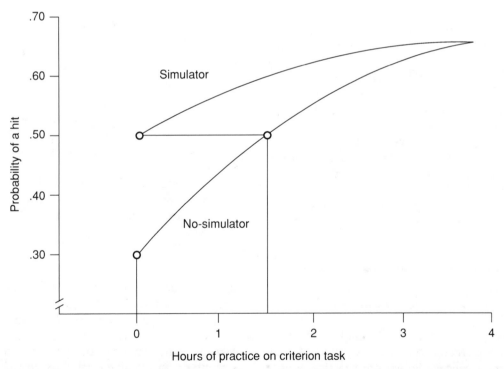

Figure 9.6 Hypothetical performance curves of two groups of learners on a baseball batting task. The simulator group practiced on a batting simulator for 3 hours prior to initial task practice, whereas the no-simulator group did not.

on the batting task to achieve. However, remember that the simulator group had already spent 3 hr of practice on the simulator! Other things being equal, this simulator situation was not very effective because practice on the simulator did not generate enough transfer to the criterion task to justify the extra time spent.

Time is not the only relevant factor here, though. The effectiveness of a simulator must also be judged in relation to the relative costs of simulator practice and criterion task practice, the availability of resources and facilities, safety, and so on. Relative to practice in a flight simulator, practice in an actual jetliner would cost a staggering amount, and there are additional concerns for the safety of people and equipment. Thus, evaluating simulators in a large instructional setting can be relatively complicated.

Overall, various simulators can be a part of most instructional programs in physical education, sports, and therapy. Practice facilities are usually seriously limited, so ways to mimic the skills with inexpensive but realistic simulators should be sought. Simulations can be very effective in the early stages of practice, where rules and strategies, among other cognitive and decision-making aspects of the activities, are learned in the simulator. As soon as movement-control learning begins to dominate, though, the effectiveness of simulators generally drops considerably unless they are nearly identical to the specific criterion task.

PRACTICAL APPLICATIONS

1. Transfer of conceptual and strategic skill elements in early learning is great, so teach to maximize this transfer.
2. In later learning, where movement patterning is being acquired, do not expect much transfer from even similar-appearing skills.
3. Later in learning, treat each class of skills (e.g., throwing) as a specific activity and do not encourage transfer from a somewhat related skill (e.g., volleyball spiking).
4. Drills and lead-up activities take considerable practice time and do not produce much transfer, so use them sparingly in later practice stages.
5. It is fruitless to try to train fundamental abilities (e.g., quickness, balance), so concentrate on the fundamental skills instead.
6. Except in very early practice, do not be concerned about negative transfer from similar-appearing skills.
7. Realistic simulators can be useful additions to the teaching program when the criterion task is expensive, is dangerous, or requires facilities that are limited.
8. Evaluate simulator effectiveness by comparing the time spent on the simulator to the time saved on the criterion task.

◇ CHAPTER SUMMARY

Large learning gains can be made by effective practice organization and scheduling. An important concept is random practice, where trials of several tasks are mixed during acquisition. Relative to blocked practice, where trials of a single given task are repeatedly presented, random practice produces far better performance at retention. Random practice probably operates by preventing the learner from simply repeating the movement output on successive trials, requiring the learner to generate the entire movement process on each trial.

Variable practice involves intentional variations of a given task, such as practicing different distances in putting. Compared to constant practice, where only a single variant is practiced, varied practice facilitates retention and generalizability, particularly to a novel situation whose specific variant has not received prior practice. Variable practice is thought to operate by generating stronger schemas, which define the relationship between parameters for a motor program and the movement's outcome.

In addition to producing criterion movements, several alternative goals of practice are producing more automatic movements, detecting and correcting one's own errors after completing the movement, and generalizing learning to different tasks and contexts. Transfer between skills depends on their movement or perceptual similarity and can be facilitated by effective instructional methods. Transfer can be quite high in early learning, but it drops considerably after practice because of the more specific nature of later movement skills. Simulators of various kinds can efficiently mimic important elements of a skill when practicing the actual skill would be too costly, dangerous, or impractical.

◇ Checking Your Understanding

1. What does it mean to say that, relative to blocked practice, random practice is detrimental to performance but beneficial to learning?
2. What is the essential difference between the methods of blocked/random practice and variable/constant practice?
3. With two skills to teach in a 1-hr lesson, how would you structure their practice trials to maximize learning?
4. Choose a skill with which you are reasonably familiar. How would you

teach automaticity in various components of this skill?
5. Describe three simulators currently used in sports or athletics. Choose one and describe its strengths and weaknesses as a training device.

◇ Key Terms

Definitions of the following terms appear on the page(s) shown in parentheses:

blocked practice (p. 200)
constant practice (p. 213)
error detection capability (p. 216)
generalizability (p. 212)
lead-up activities (p. 221)
random practice (p. 200)
retrieval practice (p. 203)
schema (p. 209)
simulator (p. 222)
variable practice (p. 207)

◇ Suggestions for Further Reading

Interesting reviews of the issues related to blocked and random practice can be found in Magill and Hall (1990), and in T.D. Lee (1988) and Shea and Zimny (1983). For more on variable practice and schema development, see Schmidt (1975). Automaticity and its enhancement with practice is reviewed by Schneider (1985), with interesting applications to part practice in various skills. Information about the principles of transfer for motor control can be found in Schmidt and Young (1987; see also Cormier & Hagman, 1987), and more general reading about the other topics in this chapter can be found in Schmidt (1988b, chapter 13).

Feedback for
Skill Learning

PREVIEW

The instructor is overwhelmed, and feeling a little guilty, while watching his class of beginning hockey players struggle to learn. With 25 students he simply does not have time to give each one much information about his or her errors and how to correct them, so the students spend a great deal of time practicing on their own without corrections during class. How can the instructor provide more feedback about errors in this situation? What information should this feedback contain, and is it efficient to give feedback about more than one fault in the action at a time? When watching a given student, should the instructor give feedback on each trial, or is it better to withhold some of this information?

This chapter can be considered an extension of chapters 8 and 9 because it also concerns organizing practice. Here, though, the focus is on how an instructor organizes and delivers feedback, information about performance or errors the learner can use for making future corrections. An instructor's feedback produces learning in several ways simultaneously. The text turns to some principles of how feedback enhances learning, examining questions about feedback frequency, feedback timing, and the most effective kinds of feedback.

1. To become familiar with the var~~ious classifications of feedback~~
2. To understand how feedback en~~hances learning~~
3. To appreciate the role of feedback ~~frequency, timing, and content~~ for enhancing learning
4. To apply the principles of feedback to many real-world teaching settings

Without a doubt, one of the most important learning processes concerns the use of feedback about actions attempted in practice. As discussed in chapter 3, feedback may be a natural consequence of the movement, as in seeing the flight of the golf ball or feeling the bat make contact with the baseball. Feedback can also be given in various "artificial" forms that are not so obvious to the learner, such as the performer's score in a diving competition or a comment about the golfer's backswing. Of course, verbal feedback is frequently under the instructor's direct control; thus, it makes up a large part of practice organization.

Verbalized feedback may convey many different kinds of information simultaneously, each of which could involve very different learning processes. For example, consider each of the following possibilities:

1. Halfway through a tiring practice, the coach says to his wrestler, "Keep it up, Bill—you're doing fine."
2. After a daring but successful pass to the open player under the basket, the coach shouts, "Good work, Mary!"
3. The coach informs his star runner that he is benched for this week's meet because his grades are too low.
4. A class instructor tells a beginning tennis player she needs to make the backswing longer and more slowly.

Each of these statements is a form of feedback about some aspect of the learner's per-

formance. As you will see, each conveys a different message, a different kind of information, and they function very differently to influence future performance and learning.

FEEDBACK CLASSIFICATIONS AND FUNCTIONS

The term **feedback** originally emerged from the analysis of closed-loop control systems (see chapter 3), referring to information about the difference between some goal state and performance. Feedback in such systems is information about error. More recently, *feedback* has taken on the general meaning of any kind of sensory information about the movement, not just that concerning errors.

Feedback Classifications

It is helpful to form a clear feedback classification system because many of the different kinds of feedback follow somewhat different principles. One system appears in Figure 10.1, where the global category of sensory information is divided into several subclasses. First, of course, there is a great deal of sensory information "out there," most of which is not related to the movement the person is learning. But of the information related to the movement, it is useful to categorize it as either available before the movement or available after the movement. Information before action is critical for move-

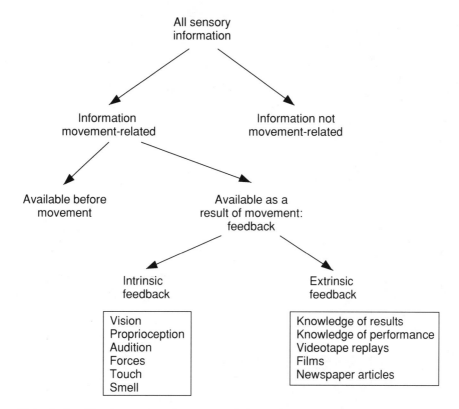

■ **Figure 10.1** A classification system for sensory information.

ment planning (discussed in chapters 3 and 4), affecting anticipation, decision making, parameter selection, and so on. However, it is the information provided as a result of the movement (*fed back* to the performer) that is considered as feedback. Feedback may be further divided into two main categories: intrinsic and extrinsic feedback.

Intrinsic Feedback

Sometimes called inherent feedback, **intrinsic feedback** is information provided as a natural consequence of making an action. When I swing at a tennis ball, I feel my hips, shoulders, and arms moving, I see the racquet travel, I hear and feel the ball's contact, and I see and hear the ball travel and whack my opponent on the leg. All these movement

features are intrinsic to the task, and I can perceive them more or less directly, without special methods or devices. Other kinds of intrinsic information might be crowd noise in basketball, particular smells in driving a race car, or finger sensations from fine control in playing a video game. This general class of feedback has been discussed throughout the text during the development of the conceptual model of human performance.

Extrinsic Feedback

Now it is time to finalize the conceptual model of human performance by adding **extrinsic feedback**, shown as the highlighted section of the conceptual model in Figure 10.2. Sometimes called enhanced feedback

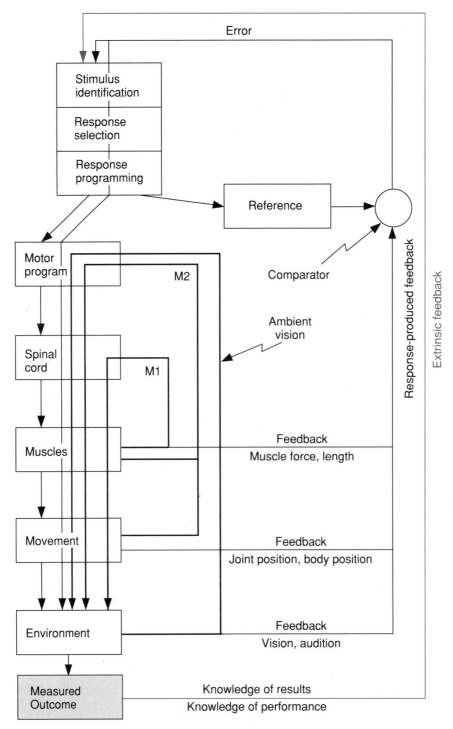

Figure 10.2 The conceptual model of human performance. Extrinsic feedback, the loop from the measured outcome to the executive, is added to complete the diagram.

or **augmented feedback**, it consists of information from the measured performance outcome that is fed back to the learner by some artificial means, such as a teacher's voice giving corrections, a stopwatch after a 100-m race, a diving judge's score, game films, videotape replays, and so on. Thus, extrinsic feedback is supplied beyond intrinsic feedback. The common feature in all these examples is that the feedback augments, or supplements, the information naturally available. Most important, this feedback is information over which the coach or instructor has control; thus, it can be given or not given, given at different times, and given in different forms to influence learning. Scientists in motor learning tend to use the term *feedback* as shorthand for augmented or extrinsic feedback as defined here, and this text will use *feedback* this way as well.

Knowledge of Results (KR). Knowledge of results (KR) is a particularly important category of extrinsic feedback. KR is extrinsic, usually verbal (or verbalizable) information about the success of an action with respect to the environmental goal. In many real-world tasks, KR is redundant with the intrinsic information. Telling the gymnast she fell on her back that time, or telling the basketball player he missed the free throw are examples of KR (the verbal information) duplicating the information that the performer receives anyway.

However, KR is not always redundant with intrinsic feedback. Gymnasts, divers, and dancers must wait for the judges' scores to know exactly how well they did. In riflery and archery it is not always possible to see where the missile hit the target area, so extrinsic KR information must be received from a coach or a scoring device. In these latter cases, KR is critically important for performance and learning because the learner cannot know about errors without it.

KR is frequently used in research, where the information given to learners in a laboratory task can be controlled. Using this general method, researchers have examined how feedback processes generate learning, and theories of feedback operation are currently being evaluated with these research paradigms. Earlier research was often conducted with very simple tasks where learners could not detect their errors by themselves, such as blindfolded limb-positioning tasks. These experiments generally showed that without KR there was no learning at all (e.g., Trowbridge & Cason, 1932). On the other hand, giving KR about errors allowed rapid improvement across practice, which remained in retention tests even when KR was withdrawn. These results suggest that when the learner cannot detect his or her own performance errors through intrinsic feedback, then no learning at all occurs unless KR is provided.

This is not to say learning cannot occur without KR. You have probably learned many real-world tasks with no KR provided by an instructor, as in practicing free throws by yourself. You received goal achievement information (i.e., whether the ball went in the basket) through intrinsic feedback, though, and this feedback was the basis of your learning. Thus, the principle is that *some* error information must be received, either intrinsically or extrinsically, for learning to occur.

Some of these findings can be summarized as follows:

- If learners have no knowledge of their own errors (from either extrinsic or intrinsic feedback), then practice results in no learning.
- However, extrinsic feedback in the form of KR generates rapid and permanent learning.
- Generally, information about errors, either from extrinsic or intrinsic sources, is essential for learning to occur.

1. State movement pattern goals clearly and early in practice so feedback about the movement can indicate how to make corrections.
2. Decide whether learners can detect their errors on their own. If they can't, provide some form of feedback.
3. In tasks where learners can detect their own errors, information from the instructor is not critical for learning, so don't be overly concerned about practice without instructor feedback.

Knowledge of Performance (KP). Knowledge of performance (KP), sometimes referred to as kinematic feedback, is augmented information about the movement pattern the learner has just made. It is frequently used by teachers and coaches in real-world settings. For example, you often hear coaches say things like "That movement was a little too late," "Your tuck was not tight enough," or "Your backswing was too long." Each of these forms of KP tells about kinematics (movement or movement patterns). Note that KP information, unlike KR, does not necessarily tell about movement success in terms of meeting the environmental goal. Rather, kinematic feedback tells about the success of the pattern that the learner actually produced. Some of the main similarities and differences between KR and KP are summarized in Table 10.1.

How Extrinsic Feedback Functions

After a movement attempt, a teacher says to the learner, "You made your backswing just right that time." Think of all the meanings that such a simple statement could have to the learner. First of all, there is a motivating, energizing, function to this feedback: It

Table 10.1 Comparison of Knowledge of Results and Knowledge of Performance

Knowledge of Results (KR)	Knowledge of Performance (KP)
Similarities	
Verbal, or verbalizable	Verbal, or verbalizable
Extrinsic	Extrinsic
Postresponse	Postresponse
Differences	
Information about outcome in terms of environmental goal	Information about movement production or patterning
Usually redundant with intrinsic feedback	Usually distinct from intrinsic feedback
Information about the score or goal	Information about kinematics
Most useful in the laboratory	Most useful in teaching

makes the learner slightly more enthusiastic about the activity and encourages trying harder. Second, there is a reinforcing function: Knowledge that the movement was okay acts as a reward, and that movement tends to be repeated in future attempts. Although it is not present in this example, you can also imagine mild punishment from a statement that the backswing was too short, especially if the instructor gives it in a menacing way. Third, there is of course the information that the backswing was of the proper length, which allows the learner to form associations with other information (e.g., how the movement felt). If the backswing had been too short, the information about this error specifies corrections on the next trial. Finally, feedback can produce a dependency function that enhances performance when feedback is present but allows performance to deteriorate when feedback is later withdrawn.

Generally, feedback in real-world settings operates simultaneously in these four interdependent ways, which are often very difficult to separate. To summarize, extrinsic feedback does these things:

1. Produces motivation, or energizes the learner to increase effort
2. Supplies reinforcement for correct and incorrect actions
3. Provides information about errors as a basis for corrections
4. Creates a dependency, leading to problems at feedback withdrawal

Motivational Properties of Feedback

In the first example given near the start of the chapter, the coach tells the tired wrestler, "Keep it up, Bill—you're doing fine." This casual comment kept Bill going a little longer in practice. Certainly, one important function of feedback is to motivate the learner, helping the tired learner bring more effort to bear on the task. In addition, early research revealed that when feedback was given during boring, repetitive tasks of long duration where performance was deteriorating, performers showed an immediate increase in proficiency, as if the feedback was acting as a kind of stimulant to get them going again. In addition, learners given feedback say they like the task more, try harder at it, and are willing to practice longer. In short, unless it is overdone, learners seem to like feedback. Even when an instructor has another primary reason for giving feedback (e.g., to correct an error), this extra motivational benefit is achieved for free.

You can capitalize on this feedback feature in practice. Think of ways to give learners feedback relatively frequently. This is not as simple as it sounds, though, because giving too much feedback (e.g., on every trial) can

cause the informational component of feedback to be relatively ineffective (see the section on How Learning Is Affected by Feedback Scheduling later in this chapter). In any case, try to avoid long periods where you give no feedback because motivation can sag and practice can either be very inefficient or cease altogether. Keeping learners informed of their progress usually translates into their bringing more effort to the task, which can only benefit them in terms of increased learning.

Feedback is particularly effective if it is public. Posting people's scores on a particular activity can generate strong motivation to succeed, at least in some learners. Display scores on a bulletin board near the gymnasium so all can see their own progress in relation to the other students. There is a potential ethical problem here, though: You must be sensitive to the influences that such public knowledge has on students who do not or cannot perform so well. At UCLA it is illegal to post students' grades and test scores by name, so codes (e.g., a student ID number) are used instead so a given student can identify only his or her own scores. This still provides a basis for evaluating one's own performance in relation to the group, which creates a great deal of motivation.

Finally, feedback contingent on performance or effort can, at least in some learners, have powerful effects on behavior. Certainly, giving verbal praise for a job well done can produce strong motivation to try harder, and students usually appreciate the recognition. Even publicly displaying gold stars, or other symbols to signify the number of miles run across the season, as shown in Figure 10.3, makes runners expend extra effort, benefiting training. Football coaches often give rating points for good plays in a practice or in a game, sometimes giving little stickers to wear on helmets for public display. Giving jelly beans (healthy, high fiber oat-bran

Kennedy High School track team
Miles run in December

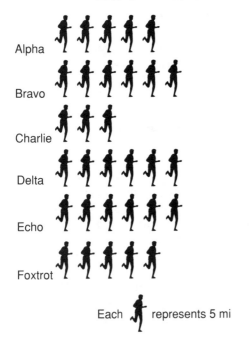

Each represents 5 mi

Figure 10.3 An example of publicly presented feedback for aiding motivation.

cookies) or other inexpensive tokens for extra effort enhances performance, leading to more practice attempts and thus to greater learning. The creative teacher or coach can produce large gains in motivation with very simple, inexpensive methods like these.

Reinforcing Properties of Feedback

In the second example given earlier, the coach shouts "Good work, Mary!" when the basketball player completes the daring pass. This represents a second major effect of feedback—its reinforcing properties. The feedback given after an action leads to an improved chance that this action will be produced in similar circumstances in the future.

In the laboratory, psychologists have studied instrumental learning. In one example of this method, if a hungry animal presses a lever within 5 s of hearing a signal, it is given a food reward. The animal gradually learns to press the lever very reliably when the sound occurs in future trials. Your new puppy quickly learns to sit on command if you give a biscuit or a friendly pat when the puppy performs the action.

Sometimes a punishing stimulus, such as a shock, is presented; here the animal learns to avoid repeating the actions that led to the shock. My childhood horse, Blackie, learned in about 2 min not to touch the new electric fence (which gave a weak but unpleasant shock), especially with the tender nose.

Very early, scientists realized that the nature and timing of the feedback has a marked influence on learning the goal response. These findings were captured and summarized by Thorndike (1927) in his empirical law of effect, which goes essentially as follows:

The law of effect: An action elicited by a stimulus and followed by pleasant, or rewarding, consequences tends to be repeated when that stimulus appears again; an action followed by unpleasant, or punishing, consequences tends not to be repeated.

In this view the focus is on feedback's giving reinforcement. Reinforcement is positive if it increases the probability of a future response, as with the biscuit for sitting on command. Reinforcement is negative if it decreases the probability of a future response, as with the shock for touching the electric fence. Thus, instrumental learning involves strengthening (by positive reinforcement) the associations between a given stimulus and the "correct" response, at the same time weakening (by negative reinforcement) the associations between that stimulus and all "incorrect" responses. When that stimulus is presented again, the correct response will tend to be produced, and competing incorrect responses will tend to be inhibited, leading to more effective performance overall. Mary, the basketball player, is more likely to attempt this kind of pass in the future because of her coach's positive reinforcement.

In the third example given earlier, the coach informs the star runner that he is benched because his grades are too low. This is an example of negative reinforcement. The feedback (being benched) should lead to decreased future probability of the behavior that led to this feedback (failing to study). This should then reduce the chances that low grades will occur in the future.

Reinforcement and Choice Behavior.
Thorndike's law of effect has had a major influence on research and thinking in education and skill training. In one way, skill learning was usually regarded as a form of instrumental learning because the learner typically must make a correct response (a skilled movement) when a stimulus was presented and avoid making incorrect ones.

Feedback, such as knowledge of results, was thought of as reinforcement, strengthening or weakening the associations between stimulus events and potential movements, thus leading to more effective performance. As summarized in Figure 10.4, reinforcement is a feature of choice behavior in most of the sports and games that are of interest here, including choosing to throw a baseball to first base rather than second, to catch a football pass, or to guard the dribbler on a basketball play. It can also have strong effects on effort, for example, when extra effort in practice some week is reinforced by recognition from the coach. It is clear that reinforcement by the instructor about the learner's choices have powerful influences on the pattern of future choices.

Intermittent Reinforcement.
A very important principle of instrumental learning is that **intermittent reinforcement**, feedback given only occasionally, is generally more effective for learning than feedback given on every trial. In research, enhanced learning is usually estimated by performance on an extinction test, where behavior is evaluated after all reinforcement is taken away. Subjects having received intermittent reinforcement continue to respond adequately far longer than subjects having received reinforcement after every trial. Also, fading, gradually reducing the amount and frequency of reinforcement in training as the learner acquires the proper behavior, generally strengthens performance when reinforcement is completely withdrawn later. These principles have considerable applicability to human motor learning—particularly the learning of choices—where a coach or an instructor provides reinforcement during training but the ultimate goal is the correct test performance (in a game, a contest, or a match) where the reinforcement must be totally withdrawn. There can be little doubt that reinforcement principles are applicable

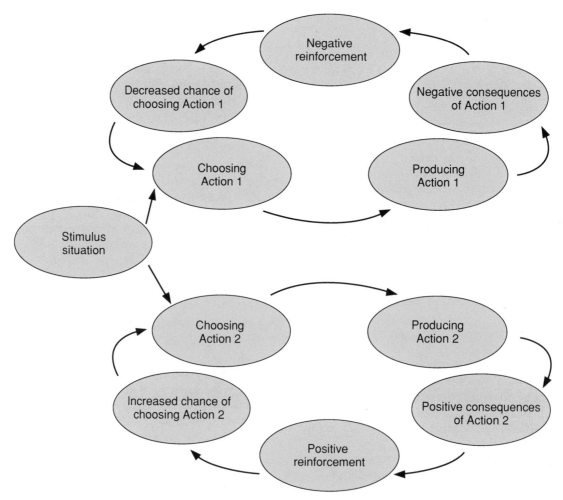

Figure 10.4 Facilitation and inhibition of choices based on feedback about their consequences. After several trials, given the stimulus situation, Action 2 will be clearly favored over Action 1.

to many aspects of motor skill learning, particularly in learning to make choices.

Informational Properties of Feedback

As just summarized, reinforcement is clearly related to the choice of actions. However, these principles are not particularly relevant to enhancing movement control in skill learning, primarily because the problems of choice are usually minimized in movement skills, although this is not always the case.

In fact, the minimization of choice is what makes movement skills different from other kinds of human skilled behavior. In cognitive learning, such as learning to speak a foreign language, the problem is which previously learned word to choose. In motor learning, however, the problem is how to produce an action. For example, in making a basketball free throw, no choice behavior seems necessary; rather, the problem is creating a pattern of movement to accomplish the single,

1. Employ reinforcement principles to maximize the learning of choices among already acquired actions; this is a critical determinant of skill in many activities.
2. Provide positive reinforcement such as praise, recognition, or tokens (e.g., gold stars) for correct choices to enhance the probability of their occurring in the future.
3. Use negative reinforcement to indicate ineffective choices but, to enhance learning, couple it with clear information about what choice should have been made.
4. Give reinforcement intermittently in practice to maximize its long-term effectiveness when reinforcement must later be withdrawn.
5. Gradually withdraw, or fade, reinforcement as the performer achieves the correct choices so that he or she learns to perform independently.

that makes the instructor so important for motor learning. Whereas a machine can give out jelly beans for effective performance, only a skilled instructor can know the proper patterns of action to provide information feedback. Because of the importance of this component of feedback, the remainder of the chapter deals with the principles of its operation for learning.

Consider now the fourth example mentioned earlier, where the instructor tells the tennis player she should make her backswing somewhat longer and slower. This information about correctness defines clearly what was wrong and can be a basis for making corrections on the next movement, bringing the movement closer to the goal values that characterize the most effective performance. There is no doubt that giving information guides the learner toward the movement goal. Continued use of this feedback keeps errors to a minimum and ensures that errors are corrected quickly, thus holding the movement pattern very near to the goal.

Recognizing that extrinsic feedback is mainly informational raises many interesting

clearly defined goal. In pitching a baseball, it is clear what you have to do (throw a curve ball in the strike zone), but the problem is how to create a limb movement pattern to generate high velocity with sufficient accuracy. Thus, choice among actions is minimized, and the problem becomes how to optimally produce an already selected action. In this sense, speaking a new foreign word whose sounds have not been produced before, *ausgezeichnet*, for example, is a problem for motor learning.

Therefore, the most important component of feedback for motor learning is the information it provides about patterns of action. This feedback about errors, giving direction for modifying future performance, is the focus

Feedback from a knowledgeable instructor is critical for learning.

and important questions for the instructor. For example, what kind of information can the learner use most effectively (e.g., information about limb position, limb timing, coordination), in what form should it be presented (verbally, in videotape replays, graphically), when should it be presented (immediately after an action, delayed somewhat), and how often should it be presented (every trial, only some trials)? However, there is a side effect of informational, guiding feedback properties—the tendency for the learner to become dependent on feedback in various ways, leading to possible performance problems when feedback is withdrawn. Because this set of issues about the informational content of feedback is so large, the next sections are devoted to these and similar questions.

For now, these ideas about extrinsic feedback can be summarized as follows:

- A major component of feedback is information about errors.
- This information leads to corrections and improves performance.
- Continued feedback tends to hold performance errors to a minimum.
- Too-frequent feedback can produce learner dependency.

Dependency Producing Properties of Feedback

Recently, scientists have realized that feedback can act in the same general way as guidance (discussed in chapter 8). When feedback containing information for error correction is given frequently, it tends to guide behavior toward the goal movement. In a sense, this process is very much like the way that guidance operates. When physically directing a learner through a golf swing, guidance acts very powerfully to reduce errors, sometimes preventing them completely. This is fine as long as the guidance is present, but the golfer can learn to depend on the guidance. Performance can deteriorate markedly when the guidance is removed and the golfer attempts to swing without it.

Just as with physical guidance, augmented feedback tends to hold the movement at the goal, allowing the learner to correct errors quickly and thereby maintain the movement's correct form or outcome. The difficulty is, as with guidance, the learner can become dependent on the feedback, using it rather than some internally generated processes for keeping the movement on target. When the instructor's feedback is removed on a retention test, the performance could suffer markedly if the learner has not developed the capability to produce the movement independently. Various ways have been developed to structure feedback to minimize dependency producing effects as discussed later.

HOW INFORMATION FEEDBACK IS USED FOR LEARNING

This section discusses some of the most important principles of using information feedback for learning, such as issues surrounding the content of feedback presentations.

What Should Feedback Information Contain?

Which of the nearly countless features of a learner's movement are usefully reported as feedback? Clearly, some of these movement features are more useful to the learner than others, and some could be useless—or worse, even detrimental. In what form should this information be presented?

Match Feedback to What Is Controlled

One important idea is that feedback content should match what the learner can control.

This is perhaps obvious: The information should change the movement somehow, but this information will be useful only if the learner has control over the movement features signaled. Here is another way that understanding how movements are controlled—as discussed in the first part of this book and based on the conceptual model in Figure 10.2—provides an advantage in giving feedback for learning.

Feedback About Motor Program Variables. A fundamental problem is how to facilitate adjustment of a faulty generalized motor program, as discussed in chapters 4 and 9. For example, the tennis player performs a groundstroke with the arm swing too early with respect to the hip rotation. Adjusting the underlying temporal structure of a movement is far more difficult than simply changing a parameter that speeds or slows the entire movement.

The processes in making such changes are not very well understood, but there are a few guidelines that can be followed. Feedback should be about some movement feature that the learner can control. For example, the learner can control when to trigger a new unit of action (e.g., a throw) or how long to make a tennis backswing. On the other hand, asking the learner to generate a certain pattern of muscular force might be impossible because such patterns are limited by the properties of muscle tissue itself. Similarly, feedback about responding to certain sensory events, such as watching the baseball as it strikes the bat (which is probably not possible) might be useless, because the learner is limited by the characteristics of sensory receptors and fundamental information-processing capabilities.

In addition, feedback describing movement features, such as the timing of the arm movement and the hip action in the tennis stroke, can be very difficult to use. Some features occur essentially simultaneously and require modifications to a fundamental, usually very well-learned pattern of action that controls multiple events. Therefore, expect progress to be slow, performance to be inconsistent, and with frequent setbacks before the learner comes to generate the desired pattern. These improvements are very difficult, they run to the heart of the problem of motor learning, and they are very poorly understood.

Learning to Specify Parameters. Other ways to change movements are far easier, especially selecting parameters for a generalized motor program (see also chapters 4 and 9). Once the generalized motor program is specified, parameters must be specified to define the superficial movement features, such as duration, direction, or amplitude. These parameters are quickly and easily changed to make the action fit the environmental requirements, as is obvious when you consider the ease with which you can throw faster, then slower, then faster again on consecutive trials.

Parameters are almost always useful as feedback as long as the movement patterning is essentially correct. Information such as "Make the movement faster," "Make the movement larger," or "Pull the bar harder" is useful as feedback because it tells the learner how to select the parameters more effectively next time. The learner can make these changes easily from trial to trial. Because the problem for the learner is to discover rules for parameter selection, feedback about parameter appropriateness is an essential aspect of motor learning.

Give Program Feedback Before Parameter Feedback. In general, it is best to give feedback directed at the correction of errors in fundamental movement patterns before giving feedback about parameter variables. In teaching the learner to make free throws, try giving such feedback about the movement patterning as the rotation of the ball, the arc on the ball, the coordination of the wrist and knee actions, and so on. Tell the learner not to worry about whether the shot was too long or short (a parameter variable) until the proper pattern is achieved. Then, feedback about parameter variables will be easy to apply to the solid, effective generalized motor program, and good accuracy in shooting should result. Allowing the learner to practice an ineffective pattern causes the improper action to be learned relatively well, making pattern corrections even more difficult in the future.

Summary ◇ Break

These principles can be summarized as follows:

- Feedback about movement pattern timing or sequencing demands modifications in the fundamental program structure.
- Feedback about program features is difficult for learners to use but is critical in modifying faulty movement programs.
- Feedback about the overall speed, distance, or force of a given movement pattern contributes to parameter learning.
- Feedback about parameters leaves the program's structure intact and is easily used by learners to match the environmental demands.

How Much Feedback Information?

Because you could give feedback about countless features on every trial, the potential for overloading the learner with too much information is very real. Information processing and memory capabilities of the learner—particularly a child—is limited, so it is doubtful that the learner can take in and retain very much information during a feedback presentation. It is also doubtful that the learner can be very effective in correcting the next action in more than one way, particularly with feedback about a motor patterning variable. Feedback such as ''Make the arm action more forcefully than the hip turn, and start the hip action earlier'' would be very difficult to translate into an effective correction; see if you could follow the advice given in Figure 10.5. Decide what error is most fundamental and give feedback only about it. When this aspect is mastered, then start giving feedback about the next most important feature, and so on.

In general, do not give feedback about several features at once because too much information is generally not useful. However, if the feedback is about a parameter variable, which is more easily implemented, you could profitably give feedback on more than one variable at the same time. For example, the learner with an already effective motor program could relatively easily implement your feedback to ''Move faster and farther next time.''

Direction, Magnitude, and Precision of Feedback

Feedback about movement errors can be expressed in terms of either the direction of the error, the magnitude of the error, or both, and with varying levels of precision. Here are some of the principles involved.

Direction Versus Magnitude of Error. Information about the direction of the learner's error (early vs. late, high vs. low, left vs. right, etc.) is critical to bring the movement into line with the goal. In addition, it is generally helpful to report the magnitude of the errors as part of the feedback, such as ''Your movement was 2 cm to the left of the target.'' Of the two, direction is far more important than magnitude. Magnitude feedback alone is difficult to use because the learner does not know which direction to make the change. As discussed later, when the error size is

Figure 10.5 Feedback should be easy to understand and limited to one feature of the action.

within acceptable limits of correctness, generally avoid giving any information about these movement features at all (see Bandwidth Feedback).

Feedback Precision. Feedback precision is based on how close the reported feedback information is to the actual performance value. You could imagine feedback only roughly approximating the movement feature, such as ''Your backswing was a little too long,'' or some that more precisely reported, ''Your backswing was 5.5 cm too long.'' Beyond relatively coarse levels, though, there appears to be little advantage in increasing feedback precision. This seems to depend on the level of learning. Early on, the learner's errors are so large that precise information about the exact size of the errors simply does not matter. At a high level of

skill, somewhat more precise information might be good because the performance errors are much smaller and imprecise feedback reports could be misleading. This overall lack of importance for feedback precision is fortunate, in a way, because it reduces the need for very accurate (and expensive) devices for measuring performance and giving feedback. Of course, the instructor should be well schooled in the proper form of the action and in how to detect errors for the feedback to describe the important movement aspects well.

Prescriptive Feedback

All of this implies that the instructor needs to provide **prescriptive feedback** for effective corrections to occur (Newell & McGinnis, 1985). The instructor's feedback should prescribe a solution to the movement error, just as the physician prescribes medicine. Many kinds of feedback have this characteristic, such as the statement "Your backswing was too long that time." Of course, saying that the backswing was 88° when the learner does not know that the goal is 100° is not useful. Also, feedback such as "Not so good that time" contains no useful information for making prescriptive movement changes, so it should be avoided. Try to direct the learner toward the effective solution.

Summary Break

These are some of the most important principles to remember about these feedback variations:

- Feedback about direction of errors is most useful for learning.
- Feedback about magnitude of errors is generally useful only if it also indicates direction of the error.
- Feedback precision is important to a point, but further efforts to increase precision do not provide additional learning gains.
- Feedback should be prescriptive in nature, so the learner knows how to modify the movement on the next attempt.

Films, Videotape Replays, and Other Feedback Aids

An effective way to provide feedback about the learner's performance is through various recording devices that capture the essentials of the actions. These records can then be used later as feedback.

Stripchart Paper Records. Early pioneers in feedback methods recorded a performer's movement on stripchart paper, such as force-time tracings in sprint starts (Howell, 1956) and in industrial tasks (Tiffin & Rogers, 1943). This information was then displayed to the learner as feedback, with the correct action's tracing superimposed over the learner's actual movement tracing. More recently, investigators have used computer-aided instruction, which presents feedback about a certain movement feature immediately on a computer screen, directing the learner toward a more effective action.

Films. Films of performances, particularly involving American football games, have been popular for many years. Of course, films allow a team to view next week's opponent to develop a game plan. But these procedures can also be used as feedback for your own team, so that a player can see the consequences of his actions, can analyze his mistakes, and can detect the most effective movement patterns to use next time. Films can be motivating, also, because performers enjoy seeing themselves in action and laughing at their errors.

As learning tools, though, films are limited because the time required for developing film is usually quite long, so many events come between a given action and the feedback. Thus, it becomes difficult for the learners to remember what they did to produce particular errors, and how to avoid making those errors the next time.

Videotape. Videotape is a very popular means of giving feedback. Soon after video recorders became commercially available in the 1960s, gymnastics coaches used them for feedback during practices as well as for recording meet performances. Videotape solved many of the problems of films: Feedback about whole performances could be viewed after only a few seconds of tape rewind, and the replays captured the dynamics of the movement in relatively good detail and, more recently, in color with sound.

However, Rothstein and Arnold (1976) reviewed the evidence on videotape replays and, surprisingly, found that such feedback was not always useful for learning. Perhaps videotape replays provide too much information, so the learner does not know what to extract as feedback. As discussed earlier, giving several sources of feedback at once is not effective, and the learner can change only a minimal number of features of the movement at a time. This leads to the suggestion that cuing, where the instructor directs the learner to examine some particular feature of the movement as feedback, should be an effective technique. Rothstein and Arnold found that those videotape feedback experiments in which some form of cuing was used showed more benefits than those where cuing was not used. Videotape can be an effective additional tool in the learning environment, but additional research needs to be done to understand how to use it most effectively.

How Learning Is Affected by Feedback Scheduling

Having examined what information to give the learner, we now turn to feedback scheduling, focusing on when and when not to give feedback, how quickly to give it, and so

Videotape replays, when used with cuing to direct the learner to the important feature, can be very effective as feedback.

| PRACTICAL APPLICATIONS |

1. When possible, try comparing the goal pattern to various kinds of records of the learner's movement patterns to increase motivation and demonstrate errors most clearly.
2. Use films as feedback sparingly because they are relatively expensive and have generally long feedback delays filled with other competing activities.
3. Employ videotape replays when possible because they are effective for enhancing motivation, have short feedback delays, and clearly indicate the dynamic aspects of the movement.
4. Use stop-action in videotape replays to signal errors in particular parts of a movement.
5. When viewing a videotape replay, use cuing to direct the learner's attention to the relevant aspect of the replay, and give instructions to ignore irrelevant features.

on. These important variables have profound effects on learning and are under the instructor's control in the practice session.

Over the past several decades, much of the understanding of how feedback operated for skill learning was based on Thorndike's law of effect, discussed earlier in this chapter. This view of learning implied that certain feedback schedules should be most effective. Even though scientists now believe that Thorndike was incorrect, his ideas—particularly those about scheduling—continue to have a strong influence in numerous applied learning settings. For this reason, you need to understand these earlier views of learning as a basis for comparison with the newer views.

Thorndike's Perspective

Recall that the basic interpretation of the law of effect was that feedback strengthens associations (or bonds) between stimulus events and particular movements, thus forming the basis of learning (review Figure 10.4). Factors that increase the amount or frequency of such feedback presentations strengthen these bonds to an increased degree, further increasing learning. This basic notion naturally gave rise to the general idea that feedback should be presented as often as possible, which quickly became a standard belief in the movement skills literature. Viewed another way, if feedback should be withheld after a particular trial and the learner cannot know the outcome from intrinsic feedback, there can be no increment of bond strengthening for that trial, making the practice essentially useless for enhancing learning.

Over the next few decades, scientists saw little in the literature that would contradict this basic viewpoint about feedback for skill learning. Gradually, based on Thorndike's ideas, a set of feedback principles emerged, suggesting that any variation of feedback during practice making the information more immediate, more precise, more frequent, more informationally rich, or generally more useful is beneficial for learning. Such a view made good common sense—it just seems logical that giving more information to the learner should benefit learning—and it became widely adopted as a result. This principle makes strong implications for the structure of practice, encouraging just about anything that would provide more information to the learner.

As you will see, though, the generalization is probably wrong in several ways. One of the major difficulties for this principle emerged with recent research on the absolute and relative frequency of feedback, key variables that define how feedback is scheduled in a learning session. These variables failed to operate in ways predicted by Thorndike's views.

Absolute Frequency and Relative Frequency of Feedback

The feedback literature has defined two general descriptors of feedback scheduling. **Absolute frequency** refers to the number of feedback presentations given to a learner across a set of trials in practice. If there are 300 trials and the instructor gives feedback on 100 of them, the absolute frequency is 100—simply the total number of feedback presentations. **Relative frequency**, on the other hand, refers to the percentage of trials receiving feedback. The number of feedback presentations is divided by the number of trials and multiplied by 100. In the example, $100/300 = .33 \times 100 = 33\%$, where the feedback was presented on 33% of the trials.

What are the principles that describe the roles of absolute and relative frequency of feedback for learning? In general, increasing the number of trials that receive feedback enhances learning. This is especially true if the learner cannot detect his or her own errors without feedback, such as when the achievement goal is difficult to detect (e.g., shooting arrows at a distant target) or when the score must be computed in some way after the movement (e.g., a score from gymnastics judges). This is certainly the case in large classes, where one instructor is spread between 15 to 30 learners, so the amount of feedback provided to each learner is generally very small. Increasing the feedback here will aid performance and learning strongly. There are some limitations to this rule, especially in one-on-one learning situations where feedback can be very frequent, and this issue is discussed in the next section. Generally speaking, though, in most class-

oriented learning situations where feedback is relatively infrequent, increasing feedback frequency benefits learning.

PRACTICAL APPLICATIONS

1. In a large class, where frequent feedback is impossible, work hard to maximize the number of practice trials for which each learner receives feedback.
2. Mix encouragement, such as positive reinforcement about effort or correct actions, with information about errors to maintain motivation and interest between feedback trials.
3. In a large class, move between the learners relatively quickly; give feedback on only one trial, or two trials at most, before moving to the next learner.
4. In a large class, it is often effective to use assistants, volunteers, or other students to help give feedback on the simpler parts of the actions.

Decreased Relative Frequency Enhances Learning. Consider this situation: A learner practices a task such as rifle shooting to a distant target, where errors cannot be detected without extrinsic feedback. Because the instructor is busy giving feedback to other students, information about the performances can be given only occasionally. We have discussed the learning benefits of the trials that actually receive feedback, but what about the no-feedback trials in between? Are they useful for learning? Do these so-called blank trials between feedback trials have any function for learning at all, or are they simply a waste of time? Instructors have suspected that no-feedback trials were generally ineffective, which has led to the development of a number of artificial (and expensive) methods to give feedback about performance when the instructor was occupied. What are the issues here?

Such questions about blank trials can be answered by examining the effect of relative frequency of feedback for learning. Recent research has shown that blank trials can be actually beneficial for learning, even though subjects receive no feedback on them and cannot detect their errors for themselves (Winstein & Schmidt, 1990). This can be seen in Figure 10.6, where the 100% group received feedback after every trial (100% relative frequency) and the 50% group received feedback after only half the trials (50% relative frequency), with the same number of total trials. The groups improved at about the same rate in acquisition. However, in the tests of learning performed without any feedback, there was no tendency for the 50% group to have learned less. Even though half of their practice trials did not receive any feedback, learning was still occurring. This challenges Thorndike's perspective that

trials without feedback should produce no learning.

But there is more. When learning is evaluated by a retention test done after two days, reducing the amount of feedback given in practice actually enhances learning—not degrades it as predicted by Thorndike's view. An example of this is seen in the smaller errors for the 50% group in Figure 10.6. How, under Thorndike's view, could less feedback ever produce *more* learning? One answer given in recent theories is that withholding feedback on some trials generates different information-processing activities during practice that enhance the learning process in various ways. These processes tend to counteract the dependency producing effects of frequent feedback, allowing more effective long-term retention as a result. This idea is discussed more formally later in this chapter.

Faded Feedback. One way to reduce the dependency producing processes inherent in feedback is to use **faded feedback**. In this

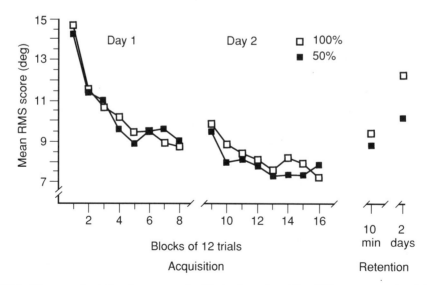

Figure 10.6 Decreased relative frequency facilitates learning. The 50% group received feedback on only half the trials yet outperformed the 100% group on a delayed retention test of learning. (From Winstein & Schmidt, 1990; reprinted by permission.)

method the learner is given feedback at high relative frequencies (essentially 100%) in early practice, which has the effect of driving the movement toward its eventual goal pattern and holding it there as long as feedback continues to be presented. To prevent the learner from developing a dependency on this feedback, the instructor gradually reduces the relative frequency of feedback as skill develops, which is the procedure used with the 50% group in Figure 10.6. With advanced skill the performance does not deteriorate very much when feedback is totally withdrawn for a few trials. If performance does begin to drop off, the instructor can give feedback again for a trial or two to bring behavior back to the target, after which the feedback can be withdrawn again. The instructor can adjust feedback scheduling to the proficiency level and improvement rate of each learner separately, thus tailoring feedback to individual differences in capabil-

ities. The ultimate goal is to generate the capability for the learner to produce the action on his or her own, without a dependency on feedback. Even though feedback is critical for developing the movement into a skilled pattern, it appears that it must be eventually removed to accomplish permanent skill learning.

Bandwidth Feedback. Another method for avoiding the dependency producing effects of frequent feedback is to use the **bandwidth feedback** method (Sherwood, 1988). The instructor gives the golfer information based on a small preset band of correctness, which might be a 20-cm range of acceptable clubhead positions at the top of the swing. If the movement falls in the correct range, no feedback is given, but if the movement falls outside the range, feedback indicating the amount and direction of the error is provided. This is illustrated in Figure 10.7,

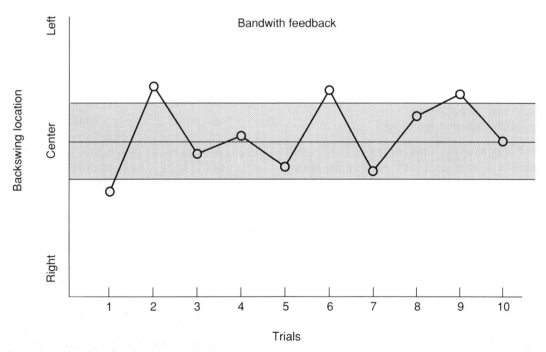

Figure 10.7 Bandwidth feedback is effective for learning. Feedback is given only if the performances fall outside the band of correctness.

showing a graph of backswing location for 10 hypothetical attempts to drive a golf ball from the tee. The band is the shaded area spanning the center. In the example here, the learner would receive bandwidth feedback only on Trials 1, 2, 6, and 9, and no information would have been provided about the other trials.

This method has several advantages. First, the method produces faded feedback as a by-product. When the learner is just beginning, the movements tend to be often outside the band, leading to frequent feedback from the instructor; with greater skill, the movements fall into the band—and feedback is withheld—more often, producing effects like faded feedback. Second, the learner receives positive reinforcement, a reward, for movements within the band; even though no feedback is given, the learner knows the previous movement was relatively good and repeats it. Finally, withholding information on a set of trials that fall within the band fosters consistent actions, so the learner is not encouraged to change the action on every trial. Eliminating these minute trial-to-trial corrections stabilizes performance, allowing more effective permanent memories.

Summary Feedback for Enhancing Learning

One way to avoid the detrimental effects of every-trial feedback is to use **summary feedback**. In this method, first studied by Lavery (1962; see the Highlight Box in this section), the feedback is withheld for a set of trials—say from 5 to 20 trials—and then is summarized for the learner in various ways. For example, a tennis instructor wants to teach a student to serve to a target position deep in the court, so he records the location of each serve in a practice session. During the practice the instructor might group the trials into sets of 15, then plot each serve's location on a graph such as in Figure 10.8. He shows the

---

PRACTICAL APPLICATIONS

1. During practice in a smaller class, avoid relative frequency larger than 50% to prevent dependency producing effects of frequent feedback.
2. Employ faded feedback: Give feedback frequently in early practice, then gradually withdraw it.
3. Use frequent feedback only until the learner achieves the basic goal movement pattern; fade the feedback presentations thereafter.
4. Adjust the schedule of fading to the individual learner, using more rapid fading for a more advanced learner and slower fading for one having problems.
5. Use bandwidth feedback as an easy way to produce fading in practice.
6. Train your students to give feedback to each other to increase the number of trials with feedback that can be given in a larger class.

---

graph to the learner only after the last trial in each 15-trial set has been completed. Notice that in this method every trial receives feedback, but the feedback is delayed, separated from the trial by several other trials.

On the surface summary feedback would seem to be particularly ineffective for learning. The informational content of the feedback would be seriously degraded because the learner wouldn't have any feedback until the summary feedback was eventually presented after the string of trials, thus receiving no basis for trial-to-trial corrections to improve performance. And when feedback is finally given, the learner would have a very difficult time relating the feedback for a particular trial with its associated movement because many other movements intervened.

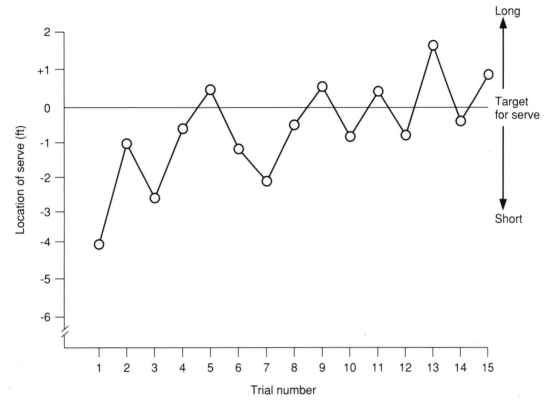

Figure 10.8 Summary feedback in learning a tennis serve. Scores are plotted on a graph, which is shown to the learner only after the last trial is completed.

Even so, early research by Lavery (1962; Lavery & Suddon, 1962) and more recent efforts have shown that summary feedback can be particularly effective for learning. Generally, even though summary feedback is less effective than every-trial feedback for performance during practice, when feedback is withdrawn in retention tests, subjects who had received summary feedback performed better than subjects who had received every-trial feedback (see the Highlight Box). These results show that, relative to every-trial feedback, summary feedback produces poorer performance in the acquisition phase but better learning, as measured on a retention test.

How Many Trials to Summarize? How many trials should you include in summary feedback? Can there be too many summarized trials? Recent evidence suggests that there is an optimal number of trials to include in summary feedback reports, with either too few or too many trials decreasing learning. Why? With every-trial feedback (a 1-trial summary), the learner is guided strongly to the goal, but this also maximizes the dependency producing effects. On the other hand, if a summary has a large number of trials (say 100), the dependency producing effects are reduced, but the learner is also less strongly guided toward the goal. This suggests an optimal number of summary feedback trials

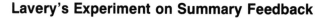

HIGHLIGHT

Lavery's Experiment on Summary Feedback

The Canadian scientist J.J. Lavery (1962; Lavery & Suddon, 1962) examined several kinds of feedback presentations during the learning of simple laboratory motor tasks, such as striking a small ball with a special hammer to propel it up a ramp to a target. All subjects performed the skill on Day 1 without any feedback, then received different kinds of feedback for the next 5 days. One group had immediate feedback, receiving KR after each trial. A second group had only summary feedback: KR was withheld for 20 trials, the individual performances were plotted on a graph, and the graph was shown to the learner after the last trial in the set (as in Figure 10.8). A third group had both kinds of feedback—feedback after each trial and a summary at the end of 20 trials. Then all subjects were tested without any feedback on the next 4 days, as well as 1 month and 3 months later.

The performance curves are shown in Figure 10.9. Notice first that the summary group performed much more poorly than the immediate and the both groups in the acquisition phase, reflecting the fact that summary feedback is difficult to use in

practice. However, on the no-feedback retention tests, the summary group was more accurate than either the immediate or the both groups. Because performance on retention tests is a measure of amount learned, we conclude that even though subjects in the summary group performed less well in acquisition, they learned more than subjects in the immediate and the both groups. These effects persisted for several months, although the differences diminished somewhat by 3 months.

One interpretation is that the groups with information after each trial (immediate and both) acquired a kind of dependency on feedback, which was prevented in the summary group. Then, when feedback was withdrawn in the retention tests, the summary subjects, who had not learned to depend on every-trial feedback, were able to repeat the movements, whereas the immediate and the both subjects were not. These results have powerful implications both for feedback scheduling to enhance learning in practical settings and for the fundamental understanding of how feedback produces learning.

where the benefits from being guided to the goal are just balanced with costs of the dependency producing influences.

This is just what was shown in an experiment by Schmidt, Lange, and Young (1990), who studied different numbers of summary feedback trials on a laboratory task resembling batting in baseball. As seen in Figure

10.10, there was an inverted-U relationship between summary length and learning, with the 5-trial summary feedback length being best. Again, even though the 1-trial condition (every-trial feedback) was best for performance during earlier practice, when feedback was being presented, the 5-trial condition was best for learning.

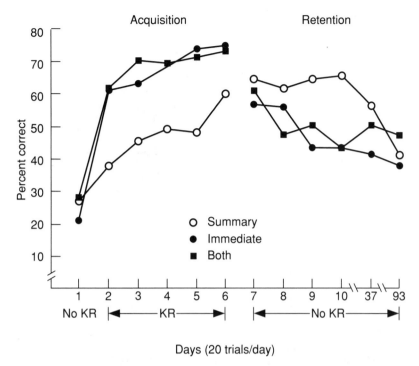

Figure 10.9 Percent correct responses for various feedback methods. Summary feedback produces poor performance in acquisition but better retention. (From Lavery, 1962; reprinted by permission.)

Summary Feedback and Task Complexity.
Does this principle hold for all kinds of motor tasks, or does it depend on task complexity? For a very simple task (e.g., Lavery's tasks in Figure 10.9), a relatively large number of trials (20 or more) can be included in summary feedback, which is far better than every-trial feedback for learning. For a more complex task, though, such as that in Figure 10.10 (analogous to batting in baseball), a shorter summary length (e.g., 5 trials) brings optimal learning. For an extremely complex task, the optimal number of trials may approach 1 (i.e., every-trial feedback), at least until the learner has mastered the essential movement elements. Generally, as the task increases in complexity, the learner needs more feedback guidance to achieve the proper actions, so fewer trials should be summarized. This general trend is depicted in Figure 10.11.

How Does Summary Feedback Work?
What are the processes behind the benefits of summary feedback? Following are three ways summary feedback could function to aid learning:

1. Summary feedback might prevent the dependency producing effects of frequent feedback because it causes the learner to perform independently for several trials before finally receiving feedback. Then the learner can make corrections to the general movement pattern produced in the earlier trials. For example, knowing that my tennis serves were generally too long, as graphed in Figure 10.8, allows me to adjust slightly, correcting the error on the next set of trials.

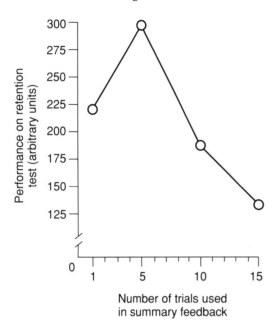

Figure 10.10 Performance on retention as a function of the number of trials used for summary feedback in acquisition. The 5-trial summary length was the most effective for learning. (From Schmidt, Lange, & Young, 1990; reprinted by permission.)

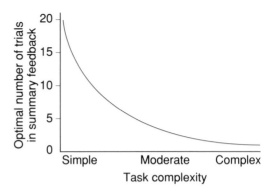

Figure 10.11 The probable relationship between task complexity and the optimal number of trials in summary feedback.

2. Summary feedback might produce more stable movements because feedback is withdrawn for several trials, giving the learner no reason to change the movement from trial to trial. Frequent feedback, on the other hand, leads the learner to change the movement on every trial, which prevents the movement from achieving the stability needed for subsequent performance.

3. Summary feedback appears to encourage learners to analyze their own response-produced (kinesthetic, visual, etc.) feedback to learn to detect their own errors (this concept was discussed in chapter 9). Frequent feedback tells learners about errors, eliminating the motivation to process response-produced feedback, so the learners do not become familiar with it. In this way, the capability of the learners to detect their own errors in future performance may be degraded by every-trial feedback.

However summary feedback enhances learning, it is *not* due to providing extra information to the learner. Return to Figure 10.8, showing the summary feedback for a hypothetical set of tennis serves. This plot offers a wealth of information, such as (a) the performance on each trial, (b) the amount of variability among the trials, (c) the improvement trend across trials, and much more.

Notice, however, in Lavery's (1962) experiment (see Highlight Box), the group that learned with immediate feedback *and* summary feedback (the both group in Figure 10.9) performed as poorly in retention as the every-trial group (the immediate group). So, if summary feedback operates because it provides more information, why did the both group learn so poorly? They received the summary information, too. My answer is that feedback is given too frequently to the immediate group (and the both group), producing one or more of the detrimental effects mentioned earlier. That is, every-trial feedback dragged down the learning in the both group to the level of the immediate group.

These are some of the issues surrounding summary feedback's usefulness for learning:

- Summary feedback could prevent the dependency producing effects of feedback, allowing learners to perform on their own.
- Summary feedback could block the learner's tendency to make corrections on every movement, thus generating movement consistency.
- Summary feedback could enhance processing of response-produced feedback, leading to more effective error-detection capabilities.
- However, summary feedback does not facilitate learning due to providing the learner with more information.

Average Feedback. In a variant of summary feedback called **average feedback**, the learner waits for several trials before receiving feedback information about his or her score (as with summary feedback), but now receives only the average score on those trials. The instructor might watch the learner make 10 golf swings, after which she reports, "Your backswing was (on the average) about 6 in. too short on those trials." Young and Schmidt (1990b) showed that average feedback was more effective for learning than feedback after every trial, in more or less the same way as summary feedback. In fact, average feedback and summary feedback could operate in the same general way—by blocking the detrimental, dependency producing effects of every-trial feedback.

Average feedback also allows the instructor to form a better idea of the learner's movement pattern. On any one attempt, just about anything can happen because performances vary greatly from trial to trial. However, by watching the performer do several trials, the instructor can filter out this variability to detect the learner's typical pattern. After viewing several trials, the instructor

could detect that the performer's usual (i.e., average) backswing is slightly too long and too rapid, even though these features may not have both been present in any particular movement. Also, average feedback gives the learner more reliable information about what to change, and how much to change it, on the next few practice trials.

When Should Feedback Information Be Given?

Assuming that you want to give feedback on a particular trial, how soon after the

---

PRACTICAL APPLICATIONS

1. Even when it is possible to give feedback on every trial, resist the temptation: Give average or summary feedback instead.
2. Give feedback in summary form if possible, graphing some feature of performance against several trials for later presentation to the learner.
3. Do not let the performer see the graph until the planned number of trials has been completed and the summary graph has been prepared.
4. Erasable marker boards or small chalkboards can effectively display summary feedback; use student help if possible to plot graphs.
5. Try giving a hard copy of summary feedback on graph paper for the learner to keep, enhancing learner motivation and interest.
6. As a variant, give feedback information based on performances averaged over several trials, the average feedback method.
7. Observe the learner for a series of trials, watching for an error pattern that you can report as average feedback.

movement should you give it? You often hear that "immediate feedback" is desirable, leading to the idea that an instructor should strive to give feedback as quickly as possible after a performance to maximize learning. What is the role, if any, of the timing of the information that you give?

Feedback timing can be described by two delay intervals, shown in Figure 10.12. The interval from a given trial until its feedback is presented is the **feedback delay**, whereas the interval from the feedback until the next trial is produced is the postfeedback delay. These two delays together form the intertrial interval, or the separation between trials. Within practical limits, these values can be as large or small as the instructor desires.

Feedback Delays and Motor Learning

An information-processing perspective about feedback holds that the learner uses feedback to correct errors. If the feedback presentation is separated in time from the action and the learner forgets various aspects of the movement by the time feedback arrives, shouldn't the feedback be less useful in making corrections? You certainly might think so, but what does the evidence say?

Empty Feedback Delays. First, consider simply lengthening the time interval between a movement and its feedback, where the interval is empty of potentially competing events (conversations, other trials, etc.). (This interval is never truly empty, of course.) When empty feedback delay has been examined in human motor learning research, scientists have almost never found systematic effects on learning (Salmoni, Schmidt, & Walter, 1984), with delays ranging from several seconds to several minutes. The lack of any degraded learning when the feedback delays were lengthened has been surprising to most scientists in the area because the information-processing view would predict that longer intervals would interfere with learning. In any case, without other activities in the interval between a movement and its feedback, the instructor doesn't need to worry about giving the feedback quickly enough.

Instantaneous Feedback. There is one exception to this generalization, however: situations where feedback is presented very quickly after a movement. Under the belief that feedback given quickly would be beneficial for learning, many instructors have tried to minimize feedback delays, essentially giving **instantaneous feedback**. This is often seen in complex simulators, where the computer delivers feedback about errors virtually instantly. It is also seen in video games, where an evil, slimy space invader is blown up instantly with a large, colorful burst of light when hit with the death ray from your

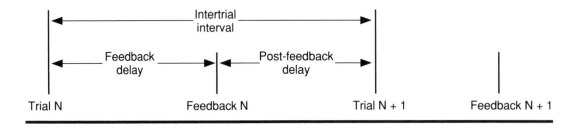

Figure 10.12 Some important intervals define the timing of feedback information during practice.

weapon, informing you that your aim and shot timing were perfect. Also, instantaneous feedback is a natural consequence of many real-world movements, where intrinsic feedback is instantly available to inform the learner about the movement outcome (e.g., seeing the flight of the golf ball).

Though it might appear that instantaneous feedback would be effective for learning, some recent research shows that giving feedback instantaneously, as opposed to delaying it a few seconds, is actually detrimental to learning (Swinnen, Schmidt, Nicholson, & Shapiro, 1990). This can be seen in Figure 10.13, where the instantaneous feedback group performed a simulated batting task more poorly than the delayed group on the second day of practice and on several reten-

tion tests given up to 4 months later. One interpretation is that feedback given instantaneously blocks the subject from processing response-produced feedback (i.e., how the movement felt, sounded, looked). Attending to this artificial feedback from the instructor retards the learning of error-detection capabilities, as discussed in chapter 9.

An interesting extension of these findings is that blocking usually instantaneous *intrinsic* feedback for a few seconds after a trial should also be effective for learning. This could be done by blocking the free throw shooter's view of the basket just after the ball release, obscuring with a screen the golfer's view of the ball's flight at a driving range, or using a blindfold for dribbling practice. However, these methods have not been

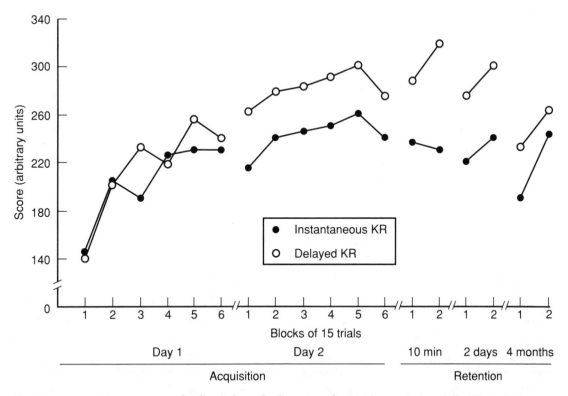

Figure 10.13 Instantaneous feedback degrades learning of coincidence-timing skills. (From Swinnen, Schmidt, Nicholson, & Shapiro, 1990; reprinted by permission.)

studied very thoroughly, so this extension of the findings should be regarded cautiously.

Interfering Activities in the Feedback Delay Interval.

When the delays are long in many real-world settings, other activities can occur between a given movement and its feedback, tending to occupy the learner's attention. These intervening activities may include conversing with a friend, practicing some other task, or attempting other trials of the given movement, as in the summary feedback method. The research findings fall into two classes, depending on the nature of the intervening task.

1. *Intervening Activity of a Different Task.* Imagine that the activity occurring between a given movement and its KR is a different task that interferes in some way. This activity could be a trial of a different motor task or even a task involving mental operations, such as recording one's scores or giving feedback to a friend. These events during the interval from the movement until feedback generally degrade learning as measured on retention tests (Marteniuk, 1986; Shea & Upton, 1976). Learning is more effective if the feedback and the movement it describes are not separated by other activities.

2. *Intervening Trials of the Same Task.* What if the intervening activity is just another trial of the same motor task? For example, the instructor might give the learner several minutes to practice a skill, then give feedback about these movements after 20 or so of the movements are completed. Feedback about a golf drive might include statements such as "Your first few drives were great, but then you started to rotate your hips too early in the later ones." This has been called trials delay of feedback, where other trials of a given action come between the movement and its feedback. Although this would seem to prevent the learner from connecting the movement and the corresponding feedback, the evidence says that it is not detrimental at all, and it is even slightly more effective for learning than presenting feedback after each trial (Lavery & Suddon, 1962). Notice that summary feedback has this feature as well, as in Figure 10.8, where Trial 1 and its feedback (in the summary graph) have Trials 2 through 15 intervening between them. You have already seen how effective summary feedback is for learning.

Random Practice and Variable Practice.

The findings in the previous sections have special implications for organizing random practice and variable practice, as discussed in chapter 9. Recall that both jumbling the order of several different tasks (random practice) and varied practice at versions of a given task (variable practice) have beneficial effects on learning. How should feedback be given during these practice sequences?

We have a good estimate of the answer from the principles we have studied so far. These principles say that it is not harmful to learning to delay feedback or even to have other trials of the same task (or task version) in the feedback delay interval. However, it is harmful to have *different* tasks in the feedback delay interval. (The notion of the "same" or "different" task refers to its temporal patterning, or relative timing, as discussed in chapter 5.) Therefore, during random practice, where several different tasks are being alternated, the instructor should provide all feedback about performances on Task A before giving any trials of Task B. A useful possibility might be to give trials of A, followed by summary feedback, then trials of B, followed by summary feedback, and so on. This is illustrated here, where "Sum FB" means summary feedback:

A, A, A, Sum FB on A,
B, B, B, Sum FB on B,
A, A, A, Sum FB on A,
and so on

Summary Break

The principles concerning feedback delays and motor learning seem relatively clear, and they can be summarized as follows:

- So-called empty delays between a given movement and its feedback have no effect on learning.
- Giving feedback instantaneously after a movement degrades learning, probably interfering with error-detection processes.
- Interfering activities in the feedback delay interval that are different from the learning task degrade learning.
- Other trials of the same task in the feedback delay interval (e.g., with summary or average feedback) are beneficial for learning.

From Feedback to Next Movement: Postfeedback Delay

After receiving feedback for one movement, in the postfeedback delay (Figure 10.12) the learner tries to generate another movement that is different from the previous one, a movement that will eliminate the errors signaled by feedback. How much time is required for processing this information, and how soon can the next movement be begun? The research on these questions shows that if this interval is too short (less than 5 s), performance on the next trial will suffer, probably because of insufficient time to plan it. However, as long as the interval is somewhat longer (say, greater than 5 s), there is no advantage to giving the learner even more time to plan and generate the next movement (Weinberg, Guy, & Tupper, 1964). The interval should probably be a little longer in a task that is relatively complex or where many different decisions have to be made about alternative movement strategies and methods. Overall, though, the postfeedback interval is not particularly powerful in determining learning, and you can focus on more important aspects of the learning environment.

PRACTICAL APPLICATIONS

1. Use relatively short feedback delays to avoid having other movements or activities separate the movement from its feedback; this also shortens the intertrial interval.
2. Do not be concerned about shortening the empty delay between a movement and its feedback because it does not markedly affect learning unless the delay is very short.
3. However, avoid having augmented, artificial feedback follow the movement instantaneously, which would degrade learning.
4. Do not intersperse practice of other learning tasks, or attention-demanding information-processing activities, between a given movement and its feedback.
5. It is effective to intersperse other trials of the same task between a given movement and its feedback, thereby approaching a summary feedback schedule.
6. When giving random practice for several tasks in the same session, give all feedback for a given task before switching practice to the next task.
7. Allow sufficient time after giving feedback (5 s should be enough) for the learner to think about and understand the errors.
8. The postfeedback intervals should be sufficiently long (e.g., 5 s) for effective planning of the next movement, but further lengthening of the postfeedback delay just wastes time.

CHAPTER SUMMARY

A learner can receive various kinds of sensory information, but augmented, extrinsic feedback about errors from the instructor is one of the most critical aspects of the learning environment. This kind of information can have several simultaneous roles: It can serve as an energizer to increase motivation; it can reinforce the probability of various future choices; it can provide information, where it signals the nature and direction of errors and how to correct them; and it can produce a learner dependency, where performance suffers when the information is withdrawn. Feedback can take on many forms, such as videotape replays, films, and, of course, verbal descriptions. Verbal feedback is best when simple and referring to only one movement feature at a time, a movement feature the learner can control.

The largest errors can be corrected in early learning with frequent feedback. After a few trials, however, learning is best if feedback frequency is gradually reduced (faded) across practice. Summary feedback, where a set of trials is described by a graph shown to the learner only after the set is completed, is particularly effective for learning, and the optimum number of trials included in the summary should decrease as task complexity increases. An early principle—that anything making feedback more frequent, accurate, and useful enhances learning—is being replaced by newer viewpoints that focus on the subtle aspects of feedback's nature and scheduling.

◇ Checking Your Understanding

1. What is the distinction between extrinsic and intrinsic feedback? Between knowledge of results and knowledge of performance? Please give examples of each.
2. Describe the four ways that extrinsic feedback modifies behavior. Select four skills situations and give a sample feedback statement that illustrates each of these modifying functions.
3. What procedures can reduce the dependency producing properties of feedback in teaching situations? Give some examples.
4. What are the benefits and limitations of videotape feedback for learning and coaching?
5. What line(s) of evidence suggests that giving feedback on every trial may actually interfere with learning? Why does this occur?

◇ Key Terms

Definitions of the following terms appear on the page(s) shown in parentheses:

absolute frequency (p. 245)
augmented feedback (p. 231)
average feedback (p. 253)
bandwidth feedback (p. 246)
extrinsic feedback (pp. 229, 231)
faded feedback (pp. 246-247)
feedback (p. 228)
feedback delay (p. 254)
feedback precision (p. 241)
instantaneous feedback (p. 254)
intermittent reinforcement (p. 235)
intrinsic feedback (p. 229)
knowledge of performance (KP) (p. 232)
knowledge of results (KR) (p. 231)
prescriptive feedback (pp. 241-242)
relative frequency (p. 245)
summary feedback (p. 248)

◇ **Suggestions
for Further Reading**

A thorough review of the published research on feedback and motor learning was done by Salmoni, Schmidt, and Walter (1984) and by Newell and McGinnis (1985), where details of the principles described here are described more fully. Some of the more recent work in this area, together with a discussion of kinesthetic feedback for motor control, was reviewed by Winstein and Schmidt (1988), and the research on videotape replays for motor learning was reviewed by Rothstein and Arnold (1976). See also Schmidt (1988b, chapter 13) for more on feedback and motor learning, and Lee and Carnahan (1990) for more on bandwidth feedback.

Part III

Applying
the Principles

Parts I and II presented many principles, processes, and mechanisms and discussed places where these could be applied to teaching and coaching situations in the real world. These various ideas have been integrated into a single conceptual model, which should help students new to this area gain a complete picture of the functioning of the human motor system. Even so, you may have the impression that these ideas are too diverse, dealing with too many different issues and situations, for effective application to occur. Chapter 11's intent is to clarify the relationships among the concepts presented earlier so that you will be able to apply them most effectively in helping others learn motor skills.

Integration and Application

PREVIEW

The instructor is beginning to panic. She has just left the administrator's office, where she learned that starting next Monday, she will be teaching a class in an activity that is relatively unfamiliar to her and that she has not taught previously. She remembers a number of seemingly scattered principles from a class in motor learning but is having trouble envisioning a course of activities that is consistent with the principles of learning, and efficient, interesting, pleasurable, and workable with the facilities at hand. How should she organize the practice? Which of the many principles are most and least important in these decisions? How should learning be evaluated? How should she begin to attack these problems?

This chapter should make these decisions easier. It reviews the principles discussed in this book and, with the kind of situation just described, provides a plan of attack to make the practice organization most effective. First comes the important problem of skill classification, because so many principles depend on what kinds of skills are being taught. Then some of the most important principles of practice are discussed as to how they influence the structure of practice at various stages of learning. Also examined are some of the learning evaluation principles so critical for education. The overall goal is to tie together all the principles in the text to facilitate application.

STUDENT GOALS

1. To integrate the various principles of organizing practice
2. To appreciate how different kinds of skills should be treated differently in practice
3. To review the principles operating at different learning stages
4. To apply principles of motor learning to defining acceptable evaluation methods

Teachers and coaches are frequently faced with the problems mentioned at the opening of this chapter, where many decisions about the organization and structure of practice need to be made, based on the instructor's knowledge and understanding of the learners, the processes and principles of learning, and of course the materials and skills that are to be taught. This final chapter is concerned with merging the many facts, principles, processes, and concepts that have been generated throughout this book into a workable whole. It is structured in a way that emphasizes the various decisions that an instructor might face. The discussion begins with the principles involved in the preparation for practice, then turns to how the principles you have learned apply to the verbal-cognitive, motor, and autonomous stages of learning. Finally, some of the principles that apply to learning evaluation are discussed.

PRE-PRACTICE PREPARATIONS

I have found that, as with most large projects in life (e.g., teaching a class or writing this book), the hardest and frequently most important part involves preparation for what is to be done. Preparation is usually agonizing for me because countless seemingly conflicting facts and principles come to mind, and it is difficult to write down essentially what will be done without a great deal of dithering, frustration, and fretting. Once I have managed to define an effective plan of action, however—even if it is not exactly finalized—the execution of this plan is relatively easy, and I often wonder why I had so much trouble preparing the plan in the first place. Assuming that the reader shares at least some of my difficulties in this regard, this chapter begins with the toughest part—the preparations for practice.

In thinking about preparations, it is useful to begin with the conceptual model of human performance that has been developed throughout this book. Most of the principles upon which the application is based depend in some way on the processes discussed throughout the text and symbolized by the conceptual model, shown in finalized form in Figure 11.1.

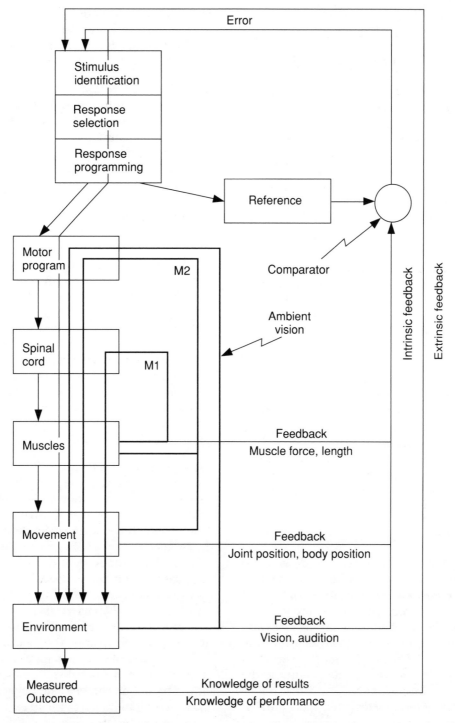

Figure 11.1 The completed conceptual model of human performance, used here as a basis for the organization of effective practice.

Classification:
A Fundamental Step

If you were to make a list of the various generalizations, principles, and applications that have been discussed in the book, you would certainly come away with the feeling, perhaps even frustration, that these statements are seldom hard-and-fast rules. Rather, the statements are often qualified in various ways. The wording frequently contains phrases such as "In the early stages of learning," or "When the class size is very small," or similar notions that limit the principle that follows to certain kinds of situations, learners, tasks, or circumstances. The science of motor control and learning is at a stage of relative infancy, so the principles and theories are not sufficiently well developed to apply to all cases and all situations, such as principles of mechanics would to engineering.

The result is that the principles that must be dealt with here tend to be somewhat specific to particular tasks, stages of practice, or types of learners—that is, specific to different classifications. Thus, it is critical to recognize these various categories and to choose the principles appropriate for them. Coming next are some of the most important classifications that make a difference for planning and teaching.

Goal of Practice: The Criterion Skill

Probably the most important decision to make involves the overall goal of practice, the **criterion skill**. In what form, or in what situation, do you want the skills you will teach to apply? Simply, what do you want your learners to be able to *do* as a result of your efforts? Of course, most instructors want their learners to be able to perform the skills well during practice, and this is certainly one criterion. However, there are several other, probably more important criteria

for learning, and the decision about which of these is most important in your situation has implications for how you organize practice. There are essentially three other criteria.

Long-Term Retention. In one case, the criterion is simply to retain for future performance the specific practiced skill. For example, in archery, platform diving, swimming, long-jumping, and so on, the skill in practice is more or less identical to the skill in competition because the task is very well standardized. Here the focus is on how well the practice produces long-term retention capabilities that can be used in some upcoming situation. You have learned about some of the variables that enhance long-term retention, such as randomizing practice, avoiding giving feedback on every trial, facilitating automatization with randomized consistent mapping practice, and so on. Also, if the criterion skill is identical with that experienced in practice (as the preceding examples are), variable practice would be of questionable value, and practice should be tailored to be as specific as possible to the actual task conditions that will be ultimately experienced.

Generalization. However, for most of the skills people practice, the goal is to apply the learning to some variation in the skill or context, that is, to generalize to novel situations. Sometimes this is seen as simple variations in the speed or force with which a given class of actions is produced, such as throwing to first base from different distances and directions. In other situations the problem is to produce novel behavior, such as deciding where to run with the football when in traffic—well after the planned portion of the play has been completed. Sometimes a person must perform in a novel environment, such as the mountain climber who never sees the same set of handholds twice. In each of these cases, the criterion skill is something different from that specifically experienced in practice.

Here practice must be tailored to meet this criterion, primarily by generating near transfer from practice to the goal skill. Relatively stereotyped practice (as with the goal of retention) will not do because this form of practice is not very effective for generalization. In this case, variable practice should be used so the learner can acquire the capability to parameterize to meet new environmental demands. Also, practice at dealing with changing environments, where decision making about what to do when new situations arise, is very important, whereas practice for automaticity and movement consistency is not. Random practice is particularly important here because it gives the learner experience at generating novel solutions to the problems, or retrieval practice.

General Performance Capabilities. Learning goals are often even more remote from practice experiences. For example, with very small children, a common goal is some gen-

The goals of practice are often more far-reaching than just achieving a single skill, having implications for future participation and learning.

eral set of capabilities to move efficiently, to be motorically effective, to have movement competence, to be confident in new situations, and so on. In teaching dance you want the learner to feel comfortable dancing in many settings and perhaps to want to learn new dances in some future situation. These benefits of practice are intended for new circumstances, and the skills in practice can be very different from those in the future criterion. Often there is the goal of facilitating future learning, so the earlier practice experiences transfer to the ease of acquiring new skills. All of this involves far transfer, transfer to tasks and situations very remote from those experienced in practice. When this goal is important, practice should be highly varied, with many different kinds of activities being experienced and the mastery of specific, individual skills being deemphasized.

Task Classifications

Having decided on the fundamental practice goals, the next step is to make decisions about the nature of the skills to be practiced. Several major classifications of skills were discussed in chapter 1 (e.g., discrete-serial-continuous, open-closed, etc.). There are many more or less global ways to classify tasks, however, each of which has a bearing on some of the decisions you must make when planning a learning environment. Following are some of them and why they matter. As you go through this list, imagine that you evaluate every task you will teach in terms of these dimensions. As you will see, knowing where these tasks lie on these dimensions has strong implications for the ways you will structure practice.

Continuous, Serial, and Discrete. This fundamental distinction has strong implications for the processes involved in performance and how to focus instruction. Discrete actions—such as a punch, a throw, a punt—

are often so quick that the movement is completed before feedback information can have much effect. The focus is on the preplanning of the movement and the production of the movement as if it were a single unit, discouraging the learner from attempting to modify the action while it is unfolding. Fatigue tends not to be a problem for learning discrete actions, so rest time can be minimized to increase the number of practice trials, at least as long as the tasks are not dangerous. Here, also, the capability for evaluating performance after the action is completed is an important goal of learning, so learners can be encouraged to attend to their own response-produced feedback to develop the capability for error detection. Of course, have them do this after the movement, not during it.

Continuous tasks—such as swimming, cross country skiing, riding a unicycle—involve a series of ongoing modifications for feedback and motor control, so focus on sensory information and how to modify behavior as a function of it. Tracking tasks (e.g., steering a race car) are important examples of continuous tasks, where learning the regularity and probability of the upcoming stimulus events and learning ways to anticipate are a large part of the process. Fatigue tends to be a larger problem with continuous tasks, so you need to budget more time for rest between practice trials. Error detection occurs *during* the action in continuous tasks and is the basis for performance, so don't attempt to develop error-detection capabilities for use after the trial, as you would with discrete actions.

Serial tasks are a curious blend of these two categories, often thought of as a set of discrete actions hooked together to form a serial chain. Sometimes you can separate the difficult pieces of the chain for part practice, which is not possible in discrete actions. The effectiveness of part practice, though, is strongly reduced if the parts are strongly in-

terdependent, as discussed later. Often a key element in the teaching process is determining the boundaries between the relatively independent parts, which then should allow part practice on each if necessary (e.g., separating the toss from the forward-swing action in a tennis serve).

Open and Closed. The open-closed dimension also has implications for teaching. If the task is open (e.g., dribbling in soccer), where the environment is unpredictable and uncertain, then instructions and emphases for learning are most effective if they focus on the nature of the environment. Trying to learn its regularities and what to do when certain events occur are typical problems for the performer in these tasks. The performer must learn to be flexible. On the other hand, learning closed skills, where the environment is stable (e.g., gymnastics), benefits from an approach that focuses on the motor control and the generation of preprogrammed actions. The performer must learn to be stable and consistent.

Motor and Cognitive. To what extent do decision making and choices among alternatives play a role in success? In highly cognitive skills (e.g., chess or coaching), high arousal levels are detrimental for performance, and probably for learning as well. With very motor skills (e.g., weight lifting), where the premium is on producing movement patterns with little decision making, higher arousal levels are tolerable, and very high levels may even be beneficial. In addition, in skills with strong cognitive elements, instruction focuses mainly on how to make the decisions, often with emphasis on minimizing errors and maximizing speed. With motor skills, though, the emphasis is more on movement control and response production.

Perceptual Emphases. How important for performance success are the various analyses of sensory information patterns? In some skills, being able to detect changes in the environmental patterns is all-important, such as seeing a play unfolding in football, so you can direct much emphasis to practice at such processes. Other skills hardly have this feature at all, such as performing a javelin throw, where the focus is mainly on movement control once the approach is begun. Deciding how much emphasis to place on sensory information determines the nature of practice activities that you want to schedule.

Sequential Dependencies. Do the parts (either successive or simultaneous) of the task interact strongly, where the control needed for the production of one part depends on the way in which another part was performed? If so, then part practice is not an effective method for teaching this skill. In serial skills, focus the learner on making the earlier parts more consistently, which simplifies the control needed on the subsequent parts. Also, these parts will never be completely consistent, so much of the learning in these skills involves ways of compensating for variations in earlier parts. Skilled gymnasts modify later parts based on variations in body position from earlier parts, and they must do so without alerting the judges that anything has gone wrong.

Possibility for Automatization. Can the skill, or perhaps a part of the skill, be automated to free attention for higher-order aspects of the skill (e.g., strategy in a game or expressive elements in dance)? The key question is whether these elements are performed under consistent-mapping conditions, where a given stimulus situation always leads to the same action. If so, you could single out these elements for special consistent-mapping practice, and you would expect this experience to contribute to skill in the overall task. However, if the action must be produced in response to various stimulus situations (e.g., for a defensive lineman in football), then practice for automatization is less effective.

Importance of Errors. How costly are errors in your task? If errors are not costly, organize instruction to automate movements in consistent environments to reduce reaction-time delays. If errors are very costly, though, such as a move in the wrong way in a football game that allows the other team to score, then practice for automatization is less important than an emphasis on sensory analysis to detect the other team's movements quickly.

Program and Parameter Learning. Do a number of the tasks you are to teach share a common relative timing structure (e.g., backhand strokes in racquetball and paddleball), or are they fundamentally different? If your analysis suggests they are members of the same class, you can tailor teaching to capitalize on these similarities, emphasizing positive transfer. For different-speed versions of a groundstroke in tennis, for example, be sure to allow for variable practice once the skills have reached the motor stage of mastery. If the learner needs to acquire a new pattern of action (new **program learning**), where the pattern is not a simple variant of any learned previously, then budget a great deal of time for practice in this phase because the rate of improvement will be relatively slow. On the other hand, if the movement is a simple variant of one learned earlier (e.g., throwing a different ball or throwing to a different location), then the improvement will be much faster because it is based mainly on **parameter learning**. In such a case, be certain to schedule varied practice of several parameters to facilitate learning the schemas that allow accurate future parameter selection.

Complex and Simple. Is the movement relatively simple, or is it complex? This is a difficult dimension because there are several ways that you can conceptualize complexity. If you think of complexity as some aspect of the number of limbs involved and/or the amount of coordination required among them, then estimating this variable is at least reasonable. For a **complex skill** defined this way, keep the arousal level fairly low; a simpler skill can actually benefit from an elevated arousal level. Complex skills also require additional thought in terms of the way you describe them in demonstrations and in the ways you give feedback when errors are made. Of course, you need to budget more time for the learning of complex skills.

Dangerous and Safe. How safe is a task with respect to possible physical injury from a performance? If you judge the task to be dangerous (e.g., swimming for beginners), it is wise to employ guidance procedures that prevent a serious error, such as a partner on the pool deck with a pole or spotting belts in gymnastics. A dangerous task tends to produce fear and anxiety in the learner, so guid-

In many tasks, the criterion skill cannot be experienced in training, so practice must be organized to facilitate transfer.

ance techniques also allow the learner to relax and concentrate on the task to be learned. A dangerous task also produces perceptual narrowing, where peripheral or rare signals are apt to be missed, so emphasis can be directed to detecting such signals.

Meaningfulness of Intrinsic Feedback. Another important consideration is whether the intrinsic information the learner receives from the task when practicing is sufficient to ensure learning. In some tasks, learners cannot detect the outcome of their own actions very well, such as in rifle shooting to distant, unseen targets or in springboard diving, where a judge is usually needed to generate the score. In such situations, you should devise a way to provide extrinsic feedback information, or knowledge of results (KR). In other tasks, where learners can detect the outcomes relatively well for themselves (e.g., fielding or batting in baseball), this need to supply outcome information is not nearly so strong.

A second consideration about feedback is the extent to which the learner needs information about the patterns of action that lead to the environmental goal. A batter may be able to detect how well she hit the ball, but she cannot easily detect errors in the fundamental patterning (e.g., the timing of the hip and shoulder action, the details of the stance, etc.). In such cases, you need to consider ways of providing this kind of information. Certainly, the nature of the task determines the use of feedback and the type of feedback information you provide.

Checklist for Practice Organization

Table 11.1 is a checklist giving the shorthand labels for the dimensions listed in the section above. In the table are my own estimates of these dimensions for just one example, a tennis serve. You might not agree completely with all of my decisions, perhaps depending

Table 11.1 Checklist of Critical Dimensions Determining Practice Organization

Task example: Tennis serve.

Dimension	Strongly present				Strongly absent
Criteria or goals for learning					
Long-term retention	X				
Generalization			X		
General performance capabilities				X	
Task classifications, dimensions, other features					
Continuous					X
Serial				X	
Discrete	X				
Open			X		
Closed	X				
Motor	X				
Cognitive			X		
Perceptual emphasis dominates			X		
Sequential dependencies present		X			
Possibility for automatization	X				
Errors critical		X			
Involves program learning	X				
Involves parameter learning			X		
Complex		X			
Dangerous					X
Intrinsic feedback useful		X			

on the age of the learners, the skill levels, and other factors. The notion is that you could rate any skill on each of these dimensions, with the judgment pattern helping you with decisions about how to organize practice. Try this rating process yourself with several other skills that you know relatively well, and notice the difference in patterns that emerge when you compare different skills.

I think it would be useful to perform this process for every skill to be taught in a unit of instruction. At least, you could do this in a relatively informal way. Thinking about skills sufficiently deeply that you can rate them on this checklist should generate an awareness of the many differences between them, leading to different decisions about procedures in teaching them, ways to organize class time and rest, how to group the activities for instruction, and so on.

Individual Differences: Grouping for Practice

One of the most troublesome problems for the instructor with a large class is how to deal with individual differences, the pervasive tendency for learners to be different from each other. Such differences can arise through differences in the patterns of inherited abilities possessed by the learners when they first come to class. Also, many of these differences come from marked variations in the amount of experience the learners have had on the tasks to be taught, especially if the learners are heterogeneous in ethnic backgrounds and prior experiences. In either case, the problem is that learners are different, requiring you to take several steps to make practice efficient for all.

Grouping for Practice

It is obvious, I suppose, that for classes to be most efficient there should be some **grouping for practice** of students according to their capacities to perform. This process most frequently results in beginning, intermediate, and advanced designations for the learners, with class activities tailored to meet these differences. In many ski-school classes at mountain resorts, I have seen as many as 10 divisions of learners, ranging from tiny children (and some adults) who are absolute beginners to race-level performers.

Usually, learners are asked to classify themselves, often by no more than signing up for intermediate lawn bowling, for example. But it is more effective if learners are provided with some more objective way to classify themselves. A checklist, with anchor points, could be used. For example, a beginning swimmer could be defined as one who, by any possible means, cannot swim more than 10 feet; intermediate swimmers might be those who can swim a pool length but need work on techniques. In many well-run ski schools, grouping is performed through a screening test at the start of a day, where the instructors evaluate everyone on a few simple turns and then direct them to the appropriate groups for the lesson.

On what basis is this grouping to be done? In the method just indicated, the grouping is based on the performer's level of *skill*. A test or evaluative process of some kind is given, and the grouping is based on its results. This tends to mix the factors of inherent abilities with those of experience, but in general it is not too bad for defining classes that are homogeneous.

Sometimes instructors are tempted to group on the basis of measures of *ability*, estimated in various ways. On the surface this sounds great: If you can group people according to fundamental abilities for the activity to be taught, more or less independently of their actual skill levels, you will have homogeneous classes in terms of the final capabilities to perform. Many years ago instructors would group on the basis of so-called general motor ability tests, motor fitness tests, or other such measures, with the same general idea of equating abilities to perform.

There are too many problems for you to use such methods today, however. The measures of general motor ability, motor fitness, and so on do not relate well enough with the many abilities involved in a given activity to allow a meaningful separation. First of all, no such thing as a general motor ability exists, as discussed in chapter 6. A given course in, say, track and field probably involves a wide range of different activities (javelin, high jumping, running, etc.), each with its own collection of abilities. If so, how can one test presume to measure an ability that underlies all these skills? Schemes for this kind of prediction do not work very well, and grouping is probably better by using the actual skill levels.

In general, then, base the grouping on the learners' skill levels, not on supposed underlying abilities. This often means that the classes have a mixture of ages because some younger children perform better than older ones; there could of course be a mixture of genders because many female students outperform many males. This is fine because it leads to the goal of directing the instruction to people with common levels of proficiency.

PRACTICE ORGANIZATION BY STAGE OF LEARNING

Having made these preliminary decisions about your practice situation, the types of learners, and the kinds of skills to be taught, it is time to organize practice. This section discusses some of the determinants of effective practice organization. It will be helpful to treat separately the three stages of practice—the verbal-cognitive, motor, and autonomous stages—because the practice principles are somewhat different depending on the levels of the learners.

Verbal-Cognitive Stage

In this first stage of learning, the task is completely new to the learner, so verbal-cognitive processes predominate in determining performance. Following are some of the principles that guide practice in this stage.

Practice Preparations

Before actual physical practice, you can generate a number of important events to facilitate what comes later. Planning practice can be simpler if you identify a number of skills, ranging in difficulty from simple through relatively difficult, as the total set of skills to be taught in the unit. In this first stage, select several relatively fundamental, **simple skills**, involving a small number of joint motions and where coordination among limbs is minimized, for first presentation. Your major goal as instructor at this stage is to arrange practice so that the learner acquires the capability to perform a rough approximation of these first skills.

Motivation. A first step usually involves some form of motivation for learning. Unless it is already obvious, the learner needs to have some good reason to learn a skill. This can come in the form of films, videotapes, photos, or a motivating short description of the activity. In teaching gymnastics I would ask a member of the gymnastics team to come give a short motivating demonstration of some simple skills, and some advanced ones, too. These efforts not only can familiarize the student with the nature of what is to be learned but also can increase the student's desire to learn this activity, particularly if it is not very common in the student's culture.

Instructions. Then, instructions, demonstrations, and modeling can be used with each skill, capitalizing on humans' remarkable observational learning capabilities. These procedures have the benefit of being motivating as well as providing the initial steps toward performance. The focus is on what the student should try to do, how performance is evaluated, how to stand and grasp the apparatus, what to look at, and what *not* to do. The main consideration is that these instructions be relatively simple and short, pointing out only a few important features because verbal descriptions are very difficult to translate into actions.

Structuring Practice

You can use several steps to allow the learner to perform a rough approximation of each skill. The principles here involve several performance variables, which enhance performance mainly temporarily during practice. Later on, in the motor stage, you can focus on procedures that make these performance gains relatively permanent, but for now your main emphasis is to have the performer generate a crude approximation of the skill.

Initial Practice. Simple as it may sound, a useful method seems to be uttering the statement "Do this," followed by a wordless demonstration. A learner can often approximate the action on the first try; then instruction can move on to more subtle aspects. If performance cannot be achieved, try various alternative methods. Break down a skill into meaningful segments, provided that the component interactions are small, to simplify it for part practice. Also, you can use guidance effectively, such as physically moving a learner through the actions, verbally guiding the learner in serial skills, or using various artificial means of preventing errors (flotation devices in swimming, training wheels on a child's bicycle). Such methods can easily be overdone and should be used cautiously, however.

Blocked and Random Practice. Blocked practice, where you present a number of trials of a given skill in sequence, is most effective at this early stage of practice. Random practice is important later on, in the motor stage, but for now the goal is simply to get the student performing. If there are several elementary skills to learn, set them up into small blocks and alternate between the skills through the hour. This maximizes the student's capability to make the necessary adjustments to approximate the skill in early practice.

Constant and Variable Practice. In those skills where the output of a given pattern must vary to accomplish different environmental goals (e.g., throwing a football different distances), opt for constant practice of just one variant so that the basic pattern can be achieved most easily. Once the learner can produce the pattern acceptably well, provide experience at different variations of this skill in the motor stage that comes next.

Feedback. More than any other level of practice, this first stage requires frequent feedback. The goal is to correct large errors in movement patterns early; feedback after every trial (if possible) is effective in directing the learner to the performance goal. Give feedback about patterns of action (knowledge of performance, KP), rather than about

the action outcome in terms of the environmental goal (knowledge of results, KR), so the learner can begin to acquire the generalized motor program for the movement. Be sure that feedback is prescriptive, indicating what to do next time to improve the pattern. And feedback should be simple, indicating at most one kind of pattern change. Try also to make feedback encouraging and positive, giving a few motivating comments when possible: "Nice try, but next time hold your head up." When possible in this stage, employ several people to give feedback, using each one for a different group of students who are working on different skills.

Generally, here are some points to remember for maximizing success in the verbal-cognitive stage:

- The goal is a rough approximation of several simpler skills.
- Employ interesting motivational techniques.
- Make instructions and demonstrations simple.
- Have learners "Do this" first, and use part practice or guidance later if this fails.
- Use blocked practice and constant practice.
- Use frequent feedback about errors in movement patterning (KP).

Motor Stage

After the initial stage of practice, which should not require very much time, the learner can produce a general approximation of the desired skill. Now the learner is ready to enter the motor stage of practice, where further improvements in movement patterns are developed. Compared to the methods in the verbal-cognitive stage, somewhat different principles and procedures are most applicable in the motor stage. Generally, as you read through the next section, notice that the goal of effective performance during practice is minimized in favor of producing a type of practice that leads to long-term retention capabilities.

Structuring Practice

As soon as the learner can perform the skill at all, it is time to alter the practice schedule to facilitate development of more effective patterning and the capabilities for long-term retention. As discussed earlier in the text, a number of practice variables can help achieve these goals.

Program and Parameter Learning. In focusing on constant rather than variable practice in the verbal-cognitive stage, you facilitated the basic action pattern without complicating matters by also requiring different environmental goals (throwing different distances, for example). This trend should probably continue, at least for a while, in the motor stage. Here the focus is on learning an effective motor program, which has the proper underlying temporal and spatial structure. However, when an action pattern is being produced consistently and effectively, it is time to focus on the capabilities to generalize to different environmental situations, to learn to select parameters for the programs, chiefly by using variable practice. However, the following general principle is a good one at this stage: Stress program (or pattern) learning first, followed by parameter learning later on when the pattern is well developed.

Variable and Constant Practice. For a skill whose pattern is to be adjusted for various environmental demands, or a criterion skill that involves a performance that is novel in some way, variable practice is an effective tool in this practice stage. Arrange repetitions of a given skill so a different variant is practiced on each trial if possible. Attempt to give experience in all the different dimensions of the skill—such as a throw's speed, distance, direction, and trajectory—as well as in various combinations of these dimensions. This variable is not as important in a skill whose criterion version is always performed in a constant way (e.g., bowling, archery), but at least variable practice does not seem to detract from learning these skills.

Blocked and Random Practice. In the verbal-cognitive stage, blocked practice was preferred because it facilitated performance. Now, however, random practice is most effective because of its capabilities to generate long-term retention. The most basic rule is to avoid many repetitions of a given action without interruption from other activities. Random practice can be used further to make learning more effective. As instructor, say that you must teach several different skills simultaneously, such as several moves in wrestling or different shots in racquetball. Then, you must devise some procedure so the learner can shift between skills, avoiding repetitions. Often this is easy, such as never having a diver repeat the same dive twice in a row. It is more difficult sometimes because of space or equipment limitations, but much can usually be done to minimize repetitious practice even here. Try to have your football team not run the same play twice in a row, alternate between shots in tennis, and rotate frequently between pieces of apparatus in gymnastics. Random practice is one of the most powerful determinants of learning, and the effective instructor works hard to use it in teaching settings.

Feedback. In the motor stage, feedback is highly effective in improving performance. Feedback can be presented about the movement's outcome in the environment, especially if this information is not available through intrinsic feedback (e.g., rifle shooting to a distant target). Usually an effective kind of information is extrinsic feedback (verbalized by the instructor) about the movement patterning. You should present feedback clearly, targeting one feature at a time and in a prescriptive way so the learner knows how to change the movement on the next attempt.

However, feedback in the motor stage can be presented too frequently or with too much information. Long-term retention then suffers because the learner develops a dependency on its guiding properties. In general, as the level of learning advances, somewhat less feedback is needed for effective learning. This should encourage you to use faded feedback, where you give information frequently in early practice and less often later as proficiency develops. Summary or average feedback methods are effective also, where the learner completes a set of trials before being allowed to see the feedback that describes the entire set. Bandwidth feedback, where you give information only if the movement is in error by some amount, is effective because it reduces feedback frequency, fading it automatically. All of these procedures are effective at least in part because they force the learner to perform on his or her own, without relying on the crutchlike properties of feedback.

Mental Practice. Practicing skills mentally is effective in this stage as well, and it has two main advantages. First, it is relevant for learning the decision-making and conceptual elements of a skill, such as the sequences of actions in a serial task, like a play in basketball. Second, it is an efficient way to use practice time when facilities are scarce. Half the group can practice physically for a short while, with the other half practicing mentally; then the groups can switch. Mental practice can also take place between trials of physical practice. In this sense, mental practice might operate much like random practice, breaking up a long sequence of blocked repetitions.

Simulators and Transfer. Because in the motor stage the problem is to refine the movement skill, simulators can often be effective at this point. This is particularly important where the criterion skill is dangerous or costly to operate or where facilities are limited. The difficulty is that you need to be reasonably certain that the simulation skill transfers to the criterion skill. Often this transfer can be large, but you can probably think of many examples where the simulated skill is not strongly related to the criterion skill, such as using blocking dummies in football or training wheels on bicycles. It is difficult to know when transfer will and will not be large, but based on your knowledge of the specificity of abilities (chapter 6), you should probably be skeptical about simulators.

Training for Error Detection

Often the concern in the motor stage is too strongly focused on the individual's performance during practice, and other aspects of learning are neglected. After all, the well-meaning instructor's or therapist's job is to facilitate performance, so he or she is apt to do everything possible to increase performance in practice, such as using frequent feedback or blocked practice. You have seen that this strategy, used blindly, can lead to deficiencies in long-term retention or in the capability to generalize.

There are other situations that fall into this category as well. One of these is learning error-detection capabilities. The learner is taught not only to perform but to evaluate his or her own performance in the future. Certain key phrases or concepts can describe a particular kind of error, such as "bent elbow" as a cue for a particular problem with the learner's golf backswing. Perceptual cues describing preparatory stance in tennis, posture after the shot, and the ball's trajectory can be developed in class, and remedies can be taught for errors in each of them. The benefit will probably not be very evident during class, when you are present. But remember that learners do not always have an instructor nearby, especially when the class is over and they must perform on their own. If the learners can acquire the capability to detect their own errors, retention performance will improve because errors are detected and corrected quickly. More importantly, being able to detect their own errors leads to the possibility that additional *learning* will occur when the instructor is not present. What a great way to improve the efficiency of practice!

Several practice variables are related to the development of error detection. Asking learners to evaluate their own errors after an action (but before giving KR or KP) focuses them on response-produced, intrinsic feedback, presumably building a heightened sensitivity to errors in movement patterning. On the other hand, giving feedback instantaneously or too frequently seems to block these analyses of intrinsic feedback, degrading error-detection capabilities and reducing retention. Having a good postmovement error-detection capability is most useful in rapid, discrete tasks, but it is hardly useful at all in long-duration continuous tasks where feedback during the action can lead to moment-to-moment adjustments.

Following are some of the most important points that determine the activities in the motor stage of practice:

- Teach fundamental movement patterns (programs) first, then parameters.
- Use variable practice for schema learning and parameter selection.
- Use prescriptive feedback (KR and KP) about movement errors.
- Avoid giving feedback on every trial; use faded, summary, average, and bandwidth feedback instead.

- Employ random practice for skills, never blocked practice.
- Use mental practice and imagery to enhance learning.

Autonomous Stage

After considerable practice, which might continue for months or years, learners finally enter the autonomous learning stage. By this point, they have well-developed movement patterns, and the focus now shifts to several higher-order aspects of performance. Because this level of practice is generally far beyond that usually experienced in physical education classes, most of the principles at this skill level are probably best applied to advanced-level coaching settings.

Two important issues in the autonomous stage are developing automaticity and using mental skills training.

Practice for Automaticity

Automaticity implies high-level physical performance produced without attention—or certainly with greatly reduced attention demand, compared to that required in lower skill levels. This capability to produce skills automatically means component parts (e.g., dribbling and running in basketball) do not require much attention, which then frees attention capacity for other important elements in a game (where to pass) or for style or form in dance. Also, automatic processes are faster than controlled processes, allowing the performer to respond more quickly and certainly. Skills that require stereotyped responses to relatively fixed patterns of stimuli (reacting to a tennis serve) or which are performed in essentially closed and predictable environments (a gymnastics routine) benefit most from automaticity.

Automaticity is produced most quickly under consistent-mapping conditions, where a given stimulus pattern always leads to the same response. A particular action of offensive football linemen always requires a defensive player to drop back in anticipation of a pass. In a situation where a given stimulus pattern can lead to two different responses, automaticity is difficult to develop, and attempts to automate will surely lead to errors when the wrong response is selected. Automatic responding can develop with several hundred trials of practice under the most favorable conditions, but it appears that many more trials than this are needed in less optimal real-world settings. A key feature of this practice is identifying (with the coach's help) which stimulus pattern leads to, or is predictive of, which response.

Practice for automaticity can also be employed with consistently performed components of serial skills, such as difficult moves in dance or gymnastics. Consistently mapped part-practice can develop these components to very high levels, with the expectation that these parts can be performed essentially automatically in the context of the whole skill. For several different elements to be automated, random practice among them will be most effective. Again, even at this stage, avoid repetitious practice. This part-practice is especially efficient because the whole serial skill (including the easy parts) does not have to be practiced in each trial.

Psychological Skills Training and Mental Practice

You often see performers who can execute the relevant movements in their sports very well in practice but who do not do well in serious competition. Another important set of processes in the autonomous stage involves very high-level processes that come under the heading of **psychological skills training**. These are strongly related to **sport psychology**, a part of which is concerned with many different methods for contributing to the mental part of performance at high levels. Mental practice, as discussed earlier, is a part of these training procedures. It allows for the rehearsal of the sequential features of a task, such as the order of turns in a ski race; for learning to gain control of emotional states so that arousal levels do not exceed those needed for effective performance; and for gains in confidence and a positive attitude toward what to do to win. Mental practice and imagery are used strongly at this level of proficiency for many world-class athletes interested in improving the mental part of their game. Other exercises can decrease uncertainty about upcoming events, the worry and fear of losing, and negative self-talk, which is often damaging to performance. There are many such methods, and they are reviewed by Martens (1988).

Here are some principles that are important for the final, autonomous stage of practice:

- Practice for automaticity to reduce attention demands.
- Tasks with consistent mapping are most easily automated.
- Use part-practice to automate stereotyped elements in a series.
- Various psychological skills training methods, including mental practice, are effective for higher level competitive situations.

EVALUATION OF LEARNING

After you have completed your unit of instruction, you must evaluate how well the learners (and, of course, you) have succeeded in meeting the goals you defined earlier. Certainly, learning evaluation implies a test of some kind, which should require that the learner perform some or all of the skills in a special session. A number of considerations should be kept in mind when deciding on the nature and scheduling of the examination.

When to Test?

The question of when to test should reflect back to your original goals of practice—the generation of learning, the relatively permanent capability for performing. This implies strongly that evaluation should not be done during the practice sessions themselves, but that it be conducted in a special session later on. I have repeatedly emphasized that the conditions of practice that generate the most effective learning are sometimes those that produce relatively poor performance during practice. For example, random practice degrades practice performance relative to blocked practice, but it is more effective for learning. Infrequent feedback often degrades performance relative to frequent feedback, but it leads to better learning. Thus, evaluating performance in practice, when performance is depressed somewhat because of the use of such scheduling or feedback methods, will not give a good estimate of how much has been learned.

Rather, evaluation is probably best done on some kind of retention test. It is even possible to model this process after other aspects of school learning, where progress in a given subject matter is evaluated on a test given at a future time known to all the students. It is often useful to declare a given day as Exam Day, where everyone knows it is the time when students' skills are evaluated.

What to Test?

An example of a scoresheet completed on Exam Day is shown in Figure 11.2. The performances are scored on some absolute scale, where the instructor knows how well a tumbling skill should be produced for a 5 to be awarded, for example. Many different kinds

Tumbling skills — final examination

	Headstand	Mat kip	Forward roll	Backward roll	Walkover	Total
Adams, J.	6	2	6	6	2	22
Henry, F.	3	9	4	2	7	25
Lee, T.	1	7	2	9	9	28
Magill, D.	5	3	1	3	5	17
Newell, K.	4	1	3	8	4	20
Singer, B.	4	2	5	5	3	19
Wade, M.	3	4	2	5	3	17

Figure 11.2 Retention scores on a "final examination" in a class in tumbling, which is typical of many measurement methods in motor learning.

of scales could have been used, such as one ranking the students from most to least proficient or even one based on the results of a round-robin tournament done in the final hour of a wrestling class. There are many ways to evaluate, and they can be fun as well as informative.

It is troubling to some that the performance on this test is based on (a) the student's fundamental abilities, (b) prior experiences, (c) the practice activities in class, (d) extraclass practice, and (e) several other factors. Notice that in-class practice, where you have some control over the teaching-learning process, is only a part of the many elements that determine test performance. With homogeneous grouping of students in terms of age, prior experiences, and so on, you can minimize many of these other factors. Then, the performances on the exam will represent the capabilities produced as a result of the teaching that you have done. This is far from perfect—for cognitive or motor learning—but it is about the best that can be done.

One alternative, which is clearly worse in my view than the delayed test method just mentioned, is to evaluate on some kind of improvement score. This is based on the performance at the end of the class, corrected for the performance at the beginning of class (e.g., subtracting the initial score from the final score). On the surface, this method seems to produce a measure of learning that compensates for a student's initial skill and ability levels. This is a complicated question, both logically and statistically, but it is not generally regarded as a sound procedure for a number of reasons. In any case, if one is to use the academic model as a way to evaluate learning, then performance on the final exam—regardless of how the learner may have performed at the start of class—is what is important. The critical part is how well the learner can perform at the end, and it is on this that grading is presumably most effectively based.

 ## CHAPTER SUMMARY

The instructor frequently faces the situation where a unit of activity, often relatively unfamiliar to the teacher, must be organized for class presentation in such a way that it is consistent with the scientific principles of effective practice as well as being efficient and interesting for the students. Some of the most important factors that determine the decisions about how to structure practice, presented throughout the earlier chapters of the text, are collected here. A first consideration is classification in terms of the criteria,

or overall goals, for practice because different criteria have different implications for practice. A second issue is the classification of the individual task(s) to be learned along a dozen or so dimensions—critical because the principles of learning frequently differ markedly for the different task types.

Next the instructor prepares for actual practice by selecting and grouping students based on their initial skill (not ability) levels and by employing various methods that motivate or enhance interest in the skills. The organization and scheduling of the actual practice activities are determined next. The instructor plans the nature of instructions and demonstrations, when practice is most effectively blocked or randomized, how and when to present feedback, whether to employ simulators, and so on. These principles of organization are somewhat different for the verbal-cognitive, motor, and autonomous stages of learning, however, so they are separated here as a function of learner proficiency.

Finally, learning is evaluated. Based on the original goals of learning, an evaluation is most effective when it is free of the temporary effects on performance that may be present in a practice session.

◇ Checking Your Understanding

1. Choose two skills with which you are familiar, and classify them on the dimensions mentioned in Table 11.1. What do you see as the largest difference(s) between them? How does this influence your decisions about their organization for effective practice?
2. What is the difference between grouping for practice on the basis of skills and grouping on the basis of abilities? Which one is to be preferred? Why?
3. Name two principles of practice organization that differ as a function of the

level of learning proficiency. Describe the most effective practice methods for each learning level.

4. Why is it important to perform evaluations well after practice sessions? Give two reasons that justify this decision.

◇ Key Terms

Definitions of the following terms appear on the page(s) shown in parentheses:

complex skill (p. 270)

criterion skill (p. 266)

grouping for practice (p. 272)

parameter learning (p. 269)

program learning (p. 269)

psychological skills training (p. 278)

simple skill (p. 273)

sport psychology (p. 278)

◇ Suggestions for Further Reading

Additional treatments of the organization of practice for instruction can be found in an excellent elementary-level text by Christina and Corcos (1988). More details about the research on the organization of practice are in Schmidt (1988b, chapters 12 and 13) and T.D. Lee (1988), and a review of the principles for blocked and random practice was done by Magill and Hall (1990). Issues in sport psychology, motivation for performance, and particularly psychological skills training in athletic situations are covered in a very readable way by Martens (1988). More general issues about coaching children can be found in Martens, Christina, Harvey, and Sharkey (1981), and in the second edition by Martens (1990).

Glossary

ability—A stable, enduring, mainly genetically defined trait that underlies skilled performance.

absolute frequency—The actual number of feedback presentations given in a series of practice trials.

ambient vision—The visual system that is full-field, nonconscious, and organized to detect orientation of the body in an environment.

amplitude—In aiming tasks, the distance between the two target centers (''A'' in Fitts' Law).

arousal—An internal state of alertness or excitement.

attention—A limited capacity, or a set of capacities, to process information.

augmented feedback—See extrinsic feedback.

automatic processing—A mode of information processing that is fast, done in parallel, not attention demanding, and often involuntary.

autonomous stage—An advanced stage of learning in which the learner develops automaticity in action and information processing.

average feedback—Feedback based on the average of several trials rather than on any one of them.

bandwidth feedback—A procedure for delivering feedback where errors are signaled only if they fall outside some range of correctness.

blocked practice—A practice sequence in which a given task is practiced on many consecutive trials.

capability—The internal representation of skill, acquired during practice, that allows performance on some task.

central pattern generator—A centrally located control mechanism that produces mainly genetically defined actions; analogous to a motor program.

closed-loop control—A mode of system control involving feedback and error detection and correction which is applicable to motor behavior.

closed skill—A skill for which the environment is stable and predictable, allowing advance organization of movement.

cognitive skill—A skill in which the primary determinants of success are related to decision making and intellectual functioning.

complex skill—A skill that requires the movements of many body parts as well as the coordination among them in time.

constant practice—A practice sequence in which only a single variation of a given class of tasks is experienced.

continuous skill—A skill where the action unfolds continuously, without a recognizable beginning and end.

controlled processing—A mode of information processing that is slow, serial, attention demanding, and voluntary.

correlation—A statistical method that evaluates the degree of relationship between two variables (r). This relationship does not imply causality.

criterion—The goal behavior, task, or score that is to be predicted.

criterion skill—The ultimate version or situation in which the skill learned in practice is to be applied; the goal of practice.

deafferentation—Cutting an afferent sensory pathway, preventing nerve impulses from the periphery from traveling to the spinal cord.

deep structure—The fundamental structure of an action, involving sequencing and relative timing (or rhythm) that defines the movement pattern.

differential approach—A method of understanding behavior focusing on individual differences and abilities.

discrete skill—A skill in which the action is usually brief and with a recognizable beginning and end.

distributed practice—A practice schedule in which the amount of rest between practice trials is long relative to the trial length.

effective target width—In aiming, the amount of spread, or variability, of movement end points about a target; the "effective" target size (W_e).

error detection capability—The learned capability to detect one's own errors through analyzing response-produced feedback.

experimental approach—A method of understanding behavior emphasizing common principles among people.

exteroceptive—Sensory information derived primarily from outside the body.

extrinsic feedback—Feedback provided artificially over and above that received naturally from a movement.

faded feedback—A feedback schedule where the relative frequency is high in early practice and diminishes in later practice.

far transfer—Transfer of learning from one task to another very different task or setting.

feedback—The difference between the state of a system and its goal, often meaning augmented or extrinsic feedback in motor learning.

feedback delay—The interval from the end of the movement until the feedback is presented.

feedback precision—The level of accuracy with which the feedback describes the movement outcome.

Fitts' Law—The principle that movement time in aiming tasks is linearly related to the $\text{Log}_2(2A/W)$; A = amplitude, W = target width.

focal vision—The visual system that primarily involves central vision, is conscious, and is specialized for object identification.

generalizability—The process of applying what is learned in a class of tasks to other, unpracticed members of the same class.

generalized motor program—A motor program whose output can vary along certain dimensions to produce novelty and flexibility in movement.

general motor ability—An older, incorrect view in which a single general ability was thought to underlie all motor behavior.

goal setting—A procedure in which the learner is encouraged to set personal performance goals during practice.

grouping for practice—The process of dividing learners into relatively homogeneous groups to make practice more workable and efficient.

guidance—A procedure used in practice where the learner is physically or verbally directed through the performance to reduce errors.

Hick's Law—The principle that choice reaction time is linearly related to the logarithm of the number of stimulus-response alternatives.

hypervigilance—A heightened state of

arousal that leads to ineffective decision making and poor performance; panic.

individual differences—The stable, enduring tendency for individuals to be different from each other in performance.

instantaneous feedback—Feedback delivered with no feedback delay at all.

intermittent reinforcement—A schedule of reinforcement where feedback is given only occasionally.

intrinsic feedback—Feedback naturally received from producing a movement.

invariance—A feature of a set of movements that remains constant, or invariant, while surface features change.

inverted-U principle—The law that increased arousal improves performance only to a point, with degraded performance as arousal is increased further.

kinesthesis—The sense derived from muscular contractions and limb movements; related to proprioception.

knowledge of performance (KP)—Augmented feedback that describes a feature of the movement pattern produced.

knowledge of results (KR)—Augmented, postresponse, verbalizable information about success in meeting the movement goal.

lead-up activities—Special tasks designed to be learned prior to the practice of a more complicated or dangerous criterion task.

M1 response—The monosynaptic stretch reflex, with a latency of 30 to 50 ms.

M2 response—The polysynaptic, functional stretch reflex, with a latency of 50 to 80 ms.

M3 response—The voluntary reaction-time response, with a latency of 120 to 180 ms.

massed practice—A practice schedule in which the amount of rest between trials is short relative to the trial length.

memory—The systems allowing persistence of the acquired capabilities for responding: short-term sensory store, short-term memory, and long-term memory.

mental practice—A practice procedure where the learner imagines successful action without overt physical practice.

model—An analogy or simulation, in which concepts are related to a familiar device or system to facilitate understanding.

modeling—A practice procedure where another person demonstrates the correct performance of the skills to be learned.

motor learning—A set of internal processes associated with practice or experience leading to a relatively permanent gain in performance capability.

motor program—Centrally located structure that defines the essential details of skilled action; analogous to a central pattern generator.

motor skill—A skill where the primary determinant of success is the movement component itself.

motor stage—The second stage of learning, in which motor programs are developed and the performance becomes increasingly consistent.

movement time (MT)—The interval from the initiation of a movement until its termination.

near transfer—Transfer of learning from one task to another that is very similar.

novelty problem—The concern that simple program theories cannot account for the production of novel, unpracticed movements.

observational learning—The process by which the learner acquires the capability for action by observing others.

open-loop control—A mode in which instructions for the effector system are determined in advance and run off without feedback.

open skill—A skill for which the environment is unpredictable or unstable, preventing advance organization of movement.

optical flow—The tendency for patterns of light rays from the environment to flow over the retina, allowing perception of motion, position, and timing.

parameters—Values that determine a movement's surface features, such as speed or amplitude, in a generalized motor program.

parameter learning—Learning to assign parameters for a given generalized motor program to meet different environmental demands.

part practice—A procedure in which a complex skill is broken down into parts that are practiced separately.

percentage transfer—A measure of transfer; the percentage of total improvement or loss on a criterion task produced by practice on some other task.

perceptual narrowing—The narrowing of attentional focus as arousal level increases.

performance curves—Plots of average performance of an individual or a group against practice trials.

prediction—The process of using people's abilities to estimate their probable success in various occupations or sports.

predictor tests—In prediction, the test or tests used to estimate the criterion score.

prescriptive feedback—Feedback that directs the learner toward error correction.

program learning—The acquisition of new patterns of action, or new generalized motor programs.

progressive part practice—A procedure in which parts of a skill are gradually integrated into larger units approaching the whole action.

proprioception—Sensory information arising from within the body, resulting in the sense of position and movement; similar to kinesthesis.

psychological refractory period (PRP)—The delay in responding to the second of two closely spaced stimuli.

psychological skills training—A collection of methods used to improve the mental approach to skills, especially for higher level performers.

random practice—A practice sequence in which tasks from several classes are experienced in random order over consecutive trials.

reaction time (RT)—The interval from presentation of an unanticipated stimulus until the beginning of the response.

reflexes—Stereotyped, involuntary, usually rapid, responses to stimuli.

relative frequency—The proportion of trials during practice on which feedback is given; absolute frequency divided by the number of trials.

relative timing—The temporal structure of action; the durations of various segments of an action divided by the total movement time.

retention test—A performance test on a given task provided after some retention interval without practice.

retrieval practice—Practice at retrieving the motor program and parameters from long-term memory; facilitated by random practice.

schema—A rule relating the various outcomes of members of a class of action to the parameters that determine the outcomes.

serial skill—A skill composed of several discrete actions strung together, often with the order of actions being critical for success.

simple skill—A skill involving a small number of joint motions and where coordination among limbs is minimized.

simulator—A training device that mimics various features of some real-world task.

skill—A capability to bring about an end result with maximum certainty, minimum energy, or minimum time.

specificity hypothesis—A view of motor abilities holding that tasks are composed of many unrelated abilities.

speed-accuracy trade-off—The tendency for accuracy to decrease as the movement speed or velocity of a movement increases.

sport psychology—A field emphasizing the discovery and application of psychological principles to sport performance.

stages—Hypothetical collections of information processes that make up the operations involved in reaction time: stimulus identification, response selection, and response programming.

stimulus-response (S-R) compatibility—The naturalness of the relationship between the stimulus and the response assigned to it.

storage problem—The concern that simple program theories cannot handle the fact that vast storage would be needed for nearly countless different movements.

summary feedback—Information about a set of trials presented only after the set has been completed.

superability—A weak general ability thought to contribute to all tasks.

surface features—An easily changeable aspect of a movement, such as movement time or amplitude, that holds the deep structure constant.

target amplitude—The linear distance a limb travels from movement initiation to termination in aiming tasks ("A" in Fitts' Law).

target width—In aiming tasks, the size of the target measured parallel to the overall movement direction ("W" in Fitts' Law).

task analysis—The process of determining the ability composition of a task or an occupation.

tau—An optical variable proportional to time until contact, figured as the size of the retinal image divided by the rate of change of the image.

tracking—A class of tasks in which a moving track must be followed, typically by movements of a manual control.

transfer of learning—The gain or the loss in proficiency on one task as a result of practice or experience on another task.

triggered reaction—Reaction to perturbations that are flexible, yet faster than the M3 response, with latency of 80 to 120 ms.

variable practice—A schedule of practice in which many variations of a class of actions are practiced.

verbal-cognitive stage—The initial stage of learning, in which verbal and cognitive processes predominate.

visual capture—The tendency for visual information to attract attention more easily than other forms of information.

visual dominance—The tendency for vision to dominate the other senses in perception.

References

Abbs, J.H., Gracco, V.L., & Cole, K.J. (1984). Control of multi-joint movement coordination: Sensorimotor mechanisms in speech motor programming. *Journal of Motor Behavior, 16*, 195-231.

Adams, J.A. (1953). *The prediction of performance at advanced stages of training on a complex psychomotor task* (Research Bulletin 53-49). Lackland Air Force Base, TX: Human Resources Research Center.

Adams, J.A. (1956). *An evaluation of test items measuring motor abilities* (Research Rep. AFPTRC-TN-56-55). Lackland Air Force Base, TX: Human Resources Research Center.

Adams, J.A. (1987). Historical review and appraisal of research on the learning, retention, and transfer of human motor skills. *Psychological Bulletin, 101*, 41-74.

Allard, F., & Burnett, N. (1985). Skill in sport. *Canadian Journal of Psychology, 39*, 294-312.

Annett, J. (1959). *Feedback and human behavior.* Middlesex, England: Penguin.

Armstrong, T.R. (1970). *Training for the production of memorized movement patterns* (Tech. Rep. No. 26). Ann Arbor: University of Michigan, Human Performance Center.

Baddeley, A.D., & Longman, D.J.A. (1978). The influence of length and frequency of training session on the rate of learning to type. *Ergonomics, 21*, 627-635.

Bahrick, H.P., Fitts, P.M., & Briggs, G.E. (1957). Learning curves—Facts or artifacts? *Psychological Bulletin, 54*, 256-268.

Bartlett, F.C. (1932). *Remembering: A study in experimental and social psychology.* Cambridge, England: Cambridge University Press.

Battig, W.F. (1966). Facilitation and interference. In E.A. Bilodeau (Ed.), *Acquisition of skill* (pp. 215-244). New York: Academic Press.

Belen'kii, V.Y., Gurfinkel, V.S., & Pal'tsev, Y.I. (1967). Elements of control of voluntary movements. *Biofizika, 12*, 135-141.

Bernstein, N. (1967). *The co-ordination and regulation of movements.* Oxford, England: Pergamon Press.

Bjork, R.A. (1975). Retrieval as a memory modifier. In R. Solso (Ed.), *Information processing and cognition: The Loyola Symposium* (pp. 123-144). Hillsdale, NJ: Erlbaum.

Bjork, R.A. (1979). *Retrieval practice.* Unpublished manuscript, University of California, Los Angeles.

Bliss, C.B. (1892-1893). Investigations in reaction time and attention. *Studies from the Yale Psychological Laboratory, 1*, 1-55.

Boder, D.P. (1935). The influence of concomitant activity and fatigue upon certain forms of reciprocal hand movement and its fundamental components. *Comparative Psychology Monographs, 11*, article 54.

Brace, D.K. (1927). *Measuring motor ability.* New York: A.S. Barnes.

Bridgeman, B., Kirch, M., & Sperling, A. (1981). Segregation of cognitive and motor aspects of visual information using induced motion. *Perception & Psychophysics, 29*, 336-342.

Brooks, V.B. (1986). *The neural basis of motor control.* New York: Oxford University Press.

Carron, A.V. (1967). *Performance and learning in a discrete motor task under massed versus distributed conditions.* Unpublished doctoral dissertation, University of California, Berkeley.

Catalano, J.F., & Kleiner, B.M. (1984). Distant transfer and practice variability. *Perceptual and Motor Skills*, **58**, 851-856.

Christina, R.W., & Corcos, D.M. (1988). *Coaches guide to teaching sport skills*. Champaign, IL: Human Kinetics.

Cormier, S.M., & Hagman, J.D. (Eds.) (1987). *Transfer of learning*. New York: Academic Press.

Crossman, E.R.F.W. (1959). A theory of the acquisition of speed skill. *Ergonomics*, **2**, 153-166.

Cuddy, L.J., & Jacoby, L.L. (1982). When forgetting helps memory. Analysis of repetition effects. *Journal of Verbal Learning and Verbal Behavior*, **21**, 451-467.

Dewhurst, D.J. (1967). Neuromuscular control system. *IEEE Transactions on Biomedical Engineering*, **14**, 167-171.

Drowatzky, J.N., & Zuccato, F.C. (1967). Interrelationships between selected measures of static and dynamic balance. *Research Quarterly*, **38**, 509-510.

Easterbrook, J.A. (1959). The effect of emotion on cue utilization and the organization of behavior. *Psychological Review*, **66**, 183-201.

Feltz, D.L., & Landers, D.M. (1983). The effects of mental practice on motor skill learning and performance: A meta analysis. *Journal of Sport Psychology*, **5**, 1-8.

Fitts, P.M. (1954). The information capacity of the human motor system in controlling the amplitude of movement. *Journal of Experimental Psychology*, **47**, 381-391.

Fitts, P.M. (1964). Perceptual-motor skills learning. In A.W. Melton (Ed.), *Categories of human learning* (pp. 243-285). New York: Academic Press.

Fitts, P.M., & Posner, M.I. (1967). *Human performance*. Belmont, CA: Brooks-Cole.

Fleishman, E.A. (1956). Psychomotor selection tests: Research and application in the United States Air Force. *Personnel Psychology*, **9**, 449-467.

Fleishman, E.A. (1957). A comparative study of aptitude patterns in unskilled and skilled psychomotor performances. *Journal of Applied Psychology*, **41**, 263-272.

Fleishman, E.A. (1964). *The structure and measurement of physical fitness*. Englewood Cliffs, NJ: Prentice-Hall.

Fleishman, E.A. (1965). The description and prediction of perceptual motor skill learning. In R. Glaser (Ed.), *Training research and education* (pp. 137-175). New York: Wiley.

Fleishman, E.A., & Bartlett, C.J. (1969). Human abilities. *Annual Review of Psychology*, **20**, 349-380.

Fleishman, E.A., & Parker, J.F. (1962). Factors in the retention and relearning of perceptual motor skill. *Journal of Experimental Psychology*, **64**, 215-226.

Fleishman, E.A., & Stephenson, R.W. (1970). *Development of a taxonomy of human performance: A review of the third year's progress* (Tech. Rep. No. 726-TPR3). Silver Springs, MD: American Institutes for Research.

Forssberg, H., Grillner, S., & Rossignol, S. (1975). Phase dependent reflex reversal during walking in the chronic spinal cat. *Brain Research*, **85**, 103-107.

Frey, H.J., & Keeney, C.J. (1964). *Elementary gymnastics apparatus skills*. New York: Ronald Press.

Gabriele, T., Hall, C.R., & Lee, T.D. (1989). Cognition in motor learning: Imagery effects on contextual interference. *Human Movement Science*, **8**, 227-245.

Gallwey, T. (1974). *Inner game of tennis*. New York: Random House.

Gentner, D.R. (1987). Timing of skilled motor performance: Tests of the proportional duration model. *Psychological Review*, **94**, 255-276.

Gibson, J.J. (1966). *The senses considered as per-*

ceptual systems. Boston: Houghton Mifflin.

Goode, S., & Magill, R.A. (1986). The contextual interference effects in learning three badminton serves. *Research Quarterly for Exercise and Sport*, **57**, 308-314.

Graw, H.M.A. (1968). *The most efficient usage of a fixed work plus rest practice period in motor learning*. Unpublished doctoral dissertation, University of California, Berkeley.

Grillner, S. (1975). Locomotion in vertebrates: Central mechanisms and reflex interaction. *Physiological Reviews*, **55**, 247-304.

Guthrie, E.R. (1952). *The psychology of learning*. New York: Harper & Row.

Henry, F.M. (1959). Reliability, measurement error, and intra-individual difference. *Research Quarterly*, **30**, 21-24.

Henry, F.M. (1961). Reaction time–movement time correlations. *Perceptual and Motor Skills*, **12**, 63-66.

Henry, F.M. (1968). Specificity vs. generality in learning motor skill. In R.C. Brown & G.S. Kenyon (Eds.), *Classical studies on physical activity* (pp. 331-340). Englewood Cliffs, NJ: Prentice-Hall. (Original work published 1958.)

Henry, F.M., & Rogers, D.E. (1960). Increased response latency for complicated movements and a "memory drum" theory of neuromotor reaction. *Research Quarterly*, **31**, 448-458.

Heuer, H. (1985). Wie wirkt mentale Übung? [How does mental practice work?]. *Psychologische Rundschau*, **36**, 191-200. [English translation: Report No. 44/1985, Research Group on Perception and Action, Center for Interdisciplinary Research (ZiF), Universität Bielefeld, Germany.]

Hick, W.E. (1952). On the rate of gain of information. *Quarterly Journal of Experimental Psychology*, **4**, 11-26.

Hollerbach, J.M. (1978). *A study of human motor control through analysis and synthesis of handwriting*. Unpublished doctoral dissertation, Massachusetts Institute of Technology, Cambridge.

Houk, J.C., & Rymer, W.Z. (1981). Neural control of muscle length and tension. In V.B. Brooks (Ed.), *Handbook of physiology: Sec. 1: Vol. 2. Motor control* (pp. 257-323). Bethesda, MD: American Physiological Society.

Howell, M.L. (1956). Use of force-time graphs for performance analysis in facilitating motor learning. *Research Quarterly*, **27**, 12-22.

Hubbard, A.W., & Seng, C.N. (1954). Visual movements of batters. *Research Quarterly*, **25**, 42-57.

Hyman, R. (1953). Stimulus information as a determinant of reaction time. *Journal of Experimental Psychology*, **45**, 188-196.

James, W. (1890). *The principles of psychology* (Vol. 1). New York: Holt.

Jeka, J., & Kelso, J.A.S. (1989). The dynamic pattern approach to coordinated behavior: A tutorial review. In S.A. Wallace (Ed.), *Perspectives on the coordination of movement* (pp. 3-45). Amsterdam: North-Holland.

Johansson, R.S., & Westling, G. (1984). Roles of glabrous skin receptors and sensorimotor memory in automatic control of precision grip when lifting rougher or more slippery objects. *Experimental Brain Research*, **56**, 560-564.

Jordan, T.C. (1972). Characteristics of visual and proprioceptive response times in the learning of a motor skill. *Journal of Experimental Psychology*, **24**, 536-543.

Kahneman, D. (1973). *Attention and effort*. Englewood Cliffs, NJ: Prentice-Hall.

Keele, S.W. (1981). Behavioral analysis of motor control. In V.B. Brooks (Ed.), *Handbook of physiology: Sec 1: Vol. 2. Motor control* (pp. 1391-1414). Bethesda, MD: American Physiological Society.

Keele, S.W. (1986). Motor control. In K. Boff, L. Kaufman, & J.P. Thomas (Eds.), *Handbook of perception and human performance: Vol. 2. Cognitive processes and performance. Section V. Information processing* (pp. 30-1–30-60). New York: Wiley.

Keele, S.W., & Posner, M.I. (1968). Processing of visual feedback in rapid movements. *Journal of Experimental Psychology, 77*, 155-158.

Kelso, J.A.S. (Ed.) (1982). *Human motor behavior: An introduction.* Hillsdale, NJ: Erlbaum.

Kelso, J.A.S., & Kay, B.A. (1987). Information and control: A macroscopic analysis of perception-action coupling. In H. Heuer & A.F. Sanders (Eds.), *Perspectives on perception and action* (pp. 3-32). Hillsdale, NJ: Erlbaum.

Kelso, J.A.S., Tuller, B., Vatikoitis-Bateson, E., & Fowler, C.A. (1984). Functionally specific articulatory cooperation following jaw perturbations during speech: Evidence for coordinative structures. *Journal of Experimental Psychology: Human Perception and Performance, 10*, 812-832.

Kerr, R., & Booth, B. (1978). Specific and varied practice of motor skill. *Perceptual and Motor Skills, 46*, 395-401.

Klapp, S.T., Hill, M.D., Tyler, J.G., Martin, Z.E., Jagacinski, R.J., & Jones, M.R. (1985). On marching to two different drummers: Perceptual aspects of the difficulties. *Journal of Experimental Psychology: Human Perception and Performance, 11*, 814-827.

Konzem, P.B. (1987). *Extended practice and patterns of bimanual interference.* Unpublished doctoral dissertation, University of Southern California, Los Angeles.

Kottke, F.J., Halpern, D., Easton, J.K., Ozel, A.T., & Burrill, B.S. (1978). The training of coordination. *Archives of Physical Medicine and Rehabilitation Medicine, 59*, 567-572.

Kugler, P.N. (Ed.) (1988). Self-organization in biological workspaces. *Human Movement Science, 7*(Entire 2-4).

Kugler, P.N., & Turvey, M.T. (1986). *Information, natural law, and the self-assembly of rhythmic movement.* Hillsdale, NJ: Erlbaum.

Landauer, T.K., & Bjork, R.A. (1978). Optimum rehearsal patterns and name learning. In M.M. Gruenberg, P.E. Morris, & R.N. Sykes (Eds.), *Practical aspects of memory* (pp. 625-632). London: Academic Press.

Lavery, J.J. (1962). Retention of simple motor skills as a function of type of knowledge of results. *Canadian Journal of Psychology, 16*, 300-311.

Lavery, J.J., & Suddon, F.H. (1962). Retention of simple motor skills as a function of the number of trials by which KR is delayed. *Perceptual and Motor Skills, 15*, 231-237.

Lee, D.N. (1980). Visuo-motor coordination in space-time. In G.E. Stelmach & J. Requin (Eds.), *Tutorials in motor behavior* (pp. 281-285). Amsterdam: North-Holland.

Lee, D.N., & Aronson, E. (1974). Visual proprioceptive control of standing in human infants. *Perception and Psychophysics, 15*, 527-532.

Lee, D.N., & Young, D.S. (1985). Visual timing of interceptive action. In D. Ingle, M. Jeannerod, & D.N. Lee (Eds.), *Brain mechanisms and spatial vision* (pp. 1-30). Dordrecht: Martinus Nijhoff.

Lee, T.D. (1988). Testing for motor learning: A focus on transfer-appropriate processing. In O.G. Meijer & K. Roth (Eds.), *Complex motor behavior: The motor-action controversy* (pp. 201-215). Amsterdam: Elsevier Science.

Lee, T.D., & Carnahan, H. (1990). Bandwidth knowledge of results and motor learning: More than just a relative frequency effect. *Quarterly Journal of Experimental Psychology*, **42A**, 777-789.

Lee, T.D., & Genovese, E.D. (1988). Distribution of practice in motor skill acquisition: Learning and performance effects reconsidered. *Research Quarterly for Exercise and Sport*, **59**, 277-287.

Lee, T.D., Wulf, G., & Schmidt, R.A. (1990). Manuscript in preparation, McMaster University.

Lee, W.A. (1980). Anticipatory control of postural and task muscles during rapid arm flexion. *Journal of Motor Behavior*, **12**, 185-196.

Lersten, K.C. (1968). Transfer of movement components in a motor learning task. *Research Quarterly*, **39**, 575-581.

Locke, E.A., & Bryan, J.F. (1966). Cognitive aspects of psychomotor performance: The effects of performance goals on level of performance. *Journal of Applied Psychology*, **50**, 286-291.

Locke, E.A., & Latham, G.P. (1985). The application of goal setting to sports. *Sport Psychology Today*, **7**, 205-222.

Locke, E.A., Shaw, K.N., Saari, L.M., & Latham, G.P. (1981). Goal setting and task performance: 1969-1980. *Psychological Bulletin*, **90**, 125-152.

Lotter, W.S. (1960). Interrelationships among reaction times and speeds of movement in different limbs. *Research Quarterly*, **31**, 147-155.

Magill, R.A. (1989). *Motor learning: Concepts and applications* (3rd ed.). Dubuque, IA: Brown.

Magill, R.A., & Hall, K.G. (1990). A review of the contextual interference effect in motor skill acquisition. *Human Movement Science*, **9**, 241-289.

Marteniuk, R.G. (1986). Information processes in movement learning: Capacity and structural interference effects. *Journal of Motor Behavior*, **18**, 55-75.

Martens, R. (1988). *Coaches guide to sport psychology*. Champaign, IL: Human Kinetics.

Martens, R. (1990). *Successful coaching* (2nd ed.). Champaign, IL: Leisure Press.

Martens, R., Christina, R.W., Harvey, J.S., & Sharkey, B.J. (1981). *Coaching young athletes*. Champaign, IL: Human Kinetics.

McCloy, C.H. (1934). The measurement of general motor capacity and general motor ability. *Research Quarterly*, **5**(Suppl. 5), 45-61.

McCullagh, P., Weiss, M.R., & Ross, D. (1989). Modeling considerations in motor skill acquisition and performance: An integrated approach. *Exercise and Sport Sciences Reviews*, **17**, 475-513.

McLeod, P., McLaughlin, C., & Nimmo-Smith, I. (1985). Information encapsulation and automaticity: Evidence from the visual control of finely tuned actions. In M.I. Posner & O.S.M. Marin (Eds.), *Attention and performance XI* (pp. 391-406). Hillsdale, NJ: Erlbaum.

Merkel, J. (1885). Die zeitlichen Verhaltnisse der Willenstätigkeit. *Philosophische Studien*, **2**, 73-127. (Cited in Woodworth, 1938.)

Merton, P.A. (1972). How we control the contraction of our muscles. *Scientific American*, **226**, 30-37.

Meyer, D.E., Abrams, R.A., Kornblum, S., Wright, C.E., & Smith, J.E.K. (1988). Optimality in human motor performance: Ideal control of rapid aimed movements. *Psychological Review*, **95**, 340-370.

Meyer, D.E., Smith, J.E.K., Kornblum, S., Abrams, R.A., & Wright, C.E. (1990). Speed-accuracy tradeoffs in aimed movements: Toward a theory of rapid voluntary action. In M. Jeannerod (Ed.), *Attention and performance XIII* (pp. 173-226). Hillsdale, NJ: Erlbaum.

Miller, G.A. (1956). The magical number seven, plus or minus two: Some limits on our capacity for processing information. *Psychological Review*, **63**, 81-97.

Nashner, L., & Berthoz, A. (1978). Visual contribution to rapid motor responses during postural control. *Brain Research*, **150**, 403-407.

Neumann, O. (1987). Beyond capacity: A functional view of attention. In H. Heuer & A.F. Sanders (Eds.), *Perspectives on perception and action* (pp. 361-394). Hillsdale, NJ: Erlbaum.

Newell, A., & Rosenbloom, P.S. (1981). Mechanisms of skill acquisition and the law of practice. In J.R. Anderson (Ed.), *Cognitive skills and their acquisition* (pp. 1-55). Hillsdale, NJ: Erlbaum.

Newell, K.M., Carlton, L.G., Carlton, M.J., & Halbert, J.A. (1980). Velocity as a factor in movement timing accuracy. *Journal of Motor Behavior*, **12**, 47-56.

Newell, K.M., & McGinnis, P.M. (1985). Kinematic information feedback for skilled performance. *Human Learning*, **4**, 39-56.

Noble, C.E. (1978). Age, race, and sex in the learning and performance of psychomotor skills. In R.T. Osborne, C.E. Noble, & N. Weyl (Eds.), *Human variation: The biopsychology of age, race, and sex* (pp. 287-378). New York: Academic Press.

Orlick, T. (1986). *Psyching for sport: Mental training for athletes*. Champaign, IL: Leisure Press.

Orlick, T. (1990). *In pursuit of excellence* (2nd ed.). Champaign, IL: Leisure Press.

Osborne, R.T., Noble, C.E., & Weyl, N. (Eds.) (1978). *Human variation: The biopsychology of age, race, and sex*. New York: Academic Press.

Polanyi, M. (1958). *Personal knowledge: Towards a post-critical philosophy*. London: Routledge and Kegan Paul.

Posner, M.I. (1978). *Chronometric explorations of mind*. Hillsdale, NJ: Erlbaum.

Raibert, M.H. (1977). *Motor control and learning by the state-space model* (Tech. Rep. No. AI-TR-439). Cambridge: Massachusetts Institute of Technology, Artificial Intelligence Laboratory.

Rawlings, E.I., Rawlings, I.L., Chen, C.S., & Yilk, M.D. (1972). The facilitating effects of mental rehearsal in the acquisition of rotary pursuit tracking. *Psychonomic Science*, **26**, 71-73.

Rothstein, A.L., & Arnold, R.K. (1976). Bridging the gap: Application of research on videotape feedback and bowling. *Motor Skills: Theory Into Practice*, **1**, 35-62.

Salmoni, A.W., Schmidt, R.A., & Walter, C.B. (1984). Knowledge of results and motor learning: A review and critical reappraisal. *Psychological Bulletin*, **95**, 355-386.

Sanders, A.F. (1980). Stage analysis of reaction processes. In G.E. Stelmach & J. Requin (Eds.), *Tutorials in motor behavior* (pp. 331-354). Amsterdam: North-Holland.

Sanders, A.F. (1990). Issues and trends in the debate on discrete vs. continuous processing of information. *Acta Psychologica*, **74**, 123-167.

Schmidt, R.A. (1969). Movement time as a determiner of timing accuracy. *Journal of Experimental Psychology*, **79**, 43-47.

Schmidt, R.A. (1975). A schema theory of discrete motor skill learning. *Psychological Review*, **82**, 225-260.

Schmidt, R.A. (1985). The search for invariance in skilled movement behavior. *Research Quarterly for Exercise and Sport*, **56**, 188-200.

Schmidt, R.A. (1987). The acquisition of skill: Some modifications to the perception-action relationship through practice. In H. Heuer & A.F. Sanders (Eds.), *Perspectives on perception and action* (pp. 77-103). Hillsdale, NJ: Erlbaum.

Schmidt, R.A. (1988a). Motor and action perspective on motor behavior. In O.G. Meijer & K. Roth (Eds.), *Complex movement behaviour: ''The'' motor-action controversy* (pp. 3-44). Amsterdam: North-Holland.

Schmidt, R.A. (1988b). *Motor control and learning: A behavioral emphasis* (2nd ed.). Champaign, IL: Human Kinetics.

Schmidt, R.A. (in press). Motor-learning principles for physical therapy. In *Contemporary management of motor control problems*: Proceedings of the II Step Conference. Alexandria, VA: Foundation for Physical Therapy.

Schmidt, R.A., Lange, C.A., & Young, D.E. (1990). Optimizing summary knowledge of results for skill learning. *Human Movement Science, 9,* 325-348.

Schmidt, R.A., & Sherwood, D.E. (1982). An inverted-U relation between spatial error and force requirements in rapid limb movements: Further evidence for the impulse-variability model. *Journal of Experimental Psychology: Human Perception and Performance, 8,* 158-170.

Schmidt, R.A., & Young, D.E. (1987). Transfer of motor control in motor skill learning. In S.M. Cormier & J.D. Hagman (Eds.), *Transfer of learning* (pp. 47-79). Orlando, FL: Academic Press.

Schmidt, R.A., Zelaznik, H.N., Hawkins, B., Frank, J.S., & Quinn, J.T. (1979). Motor-output variability: A theory for the accuracy of rapid motor acts. *Psychological Review, 86,* 415-451.

Schneider, W. (1985). Training high-performance skills. *Human Factors, 27,* 285-300.

Schneider, W., Dumais, S.T., & Shiffrin, R.M. (1984). Automatic processing and attention. In R. Parasuraman & D.R. Davies (Eds.), *Varieties of attention* (pp. 1-27). Orlando, FL: Academic Press.

Schneider, W., & Shiffrin, R.M. (1977). Controlled and automatic information processing: I. Detection, search, and attention. *Psychological Review, 84,* 1-66.

Scripture, C.W. (1905). *The new psychology.* New York: Scott.

Shapiro, D.C. (1978). *The learning of generalized motor programs.* Unpublished doctoral dissertation, University of Southern California, Los Angeles.

Shapiro, D.C., Zernicke, R.F., Gregor, R.J., & Diestel, J.D. (1981). Evidence for generalized motor programs using gait-pattern analysis. *Journal of Motor Behavior, 13,* 33-47.

Shea, C.H., Kohl, R., & Indermill, C. (1990). Contextual interference: Contributions of practice. *Acta Psychologica, 73,* 145-157.

Shea, J.B., & Morgan, R.L. (1979). Contextual interference effects on the acquisition, retention, and transfer of a motor skill. *Journal of Experimental Psychology: Human Learning and Memory, 5,* 179-187.

Shea, J.B., & Upton, G. (1976). The effects on motor skill acquisition of an interpolated motor short-term memory task during the KR-delay interval. *Journal of Motor Behavior, 8,* 277-281.

Shea, J.B., & Zimny, S.T. (1983). Context effects in memory and learning movement information. In R.A. Magill (Ed.), *Memory and control of action* (pp. 345-366). Amsterdam: North-Holland.

Sherrington, C.S. (1906). *The integrative action of the nervous system.* New Haven, CT: Yale University Press.

Sherwood, D.E. (1987). *A note on the effect of bandwidth knowledge of results on movement consistency* (Rep. No. 87-5). Boulder: University of Colorado, Institute of Cognitive Science.

Sherwood, D.E. (1988). Effect of bandwidth knowledge of results on movement consistency. *Perceptual and Motor Skills, 66,* 535-542.

Sherwood, D.E., Schmidt, R.A., & Walter, C.B. (1988). The force/force-variability relationship under controlled temporal conditions. *Journal of Motor Behavior, 20,* 106-116.

Slater-Hammel, A.T. (1960). Reliability, accuracy, and refractoriness of a transit reaction. *Research Quarterly, 31,* 217-228.

Snoddy, G.S. (1926). Learning and stability. *Journal of Applied Psychology*, **10**, 1-36.

Stelmach, G.E. (1969). Efficiency of motor learning as a function of intertrial rest. *Research Quarterly*, **40**, 198-202.

Swinnen, S., Schmidt, R.A., Nicholson, D.E., & Shapiro, D.C. (1990). Information feedback for skill acquisition: Instanteous knowledge of results degrades learning. *Journal of Experimental Psychology: Learning, Memory, and Cognition*, **16**, 706-716.

Taub, E. (1976). Movements in nonhuman primates deprived of somatosensory feedback. *Exercise and Sport Sciences Reviews*, **4**, 335-374.

Taub, E., & Berman, A.J. (1968). Movement and learning in the absence of sensory feedback. In S.J. Freedman (Ed.), *The neuropsychology of spatially oriented behavior* (pp. 173-192). Homewood, IL: Dorsey Press.

Thorndike, E.L. (1927). The law of effect. *American Journal of Psychology*, **39**, 212-222.

Tiffin, J., & Rogers, H.B. (1943). The selection and training of inspectors. *Personnel*, **22**, 3-20.

Trevarthen, C.B. (1968). Two mechanisms of vision in primates. *Psychologische Forschung*, **31**, 299-337.

Trowbridge, M.H., & Cason, H. (1932). An experimental study of Thorndike's theory of learning. *Journal of General Psychology*, **7**, 245-260.

Turvey, M.T. (1977). Preliminaries to a theory of action with reference to vision. In R. Shaw & J. Bransford (Eds.), *Perceiving, acting, and knowing* (pp. 211-265). Hillsdale, NJ: Erlbaum.

Wadman, W.J., Denier van der Gon, J.J., Geuze, R.H., & Mol, C.R. (1979). Control of fast goal-directed arm movements. *Journal of Human Movement Studies*, **5**, 3-17.

Weinberg, D.R., Guy, D.E., & Tupper, R.W. (1964). Variation of postfeedback interval in simple motor learning. *Journal of Experimental Psychology*, **67**, 98-99.

Weinberg, R.S., & Hunt, V.V. (1976). The interrelationships between anxiety, motor performance, and electromyography. *Journal of Motor Behavior*, **8**, 219-224.

Weltman, G., & Egstrom, G.H. (1966). Perceptual narrowing in novice divers. *Human Factors*, **8**, 499-505.

Winstein, C.J., & Schmidt, R.A. (1988). Sensorimotor feedback. In D.H. Holding (Ed.), *Human skills* (2nd ed., pp. 17-47). New York: Wiley.

Winstein, C.J., & Schmidt, R.A. (1990). Reduced frequency of knowledge of results enhances motor skill learning. *Journal of Experimental Psychology: Learning, Memory, and Cognition*, **16**, 677-691.

Woodworth, R.S. (1899). The accuracy of voluntary movement. *Psychological Review*, **3**(Suppl. 2), 1-114.

Woodworth, R.S. (1938). *Experimental psychology*. New York: Holt.

Wulf, G., & Schmidt, R.A. (1988). Variability in practice: Facilitation in retention and transfer through schema formation or context effects? *Journal of Motor Behavior*, **20**, 133-149.

Young, D.E., & Schmidt, R.A. (1990a). Units of motor behavior: Modifications with practice and feedback. In M. Jeannerod (Ed.), *Attention and performance XIII* (pp. 763-795). Hillsdale, NJ: Erlbaum.

Young, D.E., & Schmidt, R.A. (1990b). *Knowledge of performance and motor learning*. Manuscript in preparation, University of California, Los Angeles.

Credits

Figure and Table Credits

Figure 2.12 From *Extended Practice and Patterns of Bimanual Interference* (unpublished doctoral dissertation) by P.B. Konzem, 1987, University of Southern California, Los Angeles. Reprinted by permission of the author.

Figure 3.3 Adapted with permission from "Reliability, Accuracy, and Refractoriness of a Transit Reaction" by A.T. Slater-Hammel, *Research Quarterly for Exercise and Sport*, **31**, 1960, p. 226. *Research Quarterly* is a publication of the American Alliance for Health, Physical Education, Recreation and Dance, 1900 Association Drive, Reston, VA 22091.

Figure 3.4 From "Neuromuscular Control System" by D.J. Dewhurst, 1967, *IEEE Transactions on Bio-Medical Engineering*, **14**, p. 170. © 1967 Institute of Electrical and Electronics Engineers. Adapted by permission.

Figure 4.4 From "Control of Fast Goal-Directed Arm Movements" by W.J. Wadman, J.J. Denier van der Gon, R.H. Geuze, and C.R. Mol, 1979, *Journal of Human Movement Studies*, **5**, p. 10. Copyright 1979 by Lepus Books.

Figure 4.7 From *Training for the Production of Memorized Movement Patterns* (Technical Report No. 26, p. 35) by T.R. Armstrong, 1970, Ann Arbor, MI: University of Michigan Human Performance Center. Adapted by permission of University of Michigan.

Figure 4.8 From *A Study of Human Motor Control Through Analysis and Synthesis of Handwriting* (unpublished doctoral dissertation, p. 53) by J.M. Hollerbach, 1978, Massachusetts Institute of Technology. Adapted by permission of the author.

Figure 4.9 From *Motor Control and Learning by the State-Space Model* (Technical Report No. AI-TR-439, p. 50) by M.H. Raibert, 1977, Cambridge: Massachusetts Institute of Technology, Artificial Intelligence Laboratory. Copyright 1977 by M.H. Raibert. Reprinted by permission.

Figure 5.1 From *Motor Control and Learning: A Behavioral Emphasis* (2nd ed., p. 244) by R.A. Schmidt, 1988, Champaign, IL: Human Kinetics. Copyright 1988, 1982 by Richard A. Schmidt. Reprinted by permission.

Figures 5.2 and 5.3 From "Evidence for Generalized Motor Programs Using Gait-Pattern Analysis" by D.C. Shapiro, R.F. Zernicke, R.J. Gregor, and J.D. Diestel, 1981, *Journal of Motor Behavior*, **13**, pp. 38, 42. Reprinted by permission of D.C. Shapiro.

Figures 5.7 and 5.8 From "Motor-Output Variability: A Theory for the Accuracy of Rapid Motor Acts" by R.A. Schmidt, H. Zelaznik, B. Hawkins, J.S. Frank, and J.T. Quinn, Jr., 1979, *Psychological Review*, **86**, p. 428. Copyright 1979 by the American Psychological Association. Adapted (5.7) and reprinted (5.8) by permission of the publisher.

Figure 5.13 From "An Inverted-U Relation Between Spatial Error and Force

Requirements in Rapid Limb Movement: Further Evidence for the Impulse-Variability Model" by R.A. Schmidt and D.E. Sherwood, 1982, *Journal of Experimental Psychology: Human Perception and Performance, 8*, p. 167. Copyright 1982 by the American Psychological Association. Adapted by permission of the publisher.

Table 6.2 Adapted with permission from "Interrelationships Between Selected Measures of Static and Dynamic Balance" by J.N. Drowatsky and F.C. Zuccato, *Research Quarterly for Exercise and Sport, 38*, 1967, p. 510. *Research Quarterly* is a publication of the American Alliance for Health, Physical Education, Recreation and Dance, 1900 Association Drive, Reston, VA 22091.

Figure 6.4 From *Development of a Taxonomy of Human Performance: A Review of the Third Year's Progress* (Technical Report No. 726-TPR3) by E.A. Fleishman and R.W. Stephenson, 1970, Washington, DC: American Institutes for Research. Adapted by permission of American Institutes for Research.

Figure 7.2 From *Knowledge of Performance and Motor Learning* (unpublished doctoral dissertation) by D.E. Young, 1988, University of California–Los Angeles. Adapted by permission of the author.

Figure 7.3 From "Reduced Frequency of Knowledge of Results Enhances Motor Skill Learning" by C.J. Winstein and R.A. Schmidt, 1990, *Journal of Experimental Psychology: Learning, Memory, and Cognition, 16*, p. 680. Copyright 1990 by the American Psychological Association. Adapted by permission of the publisher.

Figure 8.1 From "Cognitive Aspects of Psychomotor Performance: The Effects of Performance Goals on Level of Perfor-

mance" by E.A. Locke and J.F. Bryan, 1966, *Journal of Applied Psychology, 50*, p. 289. Copyright 1966 by the American Psychological Association. Adapted by permission.

Figure 8.2 From "The Facilitating Effects of Mental Rehearsal in the Acquisition of Rotary Pursuit Tracking" by E.I. Rawlings, I.L. Rawlings, C.S. Chen, and M.D. Yilk, 1972, *Psychonomic Science, 26*, p. 71. Reprinted by permission of Psychonomic Society, Inc.

Figure 8.5 Reprinted with permission from "Efficiency of Motor Learning as a Function of Intertrial Rest" by G.E. Stelmach, *Research Quarterly for Exercise and Sport, 40*, 1969, p. 198. *Research Quarterly* is a publication of the American Alliance for Health, Physical Education, Recreation and Dance, 1900 Association Drive, Reston, VA 22091.

Figure 8.6 From *The Most Efficient Usage of a Fixed Work Plus Rest Practice Period in Motor Learning* (unpublished doctoral dissertation) by H.M.A. Graw, 1968, University of California–Berkeley. Adapted by permission of the author.

Figure 9.1 From "Contextual Interference Effects on the Acquisition, Retention, and Transfer of a Motor Skill" by J.B. Shea and R.L. Morgan, 1979, *Journal of Experimental Psychology: Human Learning and Memory, 5*, p. 183. Copyright 1979 by the American Psychological Association. Reprinted by permission.

Figure 9.5 Reproduced with permission of author and publisher from: Catalano, J.F., & Kleiner, B.M. "Distant Transfer in Coincident Timing as a Function of Variability of Practice." *Perceptual and Motor Skills*, 1984, *58*, 851-856.

Figure 10.6 From "Reduced Frequency of Knowledge of Results Enhances Motor

Skill Learning" by C.J. Winstein and R.A. Schmidt, 1990, *Journal of Experimental Psychology: Learning, Memory, and Cognition*, **16**, p. 683. Copyright 1990 by the American Psychological Association. Reprinted by permission of the publisher.

Figure 10.9 From "Retention of Simple Motor Skills as a Function of Type of Knowledge of Results" by J.J. Lavery, 1962, *Canadian Journal of Psychology*, **16**, p. 305. Copyright 1962. Canadian Psychological Association. Reprinted with permission.

Figure 10.10 From "Optimizing Summary Knowledge of Results for Skill Learning" by R.A. Schmidt, C.A. Lange, and D.E. Young, 1990, *Human Movement Science*, **9**. Copyright 1990 by Elsevier Science Publishers B.V. (North-Holland). Reprinted by permission.

Figure 10.13 From "Information Feedback for Skill Acquisition: Instantaneous Knowledge of Results Degrades Learning" by S. Swinnen, R.A. Schmidt, D.E. Nicholson, and D.C. Shapiro, 1990, *Journal of Experimental Psychology: Learning, Memory, and Cognition*, **16**, p. 712. Copyright 1990 by the American Psychological Association. Reprinted by permission of the publisher.

Photo Credits

Photo of David Kiley on page 1 by Teresa Whitehead. Courtesy of Casa Colina Centers for Rehabilitation.

Photo on page 3 by Konstantaras, *The Daily Illini*, Champaign, Illinois.

Photo of Chuck Ochoa on page 4 by Teresa Whitehead. Courtesy of Casa Colina Centers for Rehabilitation.

Photo on page 13 by Bill Scherer.

Photos on pages 15 and 45 courtesy of University of Southern California.

Photo on page 19 reprinted from *The New Psychology* (p. 151) by C.W. Scripture, 1905, New York: Scott.

Photos on pages 24, 151, and 220 by Stephen Warmowski, *The Daily Illini*, Champaign, Illinois.

Photos on pages 29 and 102 by Spencer Swanger/Tom Stack & Associates.

Photo on page 58 courtesy of the Pocono Mountains Vacation Bureau, Box K, 1004 Main St., Stroudsburg, PA 18360-1695.

Photo on page 70 reprinted from "Visual Proprioceptive Control of Standing in Human Infants" by D.N. Lee and E. Aronson, 1974, *Perception and Psychophysics*, **15**, p. 530. Reprinted by permission of Psychonomic Society, Inc.

Photo on page 77 courtesy of University of Arizona.

Photo of Ron Scanlon on page 80 by Teresa Whitehead. Courtesy of Casa Colina Centers for Rehabilitation.

Photo on page 92 by Meinhardt, *The Daily Illini*, Champaign, Illinois.

Photo on page 101 by Trojanowski, *The Daily Illini*, Champaign, Illinois.

Photos on pages 114, 168, and 171 by *The Daily Illini*, Champaign, Illinois.

Photo on page 127 courtesy of Arizona Office of Tourism.

Photo on page 129 by L. Young, *The Daily Illini*, Champaign, Illinois.

Photo on page 144 by Ellen Wermuth.

Photo on page 149 by Martha Hirsh, *The Daily Illini*, Champaign, Illinois.

Photo on page 153 by John Walbaum, *The Daily Illini*, Champaign, Illinois.

Photo on page 180 by Mark Robbins, *The Daily Illini*, Champaign, Illinois.

Photos on pages 182 and 183 by Steve Groer, *Rocky Mountain News*.

Photo on page 204 by Alex Tziortzis, *The Daily Illini*, Champaign, Illinois.

Photo on page 227 by Skjold.

Photos on pages 243 and 263 by Valerie Rose Hall.

Photo on page 237 by M. Johnson, *The Daily Illini*, Champaign, Illinois.

Photo on page 261 courtesy of the U.S. National Senior Sports Classic—The Senior Olympics.

Photo on page 270 by Brian Parker/Tom Stack & Associates.

Author Index

Subject Index